LIFECODE SERIES

PRESENTS

2015 LIFECODE #7

THE CONSCIOUSNESS OF TIME & SPIRITUALITY

BIRTHDAYS FOR LIFECODE #7					
06-January	22-March	20-May	27-July	15-October	31-December
15-January	31- March	29-May	08-August	24-October	
24-January	03-Apr	01-June	17-August	05-November	
05-February	12-Apr	10-June	26-August	14-November	
14-February	21-Apr	19-June	07-September	23-November	
23-February	30-Apr	28-June	16- September	04-December	
04-March	02-May	09-July	25-September	13-December	
13-March	11-May	18-July	06-October	22-December	

We use the Sun as a measurement that makes the day, the Moon as a measurement that makes the Month, the year is created by the movement of the Earth around the Sun in the solar system.

Using Vedic Mathematical methods of calculation the day of the Month plus the Month of the Year can be used as real number in the above equation. Let's say the baby was born on February 12, 1956 then the equation for birth will be: SUN + MOON = 12 (day) + 2 (Month) = Moment of Birth = 14 = 1 + 4 = 5

In this case the numbers above 9 are repetitions of the real numbers so in Vedic mathematics the higher numbers are reduced to real numbers so in this case 14 is really 5. This final number from the above equation is then referred to as your **Lifecode**.

Please Note: For Eastern countries, it is important that you check the book also with the day after the above day shown in the table if the Birth was in the evening in the Eastern Time zones of the world. The reason why is because the forecasts measurements in this book were calculated based on North American and South American time zones and dates. For places such as those located in Africa, Europe, Asia and the Far East, and the birth occurred in the evening local time, then the lifecode number after the above one should be consulted also.

Swami Ram Charran

For general information on our other products and services, please contact Heendu Learning Center at (305) 253-5410 or www.swamiram.com

2015 Edition
2015 Lifecode #7: Shiva

ISBN: 978-1-312-44345-7

Printed in the United States of America

Author Credits:

Editor in Chief:	LUERESA RAMCHARAN
Designed by:	SWAMI RAMCHARAN
Cover Design by:	LUANA & LUCAS RAMCHARRAN

Contents

Section 1

LifeCode #7– Vedic Deity Shiva

A General Look at Your Whole Life Karmas

❖ Your mind is running at a thousand miles an hour.

❖ You are constantly thinking and analyzing everything.

❖ Sometimes you keep most of your thoughts to yourself.

❖ You do not tell your plans very easily to others.

❖ You feel you are right in everything 33% of the time.

❖ Sometimes you think everyone is against you.

❖ You are very beautiful, or handsome in the case of males.

❖ You attract the opposite sex very easily.

❖ Your need for love and romance is very high.

❖ You experience many difficulties in your marriage.

❖ A sure key to happiness for you is meditation and music.

❖ You are very kind hearted and are sometimes deceived easily by your lovers.

❖ You should avoid the color black...wear light colors.

Seven is the most significant and magical of the numbers. It has long been held sacred, as is shown by the extraordinary frequency of seven in mythology, the Bible, and classifications of all kinds: there are seven notes in the musical scale, seven phases of the Moon, seven seas, seven heavenly bodies in the old Ptolemaic system, seven wonders of the world, seven hills of Rome, seven virtues, seven deadly sins, seven days of creation, seven plagues of Egypt, seven sentences in the Lord's Prayer, seven trumpets in the Apocalypse, and many more. The seventh son of a seventh son is believed to possess great magical powers. People who are Sevens are sometimes great thinkers and may have an occult or psychic side. They may be researchers, investigators, or inventors. They have an affinity with the sea and often travel widely. But they must use their powers wisely, avoiding pride and cynicism, and accepting that their talents will never make them materially rich.

You have a secretive and sometimes very private personality. You hardly speak about what you are thinking but your mind is running at 100 miles per hour. However, when you do speak your words are like fire ready to destroy the person you are directing it at. People around you see you as an egg shell ready to break with the slightest intimidation so your partner or lover feels like he or she is always walking on eggshells because he or she never knows when you are going to find something wrong with him or her. Your criticism of others can be very high and may prevent others from getting very close to you. You tend to hold back a lot of your personal feelings about others. Even your beloved one will ask you when you are going to say "I love you." It is very important that you do not analyze others too much for there are no such persons who are perfect in everything. The first lesson you must learn in life is that no one can be perfect. Once you have learnt this your love life and your marriage life will be much happier. You possess a very high temper and may sometimes speak very harshly to others. If this is a quality that is carried into your marriage it may surely end in divorce. Out of all others in this astrological analysis you possess the highest ego there is. You will never admit when you are wrong. You will never admit when you feel weak inside and you will always put up an outward appearance much different from the one that is inner. Your true feelings never seem to come out, even though your true feelings given to the other person will solve all the problems. If you are an extremely negative individual you may be addicted to drugs, alcohol or smoking. You may also be constantly complaining over petty or unnecessary matters. A small matter may worry you a great deal. You are constantly studying or reading if you are not sleeping or relaxing watching TV. You are very slow in your movements and may experience many delays in your life as a result of this. You may get married very late in life. If you do get married early there may be a possibility of separation. Late marriages are usually more successful. Your interests may lie in the field of medicine and if you study medical sciences you will be successful in a career associated with it. If you are a positive individual you may become a priest, a yogi or saint. If you are religious you may experience inner encounters with God and other divine manifestations of the universal deities. If you happen to find yourself a GURU you may experience a divine connection through that personality. If this path is followed most of your wishes will be fulfilled in life and your desires may become a reality. You may encounter many religious individuals in your life. You are advised to pay much attention to what they say for their advice may be very beneficial to you. Respect must be given to all holy people or elders in the family. Christians are advised to say the Lord's Prayer 11 times every day.

SPIRITUAL GENETICS YOU INHERITED FROM YOUR GENERATION

- ❖ You suppress your feelings to avoid conflicts with others.
- ❖ Your mind is constantly analyzing and rechecking things.
- ❖ Your love life is your greatest test since you do not express love.

- ❖ You could become highly religious or an alcoholic or drug addict.
- ❖ You would make a good radio announcer or news/talk show anchor.
- ❖ You have to be careful of overindulgence and excesses.
- ❖ You could be psychic as part of a mission in life.

MEDITATION RECOMMENDATIONS BASED ON YOUR LIFECODE

- ❖ Your primary meditation focus is love and godly things.
- ❖ I recommend that you meditate for at least 30 minutes, to slow your thoughts.
- ❖ While meditating you should always be in the lotus position of sitting with folded feet, with your thumb and forefinger touching.
- ❖ You should always close your eyes during meditation, as you are always looking at your inner self.
- ❖ A holy location, temple, mountain or place of worship is your best place for meditation

HOW DID YOUR PARENTS AFFECT YOUR LIFE PATH?

- ❖ Mom was very critical of Dad during the pregnancy.
- ❖ Mom was worried about Dad leaving her for someone else.
- ❖ Both Mom and Dad kept their hurtful feelings inside.
- ❖ Both Mom and Dad listened to a lot of music.
- ❖ One of them was either religious or addicted to alcohol.
- ❖ Mom was meticulous, particularly during her pregnancy.

BEFORE BEING BORN - WHAT WAS YOUR PAST LIFE LIKE?

- ❖ You could have been a king, queen, president or political leader of a country.
- ❖ You may have abused many people in your past life, as either a princess or prince of a castle, and therefore you could become an alcoholic in this life.
- ❖ You were involved in legal proceedings or may have been a lawyer.
- ❖ You could have been a criminal or a police officer or court leader.
- ❖ You may have been a soldier in the military or a warrior of the king.
- ❖ You were a very responsible person and took good care of the family or the community.
- ❖ You could have been the victim of jealousy and anger, which may carry over into this life.

Section 2

WHAT TYPE OF SHIVA ARE YOU

How Your Year of Birth Affects You?

In Section 1, we spoke of the general characteristics of Shivas. There are 9 Versions or Types of Shivas depending on their year of birth. In the table below find the year you were born and then look at the details below that distinguish your personality.

	WHAT TYPE OF SHIVA YOU ARE								
	1	2	3	4	5	6	7	8	9
Y E A R O F B I R T H	1891	1892	1893	1894	1895	1896	1897	1898	1899
	1900	1901	1902	1903	1904	1905	1906	1907	1908
	1909	1910	1911	1912	1913	1914	1915	1916	1917
	1918	1919	1920	1921	1922	1923	1924	1925	1926
	1927	1928	1929	1930	1931	1932	1933	1934	1935
	1936	1937	1938	1939	1940	1941	1942	1943	1944
	1945	1946	1947	1948	1949	1950	1951	1952	1953
	1954	1955	1956	1957	1958	1959	1960	1961	1962
	1963	1964	1965	1966	1967	1968	1969	1970	1971
	1972	1973	1974	1975	1976	1977	1978	1979	1980
	1981	1982	1983	1984	1985	1986	1987	1988	1989
	1990	1991	1992	1993	1994	1995	1996	1997	1998
	1999	2000	2001	2002	2003	2004	2005	2006	2007
	2008	2009	2010	2011	2012	2013	2014	2015	2016

VERSION 1 - LEADERSHIP –

If you are this version of Shiva you will tend to be independent, original, act individually, create new things, be ambitious and have the desire to dominate things in your life. You will possess self-confidence, assurance and pride; your life will be filled with activity. This version of Shiva indicates that you will usually be able to stand on your own feet and have the desire to be your own person as opposed to being involved with associates or partners.

Perhaps the most important lesson for you to learn is that there are other people in the world besides you. You must learn to live with others without bullying or imposing unjustly your own will power upon them. If you follow a positive path, you will find your way open for positive action and achievement.

When born under this Lifecode and following a negative path, you must learn to fall back on your own resources (i.e. your strength and your knowledge) and make your own decisions. You must work on your inner self – mind, body and spirit. You must learn to be original and to establish new ideas, new ideals and new tactics. Try to break away from the standard trends and be your own person.

Learn to be independent. Do not take advantage of others. Be a leader. Be spiritual. Enjoy being alone. Take time to meditate.

VERSION 2 - SERVICE –

If you are this version of Shiva, you will have a life full of gentle love and peace, for the karma of this Lifecode is to give and to seek love and companionship. Your best role is peacemaker but be aware because unscrupulous people can take advantage of the kindness of people in this form.

When you are this version of Shiva and following a negative path, the keyword is subservience. The lesson that you must learn is not to put yourself before others. You must learn cooperation, patience and consideration for others. Learn to overcome shyness and over-sensitivity. When following a positive path, you will find a life full of cooperation, the ability to work well with others and to follow instructions.

Be cooperative. Avoid being too kind. Marry only once. Avoid divorce. Don't be too materialistic. Take care with your words, and do not be too outspoken to others.

VERSION 3 - KNOWLEDGE –

If you are this version of Shiva, you are a being of self-expression in the way of peaceful, enjoyable activities surrounded by beauty, inner peace and harmonious atmosphere. This code will lead to many friends and companions. It will be a life of inspiration, talent and kindness.

When you are this type of Shiva and you are following a negative path, the lesson you must learn is self-expression, to give freely of the self and to share your feelings openly, without fear. One of the biggest dangers you must overcome is that of jealousy. When following the positive path, consider yourself fortunate, for this is the nicest of all codes to have.

Read and write a lot. Avoid childlessness. Accept all responsibilities in life. Avoid abortions and laziness. Learn to bow to all people of authority.

VERSION 4 - FOUNDATION –

If you are this version of Shiva and following a positive path, you might still find difficulties in your life, as it predicts a life of hard work and effort. The outstanding qualities of a Shiva under this influence are their abilities of organization, devotion, dignity, trust and loyalty. This version of Shiva will find great responsibility because of your outstanding qualities and will confer a wide range of trust, many times unwanted.

When born as this version of Shiva and following a negative path, you must be able to use your ability to apply yourself to detail work. You must learn to stay put, become the cornerstone and devote yourself in duty to your family community and country. A particular danger to overcome is that of unjust hatred. You must learn to cooperate with your spouse, as every little thing that happens to people born under this influence can irritate them easily.

Work hard. Listen to your employers. Avoid stress. Save your money. Avoid gambling, investments, and shady (unclear) deals. Do not be too harsh in your judgment of others.

VERSION 5 - CHANGE –

If you are this version of Shiva and are following a positive path, you might still find this influence to be a difficult but varied one to live under. You will experience frequent changes in all aspects of your life in which there will be much variety and travel. You will have freedom, curiosity, adventure, aloneness and progress. Above all, your life will be the center of constant change.

If you are this type of Shiva and are following a negative path, your keyword is freedom. You must learn to change your thoughtlessness and be ready to accept frequent, unwanted changes. Drinking habits, narcotics, sensuality and sex can be deadly if overindulged.

Watch your back. Avoid secret love affairs. Traveling is a must. Be careful whom you trust. Help others willingly. Do not be too narrow- minded. Listen to others.

VERSION 6 – FAMILY & RESPONSIBILITY–

If you are this version of Shiva and are following a positive path, you will find that it leads to glory and greatness. Many people born under this influence have been held back from their destinies because of negative aspects. You may realize a quick ascent to power and greatness in the material, military or political worlds. It will be a life of responsibility and service and very much the path of adjustments.

The greatest problem you face is adjusting to circumstances and accepting things for their true value without looking for perfection in everything. Adjustment is the key word, particularly concerning domestic relationships. You must develop a willingness to serve family, friends and country. You must learn to serve without using tyranny.

If you follow this path, you will be called upon time and time again to settle disputes, make adjustments and render final decisions. Avoid disobeying government laws and follow all traffic rules, for trouble with the police is predicted. If you are this version of Shiva, you and your spouse must avoid encouraging family visitors and involvement with family affairs.

Family interference is your karma. Avoid conflicts. Be responsible. Control your anger and ego. Obey rules. Learn to follow advice of older people. Realize there are laws that need to be followed. Family is your test.

VERSION 7 - SPIRITUAL –

If you are this version of Shiva and are following a positive path, you will be somewhat of a loner, especially with matters concerning the inner self. This is the influence of the philosopher, the deep thinker and dreamer. This type of Shiva will find peace, spirituality, trust, faith, research and wisdom. Your life will be restful and peaceful and will not be too concerned with material things.

If born under this form of Shiva and following a negative path, you will create coldness towards others. You must also overcome aloofness, which results from daydreaming and mentally wandering off, for this can prevent you from performing your responsibilities. You are humiliated and embarrassed easily or embarrass others and are faithless, which can lead to disbelief in God. You must learn to go through life cheerfully accepting the problems and troubles of others.

Learn to be independent. Don't take advantage of others. Be a leader. Be spiritual. Enjoy being alone. Learn to express your feelings openly. Do not hold back emotions. Develop your speech.

VERSION 8 - BUSINESS –

If you are this version of Shiva and are following a positive path, then this will lead you to power, authority, material and financial gains and success in all material aspects. Persons born under this form will be generous and dependable. There is outstanding inner strength and courage.

If born under this form of Shiva and following a negative path, your key word is to avoid greed, jealousy and overspending. You will find that you possess a love of power and money, and power for self, intolerance, abuse and revenge.

You will need is to cultivate [grow] good moral business ethics and understanding of people with less force and dynamics.

Control greed for money. Be content. Respect your mother. Control your need for luxury. Be humble. Your ego is too strong for others sometimes. Control your desire for expensive things.

VERSION 9 - TEACHERS –

If you are this version of Shiva and are following a positive path, then being born under this code is the all-encompassing destiny. You likely will be a world traveler and have a global outlook. You will be intuitive, understanding, knowledgeable and willing to sacrifice. You usually make good marriage partners and lovers and are full of kindness and consideration. It is predicted that you would do well with a career in government agencies.

If born under this form of Shiva and following a negative path, you will find the need to hold emotions in balance and your self-ego in check. A few of the pitfalls are fickleness, immortality and daydreaming. Once again, if negative, there is a possibility that you could end up in court or become a criminal. You must learn to avoid constant ego quarrels between couples and older family members and to not interfere in other's lives.

Health is your karma and it can decline if you are too suspicious, controlling and/or commanding. Believe in God at all times (not sometimes). Control your spending habits. Pay your bills first before anything else.

Section 3

YOUR NAME FOR THE YEAR *2015*

Names are sounds, and the Vedic Sciences recognizes that each one of us is a vibration at a specific frequency called a Lifecode. Letters forms sound or vibrations and so all languages are subject to sound or musical notes. All languages have "vocals" or vowels, which combine with consonants to form sounds or musical notes. Every name of a person will have these vowels and so the sound or vibration caused by the letters when combined would be part of the group of sounds that make up that name. In English it is sound that forms our unique frequency with the world, and so each one of us harmonizes in a unique way with the universe. When we are given a name by our parents, the feelings and emotional connection with the universe at that moment with the mother or father is embedded in the name of the baby when they give the baby its name. For example if a mother or father is going through a distressing time in their life, most likely the baby's name will start with an "I " or with an "R " as these letters represent distress at childhood. If the parents are happy and are doing well in life then the letter "E" or "C " or "L" will be the starting letter of the baby's name. This will affect any baby in any culture if the letter sound is the same as these letters mentioned.

You are unique! There will never be another YOU! A natal horoscope is not repeated for 25,000 years, because the planets all move at different speeds around our Sun. It is highly unlikely that two people would ever be born on the same date, in the same place, and be given the identically spelled name. An Astrologer needs your date, time, and place of birth. Vedic Mathematics needs only your birth certificate full name and birth date to tell who you are, what you have to work with and much, much more.

EACH LETTER OF YOUR NAME HAS A PROSPERITY LEVEL LOOK AT THE FOLLOWING GRAPH

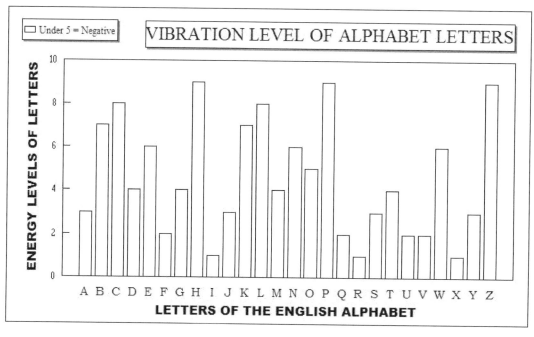

Each letter controls 9 years of your life so insert you name in the following box and you can know how your name affects you life in the age you are in now, Insert you name into the following worksheet and then find your prosperity level according to your age. A high prosperity age brings all wealth and love and happiness in your life. If you are in a low prosperity age pray, give charity and fast until the next prosperity level. If all prosperity is low, then you need to change the spelling of your name,

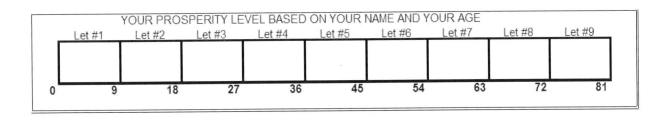

YOUR LIFE FOR THE YEAR 2015

Forecasts by the Vedic Deity Goddess Kali

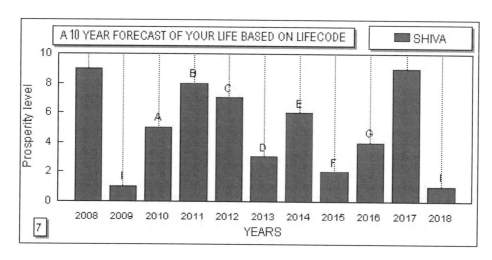

Each letter represents the period of forecast for that year. Find the letter in question and look at the Table to find the forecast for that year. With this graph, you can also check what is going to be your Karma for the year 2015 until 2018.

A.   **Achievements, loneliness, on your own, promotions, placed in charge**

B.   **Love, happiness, romance, music, relax, good foods, meeting friends**

C.   **Social enjoyment, children, new opportunities, video/TV, bargains, phone**

D.   **Hard work, coworker problems, stress, body pains, overtime, needs rest**

E.   **Travel, moves, new ideas, hyper active, driving, long-distance contacts**

F.   **Frustration, disagreements, high ego, family quarrels, authorities, debts**

G   **sleep, self analysis, astrology, spiritual connections, addiction, slow**

H.   **Investments, profits, luxury, business, payments, movies, partnerships**

I.   **Suffering, losses, sicknesses, spending, delays, hospitals, police, courts**

It is important to understand that the effects of the year will have the greatest effects in your life during this period of 2015. The monthly cycles have the second greatest effect in your life; the third effect will be the daily cycles followed by the hourly cycles.

This is a **negative** year for you. If you have led a spiritual and rightful life; the effects will be neutral-negative. Depending on the type of Shiva you are, you will have different influences throughout the year.

The positive months are: January, April, May, July and October. The neutral months are March, September and December. The neutral-negative month is June. The negative months are: February, August and November. Their specific effect on your life will be detailed in the next section

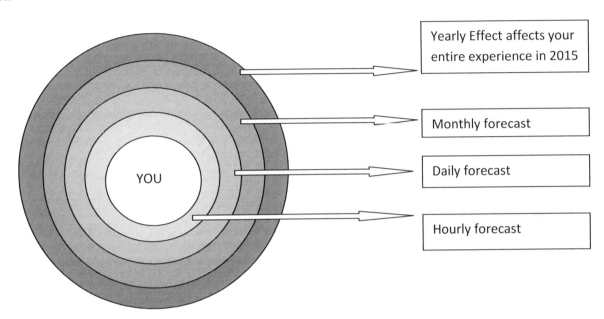

The key word is **adjustment**. Responsibility, family relationships, people in authority, and government are the influences of this period. This year is ideal for collecting monies owed to you. It is also a good year to take out a mortgage or make adjustment with creditors. It could be a year when you will be called upon to be responsible towards all those you owe. In this case, not only money but also, you may, have to pay back favors, as well as payments due on bad karmas for the past six years. If you have been involved in any illegal activities within the past six years, they will definitely catch up with you this year. If you have been involved with the government or the court in any way, you may end up losing or be penalized for your past errors. BE CAREFUL, it is an excellent year for marriage, but also a definite one for divorce. Make sure you give that little bit extra at home. It could be a year of happy domestic affairs, and many happy adjustments in the home. You will be spending a lot of time with family members and relatives. You will have many responsibilities in your career, your home and your community. I advise you to accept these without protest. This is the ideal year to purchase a new home or add to the old one. There will be many responsibilities and adjustments at this time, which may include domestic troubles, quarrels between family members, and confrontations with coworkers. These disputes will have to be resolved. Marriage and/or divorce are in the air for you or someone related to you, friend, or family. If the previous year has been positive, you will be in the forefront concerning advancement and promotion. There will be no need to be concerned about finances if your life has been positive.

All the money you need will become available this year if you are charitable and religious. If you are a responsible person, the home life will be happy and secure and the home itself will be comfortable, large and perhaps well furnished.

Those who have been negative will confront responsibilities that will not be to their liking. In addition, they will be involved in many domestic squabbles. I advise you not to impose yourself upon others at this time. To present it in a blunt manner, unless someone seeks you out for advice, keep your nose out of other people's business; keep your advice to yourself. Gossip will be disastrous for those who are influenced negatively this year and whose interference causes problems for others which will bounce right back on them in three years.

You must avoid any arguments with your spouse, your relatives or your coworkers for it will be your fault most of the time. Avoid becoming angry with your lover. Try your best to be spiritually calm, cool and collected and this will benefit you tremendously later. If not, divorce from your lover; you will experience separation from children, parents or friends. If the separation is positive, you will reunite together in the next year.

For those who would like to create good karmas for the future three years you must participate in charitable activities, go to the temple, meditate and avoid becoming angry with others. At all cost, avoid jealousy and covetousness, greed and mistrust. Vedics must do HANUMAN POOJA, pay homage to the Brahmins and Priests and perform GURU meditation. Christians must see their Priests regularly, be charitable towards the church and Catholics should go to confession.

Although the main influences of the year 2015 are described above, there are different influences that affect you according to your version of Shiva. The influences that affect you for this year depending on your Version (refer to section 2) are detailed below.

SPECIAL MESSAGE FOR VERSION 1 –SHIVA –

In 2015, Shiva Version 1 will be spending a lot of money. Money may be spent in hospital or medical bills and in funerals. You may also lose money through water and in events such as storms, hurricanes, tsunamis or tornadoes. You also have to be careful of misplacing money during this period. DO NOT gamble or play the lottery this year.

SPECIAL MESSAGE FOR VERSION 2 –SHIVA –

In 2015, Shiva Version 2 will have times of loneliness. You may be spending a lot of money on yourself this year. DO NOT gamble or play the lottery this year.

SPECIAL MESSAGE FOR VERSION 3-SHIVA –

In 2015, Shiva Version 3 will have expenses in abundance from their significant other. Avoid lending money. Avoid illicit affairs. DO NOT gamble or play the lottery this year.

SPECIAL MESSAGE FOR VERSION 4 –SHIVA –

In 2015, Shiva Version 4 will have expenses related to children or family members. You will socialize a lot; you will receive invitations to parties and gatherings but will have delays or cancellations when attending them. You will also have many opportunities for learning and you will enjoy them. DO NOT gamble or play the lottery this year.

SPECIAL MESSAGE FOR VERSION 5 –SHIVA –

In 2015, Shiva Version 5 will have to work very hard this year. They may not be very lucky with their current jobs or finding a job. You will have difficulties if you overspend. You may also have to accept extra responsibilities at work without financial compensation. Do not start any major projects this year as they will result in being cancelled or unfinished. DO NOT gamble or play the lottery this year

SPECIAL MESSAGE FOR VERSION 6 –SHIVA –

In 2015, Shiva Version 6 will have the opportunity to enjoy sexuality, beautiful people, and expensive places. You must be careful of illicit affairs that will be very hard to resist. Avoid buying anything expensive this year as it may not last long or need to be replaced later. DO NOT gamble or play the lottery this year.

SPECIAL MESSAGE FOR VERSION 7 –SHIVA –

In 2015, Shiva Version 7 will have to deal with family asking for loans. You will have a great deal of responsibilities. You will be involved with politics, powerful people, and power over money, loans, robbery or loss of money. DO NOT gamble or play the lottery this year.

SPECIAL MESSAGE FOR VERSION 8 –SHIVA –

In 2015, Shiva Version 8 will have to give donations to charitable institutions or your finances will suffer. You will be thinking and worrying about money and money may be slow in coming in. DO NOT gamble or play the lottery this year.

SPECIAL MESSAGE FOR VERSION 9 –SHIVA –

In 2015, Shiva Version 9 will have to avoid spending money on items you do not need. Do not buy anything expensive this year as this can result in you buying a replacement for that item later on. Due to the negative influences this year try to avoid lending money or borrowing money. Do not gamble or play the lottery this year.

YOUR POSITIVE, NEGATIVE AND NEUTRAL MONTHS IN THE YEAR 2015

Forecasts for the Vedic Deity Goddess Kali

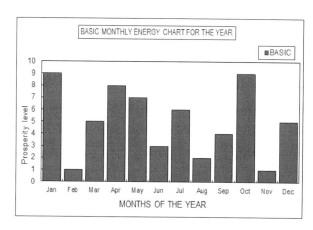
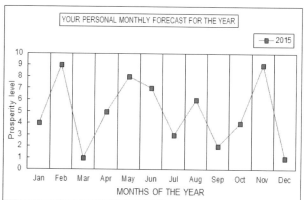

The Basic Monthly Energy Chart above shows the energy expected for every month in the year based on your birthday. The Chart on the left is the basic monthly energy chart that affects you the same way every year. Every year your **negative** months are: **February, August** and **November**, the **neutral** months are: **March, September** and **December**; the **neutral-negative** month is **June. January, April, May, July** and **October** are **positive** high energy months.

The chart on the right indicates how those months will change for 2015. If you will notice in 2015, **March, September** and **December** are **lower** energy months in this year. **July** has a **neutral-negative** energy that is highly susceptible to levels of spirituality. The Vedic New Year started in the middle of September 2014 and you commenced a year with **negative** energy. This energy will last until September 2015 when a Vedic Year with **neutral-positive** energy begins for you. You are going through a year when you have to be careful with accidents, tickets and anything related to the law. You will feel frustrated <u>often</u>. It is not a good year to start anything new to get satisfactory results. You will have many added responsibilities this year. It will be good for you to stay close to home. It is not a good to start any major projects. You should definitely avoid starting anything in **February, August** and **November**. The months of **March** and **December** also have some negative influences that you may want to avoid.

JANUARY 2015 FORECAST

LIFECODE FORECAST: Money is the main issue in your life this month. All aspects of your life connected with money may be affected such as your job, your mortgage, your prestige, your income and so on. Love and romance may be expensive but pleasurable if you are positive.

Marriage this month may be very profitable to the female partner. You may be tempted to buy yourself that expensive item you have wanted to buy for a long time but never had the money. On the other hand if you have been negative this month may bring delay, disappointment, deception or trickery pertaining to finance. It is a good time to request a promotion from your superiors and also a good time to play the lottery. Try to save some of the money that will come your way this month as you will need it in emergency next month. Real estate opportunities may seem attractive for investment purposes. It is a good time to invest in the stock market, but very little. This is a positive month for money matters and for purchasing that expensive item that is needed. Income should be high now and money will be coming from unusual quarters. If you are negative expect unforeseen expenses this month. Save some of your money for next month as you will need it. Avoid extravagance or over spending.

SPECIAL MESSAGE FOR THIS MONTH: Due to the influences of the year, you must avoid criticizing anyone or getting yourself involved in any gossip as this may become very damaging to your reputation this month. You may receive news of an older person dying far away or you may visit a sick person in the hospital or a prison. Income may be very low at this time. Do not start any business or project this month as it may be delayed. Admit your fault and apologize if necessary as this may prevent any serious confrontation with others. You may be feeling very sleepy or tired at this time. Rest and relax as much as you can as next month may be very hectic. Most of your money problems will disappear in a few weeks. If you are negative you may experience inner conflicts and worries. It is most important that you attend the temple or any religious functions this month as this will assist you in some of the problems you are experiencing. You may find the solution in those places. If you are positive you may find yourself among spiritual individuals who are very knowledgeable and who may be able to teach you a great deal about religion. See an astrologer or Guru this month. Accept any criticism.

FEBRUARY 2015 FORECAST

LIFECODE FORECAST: Be careful of accidents, conflict with police officers, negative involvement with the court and worrisome problems from all sides. At all cost you are advised to keep a low profile this month and avoid confrontations with others who are negative. Your income may be low, expenses may be high and money may be short. You may also receive sad news from afar, or news of an illness. Your personal affairs may be delayed and opportunities that may seem great at first may not be attained successfully if started this month. Of course if you are religious and charitable most of these problems may be minimized. Control your temper. Do not speak harshly and avoid conflicts with co-workers. You must go to the temple as much as you can and meditate a great deal as all these will assist you safely through this month. Any activity this month should involve spirituality, or learning. Tension may be very high and sexual feelings may be very strong. If you are having an illicit affair, you must be careful of scandal. The key word is finish. Take care of unfinished business this month. Write your ideas down and keep it for next month. Don't think of changing jobs at this time. You may be prone to accidents or have worrisome problems from all sides. Keep a low profile and avoid confrontations of a negative nature with others. Income will be low and money may be short. There is possible sad news. Delay or deception in personal affairs and opportunities will not be attained successfully. If you are religious most of these problems will be minimized.

SPECIAL MESSAGE FOR THIS MONTH: Because of the influences of the year, money will be prominent in your life this month. All aspects of your life connected with money may be affected such as your job, your mortgage, your prestige, your income and so on. Love and romance may be expensive but pleasurable if you are positive. Marriage this month may be very profitable to the female partner. You may be tempted to buy yourself that expensive item you have wanted to buy for a long time but never had the money. On the other hand if you have been negative, this month may bring delay, disappointment, deception or trickery pertaining to finance. It is a good time to request a promotion from your superiors and also a good time to play the lottery. Try to save some of the money that will come your way this month as you will need it in an emergency next month. Real estate opportunities may seem attractive for investment purposes. It is a good time to invest in the stock market, but very little. If you are having difficulties this month avoid over spending and should pray.

MARCH 2015 FORECAST

LIFECODE FORECAST: You may be feeling quite independent this month and possibly lonely. You may be very busy attending to a lot of your projects, your career or your business. You may find yourself in conflict with others as a result of your becoming too commanding or too dominating. If you are married, tension may arise at the beginning of the month where you may be denied attention from your spouse or lover. Some of your personal projects or dreams may become a reality at this time. Your inventive abilities are extremely high and you may be congratulated or honored by persons in authority. A promotion may come about at your place of employment. Your health may be affected on the 8th or 17th of the month. Quarrels may occur on the 5th, 14th and 23rd of the month. A few opportunities for promotions and advancements in your ambitions may present themselves. Take advantage of these. If you are experiencing negative feelings of loneliness, perform meditative Puja. Concentrate on yourself this month and try to do everything that you have to do on your own without requesting help from others. People will not be as cooperative as you want them to be. You may feel lonely at times. However, any new opportunities presented will make you feel good about yourself. Do not be over-confident or too competitive with others. Do not expect many invitations until next month.

SPECIAL MESSAGE FOR THIS MONTH: Because of the influence of the year, you need to be careful of accidents, conflict with police officers, negative involvement with the court and worrisome problems from all sides. At all cost you are advised to keep a low profile this month and avoid confrontations with others who are negative, so you need to decide carefully what social functions you will attend, which you will decline and most importantly be very conscious of your behavior at these functions. Even though you will make profits, your income may be low because there will be high expenses and money may be short. You may also receive sad news from afar, or news of an illness. Your personal affairs may be delayed and opportunities that may seem great at first may not be attained successfully if started this month. Of course if you are religious and charitable most of these problems may be minimized. Do not speak harshly and avoid conflicts with co-workers. You must go to the temple as much as you can and meditate a great deal as all these will assist you safely through this month. Any activity this month should involve spirituality, or learning. Tension may be very high and sexual feelings may be very strong. If you are having an illicit affair, you must be careful of scandal. Take care of unfinished business this month. Don't think of changing jobs at this time. Hindus who are experiencing trouble this month are advised to meditate, visit a guru, psychic or astrologer, and perform religious ceremonies by inviting the Brahmin Priest and feeding the homeless or older individuals. Christians are advised to do the same as above in addition to reading the 27th Psalm eleven times each day

APRIL 2015 FORECAST

LIFECODE FORECAST: Romance and love may be predominant in your mind this month. If married you will be enjoying the pleasures of the opposite sex this month. If single you may be dating that favorite person you wanted to date for a while now. Expect quite a few visitors at home or through the telephone. Your emotion may be high and you may be asked to perform good deeds. If your partner is not properly matched astrologically with you then expect a great deal of disagreements this month. Your popularity may rise now so expect quite a few requests for service from others. That invitation you have been looking forward to may come now. Expect many friends to call you or visit you this month. You may meet some new contacts or some new interests in your love affairs. That special someone, you have been thinking about may enter your life now. Married couples will be spending much more time with each other this month. Business partnerships will be profitable.

SPECIAL MESSAGE FOR THIS MONTH: Because of the influence of the year, you may be feeling quite independent this month and possibly lonely. You may be very busy attending to a lot of your projects, your career or your business. You may find yourself in conflict with others as a result of your becoming too commanding or too dominating. If married, tension may arise at the beginning of the month where you may be denied attention from your spouse or lover. Some of your personal projects or dreams may become a reality at this time. Your inventive abilities are extremely high and you may be congratulated or honored by persons in authority. A promotion may come about at your place of employment. Your health may be affected on the 8th or 17th of the month. Quarrels may occur on the 5th, 14th and 23rd of the month. A few opportunities for promotions and advancements in your ambitions may present themselves. Take advantage of these. If you are experiencing negative feelings of loneliness, perform meditative puja

MAY 2015 FORECAST

LIFECODE FORECAST: If you are a female and not pregnant at this time then you may surely hear news of pregnancy from someone related to the family. Children may need your attention this month and may demand that you spend more time with them. You may find yourself studying or reading a great deal now and if you are a student you will be successful in your exams or courses at school. You may be spending a great deal of time on the telephone and may receive lots of calls from old friends who may surprise you. If you are in business for yourself expect a great deal of profits coming to you through the telephone and an increase in clientele, but be aware that is not how much money you make, but how much you get to keep. If you are negative then expect some distress through younger individuals. You should be doing a lot of entertaining or you are being entertained a great deal this month. Your creativity is high and you will be successful with many of your undertakings. Most of your wishes will be realized. Old friends will show up at your home. Enjoy the month.

SPECIAL MESSAGE FOR THIS MONTH: Because of the influence of the year, you should expect quite a few visitors at home or through the telephone. Your emotion may be high and you may be asked to perform good deeds. If your partner is not properly matched astrologically with you then expect a great deal of disagreements this month. Your popularity may rise now so expect quite a few requests for service from others.

JUNE 2015 FORECAST

LIFECODE FORECAST: Repairs in the home, pains in the joints, overwork, tiredness, sleepiness are the influences of this month. You may be feeling very lazy and may have to put in extra time at the job for your boss. It may be a very busy time in your business or occupation. Now is the time when you may be able to fix that broken appliance or wall in your home. If you are looking for a job this month you may not find one because wherever you go the salary may not be to your satisfaction. If you are employed presently you may feel at this time that the payment received does not compensate for the work you are performing. Owners of real estate or rental properties may experience difficulty with tenants this month. In the beginning of this month your car may also require some maintenance. Contact with your mother or a female mother figure may be expected soon. Purchase of antiques or articles of those who have died may come into your possession. This is a good time for constructive activities, exercise, diet and hard work. Expect to participate in community affairs. Accept all overtime given to you at your place of employment and put in extra hours to complete your personal duties. Cut down on expenses as money is low at this time. Watch your health. This is a good time to visit the doctor.

SPECIAL MESSAGE FOR THIS MONTH: Because of the influence of the year, if you are a female and not pregnant at this time then you may surely hear news of pregnancy from someone related to the family. Children may need your attention this month and may demand that you spend more time with them. You may find yourself studying or reading a great deal now and if you are a student you will be successful in your exams or courses at school. You may be spending a great deal of time on the telephone and may receive lots of calls from old friends who may surprise you. If you are in business for yourself expect a great deal of profits coming to you through the telephone and an increase in clientele. If you are negative then expect some distress through younger individuals.

JULY 2015 FORECAST

LIFECODE FORECAST: Short travel or driving to a distant location is forecasted for you this month. If you are not taking a vacation, then you may be traveling as a result of your employment or personal business. Your romantic feelings may be extremely high at this time and single individuals may encounter an exciting month and find new romance. If married you will be enjoying the pleasures of the opposite sex this month. If single you may be dating that favorite person you wanted to date for a while now. You may be involved in a false situation where you may be accused of insincerity or you may be deceived by somebody close to you. All telephone calls coming to you from long distances should not be taken seriously. It is possible that the situation may not be as somber as you think it is. If you are negative be careful of affliction to the private organs. You must also be careful of loss of reputation. If you are making a trip you will enjoy meeting some interesting people. Your appearance may be a major topic this month. Sex, love and romance are prevalent in your mind this month. Also travel and long distance communications occupy most of your time now. You will be meeting with strangers or attractive members of the opposite sex. New changes or a possible move is the highlight of this month. Avoid impulsiveness, trickery, or dishonesty from others.

SPECIAL MESSAGE FOR THIS MONTH: Because of the influence of the year, you may have to deal with repairs in the home, pains in the joints, overwork, tiredness and sleepiness. You may be feeling very lazy and may have to put in extra time at the job for your boss. It may be a very busy time in your business or occupation. If you are looking for a job this month you may not find one because wherever you go the salary may not be to your satisfaction. If you are employed presently you may feel at this time that the payment received does not compensate for the work you are performing. Owners of real estate or rental properties may experience difficulty with tenants this month. In the beginning of this month your car may also require some maintenance. Contact with your mother may be expected soon. Purchase of antiques or articles of those who have died may come into your possession.

AUGUST 2015 FORECAST

LIFECODE FORECAST: Control your anger or your temper. It is a very tense month and you may experience some delays and difficulties at your place of employment as well as at home. Equipments may break down and traveling may be difficult. It is advisable for you to stay together with family and relatives. Do worship and meditate with them and last but not least attend services at the temple. All this will serve to assist you from having many difficulties now. Be careful of accidents and possible pain or injury to the lower back. If any disagreements develop between you and your partner, it surely is your fault for not being able to control your temper. If positive you may be promoted at your place of employment or be given more responsibility with more pay. Avoid conflicts with co-workers or being involved in discussions that are argumentative. Most of all admit when you are wrong, if you are. Avoid aggressiveness. Accept all responsibilities given to you. There is the possibility of association with negative people who will try to take advantage of you. Be calm and patient as you will be torn between your love life and your job. Be prepared for a possible quarrel with your partner or the end of a friendship. Do not cry or get angry over petty annoyances or younger individuals. Sexual activity is low.

SPECIAL MESSAGE FOR THIS MONTH: Because of the influence of the year, you should expect some short travel or driving to a distant location. If you are not taking a vacation then you may be travelling as a result of your employment or personal business. Your romantic feelings may be extremely high at this time and single individuals may encounter an exciting month in the area of romance. You may be involved in a false situation where you may be accused of insincerity or you may be deceived by somebody close to you. All telephone calls coming to you from long distances should not be taken seriously. It is possible that the situation may not be as somber as you think it is. If you are negative, you must be careful of affliction to the private organs. You must also be careful of loss of reputation. If you are making a trip you will enjoy meeting some interesting people. Your appearance may be a major topic this month.

SEPTEMBER 2015 FORECAST

LIFECODE FORECAST: Avoid criticizing anyone or getting yourself involved in any gossip as this may become very damaging to your reputation this month. You may receive news of an older person dying far away or you may visit a sick person in the hospital or a prison. Income may be very low at this time. Do not start any business or project this month as it may be delayed. Admit your fault and apologize if necessary as this may prevent any serious confrontation with others. You may be feeling very sleepy or tired at this time. Rest and relax as much as you can as next month may be very hectic. Most of your money problems will disappear in a few weeks. If you are negative you may experience inner conflicts and worries. It is most important that you attend the temple or any religious functions this month as this will assist you in some of the problems you are experiencing. You may find the solution in those places. If you are positive you may find yourself among spiritual individuals who are very knowledgeable and who may be able to teach you a great deal about religion or spirituality. See an astrologer or Guru if you are having difficulties this month. Accept gracefully when others criticize you. Avoid being hasty or too secretive about your feelings. You may be feeling lonely. If so try to read or study or meditate. Write those letters that you had planned to write last month. Financial gains are low so avoid spending. Listen to religious people and be charitable to those in need of help. You will get into trouble because of gossip or criticism this month.

SPECIAL MESSAGE FOR THIS MONTH: The influences of the year make this a very difficult time when you also need to control your anger or your temper. It is a very tense month and you may experience some delays and difficulties at your place of employment as well as at home. Equipments may break down and travelling may be difficult. It is advisable for you to stay together with family and relatives do worship and meditation with them and last but not least attend services at the temple. All this will serve to assist you from having many difficulties now. Be careful of accidents and possible pain or injury to the lower back. If any disagreements develop between you and your partner it surely is your fault for not being able to control your temper. If positive you may be promoted at your place of employment or be given more responsibility with more pay. Avoid conflicts with co- workers or being involved in discussions that are argumentative. Most of all admit when you are wrong if you are.

OCTOBER 2015 FORECAST

LIFECODE FORECAST: Money is the main issue in your life this month. All aspects of your life connected with money may be affected such as your job, your mortgage, your prestige, your income and so on. Love and romance may be expensive but pleasurable if you are positive. Marriage this month may be very profitable to the female partner. You may be tempted to buy yourself that expensive item you have wanted to buy for a long time but never had the money. On the other hand if you have been negative this month may bring delay, disappointment, deception or trickery pertaining to finance. It is a good time to request a promotion from your superiors and also a good time to play the lottery. Try to save some of the money that will come your way this month as you will need it in emergency next month. Real estate opportunities may seem attractive for investment purposes. It is a good time to invest in the stock market, but very little. This is a positive month for money matters and for purchasing that expensive item that is needed. Income should be high now and money will be coming from unusual quarters. If you are negative expect unforeseen expenses this month. Save some of your money for next month as you will need it. Avoid extravagance or over spending.

SPECIAL MESSAGE FOR THIS MONTH: Because of the influences of the year, money will be prominent in your life this month. All aspects of your life connected with money may be affected such as your job, your mortgage, your prestige, your income and so on. Love and romance may be expensive but pleasurable if you are positive. Marriage this month may be very profitable to the female partner. You may be tempted to buy yourself that expensive item you have wanted to buy for a long time but never had the money. On the other hand if you have been negative, this month may bring delay, disappointment, deception or trickery pertaining to finance. It is a good time to request a promotion from your superiors and also a good time to play the lottery. Try to save some of the money that will come your way this month as you will need it in an emergency next month. Real estate opportunities may seem attractive for investment purposes. It is a good time to invest in the stock market, but very little. If you are having difficulties this month avoid over spending and should pray.

NOVEMBER 2015 FORECAST

LIFECODE FORECAST: Be careful of accidents, conflict with police officers, negative involvement with the court and worrisome problems from all sides. At all cost you are advised to keep a low profile this month and avoid confrontations with others who are negative. Your income may be low, expenses may be high and money may be short. You may also receive sad news from afar, or news of an illness. Your personal affairs may be delayed and opportunities that may seem great at first may not be attained successfully if started this month. Of course if you are religious and charitable most of these problems may be minimized. Control your temper. Do not speak harshly and avoid conflicts with co-workers. You must go to the temple as much as you can and meditate a great deal as all these will assist you safely through this month. Any activity this month should involve spirituality, or learning. Tension may be very high and sexual feelings may be very strong. If you are having an illicit affair, you must be careful of scandal. The key word is finish. Take care of unfinished business this month. Write your ideas down and keep it for next month. Don't think of changing jobs at this time. You may be prone to accidents or have worrisome problems from all sides. Keep a low profile and avoid confrontations of a negative nature with others. Income will be low and money may be short. There is possible sad news. Delay or deception in personal affairs and opportunities will not be attained successfully. If you are religious most of these problems will be minimized.

SPECIAL MESSAGE FOR THIS MONTH: Because of the influence of the year, you need to be careful of accidents, conflict with police officers, negative involvement with the court and worrisome problems from all sides. At all cost you are advised to keep a low profile this month and avoid confrontations with others who are negative, so you need to decide carefully what social functions you will attend, which you will decline and most importantly be very conscious of your behavior at these functions. Even though you will make profits, your income may be low because there will be high expenses and money may be short. You may also receive sad news from afar, or news of an illness. Your personal affairs may be delayed and opportunities that may seem great at first may not be attained successfully if started this month. Of course if you are religious and charitable most of these problems may be minimized. Do not speak harshly and avoid conflicts with co-workers. You must go to the temple as much as you can and meditate a great deal as all these will assist you safely through this month. Any activity this month should involve spirituality, or learning. Tension may be very high and sexual feelings may be very strong. If you are having an illicit affair, you must be careful of scandal. Take care of unfinished business this month. Don't think of changing jobs at this time. Hindus who are experiencing trouble this month are advised to meditate, visit a guru, psychic or astrologer, and perform religious ceremonies by inviting the Brahmin Priest and feeding the homeless or older individuals. Christians are advised to do the same as above in addition to reading the 27th Psalm eleven times each day

DECEMBER 2015 FORECAST

LIFECODE FORECAST: You may be feeling quite independent this month and possibly lonely. You may be very busy attending to a lot of your projects, your career or your business. You may find yourself in conflict with others as a result of your becoming too commanding or too dominating. If you are married, tension may arise at the beginning of the month where you may be denied attention from your spouse or lover. Some of your personal projects or dreams may become a reality at this time. Your inventive abilities are extremely high and you may be congratulated or honored by persons in authority. A promotion may come about at your place of employment. Your health may be affected on the 8th or 17th of the month. Quarrels may occur on the 5th, 14th and 23rd of the month. A few opportunities for promotions and advancements in your ambitions may present themselves. Take advantage of these. If you are experiencing negative feelings of loneliness, perform meditative Puja. Concentrate on yourself this month and try to do everything that you have to do on your own without requesting help from others. People will not be as cooperative as you want them to be. You may feel lonely at times. However, any new opportunities presented will make you feel good about yourself. Do not be over-confident or too competitive with others. Do not expect many invitations until next month.

SPECIAL MESSAGE FOR THIS MONTH: Because of the influence of the year, you may be feeling quite independent this month and possibly lonely. You may be very busy attending to a lot of your projects, your career or your business. You may find yourself in conflict with others as a result of your becoming too commanding or too dominating. If married, tension may arise at the beginning of the month where you may be denied attention from your spouse or lover. Some of your personal projects or dreams may become a reality at this time. Your inventive abilities are extremely high and you may be congratulated or honored by persons in authority. A promotion may come about at your place of employment. Your health may be affected on the 8th or 17th of the month. Quarrels may occur on the 5th, 14th and 23rd of the month. A few opportunities for promotions and advancements in your ambitions may present themselves. Take advantage of these. If you are experiencing negative feelings of loneliness, perform meditative puja

Section 6

HIGHLIGHTS AND ADVICE FOR 2015

Forecasts by the Vedic Deity Goddess Kali

LEGAL, GOVERNMENT AND COURTS THIS YEAR

WARNING: Police, government, traffic tickets, military, city officials, and inspectors are all possible problems for you this year. You are advised to keep a disciplined and humble attitude or this could become very big problems for you. Make sure you are following all rules or regulations. Possible legal problems may involve imprisonments and fines. Fast and meditate. It is a negative year for dealing with government agencies.

ROBBERY BURGLARY AND LOSSES THIS YEAR

WARNING: It is a definite year that you will be prone to be robbed. Hide your jewelry, savings and your valuables. Safeguard your documents and your important information including your computer. Watch out for hackers. If you own a business expect the possibility of robbery. Employees make take advantage of you. Losses may occur at home or at work.

ACCIDENTS, CONFRONTATIONS AND CONFLICTS THIS YEAR

WARNING: You are very accident prone this year so you must be very careful driving, fixing, and repairing anything. If you are a contractor definitely watch out for possible injuries. If you are working with machinery or exercising you could hurt your back or shoulder. Do very little exercises this year. Do not exert or push your body too hard as this may present very bad health problems. You may face many confrontations with family, bosses or coworkers. Do not get involved in any arguments as you will lose.

FAMILY, FRIENDS AND RELATIVES THIS YEAR

WARNING: Avoid family contact as much as possible for the sake of peace. Visiting relatives may create problems. You may experience conflicts with friends you made last year. Prepare for separation as that may be better for you. Do not argue with in-laws or parents, you will be unhappy if you oppose them.

CHILDREN THIS YEAR

WARNING: There will be many conflicts with children. It may be because you are putting too much pressure on them or because they have become disrespectful. You may experience disobedience but by the end of the year the children will be a lot more calmed.

SEXUALITY AND ENERGY THIS YEAR

WARNING: Sexual Energy is low and you may have problems with your back and spine. Women will experience menstrual problems and pain on their back. You could experience separation from a lover and sexual contact may be denied. Avoid conflicts with lovers over lies and accusations.

PRAYERS, MEDITATION AND YOGA

WARNING: Much prayer and meditation is needed this year. It is important that you spend lots of time alone. You may feel like you do not believe God or that you do not want to approach the altar or go to the temple, try to fight this feeling as this will not help you this year. Music and listening to your favorite chants or songs and watching uplifting videos will help you cope with the great deal of frustration you will have this year.

TRAVEL, MOVING AND MAJOR CAREER CHANGES

WARNING: Traveling this year will be very difficult and you may experience delays, conflicts, accidents or break downs. Do not move this year until after September. You should not make any career changes. You need to respect your bosses and accept all duties given to you humbly. You need to be prepared for a great deal of responsibilities at the job. At the end of the year you may be promoted. It is a good year to apply for a government job.

OPENING A BUSINESS, PROFITS. NEW PRODUCTS, MARKETING, AGREEMENTS AND CONTRACTS THIS YEAR

WARNING: This is not a good year for opening a business; this should be delayed after September. It is a negative year to invest in the market, launch a new product or make any sales or marketing efforts. You should not be signing any agreements or contracts this year until after September.

REAL ESTATE BUYING AND SELLING THIS YEAR

WARNING: Avoid purchasing or selling Real Estate properties. It is a good year to refinance or take out a mortgage. Pay off your credit cards and do not incur additional debt. Perform repairs on properties.

GAMBLING THIS YEAR

WARNING: It is a very bad year for gambling. You will lose your shirt, your pants and your money! Do not go to the casino, invest in the stock market, get involved in any business partnership or "too-good-to be-true" deals. Keep your money; donate to the temple any 'gambling money' and pray so your money stays with you.

Section 7

WHAT IS THE BEST TIME (HOUR) TO SET APPOINTMENTS OR DO SPECIAL PROJECTS?

In this book, you have a yearly, monthly and daily personal forecast for 2015. To take advantage of the energy changes throughout the day, I have created this hourly forecast. The purpose is to help you set appointments, take naps, avoid stress, make business deals, or call a lover at a specific time of the day that will create success and happiness for you. There are certain hours when you will feel very sleepy and others you will feel very frustrated. It is advisable to take the hours that are "Sleepy" or "Stressful" as a point in time where you need to relax, meditate, and pray. In the hour of "Business", "Enjoyment," or "Creativity," you should use that time to do interviews, make deals, or involve yourself in creative projects. After some trial and error, because of the EST (Eastern Standard Time) you will be able to successfully determine all the hours of the day that will be successful for you, when to sleep, and so on.

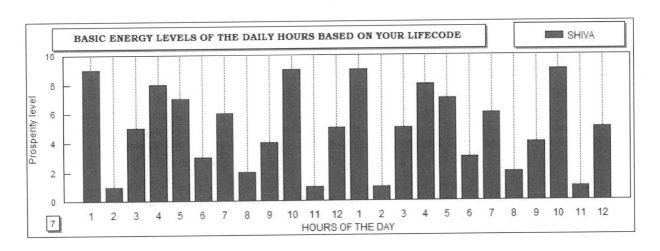

01:00 THE HOUR OF FINANCIAL GAINS AND LOSSES - Dealing with money, investments, business or gambling, are good at this time of the day. If anybody owes you, now is the time to collect that money owed. Ask for a raise now, or buy that expensive item you wanted. Good time to sign contracts and to do business deals..

02:00: THE HOUR OF CONFUSION AND TENSION – Do not make any appointments at this time, energy is low. Relax take a nap or watch TV during this hour. Do not make any decisions, do not sign any contracts or perform any business transactions. It is a good hour to pray and meditate.

03:00: THE HOUR OF ACHIEVEMENT , LONELINESS AND CREATIVITY – A good time to write, work or plan that project you had in mind. Sit , relax and think about all the ideas you have to carry out your plans, and write any new ideas down for later. This hour is good for meetings and appointments.

04:00: THE HOUR OF LOVE AND ROMANCE – A good time to meet with a friend or to have a lunch date with a partner. A good hour to discuss any problems or ideas with others. You will get good cooperation from everyone and your ideas will be accepted happily. Eat your favorite foods at this time.

05:00: THE HOUR OF CHILDREN, EDUCATION & ENERGY – You will be filled with energy at this time. A good hour to play, socialize, get some attention and mix with young children. Buy gifts for friends, go shopping for bargains and see a movie if you can. At work, study a course or training lesson, you will learn fast.

06:00: THE HOUR OF WORK AND STRESSFUL PRESSURE - Relax a little, do not strain too much. Do not worry it will get done. Avoid co-workers or company at this hour. Devote yourself to completing you tasks and your jobs. Do not ask for a raise in this hour.

07:00 THE HOUR OF TRAVEL AND ENJOYMENT – A good time to take a walk outside of the building. Enjoy a short drive or quick session with your lover. Make all your phone long distance phone calls now. Do not be false in your actions as it will backfire on you the next hour. Do not make any promises, you will be busy

08:00: THE HOUR OF RESPONSIBILITY AND FRUSTRATION – Avoid meetings, confrontations and family in this hour. You will face disagreements or lots of responsibilities at this time. Machine or cars can breakdown. Watch out for delay in traffic, accidents or late arrival for meetings or appointments.

09:00: THE HOUR OF SLEEP & RELAXATION - A good time to take a rest and get a cat-nap or short sleep. You will be feeling sleepy at this time. If you try to work you body will slow down, sit down , relax for an hour or meditate and your body will feel energetic again after an hour.

10:00 THE HOUR OF FINANCIAL GAINS AND LOSSES - Dealing with money, investments, business or gambling, are good at this time of the day. If anybody owes you, now is the time to collect that money owed. Ask for a raise now, or buy that expensive item you wanted. Good time to sign contracts and to do business deals.

11:00: THE HOUR OF CONFUSION AND TENSION – Do not make any appointments at this time, energy is low. Relax take a nap or watch TV during this hour. Do not make any decisions, do not sign any contracts or perform any business transactions. It is a good hour to pray and meditate.

12:00: THE HOUR OF ACHIEVEMENT , LONELINESS AND CREATIVITY – A good time to write, work or plan that project you had in mind. Sit , relax and think about all the ideas you have to carry out your plans, and write any new ideas down for later. This hour is good for meetings and appointments.

YOUR MONEY FOR 2015

Your Life Will Be Affected By: Mars Known As Mangal in Vedic Science

MONEY

It is a good time to spend money on the home, family and children. Do not lend or borrow at this time as family may be asking you for money. Avoid any partnerships. Credit cards or mortgages loans may run penalties and late charges. Prepare to spend some money also on court or government agencies.

You are very secretive about money. Even though money may not be important to you, you need it. You spend lots of money on your parents. Using money for real estate is lucky for you. You do not like when other people owe you money. You become very emotional about your savings and your earnings. Raises and bonuses come to you slowly but surely. You do well in business money wise. You may secretly spend or earn money from bars or clubhouses. Very few people know about your finances. You are lucky with the stock market and any farming business.

2015 MONEY FORECAST

POSITIVE MONTHS

The positive money months for you this year are JANUARY, APRIL, MAY, JULY and OCTOBER. You will find great bargains if you shop in MAY; the best days to shop for bargains are the 5th, 14th and 23th. JANUARY and OCOTBER are the best months to play the lotto. In APRIL and DECEMBER, you will also want to get luxury items that are very expensive, but is not recommended that you do in APRIL.

NEUTRAL MONTHS

The neutral months are MARCH, JUNE, SEPTEMBER and DECEMBER. MARCH, SEPTEMBER are good months to give donations to your temple or charitable organizations. This will bring you prosperity.

NEGATIVE MONTHS

Although this should be a NEGATIVE financial year, the karmic results of this depend on your previous actions. If you have not been spiritually disciplined, religious, devoted and humble you may suffer heavy losses during this year. The losses may come through expenses, purchases or any other type of loss. The months that you will be most affected by this influence will be FEBRUARY, AUGUST and NOVEMBER.

Section 9

AVOID NEGATIVE EXPERIENCES FROM THE UNIVERSE IN 2015

Your Life Will Be Affected By: Mars Known As Mangal in Vedic Science

1. Watch out for police, traffic tickets, fights with partners, government problems, credit problems, foreclosures, hospitalization, back or stomach problems, job pressures, arguments with bosses, robbery, thieves, separation and possible court problems.

2. Meditate, keep a low profile, avoid arguments with bosses & family members and go to the temple regularly. Perform chanting of Mantras and Pujas to Shiva and Hanuman. Avoid the colors red and black. Avoid all meat, if possible. Being a vegetarian this year could be very beneficial to you. If you are frustrated, listen to music and bajans.

3. For court problems etc. see your priest, perform Hanuman Puja on a Tuesday. Place 4-limes around you bed area in each corner. Avoid the feeling that you are higher than others are, act humble and chant "KALI DURGE NAMO NAMA" all day if you can.

MANTRAS YOU CAN CHANT TO AVOID NEGATIVE EXPERIENCES

OM SRAAM SREEM SROWM SA: CHANDRAMASE NAMA DADHI-SANKHA-TUSAABHAM KSTRODARNAVA-SAMBHAVAM NAMAAMI SAASINAAM SOMAM SAMBHOOMA MUKTI BHUSHANAM.

I bow to that moon-God who is bright complexioned like curds, conch or snow; born of the sea of milk and resplendent in Lord Shankar's dyiadem like and ornament.

Section 10

Your Career in 2015

Your Life Will Be Affected By: Mars Known As Mangal in Vedic Science

CAREER

Many responsibilities at your place of employment may cause you to disagree with your boss or co-workers. Do not go against higher authority; accept all duties given to you. It is <u>not</u> a good time to ask for a raise. Any new jobs will be filled with additional responsibilities. If you try to change jobs now you may end up on the unemployment line for a while. Pray, rest, eat well, avoid conflicts and this year may become an excellent one.

IT'S A **NEGATIVE** YEAR SO THE OVERALL CONDITIONS ARE NEGATIVE FOR JOBS

YOUR JOB IN 2015 AS A SHIVA	
JOB CATEGORY	**JOB CONDITION FORECAST THIS YEAR**
1 Agriculture & Land	Benefits and favors will be Neutral
2 Alcohol & Tobacco	Rethinking your position will be Negative
3 Art & Entertainment	promotions - new position may be Negative
4 Automobile & Aviation	Opportunities will be Positive
5 Banking	Benefits and favors will be Neutral
6 Basic Manufacturing	Benefits and favors will be Neutral
7 Building & Construction	Benefits and favors will be Neutral
8 Business & Sales	Responsibility & disagreements are Positive
9 Capital Goods	Benefits and favors will be Neutral
10 Chemicals	Rethinking your position will be Negative
11 Children & Day Care	promotions - new position may be Negative
12 Computers & Engineering	Changes in job will be Neutral
13 Consultants & Advisors	Opportunities will be Positive
14 Consumer	Tensions & termination can be Positive
15 Cosmetics & Beauty	Responsibility & disagreements are Positive
16 Credit	Work & co-worker stress is Positive

YOUR JOB IN 2015 AS A SHIVA

JOB CATEGORY	JOB CONDITION FORECAST THIS YEAR
17 Drugs	Changes in job will be Neutral
18 Electronics	Work & co-worker stress is Positive
19 Energy	Work & co-worker stress is Positive
20 Financial Services	Responsibility & disagreements are Positive
21 Food & Groceries	Tensions & termination can be Positive
22 Fuel & Gas Services	Rethinking your position will be Negative
23 Funeral & Death	Rethinking your position will be Negative
24 Health & Medical	Work & co-worker stress is Positive
25 Insurance	Opportunities will be Positive
26 Investing	Responsibility & disagreements are Positive
27 Tech Services	Changes in job will be Neutral
28 Jewelry & Crafts	Responsibility & disagreements are Positive
29 Legal & Court	Work & co-worker stress is Positive
30 Manufacturing & Industrial	Benefits and favors will be Neutral
31 Masseuse & Fitness	Opportunities will be Positive
32 Media	promotions - new position may be Negative
33 Metals	Work & co-worker stress is Positive
34 Modeling & Fashions	Responsibility & disagreements are Positive
35 Music & Dance	promotions - new position may be Negative
36 Photographers & Painters	Work & co-worker stress is Positive
37 Police & Military	Work & co-worker stress is Positive
38 Real Estate	Benefits and favors will be Neutral
39 Mortgages	Work & co-worker stress is Positive
40 Religion & Spirituality	Changes in job will be Neutral
41 Sanitation & Maintenance	Rethinking your position will be Negative
42 Services	Tensions & termination can be Positive
43 Shipping & Importing	Opportunities will be Positive
44 Social & Educational	promotions - new position may be Negative
45 Software	Money increases will be Neutral
46 Technology	Benefits and favors will be Neutral
47 Textile & Clothes	Tensions & termination can be Positive
48 Transport	Opportunities will be Positive
49 Utilities	Rethinking your position will be Negative
50 Writing & Publishing	promotions - new position may be Negative

Section 11

INVESTMENTS AND BUSINESSES IN 2015

WHAT IS A GOOD INVESTMENT FOR ME?

Like everything in the universe, investments have a specific type of energy, and depending on your particular code, some investments may be more profitable than others. To find out how compatible you are with different types of investments check the table below and read the details below.

This year, your investments require research, responsibility and power. This year, you should not invest with a partner. Avoid confrontation, conflicts and disagreements in investments this year as you may lose your money. Watch out for thieves and robbers.

INVESTMENT OPPORTUNITES RATING TABLE FOR SHIVA			
Seq	Type Of Investment	Life Effect	How It Will Affect You
1	SILVER	NEGATIVE	Watch out for big losses. Avoid this as it may be risky
2	GOLD	POSITIVE	Great profits, Good deals and you will make money
3	DIAMOND	POSITIVE	Great profits, Good deals and you will make money
4	REAL ESTATE	NEUTRAL	Be careful of this investment as it can hurt you
5	STOCK MARKET	NEUTRAL	Be careful of this investment as it can hurt you
6	BOND MARKET	NEGATIVE	You will have many losses - possible litigation
7	BANKING INDUSTRY	NEUTRAL	Be careful of this investment as it can hurt you
8	COMPUTER INDUSTRY	NEUTRAL	Put a lot of thoughts into it before investing in it
9	GOVERNMENT OPPORTUNITIES	NEGATIVE	Watch out for big losses. Avoid this as it may be risky
10	LAND PURCHASE/SALE	NEUTRAL	Be careful of this investment as it can hurt you
11	GAMBLING AND CASINOS	POSITIVE	Great profits, Good deals and you will make money

INVESTMENT OPPORTUNITES RATING TABLE FOR SHIVA

Seq	Type Of Investment	Life Effect	How It Will Affect You
12	MOVIE MAKING	POSITIVE	Many good opportunities with this investment
13	DOW JONES	POSITIVE	Great profits, Good deals and you will make money
14	WEB SERVICES	NEUTRAL	Put a lot of thoughts into it before investing in it
15	INSURANCE COMPANIES	POSITIVE	Many Good gains , but watch out for false deals
16	NETWORK MARKETING	POSITIVE	Great profits, Good deals and you will make money

HOW WILL MY INVESTMENTS PERFORM THIS YEAR FOR SHIVA

Seq	Type Of Investment	Year Effect	Performance Comment and Forecast
1	SILVER	NEGATIVE	Do not be impulsive; seek an advisor as it is not a good time to invest heavily in anything. Avoid partnerships. Do not sign unread contracts. Avoid legal conflicts
2	GOLD	POSITIVE	Some of your investments will pay off this year, but watch out for deceiving individuals. It may look very good but it may be too good to be true. Be cautious
3	DIAMOND	POSITIVE	Some of your investments will pay off this year, but watch out for deceiving individuals. It may look very good but it may be too good to be true. Be cautious.
4	REAL ESTATE	NEUTRAL	Try to do it all yourself this year and you will make more money and receive profits. Your ideas are creative and original, use these now. Start new.
5	STOCK MARKET	NEUTRAL	Try to do it all yourself this year and you will make more money and receive profits. Your ideas are creative and original, use these now. Start new.
6	BOND MARKET	POSITIVE	Many opportunities will knock at your door. Take advantage of these. New Investments are lucky now. Read more, research, take risks if necessary, it pays

Seq	Type Of Investment	Year Effect	Performance Comment and Forecast
	HOW WILL MY INVESTMENTS PERFORM THIS YEAR FOR SHIVA		
7	BANKING INDUSTRY	NEUTRAL	Try to do it all yourself this year and you will make more money and receive profits. Your ideas are creative and original, use these now. Start new.
8	COMPUTER INDUSTRY	NEUTRAL	Watch your investments carefully. If they go down in value, do not panic, it will go up again by year end. You may be have to struggle to keep it profitable
9	GOVERNMENT OPPORTUNITIES	NEGATIVE	Some of your investments will pay off this year, but watch out for deceiving individuals. It may look very good but it may be too good to be true. Be cautious
10	LAND PURCHASE/SALE	NEUTRAL	Try to do it all yourself this year and you will make more money and receive profits. Your ideas are creative and original, use these now. Start new.
11	GAMBLING AND CASINOS	POSITIVE	Some of your investments will pay off this year, but watch out for deceiving individuals. It may look very good but it may be too good to be true. Be cautious
12	MOVIE MAKING	NEGATIVE	Avoid this investment at this time, as any long term investments may result in losses. Money gains will be low. Wait until after September - Investments are better
13	DOW JONES	POSITIVE	Some of your investments will pay off this year, but watch out for deceiving individuals. It may look very good but it may be too good to be true. Be cautious
14	WEB SERVICES	NEUTRAL	Watch your investments carefully. If they go down in value, do not panic, it will go up again by year end. You may be have to struggle to keep it profitable
15	INSURANCE COMPANIES	POSITIVE	Investing with partners or friends may be lucky now. You will receive good offers or deals, take them. Any investments now will pay off gainfully later.
16	NETWORK MARKETING	POSITIVE	Some of your investments will pay off this year, but watch out for deceiving individuals. It may look very good but it may be too good to be true. Be cautious

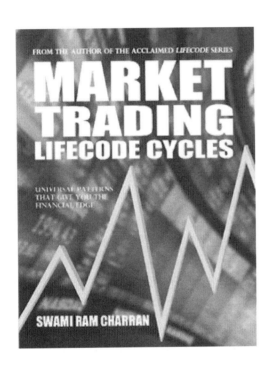

MARKET TRADING: LIFECODE CYCLES: Have you made money in the stock market during the last two years? If not you should not invest without following some sort of system or mathematical order. When we follow a system or program, we can never lose the benefit of such a system.

This book uses a unique LifeCode Trading System based on a combination of Elliott Wave, Fibonacci, Vedic Mathematics and Western Physics to identify trading opportunities in the precious metals and financial markets. This revolutionary trading tool identifies major cyclical changes and trading opportunities in the commodities and financial markets with unprecedented accuracy.

AVAILABLE FROM THE HEENDU LEARNING CENTER

http://shop.swamiram.com/mark eting-trading.html

ONLY $199.99

Section 12

YOUR LOVE LIFE IN 2015

Your Life Will Be Affected By: Mars Known As Mangal in Vedic Science

LOVE

There may be possible disturbances in your marriage life because of family interference. Do not gossip or get angry with in-laws or family. Most people will be difficult at times, so try to keep very calm and stay home and mind your own business as much as you can. People will talk bad about you, try to ignore it. Single lovers may experience separation from a very passionate and romantic lover from the last year. Do not force anyone to love you. Any marriage this year will have to deal with in-law problems and frustrations.

AM I COMPATIBLE WITH MY LOVER OR SPOUSE?

If you ever wonder about your current or future relationship and how you get along with your significant other or what are the areas that are your strength and weaknesses, find out your love match number below and then look for the explanation that follows.

PARTNER CODE # 1 (BRAMHA): EXCELLENT-You will enjoy a prosperous marriage life; money will be your test in marriage. Relationship will be business like, more material than spiritual and this can make you lose each other.

PARTNER CODE # 2 (DURGA): VERY BAD - Struggle, tests, and abuse are the characteristics of this marriage life. You will need a lot of faith.

PARTNER CODE # 3 (VISHNU): NEUTRAL - If not independent, you will feel lonely in marriage or in relationship. Do not be demanding or controlling. Avoid forcing people. Respect all.

PARTNER CODE # 4 (RUDRA): EXCELLENT - A happy married life or relationship only if words and excess desires are under control. Watch your words you could get into trouble.

PARTNER CODE # 5 (NARAYAN): GOOD - You will enjoy a marriage life of comfort and will prosper only through your children. Make them great in life. This relationship has a lot of ego each partner wants to be heard.

PARTNER CODE # 6 (KALI): NEUTRAL - You will have to work very hard to please your partner. There will be many stresses but you must not complain. Just do it.

PARTNER CODE # 7 (SHIVA): SOULMATES - Soul mates, they will always think of each other and can never forget their lovemaking moments. Highly egotistical relationship and can separate because of ego, but will constantly come back because of ego, because each partner wants to possess the other. Love connection is highly recommended for this combination.

PARTNER CODE # 8 (LAXMI): VERY BAD-You will have to keep your ego down or separation will take placed, be humble and avoid high temper and criticizing others

PARTNER CODE # 9 (INDRA): GOOD-You will have a difficult love life, but being spiritual will overcome all obstacles. People will become jealous of you quickly.

WHAT IS A GOOD YEAR TO MARRY?

After you find out that you make a good match with your partner and take the next step and decide to marry, it is important to choose a year that is suitable for you and your significant other. Following is a table with the effects of the marriage year for your Lifecode. On the next page you will find the table for the best days to marry. Since marriage is such an important step it is also recommended that you verify the dates with a knowledgeable Pundit.

GOOD YEARS TO MARRY: 1980, 1981, 1984, 1985, 1989, 1990, 1993, 1994, 1998, 1999, 2002, 2003, 2007, 2008, 2011, 2012, 2016, 2017, 2020 and 2021 before the middle of September.

FAIR YEARS TO MARRY: 1983, 1986, 1987, 1992, 1995, 1996, 2001, 2004, 2005, 2010, 2013, 2014, 2019, 2022, 2023 before the middle of September.

BAD YEARS TO MARRY: 1982, 1988, 1991, 1997, 2000, 2006, 2009, 2015, 2018, 2024 before the middle of September.

WHAT IS A GOOD DAY TO MARRY?

GOOD DAYS TO MARRY: 1, 4, 5, 9, 10, 13, 14, 18, 19, 22, 23, 27, 28 and 31.

FAIR DAYS TO MARRY: 3, 6, 7, 12, 15, 16, 21, 24, 25 and 30.

BAD DAYS TO MARRY: 2, 8, 11, 17, 20, 26 and 29.

The above information applies to the day of any month in any year. For the most appropriate date for marriage a competent priest should be consulted.

AM I GOING TO BE PREGNANT?

If you ever wondered what your chances are of getting pregnant, based on your Lifecode the predictions are below. If you want to get pregnant and are having problems, consult Swami Ram. He has natural remedies and mantras that can help you get pregnant, stay pregnant and avoid miscarriages.

It is advisable that the first child should never be aborted, as this pregnancy is the planting of the first seed, so to speak, and is the first flower of love that comes from the newly married lovers. The first baby will contain the essence of their love connections.

In my experience, I have also noticed a hereditary trait that affects the outcomes of pregnancy and that is that if a female child was abused, molested sexually or if she eats a great deal of red meat then the womb somehow becomes traumatized. Thus, she is unable to become pregnant after she gets married. In addition, if the father of any boy was a sexually illicit or perverse person, his sons will be denied female children. My advice is always to make sure you check your family history thoroughly before assessing why you may be having problems with pregnancy.

For Number 7's
The fertility level is average and is considered positive. The chances of becoming pregnant are 80%. Women in this category have weak wombs, which act dormant or barren sometimes. The reason for that is that there are more male hormones than female hormones in her body. Usually the hairier the body, the lower the fertility level, and the less hairy the more fertile she is. She must take hormonal treatment to increase estrogen. Special herbs can be taken to increase chances of pregnancy. Sitting in a tub of seawater can increase fertility level. Sit-up exercises or massaging of the lower belly with oils can increase the chance of pregnancy. Loss of head hair indicates low infertility.

Section 13

MY HOME IN 2015

What does the place where you live have to do with anything? Most people do not realize that the energy of the place where they live affects them in different aspects of their lives, affects them differently every year and additionally, these influences are felt differently in specific areas of their home. I have designed this Section to help you determine what Vedic number is the energy of your house and how that affects you personally. Additionally, I will let you know the energy that your house will have for this current year. Finally, how the energy is distributed within your home to help you use spaces for your own benefit.

If you already know your home's Vedic Code, proceed to the section of the explanations for the Vedic Location Code; otherwise, follow the instructions below to determine the Location Code for your home.

> **What Is My Location Code?** Add up the digits of the apartment number, building or home number to get a single digit as the Vedic Building or Location Code. For example, if your house address is 3149 Macabee Drive, add the 3+1+4+9 and then reduce the results (17) to a single digit to get the Vedic Building Code, i.e. 1+7=8. The #8 is the Vedic Building Code for this address.

Location Code 1: Loneliness, separation rejection and worry, promotions and progress, don't be too bossy or dominating, you may get into trouble, good for starting projects or businesses.

Location Code 2: Weddings, marriages, romance may take place at this location, lots of visitors and guests at this location, enjoy good food, lots of shopping and a rewarding love life, clean, decorate, repair, remodel and enjoy,

Location Code 3: Children visit, pregnancy, news of birth, menstrual cycle or uterus problems, studies, writing and reading books, too much TV and computer, childishness, immaturity, irresponsibility, social events, children's problems.

Location Code 4: Possible job problems, hard work, overtime, low pay, tension, high-blood pressure, high temper, gossip will create arguments, and home may experience construction and repairs that will improve its value.

Location Code 5: Travel, vacations, unauthentic visitors, long distance calls and relationships, possibility of illicit affairs or some fraudulent transactions, conscious of physical appearance. Common ailments are feet or sexual organs.

Location Code 6: Conflicts, disagreements, power struggles, frustration and responsibility, be careful of visits from family, possible police, court, or collection agencies, divorce, separation, accidents, surgeries, in-law problems.

Location Code 7: Inhabitants feel tired, sleepy, worry about life path, goals, objectives, and future, feel the need to meet with astrologers, psychics, Hindu priests and Swamis, are very secretive, house will be visited by lots of snakes.

Location Code 8: Inhabitants receive or spend a lot of money, changes to expensive furniture or fixtures, renovations, starting profitable business, people in this house are beautiful and presentable, expensive parties or purchases.

Location Code 9: Possible sewer, flooding, boiler, water problems, death, sickness, operations, government problems, accidents, money spent unexpectedly, spouses sleep separate, failed businesses, delays selling house, job frustrations

AM I COMPATIBLE WITH THE PLACE WHERE I LIVE?

How a particular location affects each individual depends on the Location Code of the place in combination with the Lifecode of the individual. The table below will give you the effect of your home.

LOCATION CODE COMPATIBILITY FOR # 7'S								
LOCATION CODE	1	2	3	4	5	6	7	8	9
LOCATION CODE COMPATIBILITY	8	9	1	2	3	4	5	6	7

Location Code Compatibility 1: While you live here you will be independent, bossy, worried, dominant, mentally nervous, and achieve high status in career.

Location Code Compatibility 2: While you live here you shop and look for bargains, cook tasty foods, romance, visitors, decorate, repair, remodel and enjoy, partner demands lots of attention.

Location Code Compatibility 3: While you live here you are argumentative and think you are right, may experience loss of children, children visit, publishing books, too much TV and computer.

Location Code Compatibility 4: While you live here you will work hard, conscientious, stress, high temper, determined, health may be affected, income and expenses equal, follow spiritual life.

Location Code Compatibility 5: While you live here you change your mind often, travel, unauthentic visitors, possibility of illicit affairs or some fraudulent transactions, unlucky with family.

Location Code Compatibility 6: While you live here you're egotistical, conflicts, power struggle, frustration, responsibility, family difficulties, police, court, collection agencies, separation, and accidents.

Location Code Compatibility 7: While you live here, you will think a lot, be tired, sleepy, secretive, critical, and gossipy, worry about life, goals, objectives, and future, feel the need for spirituality.

Location Code Compatibility 8: While you live here money is very important, may quarrel, and if positive stays. You may have a strong ego, business, and investments, attracted to luxury.

Location Code Compatibility 9: While you live here, you will have high temper, traffic tickets, financial problems, mental or physical abuse, fickle, impulsive, spiritual awakening, confused, death.

How Will My Home Be in 2015?

Every year your home goes through a cycle of influence that harmonizes with the universe. The position of the sun, moon, planets and the gravitational effects of other bodies in the universe can create the vibration that can make your location positive or negative. The number or Vedic Location Code can be used to identify this vibration. In the following table the years are indicated in the rows above, which will cross the Vedic Location code as it matches with your Vedic Building Code. This Vedic Location Code for the year in question will describe the influences for the location that year.

Your Vedic Building Code	2015
1	9
2	1
3	2
4	3
5	4
6	5
7	6
8	7
9	8

Location Year Code # 1: During this year in this house people will experience loneliness, separation and worry, promotions and progress may affect the inhabitants, some people could experience rejection from others while living here at this time, avoid being too bossy or dominating, you may get into trouble. It is a good time to start new projects or business at this home or location

Location Year Code # 2: During this year in this house people will experience weddings, marriages or romance; there will be many visitors and guests; people in this house will be enjoying good food, lots of shopping and a rewarding love life during this year. It is a good time to clean, decorate, repair, remodel and to enjoy this home. Lots of dressing up, new clothes and eating of sweets will be some of the activities in this house now.

Location Year Code # 3: During this year in this house many children will visit; possible pregnancy or news of birth; menstrual cycle or uterus problems; lots of studies, writing and reading of books; too much watching of television and computer activities; childishness, immaturity, and irresponsibility at this time. There will be many social parties and engagements this year. The year will bring problems of children, schools, or abortions to this home if the inhabitants are negative and also problem with telephone equipments and billing.

Location Year Code # 4: During this year in this house people will experience possible job problems, hard work, overtime, low pay and general career problems will affect the people in this home at this time. Tension, high-blood pressure, and high temper will affect the people in the home. Gossip will create lots of arguments and negative feelings. This home may experience construction and repairs which will improve the value of your house.

Location Year Code # 5: During this year in this house people will experience travel or vacations. There will be many visitors to this home; some of them may not be genuine. Long distance calls and long-distance relationships may be popular during this time. It is possible, that some inhabitants will have illicit affairs or some fraudulent deals or transactions. People in this house will be more conscious of their physical appearance and most of the women living or visiting here will appear beautiful. Common ailments in this house will affect the feet or sexual organs at this time.

Location Year Code # 6: During this year in this house people will experience conflicts, disagreements, power struggles, frustration and responsibility. Be careful of disturbing visits from family members who will have an attitude towards the inhabitants. There is the possibility of influences from police, court, or collection agencies communicating with the people living here. There may be suggestions of divorce or separation among the couples. One or more of the people living in this house may experience accidents or surgical operations. Check the forecast on Medical Services Code to make better choices for your health care. There may be possible problems from in-laws

Location Year Code # 7: During this year in this house people will experience tiredness and sleepiness. Inhabitants will worry at this time about their life path, their goals, their objectives, and their future. They will feel that they need to meet with astrologers, psychics, Hindu priests and swamis. People in this house will become very secretive at this time. This house may be visited by snakes this year

Location Year Code # 8: During this year in this house people will be receiving or spending a lot of money. This house may experience a change in furniture or fixtures, which may be very expensive. It is a good time to do reconstruction or renovations in this house. Starting a business will become very profitable in this house. People in this house will look more beautiful and presentable this year. Expensive parties or purchases may affect inhabitants of this house.

Location Year Code # 9: During this year in this house people will experience possible sewer, flooding, boiler, or water problems; possible death or news of death sickness or operations. There may be government, city, or state problems, accidents where only the vehicle is damaged; money spent unexpectedly. Husbands and wives will find themselves sleeping separately and any business started at this time will fail; attempts to sell this house will be delayed. There will be frustrations with your job; do not do any construction or rebuilding at this time

WHAT PLACES IN MY HOME ARE BEST FOR WHAT?

Different places in our home or office have different energies and that makes them more suitable for different activities anything from sleeping, cooking or meditating. Check the diagram below to check your home.

	#4- NEUTRAL *BEST LOCATION FOR:* KITCHEN DINING ROOM WORK/ REPAIRS GARAGE	**#3 – POSITIVE** *BEST LOCATION FOR:* BEDROOMS TELEVISION SOFAS PLAY ROOM LIBRARY	**#8 – POSITIVE** *BEST LOCATION FOR:* BUSINESS MONEY BUSINESS COMPUTERS DESK SLEEPING
	#9- NEGATIVE *BEST LOCATION FOR:* BATHROOM SEWER POOL STORAGE EMPTY SPACE	**#5- POSITIVE** *BEST LOCATION FOR:* MEETINGS EXERCISE KITCHEN ROMANCE SITTING ROOM	**#1- NEUTRAL** *BEST LOCATION FOR:* MEDITATION PRAYER ALTARS RELIGIOUS BOOKS
	#2- POSITIVE *BEST LOCATION FOR:* DRESSING ROOM GUEST ROOM KITCHEN SITTING ROOM DINING/ DEN	**#7- NEUTRAL** *BEST LOCATION FOR:* BEDROOMS READING LIVING ROOM MEDITATION GUEST ROOM	**#6- NEGATIVE** *BEST LOCATION FOR:* STORAGE POLITICS FOUNTAIN

POSITIVE/ NEGATIVE SECTIONS OF THE HOME /BUSINESS LOCATION

NORTH (top) — *WEST* (left) — *EAST* (right) — *SOUTH* (bottom)

Energy in Location 1: *Neutral Location.* This location is best for studies, meditation, prayer, altars and to read religious books. This is the central eastern part of the house or location.

Energy in Location 2: *Positive Location.* This is a good place for a dressing room and a kitchen, places of transformation. It is also good as a guest room or sitting room, in the southwestern corner.

Energy in Location 3: *Positive Location.* This is the best location for bedrooms, television, play rooms or a library. This is the central north part of the house or the location.

Energy in Location 4: *Neutral Location.* This is the best location for the kitchen, dining room, home office, and place for repairs or garage. This is the northwestern corner of the house or location.

Energy in Location 5: *Positive Location.* This is the best location for meetings, exercise, kitchen, romance or a sitting room. This is the central part of the home.

Energy in Location 6: *Negative Location.* This location is best used for storage, politics and fountains. This is the southeastern corner of the home or location.

Energy in Location 7: *Neutral Location.* This location is the best area to sleep, to be spiritual and to have profound thoughts. This is the central southern corner of the home or location.

Energy in Location 8: *Positive Location.* This is the best area in the house to keep money, wealth and possessions. It is also good to run a business in the northeastern area of the location.

Energy in Location 9: *Negative Location.* This is best for bathroom, pool or storage. Always have something religious and also a fountain in the central western area of the location.

Improve the energy of your home with Swami Ram's ***Home Energy Cleansing Kit*** at www.shop.swamiram.com or contact us at the Heendu Learning Center at 305-253-5410.

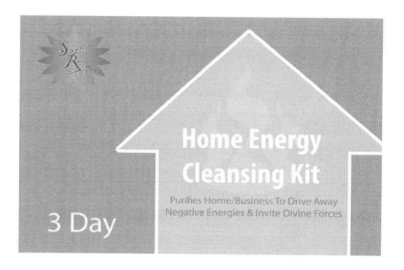

Swami Ram's Home Energy Cleansing Kit is a Life Changing product that can naturally promote tranquility and well-being in your home.

It is a scientifically proven method to drive away negative energy that causes headaches, back pain, stomach and chest pain. The results are amazing. Your aches and pains will disappear, you will sleep better and the quality of your life will dramatically improve.

This is a pure Ayurvedic mixture of herbal plant elements that have been especially prepared to help clean and improve the energy of your home to create harmony and prosperity.

Section 14

TRAVELING, MOVING AND VACATIONING

Traveling can be a positive experience, but at times it may be a difficult one as well. If you are prepared for the possible venture you will have while traveling even difficult circumstances may be viewed under a different light. When we travel, we move from one set of space to another set of space in the Universe. As we travel we replace the energy that was in the space previous to the one that we are presently occupying. Sometimes we can move into a positive space or a negative one, and our own energy can conflict with that location or space. Difficulties in travel can occur when we enter a space that conflicts with our own.

To find a proper time for traveling you must use the table below. The table is divided into Vedic Lifecodes on the left column and days of the month on the top row. To find your good or bad day for traveling, look or the day of the month when you plan to travel and cross it with the number next in line with your Vedic Lifecode.

TRAVEL DAY CODE									
	DAY OF THE MONTH YOU ARE TRAVELING								
YOUR LIFECODE	*1* *10* *19* *28*	*2* *11* *20* *29*	*3* *12* *21* *30*	*4* *13* *22* *31*	*5* *14* *23*	*6* *15* *24*	*7* *16* *25*	*8* *17* *26*	*9* *18* *27*
7	8	9	1	2	3	4	5	6	7

Travel Code 1: Fair day for traveling, most likely traveling alone, lots of time to think and meditate, worrying about things in your life. Take a book; you may need it while traveling.

Travel Code 2: Excellent day for travel, with partner or family, enjoy the company, prepare to be talking or listening to music with someone. Dress well as you may be meeting people on your trip.

Travel Code 3: Excellent day for traveling, with children or young people, educational trip, watching TV or entertainment media. Take a notepad and book, you may be writing or reading. Prepare to attend social event.

Travel Code 4: Negative day. Hard, stressful, may be job related, if not you will be tired when you arrive, extra luggage, take extra lunch and snacks as you may need them. Try to rest as much as you can after this trip.

Travel Code 5: Excellent day, fun trip, vacation, enjoyable. This may be a long distance, out of state or country. Return very satisfied and rejuvenated. Be careful of fraudulent contacts and deceptive agents.

Travel Code 6: Negative day. Trip ahead is rough. You may experience delays, frustration, anger, additional costs and losses. Be careful of accidents or of thieves. Leave home early.

Accept all delays without arguments; acceptance may save you from disaster. If visiting family, may have disagreements after. Change your date.

Travel Code 7: Fair day. Nothing exciting or interesting will happen on this trip. Inner analysis. Take time to meditate and plan your future well. Avoid getting drunk or intoxicated. You may encounter religious individuals or astrologers. Prepare to fall asleep sometime on your journey

Travel Code 8: Excellent day for traveling. If not a business trip, it will be for pleasure. Spend lots of money. If visiting casinos or gambling you may win, beautiful and handsome individuals, watch TV, look at fashions or enjoy great scenery. Business meetings and partnerships will be successful. You'll bring back lots of good stuff.

Travel Code 9: Negative day. Trip ahead is rough, delays, additional costs, accidents, thieves, baggage problems and losses. This may be a trip to funeral or hospital or court. If trip is changed, do not protest as it may be for your own good. The location that you are leaving will demand you return to it soon. Make sure you take extra money.

I hope that the above travel codes will guide you to make travel plans that will take you and bring you back safe from your journeys. Vedic Code of Science is recognized for its potential in preventing unfortunate and lucky occurrences in a person's life. Armed with the knowledge of this science, people can learn to travel safely.

The flight number of the Airline is very important. If the flight number adds up to 9, then there will be delays in the flight schedule, however there is no danger to the passengers on that flight , everyone will arrive safely. If the flight number is#6 then there is some danger of breakdown or accident. However other factors must be taken into consideration when assessing the #6 flight. The best way to avoid all airline accidents is to get airline companies to avoid placing certain flight number on certain dates. If only they will listen to this knowledge many lives could be saved.

Section 15

HOW IS MY CAR FOR ME?

The human body is made to walk on Earth. When it is elevated off the Earth in a vehicle such as an airplane or automobile, it must respond to the movements of that vehicle. The vehicle of course would respond with its own energy field together with the energy field of the human person. A measure of the resulting energy field would most likely tell how that car or vehicle would respond to your energy field when you are in it. Use your Lifecode in combination with the year the automobile was manufactured to see the effects.

YOUR LIFECODE	Vehicle Model Year								
	1981 1990 1999 2008 2017	1982 1991 2000 2009 2018	1983 1992 2001 2010 2019	1984 1993 2002 2011 2020	1985 1994 2003 2012 2021	1986 1995 2004 2013 2022	1987 1996 2005 2014 2023	1988 1997 2006 2015 2024	1989 1998 2007 2016 2025
7	8	9	1	2	3	4	5	6	7

Vehicle Code 1: This is a good car that will prove reliable, driving alone most of the time, problems with lights and ignition area. Usually have books and signs. Listen to talk shows.

Vehicle Code 2: Car transports many people, shopping, music playing, romance, love and sex will be influenced by this car. Driver always has company. Problems are seats, crowded trunk and interior.

Vehicle Code 3: Children will be transported, elaborate musical and speaker system. Most problems will be with the steering and guidance system.

Vehicle Code 4: This car will be used mostly for job. Solid car, it could experience manufacturing problems. The engine is stronger than the body of the car.

Vehicle Code 5: This car accumulates a lot of mileage. This car has wheel or transmission problems. This car will change many hands quickly.

Vehicle Code 6: This car may have lots of repairs, tickets and possible accidents now and previously. You may experience loan payment problems and spend lots of money on body repairs or exhaust system.

Vehicle Code 7: Car will be used for religious purposes. There will be oil or water problems. Driver thinks a lot. If negative owner used for drugs or alcohol, atmosphere will be quiet. Problems may be engine components.

Vehicle Code 8: Car is luxurious and expensive, some custom made. Driver experiences comfort and may even have a chauffeur. The driver may be a businessman, designer or model.

Vehicle Code 9: Car may have water and possible radiator, fuel pump problems. Possible accident will damage the car but little injury to the driver. Owner will spend lots of money on repairs and maintenance.

Section 16

HEALTH, ILLNESS AND SURGERY IN 2015

There is nothing more important to any human being that their health. When we are healthy many times we take it for granted and we abuse it by improper eating and drinking or by wearing black clothes that block our light and health, or by sleeping in an incorrect manner or not exercising, but when our health is not there, we try to look for solutions everywhere. If you have wealth and no health, you cannot enjoy it. The following table gives you an idea of how your day and month of birth influences your health.

This year you need to watch your back; be careful of high blood pressure. Avoid too much meat, eggs and fish, stick mostly to vegetables. You may experience some chest or stomach pains and could get hurt in an accident. A visit to the hospital will be either for you or to visit someone. Older people may end up being hospitalized. Avoid too much spicy food and pray as much as you can.

Your brain, heart and fluid system are the weakest parts of your body. Individuals born under this life code usually have an addiction to drugs and/or alcohol or smoking - this can lead to heart problems, insanity or physical disabilities. Common afflictions in this Life Code are mental retardation, heart diseases, diabetes, insanity or depression. Due to your high mental and brain activity, it is highly recommended for you to meditate one or two times per day for 10 to 15 minutes. Rest and relaxation will help to ease the stresses and headaches of your extremely active mind. The less meat and fish you eat the better your health will be. Your body becomes divine when you are vegetarian and you will not get sick easily. If you eat meat and drink alcohol or take drugs in your body you will be afflicted with terminal diseases. You must also avoid excesses in all things such as too much of any one type of food will be considered an excess. If not religious and calm in your temperament you can destroy yourself as well as all around you. Avoid being critical of others, the karma could distress you later on. Certainly #7 individuals are very strong headed and egotistical. You suffer from doubt and will not believe anything or anybody until you see it. It is this quality that makes you enter into arguments and disbelief. If brought up with divine qualities you will become a powerful leader and will be helpful to the world. Your diet should consist of a variety of different foods, not a concentration of any specific food. Some white meat as well as fish should accompany your meals often in small amounts as your body needs the Omega 3, 6 and 9 protein nutrients. Fruits and vegetables of all types especially Vitamin C should constantly be part of your diet.

WHEN SHOULD I GO SEE MY DOCTOR OR SCHEDULE A SURGERY?

If you ever wonder when you should visit the doctor, when is best to schedule a surgery and wish you could consult with someone, this year your Lifecode Book comes with the answer to those questions. *DO NOT have any medical procedures, particularly surgical during FULL MOON. NEW MOON is best for surgeries. A mother that gives birth during FULL MOON gets high blood pressure.

MEDICAL SERVICES CODE									
YOUR LIFECODE	**DAY OF THE MONTH YOU ARE SCHEDULING MEDICAL SERVICES**								
	1 *10* *19* *28*	*2* *11* *20* *29*	*3* *12* *21* *30*	*4* *13* *22* *31*	*5* *14* *23*	*6* *15* *24*	*7* *16* *25*	*8* *17* *26*	*9* *18* *27*
7	8	9	1	2	3	4	5	6	7

Medical Services Code 1: Positive Day for all types of medical services and surgery except if you feel depressed, postpone the appointment.

Medical Services Code 2: Excellent Day for medical services, surgery and prescriptions.

Medical Services Code 3: Positive Day to acquire knowledge about your medical conditions, to consider natural, herbal, Ayurvedic and allopathic methods.

Medical Services Code 4: Neutral Day. It is a stressful day, but at the same time is a good day to visit the doctor, have surgery or any medical treatments. Surgery will not have to be repeated.

Medical Services Code 5: Negative Day. There is the possibility of receiving false medical information, it is not recommended for surgical procedures, and problems may arise the next day.

Medical Services Code 6: Negative Day. Any diagnosis will be wrong, you will experience a great deal of pain, and the surgery will have to be repeated.

Medical Services Code 7: Excellent Day. It is a good day for medical procedures, there is no pain and usually results are good.

Medical Services Code 8: Excellent Day for medical services and procedures, but it will usually be expensive.

Medical Services Code 9: Negative Day. Definitely not a good day to visit the doctor, today the doctor will find all kinds of diseases, all diagnoses will be negative and surgery will have to be repeated or could have very negative results.

AYURVEDA AND HEALTH

"Health is the greatest treasure" this is a statement that most of us can agree with. If you have money, relationships, family and friends and have no health you will not be able to enjoy them. If you have a job, but no health, you will not be able to perform it. Therefore, health is the greatest treasure.

The secret map to this treasure is Ayurveda, the original science of health and timeless knowledge of complete health for the individual and society contained in the Veda and Vedic Literature, the most fundamental Laws of Nature governing the orderly evolution of the universe.

The use of plants as medicine is older than recorded history. The use of plants as medicines predates written human history. A 60,000-year-old Neanderthal burial site, "Shanidar IV", in northern Iraq has yielded large amounts of pollen from 8 plant species, 7 of which are used now as herbal remedies. In the written record, the study of herbs dates back over 5,000 years to the Sumerians, who described well-established medicinal uses for such plants as laurel, caraway, and thyme. Ancient Egyptian medicine of 1000 BC are known to have used garlic, opium, castor oil, coriander, mint, indigo, and other herbs for medicine and the Old Testament also mentions herb use and cultivation, including mandrake, vetch, caraway, wheat, barley, and rye.

Ayurveda or Ayurvedic medicine is estimated to have about 4,000 to 6,000 years of history. In India, Ayurveda medicine has used many herbs such as turmeric possibly as early as 1900 BC. Ayurveda has been restored for its practical value and range of application by Swami Ram Charran. Through the prevention-oriented knowledge of health care provided by Swami Ram's Ayurvedic products, every individual has the real opportunity to achieve long life in good health.

Most diseases in particular chronic ones are related in one way or another to excessive toxins in the body, a process of inflammation and malnourishment. Swami attempts to resolve most of these issues with the aid of herbs, with guidance for a healthy diet and advise about personal issues that affects our minds and then our bodies.

One of the most exciting new products that Swami Ram has available is the ***Health Maintenance Essentials Kit***. This is the key to maintaining health through natural means. These products are designed to bring balance to your body through the Ayurvedic principle of sanyong or "synergy" that teaches how to combine whole herbs in a matter that the benefits of them together is much greater than if you use each herb in isolation. Each herb has different functions, but each whole herb (instead of active ingredients) creates a holistic balance without negative side effects.

The Health Maintenance Essentials Kit includes Ashwaghanda, Ginger, Neem and Turmeric Capsules. These easy to swallow vegan capsules were designed to make it easy to ingest these herbs and receive its healing gifts. Some of the benefits that you receive from Ashwaghanda are lower cholesterol, diabetes control, stress relief, strong immune system, energy boost and sexual vigor and strength. Ginger not only helps strengthening you immune system, but also keeps your respiratory system healthy, prevents colds, reduces fever and helps with your digestion (one of the most important systems for a healthy body). The antioxidant and anti-inflammatory qualities of Turmeric are so powerful that it can be used instead of NSAID's such as Advil and Tylenol. Neem is perhaps one of the most amazing natural products available in the planet, it is called in India the "Village Pharmacy" but we will only mention its marvelous ability to detoxify your blood and internal organs, resolve all types of skin problems, helps with depression and diabetes and finally help you maintain healthy pancreas, kidneys and liver.

In Ayurveda food is medicine. Different people because of their constitution benefit from different types of foods. In Ayurveda, the five elements of space, air, earth, fire and water make up everything in the universe including the human body. These elements come together to create three different constitutional types, or doshas, known as Vata (airy), Pitta (fiery), and Kapha (earthy).

Knowing your type can help you understand what foods, exercises, and lifestyle elements can support and nurture your health and which ones can cause imbalance. The most accurate way of learning your constitution is to visit an Ayurvedic doctor. He or she can conduct a physical examination including pulse assessment and can tell you what your type is and provide specific recommendations, particularly because most people are a combination of types.

We are including a basic test for you to determine your type. Again, you must remember that most people are a combination of doshas and specific foods affect people differently.

Place a check next to the choice that best describes you. Occasionally more than one choice needs to be made.

Vatta	Pitta	Kapha
___Thin, lanky, and slender with prominent joints and thin muscles.	__Medium, symmetrical build with good muscle development.	__Large, round or stocky build. My frame is broad, stout or thick.
__Thin as a child	__Medium build as a child	__Plump or a little chunky as a child
__Tendency to lose weight or have a hard time gaining weight	__Can lose or gain weight relatively easy if you put your mind to it.	__Gain weight easily, have a hard time losing it
__Eyes are small, active and dark	__Eyes are penetrating light green, grey or amber	__Eyes are large, pleasant, attractive with thick eyelashes
__Long, angular, thin face	__Face is hear shaped with pointed chin	__Face is large, round, full
__Lips are tight, dry and thin	__Lips are smooth, usually get cold sores	__Lips are soft, pink and attractive

Vatta	Pitta	Kapha
__Teeth are irregular and protruding and gums are receding	__Teeth are medium size end gums are reddish	__Teeth are big, white and strong and gums are hearty
__Skin is dry, rough or thin	__Skin is oily, warm, reddish and prone to irritation	__Skin is thick, moist, cool, well-lubricated
__Dark complexion relative to the rest of the family	__Fair skin, sunburn easily relative to the rest of your family	__Tan slowly but usually evenly
__Hair is dry, brittle or frizzy	__Hair is fine with a tendency towards early thinning or graying	__Hair is abundant thick and oily
__Nails are dry, rough, brittle, break easily	__Nails are sharp, flexible, pink, lustrous	__Nails are thick, oily, smooth, polished
__Prefer warm climate, sunshine, moisture	__Prefer cool, well ventilated places	__Any climate is fine as long as it is not too humid
__Hands and feet are usually cold	__Usually warm regardless of the season	__ Adaptable to most temperatures
__Light Sleeper with a tendency to awaken easily	__Moderately sound sleeper usually needing less than eight hours to feel rested.	__Sleep is deep an long, I tend to awaken slowly in the morning.
__Often dream but rarely remember my dreams	__Relatively easy to remember my dreams, often dream in color.	__Generally only remember dreams if they are intense or significant
__Appetite is variable, sometimes I am hungry, and sometimes I am not.	__ Large appetite, quick digestion. May be irritable if you miss a meal or cannot eat when hungry	__Like to eat, fine appetite but you can skip meals if you have to without any physical problems
__Digestion sometimes good, sometimes not	__Usually good digestion	__Digestion is slow or sluggish
__Bowel movements can be irregular, hard, dry or constipated	__Easy and regular bowel movements. Soft, loose at least once to twice a day	__Regular steady bowel movements steady, thick, heavy
__Lively and enthusiastic nature, likes change	__purposeful and intense, likes to convince	__Easy going and accepting, like to support
__Like to stay physically active	__Enjoy physical activities, especially competitive ones	__Love leisurely activities most
__More mentally relaxed when you are exercising	__Exercise helps you control your emotions	__ Exercise helps you keep weight down in a way that diet alone doesn't
__Dislike routine	__Enjoy planning and like routine especially if you create it	__Work well with routine
__Stress makes you anxious and/ worried	__ Stress makes you irritable and/or aggressive	__Stress makes you withdrawn and/ or reclusive
__ Creative Thinker	__Good Initiator or Leader	__Good keeping organization or project running smoothly
__Variable Thirst	__Usually Thirsty	__Rarely Thirsty

Vatta	Pitta	Kapha
__Like to snack or nibble	__Like high protein foods like chicken, fish, eggs, beans	__Love fatty foods, bread, starch
__You think money is there to be spent	__You think money is best spent in special purchases or items that will advance you	__Money is easy to save for you
__Little perspiration	__Frequent perspiration	__Moderate perspiration
__Sexual interests are variable, fantasy life active	__Ready sexual interest and drive	__Steady sexual interest and drive
__Prefer sweet, sour, salty tastes	__Prefer sweet, bitter, astringent tastes	__Prefer pungent, bitter, astringent tastes
__Speaks fast and unclear	__Speaks precise, clear, to the point, sharp	__Speaks slow, gentle, long chats, monotonous

Add up all your checks. The constitution with the most checks is usually your primary constitution. If you have marked two constitutions nearly the same amount of times, you may be a dual dosha such as: Pitta-Kapha, Vatta-Kapha, etc. In rare cases, you may check the three constitutions nearly the same amount of times and in this case you have a tridosha.

NUTRITION FROM AN AYURVEDIC PERSPECTIVE

There are ten rules that the ancient sages about how to eat your food in a healthy way. These rules are:

1. Food needs to be hot
2. Food needs to be tasty and easy to digest
3. You must eat food in proper amounts (not too much, not too little)
4. You must eat food in an empty stomach, after your last meal has been digested.
5. Foods need to work with each other and not contradict each other
6. You need to eat you food in a pleasant environment and with the proper equipment for their enjoyment.
7. You should not be rushed when you eat
8. Eating should not be a long drawn out affair either
9. You should focus on your food when eating
10. Only eat foods that are nourishing and that suit you physical, mental and emotional temperament.

Section 17

CONTROL THE POSITIVE AND NEGATIVE DAYS IN YOUR LIFE

How to Control the Positive and Negative Days or Months in Your Life

When I know I have a negative day, I do not go to an interview, or I do not take an operation or schedule a surgery. When I go on a date with a lover I do not plan it on a negative day, I would enjoy my romantic moments with my partner on positive days. I pick positive days when I take a trip in my car or travel on an airline. I check the number of the place where I visit and assess the effects of the place on my mind and body. If it is a negative place for me, I would be very careful of what I eat or drink. If I have food to eat, I would pray over my food before eating. At work, I would find out the Lifecode numbers of all the people around me and determine who will work well with me and who will disagree with me. I then will act accordingly with each person in a way that will not bring me in conflict with anyone there.

LOVE & MARRIAGE

If it is a negative day for your lover then wait for another day to discuss anything important. If it is a positive day and your lover wants to spend some time with you then accept the invitations. You will feel like a miserable dog on negative days, avoid getting angry that day, accept all insults or criticism without protest…you will have your day for that. Avoid excessive sexual contact on negative days. Once is enough. If you fail on a negative day, do not worry, you will do better in a positive day.

HEALTH & FOOD

On negative days, you will feel low energy, you will feel like you want to stay home and sleep, you will feel like others do not care for you, and you can feel depressed and lazy. Listen to some music or nice chants. If you are feeling any pain try to do something natural, as going to the doctor is not a good idea. Watch what you eat as you could get indigestion, or diarrhea or fevers. Resting is always a good idea. Do not complain about your negative feelings, tell God instead. Do not do anything without knowing how it is going to help you. On negative days, avoid anything acidic. On positive days, avoid too much sugar as the body is in low metabolism.

WEALTH & MONEY

On negative days, you will receive credit calls, they may ask you to pay a bill or you will have to lend money to others. Do not address it at this time; try to address those problems on the next day, as the whole energy will change. Do not get angry. On Positive days, investments, business, any purchases will be good. Do not buy any equipment on negative days it will break.

JOB & CAREER

Your boss and other co-workers will test you on negative days. Ignore their comments and wait for another day. Remember: "every dog has its day" and you will have your opportunities on positive days. On negative days, the boss will give you more work, do not protest, accept it with great heart; this will reward you with good karma on positive days.

TRAVEL & DRIVING

Do not plan your travels on negative days, as this will create delays, baggage problems and lost or stolen articles. You will be much happier travelling on positive days. Driving on negative days can cause accidents; you have to be more cautious, say your prayers before going. On positive days, you do not have to worry. If you are planning a vacation, do it in a positive month, as it will not be a real vacation on a negative month. If someone is visiting you and they arrive at your home on a negative day for you, prepare for some conflicts. You will not feel relieved until they are gone.

MEDITATION & PRAYER

On negative days, your mind will not be able to focus. Doubts and disbelief will constantly plague your mind about God. You will have doubts about your life, your goals, and your relationships. Pray, meditate, get your thoughts together and wait for positive day. Avoid excessive exercises or strenuous yoga practices on negative days. The best way to avoid mental nervousness and tension on negative is to chant soothing meditation mantras such as "KALI DURGE NAMO NAMA". While sitting in the meditative position, think about all the things that make you angry and solve it in your mind. Do not try to clear you mind, you will get frustrated. Do longer meditation on negative days and shorter meditations on Positive days.

Now you ask the question as how I know my positive and negative days, good year, bad year, or a negative or neutral month to expect. This is the knowledge I will present in this book. Planning your life successfully does not require you to battle uselessly with the universe, but to work with the universe. Equation of life offers you the opportunity to do so with such a joy and enthusiasm that is limitless and ecstatic in its rewards and glory.

Section 18 - EXPLANATION OF THE DAILY READINGS FOR THE YEAR

DAILY INFLUENCE: (NEGATIVE, POSITIVE or NEUTRAL)

This tells you how the day is going to be in General. Some days are more negative than others, and some days are more positive than some others. You can enjoy the neutral days by doing activities that have been left back or those that do not require too much effort, as in neutral days your energy is on a middle level. It is always good to pray more on your negative days. Do more meditation or Chanting of the Mantras . Perform Charity or spiritual work as this will make you more connected to the universe. On Positive days you will be able to relax more and you will have more energy to do what you want. Its good to set up interviews and important projects for those days. If you are faced with a court date or job interview and you cannot change it , you may try talking to Swami or you may offer prayers to the Ocean or Temple before to ward off any obstacles. Of course not eating meat or wearing black clothes should be avoided on those negative days. Most of the time Court cases are postponed on negative days.

Forecast and ADVICE for the day

This is a generally close description of the day. It helps you to assess your day accordingly and lets you have an idea of some of the things that may show up in your life that day.

KEYWORDS

These are suggested words that will mostly affect your life that day. All may not apply , only some will apply. This is to let you know that some of these things may affect you . It prepares you to expect these. They may be postive or negative according to the influence of the day.

ASPECTS OF THE DAY

THERE IS A TIME FOR EVERYTHING - Many people sometimes wonder why they have problems after they move or wether they could have avoided the problems they are facing now. Well if you move the right day, travel on the best days, or get married on the wrong day, then this can affect your life. If you can do all the things in your life at the right time , then you will have very little problem harmonizing with the universe. If it says bad , then do not do it if you can avoid it.

BIBLE VERSES: (Proverbs)

These have been taken from the Book of Proverbs in the Christian St James Bible

READ PSALMS #'s:

More than Five Psalms have been recommended, but you only need to read at leats Two of those given

VEDIC MANTRAS FOR THE DAY:

These are special words which are designed to produce certain sounds and vibrations that will create positive changes in your life. Just like the bible says that " In the beginning it was the word, and the word was God and the word became one" so also the Hindus have the word "OM" which is known as the first word of Creation and is known as the vibration of birth. Dr. OZ on OPRAH recommends the Chanting of "OM" for relieving stress. So also these mantras given, will remove negativities in your life. It is sound that controls the mind, so only sound can change mental energy- good or bad.

RULING PLANET:

The Planets acts as timers in our life. Just how the Moon controls the ovulation cycle in women , the planets affect our emotions and moods, and our reaction to the Universal forces. SUN, MOON, MERCURY, VENUS and JUPITER are all Positive effects. The Negative ones are SATURN, RAHU, KETU , NEPTUNE, URANUS and PLUTO.

RULING DEITY:

Each of us is influenced by Cosmic forces and elements constantly in the Universe. The Deities are these forces and elements that affect our life every minute, hour, day, month and year. For example when there is a predominace of salt in our body, then our energy is hyper and when there is a lot of sugar, our nerves become itchy. The deities which are all the elements in the periodic table such as sodium, potassium, mercury , oxygen, copper etc. can affect our health, money and more by they way our brain and body process them. For example a predominance of Kali in our system creates frustration and destructive qualities. A presence of Shiva that day may increase our mental energy and make us more alert that day. So the ruling deity tells what elements are affecting us so when we bow to it we will harmonize with it and get some positive energy from it. Matching the mantra vibration with the elements helps to bring peace and inner happiness.

JANUARY 1, 2015

01/01/2015 THU		This is considered a POSITIVE day for you							Shiva
Moving	Shopping	Health	Investing	Gambling	Love is	Wedding	Travel	Work/Job	Planet
Good	Good	Excellent	Excellent	Excellent	Good	Excellent	Good	Excellent	Jupiter

KEYWORDS ARE: Abusive, Promotion, Fame - TV, High Pleasure, High Pleasure
Business & money gains, Major Expense, Death, Income, Investments

Lotto #'s	play 4 #s	play 3 #s	Ruling Angel:............	Color Sugestion:............	Ruling Deity
8,10,34,26,18,20	8887	887	Haniel	Yellow/White/Silver	Mahalaxmi

ADVICE & DETAILS	MANTRA FOR TODAY
You will be having a good feeling about your income and expenses. It is a good day to purchase and make investments in the market. It is also a good day to look for a new home.	Om Graam Greem Graum Sa Gurave namah swaha 21 times 0 Om Maha Laxmi Cha Vidmahae Vishu Patnayai Cha Dhi Mahi Tanno Laxmi Pracho Dayat

BIBLE VERSES: (Proverbs)

14:1. A wise woman buildeth her house: but the foolish will pull down with her hands that also which is built.

READ PSALMS #'s: 8, 17, 35 ,44, 53, 62, 80, 107, 125

JANUARY 2, 2015

01/02/2015 FRI		This is considered a NEGATIVE day for you							Shiva
Moving	Shopping	Health	Investing	Gambling	Love is	Wedding	Travel	Work/Job	Planet
Bad	Bad	Bad	Bad	Bad	Bad	Bad	Bad	Bad	Saturn

KEYWORDS ARE: Karmic debts, God - Karma, IRS - Law, Denial - Doubt,
Quarrels & lovers, Money - Profits, Sickness - cold, Legal matter, Abusive

Lotto #'s	play 4 #s	play 3 #s	Ruling Angel:............	Color Sugestion:............	Ruling Deity
10,1,33,31,18,14	9987	997	Mikael	Gold/Brown/Blue/Dark Green	Pitridev

ADVICE & DETAILS	MANTRA FOR TODAY
Death is the influence of today. This may be a physical death, the end of a project, idea, habit or thought. You must remember that death is necessary for life and that the end of something, brings new beginnings. This day is also influenced by accidents, so be aware of of your surroundings, do not text while driving or get involved in any kind of risky behavi	Om Graam Greem Graum Sa Gurave namah swaha 21 times 0 Om Maha Laxmi Cha Vidmahae Vishu Patnayai Cha Dhi Mahi Tanno Laxmi Pracho Dayat

BIBLE VERSES: (Proverbs)

14:3. In the mouth of a fool is the rod of pride: but the lips of the wise preserve them.

READ PSALMS #'s: 9, 18, 36 ,45, 54, 63, 81, 108, 126

JANUARY 3, 2015

01/03/2015 SAT		This is considered a NEUTRAL day for you							Shiva
Moving	Shopping	Health	Investing	Gambling	Love is	Wedding	Travel	Work/Job	Planet
Fair	Fair	Fair	Fair	Fair	Bad	Fair	Fair	Bad	Sun

KEYWORDS ARE: Commanding, Home Alone, Boastful, lonliness,
Meditative, Income, Legal matter, Illness - Cold, On Your Own

Lotto #'s	play 4 #s	play 3 #s	Ruling Angel:............	Color Sugestion:............	Ruling Deity
2,3,33,32,18,16	4816	179	Gabriel	White/Yellow/ Peach	Gaitree

ADVICE & DETAILS	MANTRA FOR TODAY
You can connect with the real power within you, the universal consciousness that inhabits in you. Dedicate time to meditation, prayer, religious acts of devotion and if possible visit priests, Gurus or spiritual guides.	Om Ganga mataye nama swaha Om Varuna Devta aye Pahimam 11 times Om hareem mama sarva shatru janam vashee kuru kuru swaha om hareem ksham kasham kasheem kasheem swaha 9 times

BIBLE VERSES: (Proverbs)

13:21. Evil pursueth sinners: and to the just good shall be repaid.

0

READ PSALMS #'s: 1, 10, 28 ,37, 46, 55, 73, 100, 118

JANUARY 4, 2015

| 01/04/2015 SUN | This is considered a POSITIVE day for you | | | | | | | | Shiva |

Moving	Shopping	Health	Investing	Gambling	Love is	Wedding	Travel	Work/Job	Planet
Good	Excellent	Good	Good	Good	Excellent	Good	Excelle	Good	Venus

KEYWORDS ARE: Association, Music, Partnership, romamce, Spending, Investments, Abusive, Friendships, Affection

Lotto #'s	play 4 #s	play 3 #s	Ruling Angel:............	Color Sugestion:............	Ruling Deity
3,3,33,31,18,19	8078	2710	Raziel	Red/Yellow/Pink	Durga

ADVICE & DETAILS	MANTRA FOR TODAY
Love will return to you this day. You will be able to make up back with your lover. You will be feeling very sleepy today. You will want to enjoy good food and have a quiet date.	Om Namo Bhagawate Mukhtanandaya, 108 times AUM KRSNAYA VIDMAHE DAMODARAYA DHIMAHI. TANNO VISHNU PRACODAYAT. 9 times

BIBLE VERSES: (Proverbs)
13:23. Much food is in the tillage of fathers: but for others it is gathered without judgment.
READ PSALMS #'s: 2, 11, 29 ,38, 47, 56, 74, 101, 119

JANUARY 5, 2015

| 01/05/2015 MON | This is considered a POSITIVE day for you | | | | | | | | Shiva |

Moving	Shopping	Health	Investing	Gambling	Love is	Wedding	Travel	Work/Job	Planet
Good	Excellent	Excellent	Good	Good	Good	Good	Excelle	Good	Mercury

KEYWORDS ARE: Communication, Publishing, read, children, Social Functions, Power, Karmic debts, Teacher, Expression

Lotto #'s	play 4 #s	play 3 #s	Ruling Angel:............	Color Sugestion:............	Ruling Deity
4,4,34,32,18,12	2311	372	Zadkiel	Green/Sky Blue/White	Saraswaty

ADVICE & DETAILS	MANTRA FOR TODAY
The thought of watching TV is very appealing today. Spending time with children will benefit your creativity, but you must refrain from allowing immaturity to control your actions today.	Kali Durge Namo Nama Om Durge aye nama swaha 108 times AUM TATPURUSAYA VIDMAHE VAKRATUNDAY DHIMAHI. TANNO DANTI PRACODAYAT. 9 times

BIBLE VERSES: (Proverbs)
13:25. The just eateth and filleth his soul: but the belly of the wicked is never to be filled.
READ PSALMS #'s: 3, 12, 30 ,39, 48, 57, 75, 102, 120

JANUARY 6, 2015

| 01/06/2015 TUE | This is considered a NEUTRAL day for you | | | | | | | | Shiva |

Moving	Shopping	Health	Investing	Gambling	Love is	Wedding	Travel	Work/Job	Planet
Bad	Bad	Bad	Bad	Bad	Fair	Good	Bad	Bad	Pluto

KEYWORDS ARE: Tiredness, work, career, building, Co-workers, Promotion, God - Karma, Real Estate, Industrial

Lotto #'s	play 4 #s	play 3 #s	Ruling Angel:............	Color Sugestion:............	Ruling Deity
5,6,33,31,18,13	6639	473	Metatron	Dark Blue/ Purple/ Mauve	Ganesh

ADVICE & DETAILS	MANTRA FOR TODAY
You may have to deal with problems at your job today. Deal with these difficulties keeping in mind your long-term goals and ambitons. You will have to work very hard today.	Om hareem Kleem Hreem Aem Saraswataye namaha 21 times Om Guru bramha, Guru Vishnu Guru Deva mahaeshwara guru saksha paam bramha, tasmi shri guruve nama 9 times

BIBLE VERSES: (Proverbs)
14:2. He that walketh in the right way, and feareth God, is despised by him that goeth by an infamous way.
READ PSALMS #'s: 4, 13, 31 ,40, 49, 58, 76, 103, 121

JANUARY 7, 2015

01/07/2015 WED	This is considered a POSITIVE day for you								Shiva

Moving	Shopping	Health	Investing	Gambling	Love is	Wedding	Travel	Work/Job	Planet
Excellent	Good	Excellent	Good	Good	Excellent	Good	Excelle	Good	Uranus

KEYWORDS ARE: travel, short trips, change, deception,
Belief and faith, Fame - TV, IRS - Law, Beauty - Sex, Short Trips

Lotto #'s	play 4 #s	play 3 #s	Ruling Angel:............	Color Sugestion:............	Ruling Deity
6,6,34,31,18,15	5001	574	Camael	Orange/White/Light Green/ Beige	Krishna

ADVICE & DETAILS	MANTRA FOR TODAY
The greatest influence ot this day is that of moving, taking short trips and changes. Following the divine laws of the universe will provide protection while you travel and will also protect you from deceit and trickery that others may use to gain an unfair and dishonest advantage.	*Om Jai Viganeshwaraya.. Lambodaraya Namo Namaha 21 times Om Sarva Mangal Mangalye, Shiva Sarvart Sadike, Sharan Tryambike Gowri, Narayane Namo asttute 9 times*

BIBLE VERSES: (Proverbs)

14:4. Where there are no oxen, the crib is empty: but where there is much corn, there the strength of the ox is manifest.

READ PSALMS #'s: 5, 14, 32 ,41, 50, 59, 77, 104, 122

JANUARY 8, 2015

01/08/2015 THU	This is considered a NEGATIVE day for you								Shiva

Moving	Shopping	Health	Investing	Gambling	Love is	Wedding	Travel	Work/Job	Planet
Bad	Bad	Bad	Fair	Fair	Bad	Bad	Bad	Bad	Mars

KEYWORDS ARE: frustration, family, power, electricity,
Money conflicts, Money Wasted, Accidents, Anger - Ego, responsibility

Lotto #'s	play 4 #s	play 3 #s	Ruling Angel:............	Color Sugestion:............	Ruling Deity
7,7,33,32,18,18	9621	675	Raphael	Purple/DeepBlue/Rose	Hanuman

ADVICE & DETAILS	MANTRA FOR TODAY
Today your enemies will oppose you. Enemies are not only people, but also situations and addictions. You must avoid today alcohol and drugs because they may bring very negative consequences into your life. You will be invited to socialize and share with others, but make sure you do it in a balanced manner and leave as soon as you feel sleepy or tired.	*Om Graam Greem Graum Sa Gurave namah swaha 21 times AUM VAGDEVYAI CA VIDMAHE KAMARAJAYA DHIMAHI. TANNO DEVI PRACODAYAT. 9 times*

BIBLE VERSES: (Proverbs)

14:6. A scorner seeketh wisdom, and findeth it not: the learning of the wise is easy.

READ PSALMS #'s: 6, 15, 33 ,42, 51, 60, 78, 105, 123

JANUARY 9, 2015

01/09/2015 FRI	This is considered a NEUTRAL day for you								Shiva

Moving	Shopping	Health	Investing	Gambling	Love is	Wedding	Travel	Work/Job	Planet
Good	Fair	Fair	Bad	Bad	Good	Fair	Good	Fair	Moon

KEYWORDS ARE: finish, introspection, religion, priests,
Slow Day with Tension, High Pleasure, Denial - Doubt, spiritual, sleepiness

Lotto #'s	play 4 #s	play 3 #s	Ruling Angel:............	Color Sugestion:............	Ruling Deity
8,8,34,31,18,19	10407	776	Zaphkiel	Light Blue/Purple/Peach	Ganga

ADVICE & DETAILS	MANTRA FOR TODAY
This day requires that you devote your internal power to the power of the Divine. This is a day where you are required to spend time in religious or spiritual pursuits, meditating, praying or visiting priests or holy people.	*Om Mana Swasti Shanti Kuru kuru Swaha Shivoham Shivoham 27 times om haring jawala mukhi mam sarva shatru bakshaya bakshaya hung phat swaha Om Nama shivaya pahimam 9 times*

BIBLE VERSES: (Proverbs)

14:8. The wisdom of a discreet man is to understand his way: and the imprudence of fools erreth.

READ PSALMS #'s: 7, 16, 34 ,43, 52, 61, 79, 106, 124

JANUARY 10, 2015

01/10/2015 SAT		This is considered a POSITIVE day for you							Shiva
Moving	Shopping	Health	Investing	Gambling	Love is	Wedding	Travel	Work/Job	Planet
Good	Good	Excellent	Excellent	Excellent	Good	Excellent	Good	Excellent	Jupiter

KEYWORDS ARE: Abusive, Promotion, Fame - TV, High Pleasure, Business & money gains, Major Expense, Death, Income, Investments

Lotto #'s	play 4 #s	play 3 #s	Ruling Angel:............	Color Sugestion:...........	Ruling Deity
9,10,33,32,18,22	9010	877	Haniel	Yellow/White/Silver	Mahalaxmi

ADVICE & DETAILS

You will be having a good feeling about your income and expenses. It is a good day to purchase and make investments in the market. It is also a good day to look for a new home.

BIBLE VERSES: (Proverbs)

14:10. The heart that knoweth the bitterness of his own soul, in his joy the stranger shall not intermeddle.

READ PSALMS #'s: 8, 17, 35 ,44, 53, 62, 80, 107, 125

MANTRA FOR TODAY

Jai Jai Shiva Shambo.(2)
...Mahadeva Shambo (2)
21 times
Om Jayanti Mangala Kali
Bhadrakali Kapalini Durga
Kshama Shiva Dhatri Swaha
Swadha Namostute
9 times

JANUARY 11, 2015

01/11/2015 SUN		This is considered a NEGATIVE day for you							Shiva
Moving	Shopping	Health	Investing	Gambling	Love is	Wedding	Travel	Work/Job	Planet
Bad	Bad	Bad	Bad	Bad	Bad	Bad	Bad	Bad	Saturn

KEYWORDS ARE: Karmic debts, God - Karma, IRS - Law, Denial - Doubt, Quarrels & lovers, Money - Profits, Sickness - cold, Legal matter, Abusive

Lotto #'s	play 4 #s	play 3 #s	Ruling Angel:............	Color Sugestion:...........	Ruling Deity
10,2,33,32,18,14	1736	978	Mikael	Gold/Brown/Blue/Dark Green	Pitridev

ADVICE & DETAILS

Death is the influence of today. This may be a physical death, the end of a project, idea, habit or thought. You must remember that death is necessary for life and that the end of something, brings new beginnings. This day is also influenced by accidents, so be aware of of your surroundings, do not text while driving or get involved in any kind of risky behavi

BIBLE VERSES: (Proverbs)

14:12. There is a way which seemeth just to a man: but the ends thereof lead to death.

READ PSALMS #'s: 9, 18, 36 ,45, 54, 63, 81, 108, 126

MANTRA FOR TODAY

Om Hareem Nama Swaha...Shri Maha Laxmi Aye Namah swaha
12 times
Om maha laxmi cha vidmahe vishnu pataya dhi mahi tanno laxmi pracho dayat
Om hareem namam swaha
9 times

JANUARY 12, 2015

01/12/2015 MON		This is considered a NEUTRAL day for you							Shiva
Moving	Shopping	Health	Investing	Gambling	Love is	Wedding	Travel	Work/Job	Planet
Fair	Fair	Fair	Fair	Fair	Bad	Fair	Fair	Bad	Sun

KEYWORDS ARE: God - Karma, Home Alone, Accidents, death, Illnese, children, hypertension, Income, Legal matter, Illness - Cold, Karmic debts

Lotto #'s	play 4 #s	play 3 #s	Ruling Angel:............	Color Sugestion:...........	Ruling Deity
2,3,34,31,18,17	2735	179	Gabriel	White/Yellow/ Peach	Gaitree

ADVICE & DETAILS

You can connect with the real power within you, the universal consciousness that inhabits in you. Dedicate time to meditation, prayer, religious acts of devotion and if possible visit priests, Gurus or spiritual guides.

BIBLE VERSES: (Proverbs)

14:5. A faithful witness will not lie: but a deceitful witness uttereth a lie.
0

READ PSALMS #'s: 1, 10, 28 ,37, 46, 55, 73, 100, 118

MANTRA FOR TODAY

Om Ganga mataye nama swaha
Om Varuna Devta aye Pahimam
11 times
Om hareem mama sarva shatru janam vashee kuru kuru swaha
om hareem ksham kasham kasheem kasheem swaha
9 times

JANUARY 13, 2015

01/13/2015	TUE		This is considered a POSITIVE day for you						Shiva

Moving	Shopping	Health	Investing	Gambling	Love is	Wedding	Travel	Work/Job	Planet
Good	Excellent	Good	Good	Good	Excellent	Good	Excelle	Good	Venus

KEYWORDS ARE: Association, Music, Partnership, romamce, Spending, Investments, Abusive, Friendships, Affection

Lotto #'s	play 4 #s	play 3 #s	Ruling Angel:............	Color Sugestion:............	Ruling Deity
3,3,34,31,18,18	8233	2710	Raziel	Red/Yellow/Pink	Durga

ADVICE & DETAILS	MANTRA FOR TODAY
Love will return to you this day. You will be able to make up back with your lover. You will be feeling very sleepy today. You will want to enjoy good food and have a quiet date.	Om Namo Bhagawate Mukhtanandaya, 108 times AUM KRSNAYA VIDMAHE DAMODARAYA DHIMAHI. TANNO VISHNU PRACODAYAT. 9 times

BIBLE VERSES: (Proverbs)

14:7. Go against a foolish man, and he knoweth not the lips of prudence.

0

READ PSALMS #'s: 2, 11, 29 ,38, 47, 56, 74, 101, 119

JANUARY 14, 2015

01/14/2015	WED		This is considered a POSITIVE day for you						Shiva

Moving	Shopping	Health	Investing	Gambling	Love is	Wedding	Travel	Work/Job	Planet
Good	Excellent	Excellent	Good	Good	Good	Good	Excelle	Good	Mercury

KEYWORDS ARE: Communication, Publishing, read, children, Social Functions, Power, Karmic debts, Teacher, Expression

Lotto #'s	play 4 #s	play 3 #s	Ruling Angel:............	Color Sugestion:............	Ruling Deity
4,4,34,31,18,12	7410	372	Zadkiel	Green/Sky Blue/White	Saraswaty

ADVICE & DETAILS	MANTRA FOR TODAY
The thought of watching TV is very appealing today. Spending time with children will benefit your creativity, but you must refrain from allowing immaturity to control your actions today.	Kali Durge Namo Nama Om Durge aye nama swaha 108 times AUM TATPURUSAYA VIDMAHE VAKRATUNDAY DHIMAHI. TANNO DANTI PRACODAYAT. 9 times

BIBLE VERSES: (Proverbs)

14:9. A fool will laugh at sin, but among the just grace shall abide.

0

READ PSALMS #'s: 3, 12, 30 ,39, 48, 57, 75, 102, 120

JANUARY 15, 2015

01/15/2015	THU		This is considered a NEUTRAL day for you						Shiva

Moving	Shopping	Health	Investing	Gambling	Love is	Wedding	Travel	Work/Job	Planet
Bad	Bad	Bad	Bad	Bad	Fair	Good	Bad	Bad	Pluto

KEYWORDS ARE: Tiredness, work, career, building, Co-workers, Promotion, God - Karma, Real Estate, Industrial

Lotto #'s	play 4 #s	play 3 #s	Ruling Angel:............	Color Sugestion:............	Ruling Deity
5,6,33,31,18,13	8416	473	Metatron	Dark Blue/ Purple/ Mauve	Ganesh

ADVICE & DETAILS	MANTRA FOR TODAY
You may have to deal with problems at your job today. Deal with these difficulties keeping in mind your long-term goals and ambitons. You will have to work very hard today.	Om hareem Kleem Hreem Aem Saraswataye namaha 21 times Om Guru bramha, Guru Vishnu Guru Deva mahaeshwara guru saksha paam bramha, tasmi shri guruve nama 9 times

BIBLE VERSES: (Proverbs)

14:11. The house of the wicked shall be destroyed: but the tabernacles of the just shall flourish.

READ PSALMS #'s: 4, 13, 31 ,40, 49, 58, 76, 103, 121

JANUARY 16, 2015

01/16/2015	FRI	This is considered a POSITIVE day for you								Shiva
Moving	Shopping	Health	Investing	Gambling	Love is	Wedding	Travel	Work/Job		Planet
Excellent	Good	Excellent	Good	Good	Excellent	Good	Excelle	Good		Uranus

KEYWORDS ARE: travel, short trips, change, deception, Belief and faith, Fame - TV, IRS - Law, Beauty - Sex, Short Trips

Lotto #'s	play 4 #s	play 3 #s	Ruling Angel:............	Color Sugestion:............	Ruling Deity
6,7,34,31,18,16	9588	574	Camael	Orange/White/Light Green/ Beige	Krishna

ADVICE & DETAILS	MANTRA FOR TODAY
The greatest influence ot this day is that of moving, taking short trips and changes. Following the divine laws of the universe will provide protection while you travel and will also protect you from deceit and trickery that others may use to gain an unfair and dishonest advantage.	Om Jai Viganeshwaraya.. Lambodaraya Namo Namaha 21 times Om Sarva Mangal Mangalye, Shiva Sarvart Sadike, Sharan Tryambike Gowri, Narayane Namo asttute 9 times

BIBLE VERSES: (Proverbs)

14:13. Laughter shall be mingled with sorrow, and mourning taketh hold of the ends of joy.

READ PSALMS #'s: 5, 14, 32 ,41, 50, 59, 77, 104, 122

JANUARY 17, 2015

01/17/2015	SAT	This is considered a NEGATIVE day for you								Shiva
Moving	Shopping	Health	Investing	Gambling	Love is	Wedding	Travel	Work/Job		Planet
Bad	Bad	Bad	Fair	Fair	Bad	Bad	Bad	Bad		Mars

KEYWORDS ARE: frustration, family, power, electricity, Money conflicts, Money Wasted, Accidents, Anger - Ego, responsibility

Lotto #'s	play 4 #s	play 3 #s	Ruling Angel:............	Color Sugestion:............	Ruling Deity
7,7,33,31,18,18	3199	675	Raphael	Purple/DeepBlue/Rose	Hanuman

ADVICE & DETAILS	MANTRA FOR TODAY
Today your enemies will oppose you. Enemies are not only people, but also situations and addictions. You must avoid today alcohol and drugs because they may bring very negative consequences into your life. You will be invited to socialize and share with others, but make sure you do it in a balanced manner and leave as soon as you feel sleepy or tired.	Om Graam Greem Graum Sa Gurave namah swaha 21 times AUM VAGDEVYAI CA VIDMAHE KAMARAJAYA DHIMAHI. TANNO DEVI PRACODAYAT. 9 times

BIBLE VERSES: (Proverbs)

14:15. The innocent believeth every word: the discreet man considereth his steps. No good shall come to the deceitfnl son: but the wise servant

READ PSALMS #'s: 6, 15, 33 ,42, 51, 60, 78, 105, 123

JANUARY 18, 2015

01/18/2015	SUN	This is considered a NEUTRAL day for you								Shiva
Moving	Shopping	Health	Investing	Gambling	Love is	Wedding	Travel	Work/Job		Planet
Good	Fair	Fair	Bad	Bad	Good	Fair	Good	Fair		Moon

KEYWORDS ARE: finish, introspection, religion, priests, Slow Day with Tension, High Pleasure, Denial - Doubt, spiritual, sleepiness

Lotto #'s	play 4 #s	play 3 #s	Ruling Angel:............	Color Sugestion:............	Ruling Deity
8,9,34,32,18,19	10249	776	Zaphkiel	Light Blue/Purple/Peach	Ganga

ADVICE & DETAILS	MANTRA FOR TODAY
This day requires that you devote your internal power to the power of the Divine. This is a day where you are required to spend time in religious or spiritual pursuits, meditating, praying or visiting priests or holy people.	Om Mana Swasti Shanti Kuru kuru Swaha Shivoham Shivoham 27 times om haring jawala mukhi mam sarva shatru bakshaya bakshaya hung phat swaha Om Nama shivaya pahimam 9 times

BIBLE VERSES: (Proverbs)

14:17. The impatient man shall work folly: and the crafty man is hateful.

0

READ PSALMS #'s: 7, 16, 34 ,43, 52, 61, 79, 106, 124

JANUARY 19, 2015

01/19/2015 MON		This is considered a POSITIVE day for you							Shiva
Moving	Shopping	Health	Investing	Gambling	Love is	Wedding	Travel	Work/Job	Planet
Good	Good	Excellent	Excellent	Excellent	Good	Excellent	Good	Excellent	Jupiter

KEYWORDS ARE: Abusive, Promotion, Fame - TV, High Pleasure, Business & money gains, Major Expense, Death, Income, Investments

Lotto #'s	play 4 #s	play 3 #s	Ruling Angel:...........	Color Sugestion:...........	Ruling Deity
9,9,33,32,18,21	1330	877	Haniel	Yellow/White/Silver	Mahalaxmi

ADVICE & DETAILS	MANTRA FOR TODAY
You will be having a good feeling about your income and expenses. It is a good day to purchase and make investments in the market. It is also a good day to look for a new home.	Jai Jai Shiva Shambo.(2) ...Mahadeva Shambo (2) 21 times Om Jayanti Mangala Kali Bhadrakali Kapalini Durga Kshama Shiva Dhatri Swaha Swadha Namostute 9 times

BIBLE VERSES: (Proverbs)

14:19. The evil shall fall down before the good: and the wicked before the gates of the just.

READ PSALMS #'s: 8, 17, 35 ,44, 53, 62, 80, 107, 125

JANUARY 20, 2015

01/20/2015 TUE		This is considered a NEGATIVE day for you							Shiva
Moving	Shopping	Health	Investing	Gambling	Love is	Wedding	Travel	Work/Job	Planet
Bad	Bad	Bad	Bad	Bad	Bad	Bad	Bad	Bad	Saturn

KEYWORDS ARE: Karmic debts, God - Karma, IRS - Law, Denial - Doubt, Quarrels & lovers, Money - Profits, Sickness - cold, Legal matter, Abusive

Lotto #'s	play 4 #s	play 3 #s	Ruling Angel:...........	Color Sugestion:...........	Ruling Deity
10,2,33,31,18,14	5909	978	Mikael	Gold/Brown/Blue/Dark Green	Pitridev

ADVICE & DETAILS	MANTRA FOR TODAY
Death is the influence of today. This may be a physical death, the end of a project, idea, habit or thought. You must remember that death is necessary for life and that the end of something, brings new beginnings. This day is also influenced by accidents, so be aware of of your surroundings, do not text while driving or get involved in any kind of risky behavi	Om Hareem Nama Swaha..Shri Maha Laxmi Aye Namah swaha 12 times Om maha laxmi cha vidmahe vishnu pataya dhi mahi tanno laxmi pracho dayat Om hareem namam swaha 9 times

BIBLE VERSES: (Proverbs)

14:21. He that despiseth his neighbour, sinneth: but he that sheweth mercy to the poor, shall be blessed. He that believeth in the Lord, loveth mercy.

READ PSALMS #'s: 9, 18, 36 ,45, 54, 63, 81, 108, 126

JANUARY 21, 2015

01/21/2015 WED		This is considered a NEUTRAL day for you							Shiva
Moving	Shopping	Health	Investing	Gambling	Love is	Wedding	Travel	Work/Job	Planet
Fair	Fair	Fair	Fair	Fair	Bad	Fair	Fair	Bad	Sun

KEYWORDS ARE: God - Karma, Home Alone, Accidents, death, Illnese, children, hypertension, Income, Legal matter, Illness - Cold, Karmic debts

Lotto #'s	play 4 #s	play 3 #s	Ruling Angel:...........	Color Sugestion:...........	Ruling Deity
2,3,33,31,18,17	6185	179	Gabriel	White/Yellow/ Peach	Gaitree

ADVICE & DETAILS	MANTRA FOR TODAY
You can connect with the real power within you, the universal consciousness that inhabits in you. Dedicate time to meditation, prayer, religious acts of devotion and if possible visit priests, Gurus or spiritual guides.	Om Ganga mataye nama swaha Om Varuna Devta aye Pahimam 11 times Om hareem mama sarva shatru janam vashee kuru kuru swaha om hareem ksham kasham kasheem kasheem swaha 9 times

BIBLE VERSES: (Proverbs)

14:14. A fool shall be filled with his own ways, and the good man shall be above him.

READ PSALMS #'s: 1, 10, 28 ,37, 46, 55, 73, 100, 118

JANUARY 22, 2015

01/22/2015 THU	This is considered a POSITIVE day for you								Shiva

Moving	Shopping	Health	Investing	Gambling	Love is	Wedding	Travel	Work/Job	Planet
Good	Excellent	Good	Good	Good	Excellent	Good	Excelle	Good	Venus

KEYWORDS ARE: IRS - Law, Music, Denial - Doubt, losses, Stress with Bosses, Investments, Abusive, Friendships, God - Karma

Lotto #'s	play 4 #s	play 3 #s	Ruling Angel:............	Color Sugestion:............	Ruling Deity
3,3,34,32,18,18	6855	2710	Raziel	Red/Yellow/Pink	Durga

ADVICE & DETAILS	MANTRA FOR TODAY
Love will return to you this day. You will be able to make up back with your lover. You will be feeling very sleepy today. You will want to enjoy good food and have a quiet date.	Om Namo Bhagawate Mukhtanandaya, 108 times AUM KRSNAYA VIDMAHE DAMODARAYA DHIMAHI. TANNO VISHNU PRACODAYAT. 9 times
BIBLE VERSES: (Proverbs) 14:16. A wise man feareth, and declineth from evil: the fool leapeth over, and is confident.	
READ PSALMS #'s: 2, 11, 29 ,38, 47, 56, 74, 101, 119	

JANUARY 23, 2015

01/23/2015 FRI	This is considered a POSITIVE day for you								Shiva

Moving	Shopping	Health	Investing	Gambling	Love is	Wedding	Travel	Work/Job	Planet
Good	Excellent	Excellent	Good	Good	Good	Good	Excelle	Good	Mercury

KEYWORDS ARE: Communication, Publishing, read, children, Social Functions, Power, Karmic debts, Teacher, Expression

Lotto #'s	play 4 #s	play 3 #s	Ruling Angel:............	Color Sugestion:............	Ruling Deity
4,5,33,31,18,12	1410	372	Zadkiel	Green/Sky Blue/White	Saraswaty

ADVICE & DETAILS	MANTRA FOR TODAY
The thought of watching TV is very appealing today. Spending time with children will benefit your creativity, but you must refrain from allowing immaturity to control your actions today.	Kali Durge Namo Nama Om Durge aye nama swaha 108 times AUM TATPURUSAYA VIDMAHE VAKRATUNDAY DHIMAHI. TANNO DANTI PRACODAYAT. 9 times
BIBLE VERSES: (Proverbs) 14:18. The childish shall possess folly, and the prudent shall look for knowledge.	
READ PSALMS #'s: 3, 12, 30 ,39, 48, 57, 75, 102, 120	

JANUARY 24, 2015

01/24/2015 SAT	This is considered a NEUTRAL day for you								Shiva

Moving	Shopping	Health	Investing	Gambling	Love is	Wedding	Travel	Work/Job	Planet
Bad	Bad	Bad	Bad	Bad	Fair	Good	Bad	Bad	Pluto

KEYWORDS ARE: Tiredness, work, career, building, Co-workers, Promotion, God - Karma, Real Estate, Industrial

Lotto #'s	play 4 #s	play 3 #s	Ruling Angel:............	Color Sugestion:............	Ruling Deity
5,5,33,32,18,13	9513	473	Metatron	Dark Blue/ Purple/ Mauve	Ganesh

ADVICE & DETAILS	MANTRA FOR TODAY
You may have to deal with problems at your job today. Deal with these difficulties keeping in mind your long-term goals and ambitons. You will have to work very hard today.	Om hareem Kleem Hreem Aem Saraswataye namaha 21 times Om Guru bramha, Guru Vishnu Guru Deva mahaeshwara guru saksha paam bramha, tasmi shri guruve nama 9 times
BIBLE VERSES: (Proverbs) 14:20. The poor man shall be hateful even to his own neighbour: but the friends of the rich are many.	
READ PSALMS #'s: 4, 13, 31 ,40, 49, 58, 76, 103, 121	

JANUARY 25, 2015

01/25/2015 SUN	This is considered a POSITIVE day for you								Shiva
Moving	Shopping	Health	Investing	Gambling	Love is	Wedding	Travel	Work/Job	Planet
Excellent	Good	Excellent	Good	Good	Excellent	Good	Excelle	Good	Uranus

KEYWORDS ARE: travel, short trips, change, deception, Belief and faith, Fame - TV, IRS - Law, Beauty - Sex, Short Trips

Lotto #'s	play 4 #s	play 3 #s	Ruling Angel:............	Color Sugestion:............	Ruling Deity
6,6,33,31,18,16	9533	574	Camael	Orange/White/Light Green/ Beige	Krishna

ADVICE & DETAILS	MANTRA FOR TODAY
The greatest influence ot this day is that of moving, taking short trips and changes. Following the divine laws of the universe will provide protection while you travel and will also protect you from deceit and trickery that others may use to gain an unfair and dishonest advantage.	Om Jai Viganeshwaraya.. Lambodaraya Namo Namaha 21 times Om Sarva Mangal Mangalye, Shiva Sarvart Sadike, Sharan Tryambike Gowri, Narayane Namo asttute 9 times

BIBLE VERSES: (Proverbs)

14:22. They err that work evil: but mercy and truth prepare good things.
0

READ PSALMS #'s: 5, 14, 32 ,41, 50, 59, 77, 104, 122

JANUARY 26, 2015

01/26/2015 MON	This is considered a NEGATIVE day for you								Shiva
Moving	Shopping	Health	Investing	Gambling	Love is	Wedding	Travel	Work/Job	Planet
Bad	Bad	Bad	Fair	Fair	Bad	Bad	Bad	Bad	Mars

KEYWORDS ARE: frustration, family, power, electricity, Money conflicts, Money Wasted, Accidents, Anger - Ego, responsibility

Lotto #'s	play 4 #s	play 3 #s	Ruling Angel:............	Color Sugestion:............	Ruling Deity
7,7,34,31,18,18	1075	675	Raphael	Purple/DeepBlue/Rose	Hanuman

ADVICE & DETAILS	MANTRA FOR TODAY
Today your enemies will oppose you. Enemies are not only people, but also situations and addictions. You must avoid today alcohol and drugs because they may bring very negative consequences into your life. You will be invited to socialize and share with others, but make sure you do it in a balanced manner and leave as soon as you feel sleepy or tired.	Om Graam Greem Graum Sa Gurave namah swaha 21 times AUM VAGDEVYAI CA VIDMAHE KAMARAJAYA DHIMAHI. TANNO DEVI PRACODAYAT. 9 times

BIBLE VERSES: (Proverbs)

14:24. The crown of the wise, is their riches: the folly of fools, imprudence.
0

READ PSALMS #'s: 6, 15, 33 ,42, 51, 60, 78, 105, 123

JANUARY 27, 2015

01/27/2015 TUE	This is considered a NEUTRAL day for you								Shiva
Moving	Shopping	Health	Investing	Gambling	Love is	Wedding	Travel	Work/Job	Planet
Good	Fair	Fair	Bad	Bad	Good	Fair	Good	Fair	Moon

KEYWORDS ARE: finish, introspection, religion, priests, Slow Day with Tension, High Pleasure, Denial - Doubt, spiritual, sleepiness

Lotto #'s	play 4 #s	play 3 #s	Ruling Angel:............	Color Sugestion:............	Ruling Deity
8,9,34,31,18,19	1491	776	Zaphkiel	Light Blue/Purple/Peach	Ganga

ADVICE & DETAILS	MANTRA FOR TODAY
This day requires that you devote your internal power to the power of the Divine. This is a day where you are required to spend time in religious or spiritual pursuits, meditating, praying or visiting priests or holy people.	Om Mana Swasti Shanti Kuru kuru Swaha Shivoham Shivoham 27 times om haring jawala mukhi mam sarva shatru bakshaya bakshaya hung phat swaha Om Nama shivaya pahimam 9 times

BIBLE VERSES: (Proverbs)

14:26. In the fear of the Lord is confidence of strength, and there shall be hope for his children.

READ PSALMS #'s: 7, 16, 34 ,43, 52, 61, 79, 106, 124

JANUARY 28, 2015

01/28/2015	WED	This is considered a POSITIVE day for you							Shiva

Moving	Shopping	Health	Investing	Gambling	Love is	Wedding	Travel	Work/Job	Planet
Good	Good	Excellent	Excellent	Excellent	Good	Excellent	Good	Excellent	Jupiter

KEYWORDS ARE: Abusive, Promotion, Fame - TV, High Pleasure, Business & money gains, Major Expense, Death, Income, Investments

Lotto #'s	play 4 #s	play 3 #s	Ruling Angel:............	Color Sugestion:............	Ruling Deity
9,9,33,32,18,21	10892	877	Haniel	Yellow/White/Silver	Mahalaxmi

ADVICE & DETAILS	MANTRA FOR TODAY
You will be having a good feeling about your income and expenses. It is a good day to purchase and make investments in the market. It is also a good day to look for a new home.	Jai Jai Shiva Shambo.(2) ...Mahadeva Shambo (2) 21 times Om Jayanti Mangala Kali Bhadrakali Kapalini Durga Kshama Shiva Dhatri Swaha Swadha Namostute 9 times

BIBLE VERSES: (Proverbs)

14:28. In the multitude of people is the dignity of the king: and in the small number of the people the dishonour of the prince.

READ PSALMS #'s: 8, 17, 35 ,44, 53, 62, 80, 107, 125

JANUARY 29, 2015

01/29/2015	THU	This is considered a NEGATIVE day for you							Shiva

Moving	Shopping	Health	Investing	Gambling	Love is	Wedding	Travel	Work/Job	Planet
Bad	Bad	Bad	Bad	Bad	Bad	Bad	Bad	Bad	Saturn

KEYWORDS ARE: Karmic debts, God - Karma, IRS - Law, Denial - Doubt, Quarrels & lovers, Money - Profits, Sickness - cold, Legal matter, Abusive

Lotto #'s	play 4 #s	play 3 #s	Ruling Angel:............	Color Sugestion:............	Ruling Deity
10,2,34,31,18,15	3130	978	Mikael	Gold/Brown/Blue/Dark Green	Pitridev

ADVICE & DETAILS	MANTRA FOR TODAY
Death is the influence of today. This may be a physical death, the end of a project, idea, habit or thought. You must remember that death is necessary for life and that the end of something, brings new beginnings. This day is also influenced by accidents, so be aware of of your surroundings, do not text while driving or get involved in any kind of risky behavi	Om Hareem Nama Swaha...Shri Maha Laxmi Aye Namah swaha 12 times Om maha laxmi cha vidmahe vishnu pataya dhi mahi tanno laxmi pracho dayat Om hareem namam swaha 9 times

BIBLE VERSES: (Proverbs)

14:30. Soundness of heart is the life of the flesh: but envy is the rottenness of the bones.

READ PSALMS #'s: 9, 18, 36 ,45, 54, 63, 81, 108, 126

JANUARY 30, 2015

01/30/2015	FRI	This is considered a NEUTRAL day for you							Shiva

Moving	Shopping	Health	Investing	Gambling	Love is	Wedding	Travel	Work/Job	Planet
Fair	Fair	Fair	Fair	Fair	Bad	Fair	Fair	Bad	Sun

KEYWORDS ARE: God - Karma, Home Alone, Accidents, death, Illnese, children, hypertension, Income, Legal matter, Illness - Cold, Karmic debts

Lotto #'s	play 4 #s	play 3 #s	Ruling Angel:............	Color Sugestion:............	Ruling Deity
2,2,33,32,18,17	6243	179	Gabriel	White/Yellow/ Peach	Gaitree

ADVICE & DETAILS	MANTRA FOR TODAY
You can connect with the real power within you, the universal consciousness that inhabits in you. Dedicate time to meditation, prayer, religious acts of devotion and if possible visit priests, Gurus or spiritual guides.	Om Ganga mataye nama swaha Om Varuna Devta aye Pahimam 11 times Om hareem mama sarva shatru janam vashee kuru kuru swaha om hareem ksham kasham kasheem kasheem swaha 9 times

BIBLE VERSES: (Proverbs)

14:23. In much work there shall be abundance: but where there are many words, there is oftentimes want.

READ PSALMS #'s: 1, 10, 28 ,37, 46, 55, 73, 100, 118

JANUARY 31, 2015

01/31/2015 SAT		This is considered a POSITIVE day for you							Shiva
Moving	Shopping	Health	Investing	Gambling	Love is	Wedding	Travel	Work/Job	Planet
Good	Excellent	Good	Good	Good	Excellent	Good	Excelle	Good	Venus

KEYWORDS ARE: IRS - Law, Music, Denial - Doubt, losses, Stress with Bosses, Investments, Abusive, Friendships, God - Karma

Lotto #'s	play 4 #s	play 3 #s	Ruling Angel:............	Color Sugestion:............	Ruling Deity
3,4,33,31,18,19	5393	2710	Raziel	Red/Yellow/Pink	Durga

ADVICE & DETAILS	MANTRA FOR TODAY
Love will return to you this day. You will be able to make up back with your lover. You will be feeling very sleepy today. You will want to enjoy good food and have a quiet date.	Om Namo Bhagawate Mukhtanandaya, 108 times AUM KRSNAYA VIDMAHE DAMODARAYA DHIMAHI. TANNO VISHNU PRACODAYAT. 9 times
BIBLE VERSES: (Proverbs)	
14:25. A faithful witness delivereth souls: and the double dealer uttereth lies.	
READ PSALMS #'s: 2, 11, 29 ,38, 47, 56, 74, 101, 119	

FEBRUARY 1, 2015

02/01/2015 SUN		This is considered a POSITIVE day for you							Shiva
Moving	Shopping	Health	Investing	Gambling	Love is	Wedding	Travel	Work/Job	Planet
Good	Good	Excellent	Excellent	Bad	Good	Bad	Good	Excellent	Saturn

KEYWORDS ARE: Accidents, Denial - Doubt, money, profits, Investment news , Abusive, Karmic debts, God - Karma, Money Wasted

Lotto #'s	play 4 #s	play 3 #s	Ruling Angel:............	Color Sugestion:............	Ruling Deity
9,2,34,31,19,13	3892	887	Mikael	Gold/Brown/Blue/Dark Green	Pitridev

ADVICE & DETAILS	MANTRA FOR TODAY
Today money comes in, money goes out. You will make profits, but at the same time you will have big expenses and you will enjoy high pleasure.	Kali Durge Namo Nama Om Durge aye nama swaha 108 times AUM TATPURUSAYA VIDMAHE VAKRATUNDAY DHIMAHI. TANNO DANTI PRACODAYAT. 9 times
BIBLE VERSES: (Proverbs)	
14:33. In the heart of the prudent resteth wisdom, and it shall instruct all the ignorant.	
READ PSALMS #'s: 9, 18, 36 ,45, 54, 63, 81, 108, 126	

FEBRUARY 2, 2015

02/02/2015 MON		This is considered a NEGATIVE day for you							Shiva
Moving	Shopping	Health	Investing	Gambling	Love is	Wedding	Travel	Work/Job	Planet
Bad	Bad	Bad	Bad	Fair	Bad	Fair	Bad	Bad	Sun

KEYWORDS ARE: Denial - Doubt, lonliness, losses, sadness, Family conflicts, Arguments, Karmic debts, God - Karma, Home Alone, Accidents

Lotto #'s	play 4 #s	play 3 #s	Ruling Angel:............	Color Sugestion:............	Ruling Deity
10,3,34,32,19,16	2137	988	Gabriel	White/Yellow/ Peach	Gaitree

ADVICE & DETAILS	MANTRA FOR TODAY
There will be a great deal of confusion today. There will be many bills and expenses and you may not have enough money to cover them. There could be delays in court cases. You may have to pay for something you do not want.	Om Hareem Nama Swaha..Shri Maha Laxmi Aye Namah swaha 12 times Om maha laxmi cha vidmahe vishnu pataya dhi mahi tanno laxmi pracho dayat Om hareem namam swaha 9 times
BIBLE VERSES: (Proverbs)	
14:26. In the fear of the Lord is confidence of strength, and there shall be hope for his children.	
READ PSALMS #'s: 1, 10, 28 ,37, 46, 55, 73, 100, 118	

FEBRUARY 3, 2015

02/03/2015	TUE		This is considered a NEUTRAL day for you							Shiva

Moving	Shopping	Health	Investing	Gambling	Love is	Wedding	Travel	Work/Job	Planet
Fair	Fair	Fair	Fair	Good	Bad	Good	Fair	Bad	Venus

KEYWORDS ARE: lonliness, romamce, godliness, alone, On Your Own, God - Karma, IRS - Law, Music, Confined

Lotto #'s	play 4 #s	play 3 #s	Ruling Angel:............	Color Sugestion:............	Ruling Deity
2,4,33,32,19,18	3010	189	Raziel	Red/Yellow/Pink	Durga

ADVICE & DETAILS	MANTRA FOR TODAY
This is one of those days that you want to have over and over again if you are connected with the gods. You should expect promotion, money and romance.	*Om Ganga mataye nama swaha* *Om Varuna Devta aye Pahimam* *11 times* *Om hareem mama sarva shatru janam vashee kuru kuru swaha* *om hareem ksham kasham kasheem kasheem swaha* *9 times*
BIBLE VERSES: (Proverbs)	
14:28. In the multitude of people is the dignity of the king: and in the small number of the people the dishonour of the prince.	
READ PSALMS #'s: 2, 11, 29 ,38, 47, 56, 74, 101, 119	

FEBRUARY 4, 2015

02/04/2015	WED		This is considered a POSITIVE day for you							Shiva

Moving	Shopping	Health	Investing	Gambling	Love is	Wedding	Travel	Work/Job	Planet
Good	Excellent	Good	Good	Good	Excellent	Good	Excelle	Good	Mercury

KEYWORDS ARE: romamce, children, speech, co-operation, Gifts and friends, IRS - Law, Accidents, Publishing, love

Lotto #'s	play 4 #s	play 3 #s	Ruling Angel:............	Color Sugestion:............	Ruling Deity
3,4,34,31,19,19	6923	2810	Zadkiel	Green/Sky Blue/White	Saraswaty

ADVICE & DETAILS	MANTRA FOR TODAY
Enjoy this day! If you fill it with sweet words and with kindness, you will encounter romance, good partnerships and to top it all off money.	*Om Namo Bhagawate* *Mukhtanandaya,* *108 times* *AUM KRSNAYA VIDMAHE* *DAMODARAYA DHIMAHI.* *TANNO VISHNU* *PRACODAYAT.* *9 times*
BIBLE VERSES: (Proverbs)	
14:30. Soundness of heart is the life of the flesh: but envy is the rottenness of the bones.	
READ PSALMS #'s: 3, 12, 30 ,39, 48, 57, 75, 102, 120	

FEBRUARY 5, 2015

02/05/2015	THU		This is considered a POSITIVE day for you							Shiva

Moving	Shopping	Health	Investing	Gambling	Love is	Wedding	Travel	Work/Job	Planet
Good	Excellent	Excellent	Good	Bad	Good	Good	Excelle	Good	Pluto

KEYWORDS ARE: children, building, imaturity, television, Petty quarels, Accidents, Denial - Doubt, work, children

Lotto #'s	play 4 #s	play 3 #s	Ruling Angel:............	Color Sugestion:............	Ruling Deity
4,5,34,32,19,12	5709	382	Metatron	Dark Blue/ Purple/ Mauve	Ganesh

ADVICE & DETAILS	MANTRA FOR TODAY
Today, it will feel very comfortable at your work place, at your job. Opportunities to advance may present themselves. Financial situation improves.	*Kali Durge Namo Nama* *Om Durge aye nama swaha* *108 times* *AUM TATPURUSAYA* *VIDMAHE VAKRATUNDAY* *DHIMAHI. TANNO DANTI* *PRACODAYAT.* *9 times*
BIBLE VERSES: (Proverbs)	
14:32. The wicked man shall be driven out in his wickedness: but the just hath hope in his death.	
READ PSALMS #'s: 4, 13, 31 ,40, 49, 58, 76, 103, 121	

FEBRUARY 6, 2015

02/06/2015	FRI		This is considered a NEUTRAL day for you							Shiva
Moving	Shopping	Health	Investing	Gambling	Love is	Wedding	Travel	Work/Job		Planet
Bad	Bad	Bad	Bad	Good	Fair	Good	Bad	Bad		Uranus

KEYWORDS ARE: High Temper, Exercise, Laziness, Industrial, Career improvments, Losses, Death, Distant, far, Job Problems

Lotto #'s	play 4 #s	play 3 #s	Ruling Angel:............	Color Sugestion:............	Ruling Deity
5,6,34,31,19,15	4651	483	Camael	Orange/White/Light Green/ Beige	Krishna

ADVICE & DETAILS	MANTRA FOR TODAY
There will be changes at the job, and these will be in your favor. You will enjoy engaging in new projects. Coworkers may be friendly, but you must be careful with whom you trust.	Om hareem Kleem Hreem Aem Saraswataye namaha 21 times Om Guru bramha, Guru Vishnu Guru Deva mahaeshwara guru saksha paam bramha, tasmi shri guruve nama 9 times

BIBLE VERSES: (Proverbs)

14:34. Justice exalteth a nation: but sin maketh nations miserable.

0

READ PSALMS #'s: 5, 14, 32 ,41, 50, 59, 77, 104, 122

FEBRUARY 7, 2015

02/07/2015	SAT		This is considered a POSITIVE day for you							Shiva
Moving	Shopping	Health	Investing	Gambling	Love is	Wedding	Travel	Work/Job		Planet
Excellent	Good	Excellent	Good	Fair	Excellent	Bad	Excelle	Good		Mars

KEYWORDS ARE: Exercise, Jealousy, Moving, Short Trips, Romance with lovers, Death, Sickness - cold, Family Conflicts, Deception

Lotto #'s	play 4 #s	play 3 #s	Ruling Angel:............	Color Sugestion:............	Ruling Deity
6,7,33,32,19,16	9820	584	Raphael	Purple/DeepBlue/Rose	Hanuman

ADVICE & DETAILS	MANTRA FOR TODAY
You will have delays in travel. Your business sales will be low. You need to watch out for accidents or health problems. You may experience some constipation or bad digestion from bad meals.	Om Jai Viganeshwaraya.. Lambodaraya Namo Namaha 21 times Om Sarva Mangal Mangalye, Shiva Sarvart Sadike, Sharan Tryambike Gowri, Narayane Namo asttute 9 times

BIBLE VERSES: (Proverbs)

15:1. A mild answer breaketh wrath: but a harsh word stirreth up fury.

0

READ PSALMS #'s: 6, 15, 33 ,42, 51, 60, 78, 105, 123

FEBRUARY 8, 2015

02/08/2015	SUN		This is considered a NEGATIVE day for you							Shiva
Moving	Shopping	Health	Investing	Gambling	Love is	Wedding	Travel	Work/Job		Planet
Bad	Bad	Bad	Fair	Bad	Bad	Fair	Bad	Bad		Moon

KEYWORDS ARE: Jealousy, Slow Day, Government, responsibility, Family & children, Sickness - cold, Legal matter, Sleepiness, Quarrels

Lotto #'s	play 4 #s	play 3 #s	Ruling Angel:............	Color Sugestion:............	Ruling Deity
7,8,33,32,19,18	10435	685	Zaphkiel	Light Blue/Purple/Peach	Ganga

ADVICE & DETAILS	MANTRA FOR TODAY
You will have disagreemets and frustration over your financial situation today. You will be worried about losing your position. The jealousy of coworkers may affect your performance at work. Do not be rude to bosses.	Om Graam Greem Graum Sa Gurave namah swaha 21 times AUM VAGDEVYAI CA VIDMAHE KAMARAJAYA DHIMAHI. TANNO DEVI PRACODAYAT. 9 times

BIBLE VERSES: (Proverbs)

15:3. The eyes of the Lord in every place behold the good and the evil.

0

READ PSALMS #'s: 7, 16, 34 ,43, 52, 61, 79, 106, 124

FEBRUARY 9, 2015

02/09/2015	MON		This is considered a NEUTRAL day for you							Shiva
Moving	Shopping	Health	Investing	Gambling	Love is	Wedding	Travel	Work/Job		Planet
Good	Fair	Fair	Bad	Excellent	Good	Excellent	Good	Fair		Jupiter

KEYWORDS ARE: IRS - Law, High Pleasure, Criticism, sleepiness, Inner Conflicts with Job, Legal matter, Abusive, Promotion, Alcohol - drugs

Lotto #'s	play 4 #s	play 3 #s	Ruling Angel:............	Color Sugestion:............	Ruling Deity
8,10,33,31,19,21	5150	786	Haniel	Yellow/White/Silver	Mahalaxmi

ADVICE & DETAILS
You may receive an unexpected financial windfall today. It is a good day to save money and to plan your financial future. Set up a retirement plan. Donate to charity today.

BIBLE VERSES: (Proverbs)
15:5. A fool laugheth at the instruction of his father: but he that regardeth reproofs shall become prudent. In abundant justice there is the greatest

READ PSALMS #'s: 8, 17, 35 ,44, 53, 62, 80, 107, 125

MANTRA FOR TODAY
Om Mana Swasti Shanti Kuru kuru Swaha Shivoham Shivoham
27 times
om haring jawala mukhi mam sarva shatru bakshaya bakshaya hung phat swaha
Om Nama shivaya pahimam
9 times

FEBRUARY 10, 2015

02/10/2015	TUE		This is considered a POSITIVE day for you							Shiva
Moving	Shopping	Health	Investing	Gambling	Love is	Wedding	Travel	Work/Job		Planet
Good	Good	Excellent	Excellent	Bad	Good	Bad	Good	Excellent		Saturn

KEYWORDS ARE: Accidents, Denial - Doubt, money, profits, Investment news , Abusive, Karmic debts, God - Karma, Money Wasted

Lotto #'s	play 4 #s	play 3 #s	Ruling Angel:............	Color Sugestion:............	Ruling Deity
9,1,34,31,19,13	2878	887	Mikael	Gold/Brown/Blue/Dark Green	Pitridev

ADVICE & DETAILS
Today money comes in, money goes out. You will make profits, but at the same time you will have big expenses and you will enjoy high pleasure.

BIBLE VERSES: (Proverbs)
15:7. The lips of the wise shall disperse knowledge: the heart of fools shall be unlike.

READ PSALMS #'s: 9, 18, 36 ,45, 54, 63, 81, 108, 126

MANTRA FOR TODAY
Jai Jai Shiva Shambo.(2)
...Mahadeva Shambo (2)
21 times
Om Jayanti Mangala Kali Bhadrakali Kapalini Durga Kshama Shiva Dhatri Swaha Swadha Namostute
9 times

FEBRUARY 11, 2015

02/11/2015	WED		This is considered a NEGATIVE day for you							Shiva
Moving	Shopping	Health	Investing	Gambling	Love is	Wedding	Travel	Work/Job		Planet
Bad	Bad	Bad	Bad	Fair	Bad	Fair	Bad	Bad		Sun

KEYWORDS ARE: Denial - Doubt, lonliness, losses, sadness, Family conflicts, Arguments, Karmic debts, God - Karma, Home Alone, Accidents

Lotto #'s	play 4 #s	play 3 #s	Ruling Angel:............	Color Sugestion:............	Ruling Deity
10,3,33,31,19,15	8298	988	Gabriel	White/Yellow/ Peach	Gaitree

ADVICE & DETAILS
There will be a great deal of confusion today. There will be many bills and expenses and you may not have enough money to cover them. There could be delays in court cases. You may have to pay for something you do not want.

BIBLE VERSES: (Proverbs)
14:35. A wise servant is acceptable to the king: he that is good for nothing shall feel his anger.

READ PSALMS #'s: 1, 10, 28 ,37, 46, 55, 73, 100, 118

MANTRA FOR TODAY
Om Hareem Nama Swaha..Shri Maha Laxmi Aye Namah swaha
12 times
Om maha laxmi cha vidmahe vishnu pataya dhi mahi tanno laxmi pracho dayat
Om hareem namam swaha
9 times

FEBRUARY 12, 2015

02/12/2015 THU			This is considered a NEUTRAL day for you						Shiva

Moving	Shopping	Health	Investing	Gambling	Love is	Wedding	Travel	Work/Job	Planet
Fair	Fair	Fair	Fair	Good	Bad	Good	Fair	Bad	Venus

KEYWORDS ARE: death, romamce, finish, fame, Tiredness, Low Energy, Sleepy, God - Karma, IRS - Law, Music, Denial - Doubt

Lotto #'s	play 4 #s	play 3 #s	Ruling Angel:............	Color Sugestion:............	Ruling Deity
2,3,33,32,19,18	9365	189	Raziel	Red/Yellow/Pink	Durga

ADVICE & DETAILS	MANTRA FOR TODAY
This is one of those days that you want to have over and over again if you are connected with the gods. You should expect promotion, money and romance.	Om Ganga mataye nama swaha Om Varuna Devta aye Pahimam 11 times Om hareem mama sarva shatru janam vashee kuru kuru swaha om hareem ksham kasham kasheem kasheem swaha 9 times

BIBLE VERSES: (Proverbs)

15:2. The tongue of the wise adorneth knowledge: but the mouth of fools bubbleth out folly.

READ PSALMS #'s: 2, 11, 29 ,38, 47, 56, 74, 101, 119

FEBRUARY 13, 2015

02/13/2015 FRI			This is considered a POSITIVE day for you						Shiva

Moving	Shopping	Health	Investing	Gambling	Love is	Wedding	Travel	Work/Job	Planet
Good	Excellent	Good	Good	Good	Excellent	Good	Excelle	Good	Mercury

KEYWORDS ARE: romamce, children, speech, co-operation, Gifts and friends, IRS - Law, Accidents, Publishing, love

Lotto #'s	play 4 #s	play 3 #s	Ruling Angel:............	Color Sugestion:............	Ruling Deity
3,5,33,31,19,19	5083	2810	Zadkiel	Green/Sky Blue/White	Saraswaty

ADVICE & DETAILS	MANTRA FOR TODAY
Enjoy this day! If you fill it with sweet words and with kindness, you will encounter romance, good partnerships and to top it all off money.	Om Namo Bhagawate Mukhtanandaya, 108 times AUM KRSNAYA VIDMAHE DAMODARAYA DHIMAHI. TANNO VISHNU PRACODAYAT. 9 times

BIBLE VERSES: (Proverbs)

15:4. A peaceable tongue is a tree of life: but that which is immoderate, shall crush the spirit.

READ PSALMS #'s: 3, 12, 30 ,39, 48, 57, 75, 102, 120

FEBRUARY 14, 2015

02/14/2015 SAT			This is considered a POSITIVE day for you						Shiva

Moving	Shopping	Health	Investing	Gambling	Love is	Wedding	Travel	Work/Job	Planet
Good	Excellent	Excellent	Good	Bad	Good	Good	Excelle	Good	Pluto

KEYWORDS ARE: children, building, imaturity, television, Petty quarels, Accidents, Denial - Doubt, work, children

Lotto #'s	play 4 #s	play 3 #s	Ruling Angel:............	Color Sugestion:............	Ruling Deity
4,5,34,31,19,12	8422	382	Metatron	Dark Blue/ Purple/ Mauve	Ganesh

ADVICE & DETAILS	MANTRA FOR TODAY
Today, it will feel very comfortable at your work place, at your job. Opportunities to advance may present themselves. Financial situation improves.	Kali Durge Namo Nama Om Durge aye nama swaha 108 times AUM TATPURUSAYA VIDMAHE VAKRATUNDAY DHIMAHI. TANNO DANTI PRACODAYAT. 9 times

BIBLE VERSES: (Proverbs)

15:6. The house of the just is very much strength: and in the fruits of the wicked is trouble.

READ PSALMS #'s: 4, 13, 31 ,40, 49, 58, 76, 103, 121

FEBRUARY 15, 2015

02/15/2015 SUN			This is considered a NEUTRAL day for you						Shiva

Moving	Shopping	Health	Investing	Gambling	Love is	Wedding	Travel	Work/Job	Planet
Bad	Bad	Bad	Bad	Good	Fair	Good	Bad	Bad	Uranus

KEYWORDS ARE: High Temper, Exercise, Laziness, Industrial, Career improvments, Losses, Death, Distant, far, Job Problems

Lotto #'s	play 4 #s	play 3 #s	Ruling Angel:............	Color Sugestion:............	Ruling Deity
5,6,34,31,19,14	5285	483	Camael	Orange/White/Light Green/ Beige	Krishna

ADVICE & DETAILS	MANTRA FOR TODAY
There will be changes at the job, and these will be in your favor. You will enjoy engaging in new projects. Coworkers may be friendly, but you must be careful with whom you trust.	*Om hareem Kleem Hreem Aem Saraswataye namaha* *21 times* *Om Guru bramha, Guru Vishnu Guru Deva mahaeshwara guru saksha paam bramha, tasmi shri guruve nama* *9 times*

BIBLE VERSES: (Proverbs)
15:8. The victims of the wicked are abominable to the Lord: the vows of the just are acceptable.

READ PSALMS #'s: 5, 14, 32 ,41, 50, 59, 77, 104, 122

FEBRUARY 16, 2015

02/16/2015 MON			This is considered a POSITIVE day for you						Shiva

Moving	Shopping	Health	Investing	Gambling	Love is	Wedding	Travel	Work/Job	Planet
Excellent	Good	Excellent	Good	Fair	Excellent	Bad	Excelle	Good	Mars

KEYWORDS ARE: Exercise, Jealousy, Moving, Short Trips, Romance with lovers, Death, Sickness - cold, Family Conflicts, Deception

Lotto #'s	play 4 #s	play 3 #s	Ruling Angel:............	Color Sugestion:............	Ruling Deity
6,7,34,32,19,16	5072	584	Raphael	Purple/DeepBlue/Rose	Hanuman

ADVICE & DETAILS	MANTRA FOR TODAY
You will have delays in travel. Your business sales will be low. You need to watch out for accidents or health problems. You may experience some constipation or bad digestion from bad meals.	*Om Jai Viganeshwaraya.. Lambodaraya Namo Namaha* *21 times* *Om Sarva Mangal Mangalye, Shiva Sarvart Sadike, Sharan Tryambike Gowri, Narayane Namo asttute* *9 times*

BIBLE VERSES: (Proverbs)
15:10. Instruction is grievous to him that forsaketh the way of life: he that hateth reproof shall die.

READ PSALMS #'s: 6, 15, 33 ,42, 51, 60, 78, 105, 123

FEBRUARY 17, 2015

02/17/2015 TUE			This is considered a NEGATIVE day for you						Shiva

Moving	Shopping	Health	Investing	Gambling	Love is	Wedding	Travel	Work/Job	Planet
Bad	Bad	Bad	Fair	Bad	Bad	Fair	Bad	Bad	Moon

KEYWORDS ARE: Jealousy, Slow Day, Government, responsibility, Family & children, Sickness - cold, Legal matter, Sleepiness, Quarrels

Lotto #'s	play 4 #s	play 3 #s	Ruling Angel:............	Color Sugestion:............	Ruling Deity
7,9,33,32,19,18	3945	685	Zaphkiel	Light Blue/Purple/Peach	Ganga

ADVICE & DETAILS	MANTRA FOR TODAY
You will have disagreemets and frustration over your financial situation today. You will be worried about losing your position. The jealousy of coworkers may affect your performance at work. Do not be rude to bosses.	*Om Graam Greem Graum Sa Gurave namah swaha* *21 times* *AUM VAGDEVYAI CA VIDMAHE KAMARAJAYA DHIMAHI. TANNO DEVI PRACODAYAT.* *9 times*

BIBLE VERSES: (Proverbs)
15:12. A corrupt man loveth not one that reproveth him: nor will he go to the wise.

READ PSALMS #'s: 7, 16, 34 ,43, 52, 61, 79, 106, 124

FEBRUARY 18, 2015

02/18/2015 WED			This is considered a NEUTRAL day for you						Shiva

Moving	Shopping	Health	Investing	Gambling	Love is	Wedding	Travel	Work/Job	Planet
Good	Fair	Fair	Bad	Excellent	Good	Excellent	Good	Fair	**Jupiter**

KEYWORDS ARE: IRS - Law, High Pleasure, Criticism, sleepiness, Inner Conflicts with Job, Legal matter, Abusive, Promotion, Alcohol - drugs

Lotto #'s	play 4 #s	play 3 #s	Ruling Angel:...........	Color Sugestion:...........		Ruling Deity
8,10,33,32,19,21	5240	786	**Haniel**	**Yellow/White/Silver**		**Mahalaxmi**

ADVICE & DETAILS	MANTRA FOR TODAY
You may receive an unexpected financial windfall today. It is a good day to save money and to plan your financial future. Set up a retirement plan. Donate to charity today.	*Om Mana Swasti Shanti Kuru kuru Swaha Shivoham Shivoham 27 times om haring jawala mukhi mam sarva shatru bakshaya bakshaya hung phat swaha Om Nama shivaya pahimam 9 times*

BIBLE VERSES: (Proverbs)
15:14. The heart of the wise seeketh instruction: and the mouth of fools feedeth on foolishness.

READ PSALMS #'s: 8, 17, 35 ,44, 53, 62, 80, 107, 125

FEBRUARY 19, 2015

02/19/2015 THU			This is considered a POSITIVE day for you						Shiva

Moving	Shopping	Health	Investing	Gambling	Love is	Wedding	Travel	Work/Job	Planet
Good	Good	Excellent	Excellent	Bad	Good	Bad	Good	Excellent	**Saturn**

KEYWORDS ARE: Accidents, Denial - Doubt, money, profits, Investment news , Abusive, Karmic debts, God - Karma, Money Wasted

Lotto #'s	play 4 #s	play 3 #s	Ruling Angel:...........	Color Sugestion:...........		Ruling Deity
9,2,34,31,19,13	2074	887	**Mikael**	**Gold/Brown/Blue/Dark Green**		**Pitridev**

ADVICE & DETAILS	MANTRA FOR TODAY
Today money comes in, money goes out. You will make profits, but at the same time you will have big expenses and you will enjoy high pleasure.	*Jai Jai Shiva Shambo.(2) ...Mahadeva Shambo (2) 21 times Om Jayanti Mangala Kali Bhadrakali Kapalini Durga Kshama Shiva Dhatri Swaha Swadha Namostute 9 times*

BIBLE VERSES: (Proverbs)
15:16. Better is a little with the fear of the Lord, than great treasures without content.

READ PSALMS #'s: 9, 18, 36 ,45, 54, 63, 81, 108, 126

FEBRUARY 20, 2015

02/20/2015 FRI			This is considered a NEGATIVE day for you						Shiva

Moving	Shopping	Health	Investing	Gambling	Love is	Wedding	Travel	Work/Job	Planet
Bad	Bad	Bad	Bad	Fair	Bad	Fair	Bad	Bad	**Sun**

KEYWORDS ARE: Denial - Doubt, lonliness, losses, sadness, Family conflicts, Arguments, Karmic debts, God - Karma, Home Alone, Accidents

Lotto #'s	play 4 #s	play 3 #s	Ruling Angel:...........	Color Sugestion:...........		Ruling Deity
10,2,33,31,19,15	4811	988	**Gabriel**	**White/Yellow/ Peach**		**Gaitree**

ADVICE & DETAILS	MANTRA FOR TODAY
There will be a great deal of confusion today. There will be many bills and expenses and you may not have enough money to cover them. There could be delays in court cases. You may have to pay for something you do not want.	*Om Hareem Nama Swaha..Shri Maha Laxmi Aye Namah swaha 12 times Om maha laxmi cha vidmahe vishnu pataya dhi mahi tanno laxmi pracho dayat Om hareem namam swaha 9 times*

BIBLE VERSES: (Proverbs)
15:9. The way of the wicked is an abomination to the Lord: he that followeth justice is beloved by him.

READ PSALMS #'s: 1, 10, 28 ,37, 46, 55, 73, 100, 118

FEBRUARY 21, 2015

02/21/2015 SAT		This is considered a NEUTRAL day for you							Shiva
Moving	Shopping	Health	Investing	Gambling	Love is	Wedding	Travel	Work/Job	Planet
Fair	Fair	Fair	Fair	Good	Bad	Good	Fair	Bad	Venus

KEYWORDS ARE: death, romamce, finish, fame,
Tiredness, Low Energy, Sleepy, God - Karma, IRS - Law, Music, Denial - Doubt

Lotto #'s	play 4 #s	play 3 #s	Ruling Angel:............	Color Sugestion:............	Ruling Deity
2,4,34,31,19,17	9777	189	Raziel	Red/Yellow/Pink	Durga

ADVICE & DETAILS	MANTRA FOR TODAY
This is one of those days that you want to have over and over again if you are connected with the gods. You should expect promotion, money and romance.	Om Ganga mataye nama swaha Om Varuna Devta aye Pahimam 11 times Om hareem mama sarva shatru janam vashee kuru kuru swaha om hareem ksham kasham kasheem kasheem swaha 9 times

BIBLE VERSES: (Proverbs)
15:11. Hell and destruction are before the Lord: how much more the hearts of the children of men?
READ PSALMS #'s: 2, 11, 29 ,38, 47, 56, 74, 101, 119

FEBRUARY 22, 2015

02/22/2015 SUN		This is considered a POSITIVE day for you							Shiva
Moving	Shopping	Health	Investing	Gambling	Love is	Wedding	Travel	Work/Job	Planet
Good	Excellent	Good	Good	Good	Excellent	Good	Excelle	Good	Mercury

KEYWORDS ARE: losses, children, sadness, sickness,
Financial losses & expenses, IRS - Law, Accidents, Publishing, death

Lotto #'s	play 4 #s	play 3 #s	Ruling Angel:............	Color Sugestion:............	Ruling Deity
3,5,33,32,19,20	5920	2810	Zadkiel	Green/Sky Blue/White	Saraswaty

ADVICE & DETAILS	MANTRA FOR TODAY
Enjoy this day! If you fill it with sweet words and with kindness, you will encounter romance, good partnerships and to top it all off money.	Om Namo Bhagawate Mukhtanandaya, 108 times AUM KRSNAYA VIDMAHE DAMODARAYA DHIMAHI. TANNO VISHNU PRACODAYAT. 9 times

BIBLE VERSES: (Proverbs)
15:13. A glad heart maketh a cheerful countenance: but by grief of mind the spirit is cast down.
READ PSALMS #'s: 3, 12, 30 ,39, 48, 57, 75, 102, 120

FEBRUARY 23, 2015

02/23/2015 MON		This is considered a POSITIVE day for you							Shiva
Moving	Shopping	Health	Investing	Gambling	Love is	Wedding	Travel	Work/Job	Planet
Good	Excellent	Excellent	Good	Bad	Good	Good	Excelle	Good	Pluto

KEYWORDS ARE: children, building, imaturity, television,
Petty quarels, Accidents, Denial - Doubt, work, children

Lotto #'s	play 4 #s	play 3 #s	Ruling Angel:............	Color Sugestion:............	Ruling Deity
4,5,34,32,19,12	1411	382	Metatron	Dark Blue/ Purple/ Mauve	Ganesh

ADVICE & DETAILS	MANTRA FOR TODAY
Today, it will feel very comfortable at your work place, at your job. Opportunities to advance may present themselves. Financial situation improves.	Kali Durge Namo Nama Om Durge aye nama swaha 108 times AUM TATPURUSAYA VIDMAHE VAKRATUNDAY DHIMAHI. TANNO DANTI PRACODAYAT. 9 times

BIBLE VERSES: (Proverbs)
15:15. All the days of the poor are evil: a secure mind is like a continual feast.
READ PSALMS #'s: 4, 13, 31 ,40, 49, 58, 76, 103, 121

FEBRUARY 24, 2015

02/24/2015 TUE	This is considered a NEUTRAL day for you								Shiva

Moving	Shopping	Health	Investing	Gambling	Love is	Wedding	Travel	Work/Job	Planet
Bad	Bad	Bad	Bad	Good	Fair	Good	Bad	Bad	Uranus

KEYWORDS ARE: High Temper, Exercise, Laziness, Industrial, Career improvments, Losses, Death, Distant, far, Job Problems

Lotto #'s	play 4 #s	play 3 #s	Ruling Angel:............	Color Sugestion:............	Ruling Deity
5,6,33,32,19,15	1923	483	Camael	Orange/White/Light Green/ Beige	Krishna

ADVICE & DETAILS	MANTRA FOR TODAY
There will be changes at the job, and these will be in your favor. You will enjoy engaging in new projects. Coworkers may be friendly, but you must be careful with whom you trust.	Om hareem Kleem Hreem Aem Saraswataye namaha 21 times Om Guru bramha, Guru Vishnu Guru Deva mahaeshwara guru saksha paam bramha, tasmi shri guruve nama 9 times
BIBLE VERSES: (Proverbs)	
15:17. It is better to be invited to herbs with love, than to a fatted calf with hatred.	
READ PSALMS #'s: 5, 14, 32 ,41, 50, 59, 77, 104, 122	

FEBRUARY 25, 2015

02/25/2015 WED	This is considered a POSITIVE day for you								Shiva

Moving	Shopping	Health	Investing	Gambling	Love is	Wedding	Travel	Work/Job	Planet
Excellent	Good	Excellent	Good	Fair	Excellent	Bad	Excelle	Good	Mars

KEYWORDS ARE: Exercise, Jealousy, Moving, Short Trips, Romance with lovers, Death, Sickness - cold, Family Conflicts, Deception

Lotto #'s	play 4 #s	play 3 #s	Ruling Angel:............	Color Sugestion:............	Ruling Deity
6,8,34,31,19,16	7415	584	Raphael	Purple/DeepBlue/Rose	Hanuman

ADVICE & DETAILS	MANTRA FOR TODAY
You will have delays in travel. Your business sales will be low. You need to watch out for accidents or health problems. You may experience some constipation or bad digestion from bad meals.	Om Jai Viganeshwaraya.. Lambodaraya Namo Namaha 21 times Om Sarva Mangal Mangalye, Shiva Sarvart Sadike, Sharan Tryambike Gowri, Narayane Namo asttute 9 times
BIBLE VERSES: (Proverbs)	
15:19. The way of the slothful is as a hedge of thorns: the way of the just is without offence.	
READ PSALMS #'s: 6, 15, 33 ,42, 51, 60, 78, 105, 123	

FEBRUARY 26, 2015

02/26/2015 THU	This is considered a NEGATIVE day for you								Shiva

Moving	Shopping	Health	Investing	Gambling	Love is	Wedding	Travel	Work/Job	Planet
Bad	Bad	Bad	Fair	Bad	Bad	Fair	Bad	Bad	Moon

KEYWORDS ARE: Jealousy, Slow Day, Government, responsibility, Family & children, Sickness - cold, Legal matter, Sleepiness, Quarrels

Lotto #'s	play 4 #s	play 3 #s	Ruling Angel:............	Color Sugestion:............	Ruling Deity
7,8,33,32,19,19	7829	685	Zaphkiel	Light Blue/Purple/Peach	Ganga

ADVICE & DETAILS	MANTRA FOR TODAY
You will have disagreemets and frustration over your financial situation today. You will be worried about losing your position. The jealousy of coworkers may affect your performance at work. Do not be rude to bosses.	Om Graam Greem Graum Sa Gurave namah swaha 21 times AUM VAGDEVYAI CA VIDMAHE KAMARAJAYA DHIMAHI. TANNO DEVI PRACODAYAT. 9 times
BIBLE VERSES: (Proverbs)	
15:21. Folly is joy to the fool: and the wise man maketh straight his steps.	
0	
READ PSALMS #'s: 7, 16, 34 ,43, 52, 61, 79, 106, 124	

FEBRUARY 27, 2015

02/27/2015 FRI		This is considered a NEUTRAL day for you							Shiva
Moving	Shopping	Health	Investing	Gambling	Love is	Wedding	Travel	Work/Job	Planet
Good	Fair	Fair	Bad	Excellent	Good	Excellent	Good	Fair	Jupiter

KEYWORDS ARE: IRS - Law, High Pleasure, Criticism, sleepiness, Inner Conflicts with Job, Legal matter, Abusive, Promotion, Alcohol - drugs

Lotto #'s	play 4 #s	play 3 #s	Ruling Angel:............	Color Sugestion:............	Ruling Deity
8,10,33,32,19,21	6247	786	Haniel	Yellow/White/Silver	Mahalaxmi

ADVICE & DETAILS	MANTRA FOR TODAY
You may receive an unexpected financial windfall today. It is a good day to save money and to plan your financial future. Set up a retirement plan. Donate to charity today.	Om Mana Swasti Shanti Kuru kuru Swaha Shivoham Shivoham 27 times om haring jawala mukhi mam sarva shatru bakshaya bakshaya hung phat swaha Om Nama shivaya pahimam 9 times

BIBLE VERSES: (Proverbs)
15:23. A man rejoiceth in the sentence of his mouth: and a word in due time is best.
READ PSALMS #'s: 8, 17, 35 ,44, 53, 62, 80, 107, 125

FEBRUARY 28, 2015

02/28/2015 SAT		This is considered a POSITIVE day for you							Shiva
Moving	Shopping	Health	Investing	Gambling	Love is	Wedding	Travel	Work/Job	Planet
Good	Good	Excellent	Excellent	Bad	Good	Bad	Good	Excellent	Saturn

KEYWORDS ARE: Accidents, Denial - Doubt, money, profits, Investment news , Abusive, Karmic debts, God - Karma, Money Wasted

Lotto #'s	play 4 #s	play 3 #s	Ruling Angel:............	Color Sugestion:............	Ruling Deity
9,2,33,32,19,13	2938	887	Mikael	Gold/Brown/Blue/Dark Green	Pitridev

ADVICE & DETAILS	MANTRA FOR TODAY
Today money comes in, money goes out. You will make profits, but at the same time you will have big expenses and you will enjoy high pleasure.	Jai Jai Shiva Shambo.(2) ...Mahadeva Shambo (2) 21 times Om Jayanti Mangala Kali Bhadrakali Kapalini Durga Kshama Shiva Dhatri Swaha Swadha Namostute 9 times

BIBLE VERSES: (Proverbs)
15:25. The Lord will destroy the house of the proud: and will strengthen the borders of the widow.
READ PSALMS #'s: 9, 18, 36 ,45, 54, 63, 81, 108, 126

MARCH 1, 2015

03/01/2015 SUN		This is considered a POSITIVE day for you							Shiva
Moving	Shopping	Health	Investing	Gambling	Love is	Wedding	Travel	Work/Job	Planet
Good	Good	Excellent	Excellent	Fair	Good	Fair	Good	Excellent	Sun

KEYWORDS ARE: Denial - Doubt, lonliness, investment, luxury, Loans and Mortgages, On Your Own, God - Karma, Home Alone, High Pleasure

Lotto #'s	play 4 #s	play 3 #s	Ruling Angel:............	Color Sugestion:............	Ruling Deity
9,2,34,31,20,15	7362	897	Gabriel	White/Yellow/ Peach	Gaitree

ADVICE & DETAILS	MANTRA FOR TODAY
Be very careful of wasting money today, particularly in a big ticket item. The influences of today if you are positive may help you with a promotion, but if you are negative you will feel lazy and inactive, you must overcome this tendency and accomplish your tasks.	Om Hareem Nama Swaha..Shri Maha Laxmi Aye Namah swaha 12 times Om maha laxmi cha vidmahe vishnu pataya dhi mahi tanno laxmi pracho dayat Om hareem namam swaha 9 times

BIBLE VERSES: (Proverbs)
15:18. A passionate man stirreth up strifes: he that is patient appeaseth those that are stirred up.
READ PSALMS #'s: 1, 10, 28 ,37, 46, 55, 73, 100, 118

MARCH 2, 2015

| 03/02/2015 MON | | This is considered a NEGATIVE day for you | | | | | | | Shiva | |

Moving	Shopping	Health	Investing	Gambling	Love is	Wedding	Travel	Work/Job	Planet
Bad	Bad	Bad	Bad	Good	Bad	Good	Bad	Bad	Venus

KEYWORDS ARE: death, romamce, finish, fame,
Tiredness, Low Energy, Sleepy, Commanding, IRS - Law, Music, Denial - Doubt

Lotto #'s	play 4 #s	play 3 #s	Ruling Angel:............	Color Sugestion:............	Ruling Deity
10,3,33,31,20,17	4005	998	Raziel	Red/Yellow/Pink	Durga

ADVICE & DETAILS	MANTRA FOR TODAY
Today is a great day to enjoy friends, associates, to venture into partnerships and to listen to and honor teachers. You could also lose or end a relationship with a lover.	*Om Hareem Nama Swaha..Shri Maha Laxmi Aye Namah swaha 12 times Om maha laxmi cha vidmahe vishnu pataya dhi mahi tanno laxmi pracho dayat Om hareem namam swaha 9 times*
BIBLE VERSES: (Proverbs)	
15:20. A wise son maketh a father joyful: but the foolish man despiseth his mother.	
READ PSALMS #'s: 2, 11, 29 ,38, 47, 56, 74, 101, 119	

MARCH 3, 2015

| 03/03/2015 TUE | | This is considered a NEUTRAL day for you | | | | | | | Shiva | |

Moving	Shopping	Health	Investing	Gambling	Love is	Wedding	Travel	Work/Job	Planet
Fair	Fair	Fair	Fair	Good	Bad	Good	Fair	Bad	Mercury

KEYWORDS ARE: independence, children, individuality, unique,
Commanding, Home Alone, Accidents, Publishing, lonliness

Lotto #'s	play 4 #s	play 3 #s	Ruling Angel:............	Color Sugestion:............	Ruling Deity
2,4,34,32,20,19	10020	199	Zadkiel	Green/Sky Blue/White	Saraswaty

ADVICE & DETAILS	MANTRA FOR TODAY
You may hear news of possible pregnancy of birth of a baby. Tension over children or younger people. You must watch your health today. You will be stressed.	*Om Ganga mataye nama swaha Om Varuna Devta aye Pahimam 11 times Om hareem mama sarva shatru janam vashee kuru kuru swaha om hareem ksham kasham kasheem kasheem swaha 9 times*
BIBLE VERSES: (Proverbs)	
15:22. Designs are brought to nothing where there is no counsel: but where there are many counsellors, they are established.	
READ PSALMS #'s: 3, 12, 30 ,39, 48, 57, 75, 102, 120	

MARCH 4, 2015

| 03/04/2015 WED | | This is considered a POSITIVE day for you | | | | | | | Shiva | |

Moving	Shopping	Health	Investing	Gambling	Love is	Wedding	Travel	Work/Job	Planet
Good	Excellent	Good	Good	Bad	Excellent	Good	Excelle	Good	Pluto

KEYWORDS ARE: marriage, building, Talkative, food,
Love quarrels, Boastful, Denial - Doubt, work, romamce

Lotto #'s	play 4 #s	play 3 #s	Ruling Angel:............	Color Sugestion:............	Ruling Deity
3,5,34,31,20,21	10026	2910	Metatron	Dark Blue/ Purple/ Mauve	Ganesh

ADVICE & DETAILS	MANTRA FOR TODAY
There is the possibility of tension at work with coworkers. You may have group projects that may create conflict. Coworkers are friendly but tense.	*Om Namo Bhagawate Mukhtanandaya, 108 times AUM KRSNAYA VIDMAHE DAMODARAYA DHIMAHI. TANNO VISHNU PRACODAYAT. 9 times*
BIBLE VERSES: (Proverbs)	
15:24. The path of life is above for the wise, that he may decline from the lowest hell.	
READ PSALMS #'s: 4, 13, 31 ,40, 49, 58, 76, 103, 121	

MARCH 5, 2015

03/05/2015 THU		This is considered a POSITIVE day for you							Shiva
Moving	Shopping	Health	Investing	Gambling	Love is	Wedding	Travel	Work/Job	Planet
Good	Excellent	Excellent	Good	Good	Good	Good	Excelle	Good	Uranus

KEYWORDS ARE: Childishness, Exercise, Teacher, Communication, Feeling playful, Lonliness, Death, Distant, far, Social Functions

Lotto #'s	play 4 #s	play 3 #s	Ruling Angel:............	Color Sugestion:............	Ruling Deity
4,7,33,31,20,14	9377	392	Camael	Orange/White/Light Green/ Beige	Krishna

ADVICE & DETAILS	MANTRA FOR TODAY
You will receive news of becoming pregnant or hear about someone else being pregnant or receive news about children. You will have the opportunity to buy or be somewhere related to luxury and fame. Do not begin any project today; today is a day to culminate projects of any type.	*Kali Durge Namo Nama Om Durge aye nama swaha 108 times AUM TATPURUSAYA VIDMAHE VAKRATUNDAY DHIMAHI. TANNO DANTI PRACODAYAT. 9 times*

BIBLE VERSES: (Proverbs)
15:26. Evil thoughts are an abomination to the Lord: and pure words most beautiful shall be confirmed by him.

READ PSALMS #'s: 5, 14, 32 ,41, 50, 59, 77, 104, 122

MARCH 6, 2015

03/06/2015 FRI		This is considered a NEUTRAL day for you							Shiva
Moving	Shopping	Health	Investing	Gambling	Love is	Wedding	Travel	Work/Job	Planet
Bad	Bad	Bad	Bad	Fair	Fair	Bad	Bad	Bad	Mars

KEYWORDS ARE: Low Pay, Jealousy, Real Estate, Tiredness, Job enjoyment, Meditative, Sickness - cold, Family Conflicts, High Temper

Lotto #'s	play 4 #s	play 3 #s	Ruling Angel:............	Color Sugestion:............	Ruling Deity
5,7,34,31,20,15	6234	493	Raphael	Purple/DeepBlue/Rose	Hanuman

ADVICE & DETAILS	MANTRA FOR TODAY
You may have to deal with coworker problems today. You will also have conflicts and tensions with bosses. You should keep a low profile today. Keep your nose to the grindstone and do your duty without complaining. Avoid contact with coworkers.	*Om hareem Kleem Hreem Aem Saraswataye namaha 21 times Om Guru bramha, Guru Vishnu Guru Deva mahaeshwara guru saksha paam bramha, tasmi shri guruve nama 9 times*

BIBLE VERSES: (Proverbs)
15:28. The mind of the just studieth obedience: the mouth of the wicked overfloweth with evils.

READ PSALMS #'s: 6, 15, 33 ,42, 51, 60, 78, 105, 123

MARCH 7, 2015

03/07/2015 SAT		This is considered a POSITIVE day for you							Shiva
Moving	Shopping	Health	Investing	Gambling	Love is	Wedding	Travel	Work/Job	Planet
Excellent	Good	Excellent	Good	Bad	Excellent	Fair	Excelle	Good	Moon

KEYWORDS ARE: Illicit Affairs, Slow Day, Beauty - Sex, travel, Comfort & Jokes, Worry, Legal matter, Sleepiness, Excercise

Lotto #'s	play 4 #s	play 3 #s	Ruling Angel:............	Color Sugestion:............	Ruling Deity
6,9,33,31,20,17	1544	594	Zaphkiel	Light Blue/Purple/Peach	Ganga

ADVICE & DETAILS	MANTRA FOR TODAY
This day is influenced by changes, moves and trips to close by locations. You will change your mind often and this lack of focus may cause you to get into an accident. Try to stay focused on your goals and minimize the multitasking especially when driving from one place to another.	*Om Jai Viganeshwaraya.. Lambodaraya Namo Namaha 21 times Om Sarva Mangal Mangalye, Shiva Sarvart Sadike, Sharan Tryambike Gowri, Narayane Namo asttute 9 times*

BIBLE VERSES: (Proverbs)
15:30. The light of the eyes rejoiceth the soul: a good name maketh the bones fat.

READ PSALMS #'s: 7, 16, 34 ,43, 52, 61, 79, 106, 124

MARCH 8, 2015

03/08/2015 SUN		This is considered a NEGATIVE day for you							Shiva
Moving	Shopping	Health	Investing	Gambling	Love is	Wedding	Travel	Work/Job	Planet
Bad	Bad	Bad	Fair	Excellent	Bad	Excellent	Bad	Bad	Jupiter

KEYWORDS ARE: Police, High Pleasure, Anger - Ego, frustration, Back Pain and job stress, Dominating, Abusive, Promotion, Jealousy

Lotto #'s	play 4 #s	play 3 #s	Ruling Angel:............	Color Sugestion:............	Ruling Deity
7,9,33,31,20,20	10497	695	Haniel	Yellow/White/Silver	Mahalaxmi

ADVICE & DETAILS

You will hear news of profit or gains or inheritance from far away. You will have a wealthy relative contact you or visit you. Avoid taking risks with money or signing contracts for purchases.

MANTRA FOR TODAY

Om Graam Greem Graum Sa Gurave namah swaha
21 times
AUM VAGDEVYAI CA VIDMAHE KAMARAJAYA DHIMAHI. TANNO DEVI PRACODAYAT.
9 times

BIBLE VERSES: (Proverbs)

15:32. He that rejecteth instruction, despiseth his own soul: but he that yieldeth to reproof, possesseth understanding.

READ PSALMS #'s: 8, 17, 35 ,44, 53, 62, 80, 107, 125

MARCH 9, 2015

03/09/2015 MON		This is considered a NEUTRAL day for you							Shiva
Moving	Shopping	Health	Investing	Gambling	Love is	Wedding	Travel	Work/Job	Planet
Good	Fair	Fair	Bad	Bad	Good	Bad	Good	Fair	Saturn

KEYWORDS ARE: Accidents, Denial - Doubt, spiritual, religion, Religious miracle, Illness - Cold, Karmic debts, God - Karma, Slow Day

Lotto #'s	play 4 #s	play 3 #s	Ruling Angel:............	Color Sugestion:............	Ruling Deity
8,1,33,31,20,13	3069	796	Mikael	Gold/Brown/Blue/Dark Green	Pitridev

ADVICE & DETAILS

It will be difficult, but possible to overcome your sadness today. Your mind will tend to veer towards thoughts of losses, doubts, denial and death; if you cannot control it you will be creating this in your life. Pray, meditate and place your trust in the Higher Power.

MANTRA FOR TODAY

Om Mana Swasti Shanti Kuru kuru Swaha Shivoham Shivoham
27 times
om haring jawala mukhi mam sarva shatru bakshaya bakshaya hung phat swaha
Om Nama shivaya pahimam
9 times

BIBLE VERSES: (Proverbs)

16:1. It is the part of man to prepare the soul: and of the Lord to govern the tongue.

READ PSALMS #'s: 9, 18, 36 ,45, 54, 63, 81, 108, 126

MARCH 10, 2015

03/10/2015 TUE		This is considered a POSITIVE day for you							Shiva
Moving	Shopping	Health	Investing	Gambling	Love is	Wedding	Travel	Work/Job	Planet
Good	Good	Excellent	Excellent	Fair	Good	Fair	Good	Excellent	Sun

KEYWORDS ARE: Denial - Doubt, lonliness, investment, luxury, Loans and Mortgages, On Your Own, God - Karma, Home Alone, High Pleasure

Lotto #'s	play 4 #s	play 3 #s	Ruling Angel:............	Color Sugestion:............	Ruling Deity
9,3,34,32,20,15	6779	897	Gabriel	White/Yellow/ Peach	Gaitree

ADVICE & DETAILS

Be very careful of wasting money today, particularly in a big ticket item. The influences of today if you are positive may help you with a promotion, but if you are negative you will feel lazy and inactive, you must overcome this tendency and accomplish your tasks.

MANTRA FOR TODAY

Jai Jai Shiva Shambo.(2) ...Mahadeva Shambo (2)
21 times
Om Jayanti Mangala Kali Bhadrakali Kapalini Durga Kshama Shiva Dhatri Swaha Swadha Namostute
9 times

BIBLE VERSES: (Proverbs)

15:27. He that is greedy of gain troublert his own house: but he that hateth bribes shall live. By mercy and faith sins are purged away: and by the

READ PSALMS #'s: 1, 10, 28 ,37, 46, 55, 73, 100, 118

MARCH 11, 2015

03/11/2015	WED	This is considered a NEGATIVE day for you							Shiva
Moving	Shopping	Health	Investing	Gambling	Love is	Wedding	Travel	Work/Job	Planet
Bad	Bad	Bad	Bad	Good	Bad	Good	Bad	Bad	Venus

KEYWORDS ARE: death, romamce, finish, fame, Tiredness, Low Energy, Sleepy, Commanding, IRS - Law, Music, Denial - Doubt

Lotto #'s	play 4 #s	play 3 #s	Ruling Angel:............	Color Sugestion:............	Ruling Deity
10,4,33,32,20,16	7433	998	Raziel	Red/Yellow/Pink	Durga

ADVICE & DETAILS	MANTRA FOR TODAY
Today is a great day to enjoy friends, associates, to venture into partnerships and to listen to and honor teachers. You could also lose or end a relationship with a lover.	Om Hareem Nama Swaha..Shri Maha Laxmi Aye Namah swaha 12 times Om maha laxmi cha vidmahe vishnu pataya dhi mahi tanno laxmi pracho dayat Om hareem namam swaha 9 times
BIBLE VERSES: (Proverbs)	
15:29. The Lord is far from the wicked: and he will hear the prayers of the just.	
READ PSALMS #'s: 2, 11, 29 ,38, 47, 56, 74, 101, 119	

MARCH 12, 2015

03/12/2015	THU	This is considered a NEUTRAL day for you							Shiva
Moving	Shopping	Health	Investing	Gambling	Love is	Wedding	Travel	Work/Job	Planet
Fair	Fair	Fair	Fair	Good	Bad	Good	Fair	Bad	Mercury

KEYWORDS ARE: losses, children, sadness, sickness, Financial losses & expenses, Home Alone, Accidents, Publishing, death

Lotto #'s	play 4 #s	play 3 #s	Ruling Angel:............	Color Sugestion:............	Ruling Deity
2,5,33,31,20,18	1863	199	Zadkiel	Green/Sky Blue/White	Saraswaty

ADVICE & DETAILS	MANTRA FOR TODAY
You may hear news of possible pregnancy of birth of a baby. Tension over children or younger people. You must watch your health today. You will be stressed.	Om Ganga mataye nama swaha Om Varuna Devta aye Pahimam 11 times Om hareem mama sarva shatru janam vashee kuru kuru swaha om hareem ksham kasham kasheem kasheem swaha 9 times
BIBLE VERSES: (Proverbs)	
15:31. The ear that heareth the reproofs of life, shall abide in the midst of the wise.	
READ PSALMS #'s: 3, 12, 30 ,39, 48, 57, 75, 102, 120	

MARCH 13, 2015

03/13/2015	FRI	This is considered a POSITIVE day for you							Shiva
Moving	Shopping	Health	Investing	Gambling	Love is	Wedding	Travel	Work/Job	Planet
Good	Excellent	Good	Good	Bad	Excellent	Good	Excelle	Good	Pluto

KEYWORDS ARE: marriage, building, Talkative, food, Love quarrels, Boastful, Denial - Doubt, work, romamce

Lotto #'s	play 4 #s	play 3 #s	Ruling Angel:............	Color Sugestion:............	Ruling Deity
3,5,33,32,20,21	8978	2910	Metatron	Dark Blue/ Purple/ Mauve	Ganesh

ADVICE & DETAILS	MANTRA FOR TODAY
There is the possibility of tension at work with coworkers. You may have group projects that may create conflict. Coworkers are friendly but tense.	Om Namo Bhagawate Mukhtanandaya, 108 times AUM KRSNAYA VIDMAHE DAMODARAYA DHIMAHI. TANNO VISHNU PRACODAYAT. 9 times
BIBLE VERSES: (Proverbs)	
15:33. The fear of the Lord is the lesson of wisdom: and humility goeth before glory.	
READ PSALMS #'s: 4, 13, 31 ,40, 49, 58, 76, 103, 121	

MARCH 14, 2015

03/14/2015 SAT		This is considered a POSITIVE day for you							Shiva
Moving	Shopping	Health	Investing	Gambling	Love is	Wedding	Travel	Work/Job	Planet
Good	Excellent	Excellent	Good	Good	Good	Good	Excelle	Good	Uranus

KEYWORDS ARE: Childishness, Exercise, Teacher, Communication, Feeling playful, Lonliness, Death, Distant, far, Social Functions

Lotto #'s	play 4 #s	play 3 #s	Ruling Angel:............	Color Sugestion:............	Ruling Deity
4,6,34,32,20,14	8296	392	Camael	Orange/White/Light Green/ Beige	Krishna

ADVICE & DETAILS	MANTRA FOR TODAY
You will receive news of becoming pregnant or hear about someone else being pregnant or receive news about children. You will have the opportunity to buy or be somewhere related to luxury and fame. Do not begin any project today; today is a day to culminate projects of any type.	*Kali Durge Namo Nama Om Durge aye nama swaha 108 times AUM TATPURUSAYA VIDMAHE VAKRATUNDAY DHIMAHI. TANNO DANTI PRACODAYAT. 9 times*

BIBLE VERSES: (Proverbs)

16:2. All the ways of a man are open to his eyes: the Lord is the weigher of spirits.

READ PSALMS #'s: 5, 14, 32 ,41, 50, 59, 77, 104, 122

MARCH 15, 2015

03/15/2015 SUN		This is considered a NEUTRAL day for you							Shiva
Moving	Shopping	Health	Investing	Gambling	Love is	Wedding	Travel	Work/Job	Planet
Bad	Bad	Bad	Bad	Fair	Fair	Bad	Bad	Bad	Mars

KEYWORDS ARE: Low Pay, Jealousy, Real Estate, Tiredness, Job enjoyment, Meditative, Sickness - cold, Family Conflicts, High Temper

Lotto #'s	play 4 #s	play 3 #s	Ruling Angel:............	Color Sugestion:............	Ruling Deity
5,8,33,31,20,15	4791	493	Raphael	Purple/DeepBlue/Rose	Hanuman

ADVICE & DETAILS	MANTRA FOR TODAY
You may have to deal with coworker problems today. You will also have conflicts and tensions with bosses. You should keep a low profile today. Keep your nose to the grindstone and do your duty without complaining. Avoid contact with coworkers.	*Om hareem Kleem Hreem Aem Saraswataye namaha 21 times Om Guru bramha, Guru Vishnu Guru Deva mahaeshwara guru saksha paam bramha, tasmi shri guruve nama 9 times*

BIBLE VERSES: (Proverbs)

16:4. The Lord hath made all things for himself: the wicked also for the evil day.

READ PSALMS #'s: 6, 15, 33 ,42, 51, 60, 78, 105, 123

MARCH 16, 2015

03/16/2015 MON		This is considered a POSITIVE day for you							Shiva
Moving	Shopping	Health	Investing	Gambling	Love is	Wedding	Travel	Work/Job	Planet
Excellent	Good	Excellent	Good	Bad	Excellent	Fair	Excelle	Good	Moon

KEYWORDS ARE: Illicit Affairs, Slow Day, Beauty - Sex, travel, Comfort & Jokes, Worry, Legal matter, Sleepiness, Excercise

Lotto #'s	play 4 #s	play 3 #s	Ruling Angel:............	Color Sugestion:............	Ruling Deity
6,9,34,32,20,18	10504	594	Zaphkiel	Light Blue/Purple/Peach	Ganga

ADVICE & DETAILS	MANTRA FOR TODAY
This day is influenced by changes, moves and trips to close by locations. You will change your mind often and this lack of focus may cause you to get into an accident. Try to stay focused on your goals and minimize the multitasking especially when driving from one place to another.	*Om Jai Viganeshwaraya.. Lambodaraya Namo Namaha 21 times Om Sarva Mangal Mangalye, Shiva Sarvart Sadike, Sharan Tryambike Gowri, Narayane Namo asttute 9 times*

BIBLE VERSES: (Proverbs)

16:6. By mercy and truth iniquity is redeemed; and by the fear of the Lord men depart from evil.

READ PSALMS #'s: 7, 16, 34 ,43, 52, 61, 79, 106, 124

MARCH 17, 2015

03/17/2015 TUE			This is considered a NEGATIVE day for you						Shiva
Moving	Shopping	Health	Investing	Gambling	Love is	Wedding	Travel	Work/Job	Planet
Bad	Bad	Bad	Fair	Excellent	Bad	Excellent	Bad	Bad	Jupiter

KEYWORDS ARE: Police, High Pleasure, Anger - Ego, frustration, Back Pain and job stress, Dominating, Abusive, Promotion, Jealousy

Lotto #'s	play 4 #s	play 3 #s	Ruling Angel:.............	Color Sugestion:............	Ruling Deity
7,10,34,31,20,20	8012	695	Haniel	Yellow/White/Silver	Mahalaxmi

ADVICE & DETAILS	MANTRA FOR TODAY
You will hear news of profit or gains or inheritance from far away. You will have a wealthy relative contact you or visit you. Avoid taking risks with money or signing contracts for purchases.	Om Graam Greem Graum Sa Gurave namah swaha 21 times AUM VAGDEVYAI CA VIDMAHE KAMARAJAYA DHIMAHI. TANNO DEVI PRACODAYAT. 9 times

BIBLE VERSES: (Proverbs)
16:8. Better is a little with justice, than great revenues with iniquity.
0
READ PSALMS #'s: 8, 17, 35 ,44, 53, 62, 80, 107, 125

MARCH 18, 2015

03/18/2015 WED			This is considered a NEUTRAL day for you						Shiva
Moving	Shopping	Health	Investing	Gambling	Love is	Wedding	Travel	Work/Job	Planet
Good	Fair	Fair	Bad	Bad	Good	Bad	Good	Fair	Saturn

KEYWORDS ARE: Accidents, Denial - Doubt, spiritual, religion, Religious miracle, Illness - Cold, Karmic debts, God - Karma, Slow Day

Lotto #'s	play 4 #s	play 3 #s	Ruling Angel:.............	Color Sugestion:............	Ruling Deity
8,1,34,31,20,12	8681	796	Mikael	Gold/Brown/Blue/Dark Green	Pitridev

ADVICE & DETAILS	MANTRA FOR TODAY
It will be difficult, but possible to overcome your sadness today. Your mind will tend to veer towards thoughts of losses, doubts, denial and death; if you cannot control it you will be creating this in your life. Pray, meditate and place your trust in the Higher Power.	Om Mana Swasti Shanti Kuru kuru Swaha Shivoham Shivoham 27 times om haring jawala mukhi mam sarva shatru bakshaya bakshaya hung phat swaha Om Nama shivaya pahimam 9 times

BIBLE VERSES: (Proverbs)
16:10. Divination is in the lips of the king, his mouth shall not err in judgment.
READ PSALMS #'s: 9, 18, 36 ,45, 54, 63, 81, 108, 126

MARCH 19, 2015

03/19/2015 THU			This is considered a POSITIVE day for you						Shiva
Moving	Shopping	Health	Investing	Gambling	Love is	Wedding	Travel	Work/Job	Planet
Good	Good	Excellent	Excellent	Fair	Good	Fair	Good	Excellent	Sun

KEYWORDS ARE: Denial - Doubt, lonliness, investment, luxury, Loans and Mortgages, On Your Own, God - Karma, Home Alone, High Pleasure

Lotto #'s	play 4 #s	play 3 #s	Ruling Angel:.............	Color Sugestion:............	Ruling Deity
9,2,33,31,20,14	1236	897	Gabriel	White/Yellow/ Peach	Gaitree

ADVICE & DETAILS	MANTRA FOR TODAY
Be very careful of wasting money today, particularly in a big ticket item. The influences of today if you are positive may help you with a promotion, but if you are negative you will feel lazy and inactive, you must overcome this tendency and accomplish your tasks.	Jai Jai Shiva Shambo.(2) ...Mahadeva Shambo (2) 21 times Om Jayanti Mangala Kali Bhadrakali Kapalini Durga Kshama Shiva Dhatri Swaha Swadha Namostute 9 times

BIBLE VERSES: (Proverbs)
16:3. Lay open thy works to the Lord: and thy thoughts shall be directed.
0
READ PSALMS #'s: 1, 10, 28 ,37, 46, 55, 73, 100, 118

MARCH 20, 2015

03/20/2015 FRI	This is considered a NEGATIVE day for you								Shiva

Moving	Shopping	Health	Investing	Gambling	Love is	Wedding	Travel	Work/Job	Planet
Bad	Bad	Bad	Bad	Good	Bad	Good	Bad	Bad	Venus

KEYWORDS ARE: death, romamce, finish, fame,
Tiredness, Low Energy, Sleepy, Commanding, IRS - Law, Music, Denial - Doubt

Lotto #'s	play 4 #s	play 3 #s	Ruling Angel:............	Color Sugestion:............	Ruling Deity
10,3,34,32,20,17	3254	998	Raziel	Red/Yellow/Pink	Durga

ADVICE & DETAILS	MANTRA FOR TODAY
Today is a great day to enjoy friends, associates, to venture into partnerships and to listen to and honor teachers. You could also lose or end a relationship with a lover.	*Om Hareem Nama Swaha..Shri Maha Laxmi Aye Namah swaha 12 times Om maha laxmi cha vidmahe vishnu pataya dhi mahi tanno laxmi pracho dayat Om hareem namam swaha 9 times*
BIBLE VERSES: (Proverbs)	
16:5. Every proud man is an abomination to the Lord: though hand should be joined to hand, he is not innocent. The beginning of a good way is to	
READ PSALMS #'s: 2, 11, 29 ,38, 47, 56, 74, 101, 119	

MARCH 21, 2015

03/21/2015 SAT	This is considered a NEUTRAL day for you								Shiva

Moving	Shopping	Health	Investing	Gambling	Love is	Wedding	Travel	Work/Job	Planet
Fair	Fair	Fair	Fair	Good	Bad	Good	Fair	Bad	Mercury

KEYWORDS ARE: losses, children, sadness, sickness,
Financial losses & expenses, Home Alone, Accidents, Publishing, death

Lotto #'s	play 4 #s	play 3 #s	Ruling Angel:............	Color Sugestion:............	Ruling Deity
2,5,34,31,20,19	1208	199	Zadkiel	Green/Sky Blue/White	Saraswaty

ADVICE & DETAILS	MANTRA FOR TODAY
You may hear news of possible pregnancy of birth of a baby. Tension over children or younger people. You must watch your health today. You will be stressed.	*Om Ganga mataye nama swaha Om Varuna Devta aye Pahimam 11 times Om hareem mama sarva shatru janam vashee kuru kuru swaha om hareem ksham kasham kasheem kasheem swaha 9 times*
BIBLE VERSES: (Proverbs)	
16:7. When the ways of man shall please the Lord, he will convert even his enemies to peace.	
READ PSALMS #'s: 3, 12, 30 ,39, 48, 57, 75, 102, 120	

MARCH 22, 2015

03/22/2015 SUN	This is considered a POSITIVE day for you								Shiva

Moving	Shopping	Health	Investing	Gambling	Love is	Wedding	Travel	Work/Job	Planet
Good	Excellent	Good	Good	Bad	Excellent	Good	Excelle	Good	Pluto

KEYWORDS ARE: finish, building, fame, pregnancy,
Accidents, Illness, Alcoholism, Boastful, Denial - Doubt, work, losses

Lotto #'s	play 4 #s	play 3 #s	Ruling Angel:............	Color Sugestion:............	Ruling Deity
3,5,34,31,20,20	8497	2910	Metatron	Dark Blue/ Purple/ Mauve	Ganesh

ADVICE & DETAILS	MANTRA FOR TODAY
There is the possibility of tension at work with coworkers. You may have group projects that may create conflict. Coworkers are friendly but tense.	*Om Namo Bhagawate Mukhtanandaya, 108 times AUM KRSNAYA VIDMAHE DAMODARAYA DHIMAHI. TANNO VISHNU PRACODAYAT. 9 times*
BIBLE VERSES: (Proverbs)	
16:9. The heart of man disposeth his way: but the Lord must direct his steps.	
READ PSALMS #'s: 4, 13, 31 ,40, 49, 58, 76, 103, 121	

MARCH 23, 2015

03/23/2015	MON		This is considered a POSITIVE day for you							Shiva
Moving	Shopping	Health	Investing	Gambling	Love is	Wedding	Travel	Work/Job		Planet
Good	Excellent	Excellent	Good	Good	Good	Good	Excelle	Good		Uranus

KEYWORDS ARE: Childishness, Exercise, Teacher, Communication, Feeling playful, Lonliness, Death, Distant, far, Social Functions

Lotto #'s	play 4 #s	play 3 #s	Ruling Angel:............	Color Sugestion:............	Ruling Deity
4,7,34,32,20,13	5002	392	Camael	Orange/White/Light Green/ Beige	Krishna

ADVICE & DETAILS	MANTRA FOR TODAY
You will receive news of becoming pregnant or hear about someone else being pregnant or receive news about children. You will have the opportunity to buy or be somewhere related to luxury and fame. Do not begin any project today; today is a day to culminate projects of any type.	*Kali Durge Namo Nama* *Om Durge aye nama swaha* *108 times* *AUM TATPURUSAYA VIDMAHE VAKRATUNDAY DHIMAHI. TANNO DANTI PRACODAYAT.* *9 times*

BIBLE VERSES: (Proverbs)
16:11. Weight and balance are judgments of the Lord: and his work all the weights of the bag.
READ PSALMS #'s: 5, 14, 32 ,41, 50, 59, 77, 104, 122

MARCH 24, 2015

03/24/2015	TUE		This is considered a NEUTRAL day for you							Shiva
Moving	Shopping	Health	Investing	Gambling	Love is	Wedding	Travel	Work/Job		Planet
Bad	Bad	Bad	Bad	Fair	Fair	Bad	Bad	Bad		Mars

KEYWORDS ARE: Low Pay, Jealousy, Real Estate, Tiredness, Job enjoyment, Meditative, Sickness - cold, Family Conflicts, High Temper

Lotto #'s	play 4 #s	play 3 #s	Ruling Angel:............	Color Sugestion:............	Ruling Deity
5,8,34,31,20,16	5719	493	Raphael	Purple/DeepBlue/Rose	Hanuman

ADVICE & DETAILS	MANTRA FOR TODAY
You may have to deal with coworker problems today. You will also have conflicts and tensions with bosses. You should keep a low profile today. Keep your nose to the grindstone and do your duty without complaining. Avoid contact with coworkers.	*Om hareem Kleem Hreem Aem Saraswataye namaha* *21 times* *Om Guru bramha, Guru Vishnu Guru Deva mahaeshwara guru saksha paam bramha, tasmi shri guruve nama* *9 times*

BIBLE VERSES: (Proverbs)
16:13. Just lips are the delight of kings: he that speaketh right things shall be loved.
READ PSALMS #'s: 6, 15, 33 ,42, 51, 60, 78, 105, 123

MARCH 25, 2015

03/25/2015	WED		This is considered a POSITIVE day for you							Shiva
Moving	Shopping	Health	Investing	Gambling	Love is	Wedding	Travel	Work/Job		Planet
Excellent	Good	Excellent	Good	Bad	Excellent	Fair	Excelle	Good		Moon

KEYWORDS ARE: Illicit Affairs, Slow Day, Beauty - Sex, travel, Comfort & Jokes, Worry, Legal matter, Sleepiness, Excercise

Lotto #'s	play 4 #s	play 3 #s	Ruling Angel:............	Color Sugestion:............	Ruling Deity
6,9,34,31,20,17	3737	594	Zaphkiel	Light Blue/Purple/Peach	Ganga

ADVICE & DETAILS	MANTRA FOR TODAY
This day is influenced by changes, moves and trips to close by locations. You will change your mind often and this lack of focus may cause you to get into an accident. Try to stay focused on your goals and minimize the multitasking especially when driving from one place to another.	*Om Jai Viganeshwaraya.. Lambodaraya Namo Namaha* *21 times* *Om Sarva Mangal Mangalye, Shiva Sarvart Sadike, Sharan Tryambike Gowri, Narayane Namo asttute* *9 times*

BIBLE VERSES: (Proverbs)
16:15. In the cheerfulness of the king's countenance is life: and his clemency is like the latter rain.
READ PSALMS #'s: 7, 16, 34 ,43, 52, 61, 79, 106, 124

MARCH 26, 2015

03/26/2015 THU	This is considered a NEGATIVE day for you								Shiva
Moving	Shopping	Health	Investing	Gambling	Love is	Wedding	Travel	Work/Job	Planet
Bad	Bad	Bad	Fair	Excellent	Bad	Excellent	Bad	Bad	Jupiter

KEYWORDS ARE: Police, High Pleasure, Anger - Ego, frustration, Back Pain and job stress, Dominating, Abusive, Promotion, Jealousy

Lotto #'s	play 4 #s	play 3 #s	Ruling Angel:............	Color Sugestion:............	Ruling Deity
7,10,33,32,20,20	5514	695	Haniel	Yellow/White/Silver	Mahalaxmi

ADVICE & DETAILS	MANTRA FOR TODAY
You will hear news of profit or gains or inheritance from far away. You will have a wealthy relative contact you or visit you. Avoid taking risks with money or signing contracts for purchases.	Om Graam Greem Graum Sa Gurave namah swaha 21 times AUM VAGDEVYAI CA VIDMAHE KAMARAJAYA DHIMAHI. TANNO DEVI PRACODAYAT. 9 times

BIBLE VERSES: (Proverbs)

16:17. The path of the just departeth from evils: he that keepeth his soul keepeth his way.

READ PSALMS #'s: 8, 17, 35 ,44, 53, 62, 80, 107, 125

MARCH 27, 2015

03/27/2015 FRI	This is considered a NEUTRAL day for you								Shiva
Moving	Shopping	Health	Investing	Gambling	Love is	Wedding	Travel	Work/Job	Planet
Good	Fair	Fair	Bad	Bad	Good	Bad	Good	Fair	Saturn

KEYWORDS ARE: Accidents, Denial - Doubt, spiritual, religion, Religious miracle, Illness - Cold, Karmic debts, God - Karma, Slow Day

Lotto #'s	play 4 #s	play 3 #s	Ruling Angel:............	Color Sugestion:............	Ruling Deity
8,2,34,32,20,13	8702	796	Mikael	Gold/Brown/Blue/Dark Green	Pitridev

ADVICE & DETAILS	MANTRA FOR TODAY
It will be difficult, but possible to overcome your sadness today. Your mind will tend to veer towards thoughts of losses, doubts, denial and death; if you cannot control it you will be creating this in your life. Pray, meditate and place your trust in the Higher Power.	Om Mana Swasti Shanti Kuru kuru Swaha Shivoham Shivoham 27 times om haring jawala mukhi mam sarva shatru bakshaya bakshaya hung phat swaha Om Nama shivaya pahimam 9 times

BIBLE VERSES: (Proverbs)

16:19. It is better to be humbled with the meek, than to divide spoils with the proud.

READ PSALMS #'s: 9, 18, 36 ,45, 54, 63, 81, 108, 126

MARCH 28, 2015

03/28/2015 SAT	This is considered a POSITIVE day for you								Shiva
Moving	Shopping	Health	Investing	Gambling	Love is	Wedding	Travel	Work/Job	Planet
Good	Good	Excellent	Excellent	Fair	Good	Fair	Good	Excellent	Sun

KEYWORDS ARE: Denial - Doubt, lonliness, investment, luxury, Loans and Mortgages, On Your Own, God - Karma, Home Alone, High Pleasure

Lotto #'s	play 4 #s	play 3 #s	Ruling Angel:............	Color Sugestion:............	Ruling Deity
9,3,33,31,20,15	7001	897	Gabriel	White/Yellow/ Peach	Gaitree

ADVICE & DETAILS	MANTRA FOR TODAY
Be very careful of wasting money today, particularly in a big ticket item. The influences of today if you are positive may help you with a promotion, but if you are negative you will feel lazy and inactive, you must overcome this tendency and accomplish your tasks.	Jai Jai Shiva Shambo.(2) ...Mahadeva Shambo (2) 21 times Om Jayanti Mangala Kali Bhadrakali Kapalini Durga Kshama Shiva Dhatri Swaha Swadha Namostute 9 times

BIBLE VERSES: (Proverbs)

16:12. They that act wickedly are abominable to the king: for the throne is established by justice.

READ PSALMS #'s: 1, 10, 28 ,37, 46, 55, 73, 100, 118

MARCH 29, 2015

| 03/29/2015 SUN | | | This is considered a NEGATIVE day for you | | | | | | Shiva |

Moving	Shopping	Health	Investing	Gambling	Love is	Wedding	Travel	Work/Job	Planet
Bad	Bad	Bad	Bad	Good	Bad	Good	Bad	Bad	Venus

KEYWORDS ARE: death, romamce, finish, fame,
Tiredness, Low Energy, Sleepy, Commanding, IRS - Law, Music, Denial - Doubt

Lotto #'s	play 4 #s	play 3 #s	Ruling Angel:............	Color Sugestion:............	Ruling Deity
10,3,33,32,20,17	10467	998	Raziel	Red/Yellow/Pink	Durga

ADVICE & DETAILS	MANTRA FOR TODAY
Today is a great day to enjoy friends, associates, to venture into partnerships and to listen to and honor teachers. You could also lose or end a relationship with a lover.	*Om Hareem Nama Swaha..Shri Maha Laxmi Aye Namah swaha 12 times Om maha laxmi cha vidmahe vishnu pataya dhi mahi tanno laxmi pracho dayat Om hareem namam swaha 9 times*

BIBLE VERSES: (Proverbs)
16:14. The wrath of a king is as messengers of death: and the wise man will pacify it.

READ PSALMS #'s: 2, 11, 29 ,38, 47, 56, 74, 101, 119

MARCH 30, 2015

| 03/30/2015 MON | | | This is considered a NEUTRAL day for you | | | | | | Shiva |

Moving	Shopping	Health	Investing	Gambling	Love is	Wedding	Travel	Work/Job	Planet
Fair	Fair	Fair	Fair	Good	Bad	Good	Fair	Bad	Mercury

KEYWORDS ARE: losses, children, sadness, sickness,
Financial losses & expenses, Home Alone, Accidents, Publishing, death

Lotto #'s	play 4 #s	play 3 #s	Ruling Angel:............	Color Sugestion:............	Ruling Deity
2,5,33,32,20,18	4935	199	Zadkiel	Green/Sky Blue/White	Saraswaty

ADVICE & DETAILS	MANTRA FOR TODAY
You may hear news of possible pregnancy of birth of a baby. Tension over children or younger people. You must watch your health today. You will be stressed.	*Om Ganga mataye nama swaha Om Varuna Devta aye Pahimam 11 times Om hareem mama sarva shatru janam vashee kuru kuru swaha om hareem ksham kasham kasheem kasheem swaha 9 times*

BIBLE VERSES: (Proverbs)
16:16. Get wisdom, because it is better than gold: and purchase prudence, for it is more precious than silver.

READ PSALMS #'s: 3, 12, 30 ,39, 48, 57, 75, 102, 120

MARCH 31, 2015

| 03/31/2015 TUE | | | This is considered a POSITIVE day for you | | | | | | Shiva |

Moving	Shopping	Health	Investing	Gambling	Love is	Wedding	Travel	Work/Job	Planet
Good	Excellent	Good	Good	Bad	Excellent	Good	Excelle	Good	Pluto

KEYWORDS ARE: finish, building, fame, pregnancy,
Accidents, Illness, Alcoholism, Boastful, Denial - Doubt, work, losses

Lotto #'s	play 4 #s	play 3 #s	Ruling Angel:............	Color Sugestion:............	Ruling Deity
3,5,34,31,20,20	2834	2910	Metatron	Dark Blue/ Purple/ Mauve	Ganesh

ADVICE & DETAILS	MANTRA FOR TODAY
There is the possibility of tension at work with coworkers. You may have group projects that may create conflict. Coworkers are friendly but tense.	*Om Namo Bhagawate Mukhtanandaya, 108 times AUM KRSNAYA VIDMAHE DAMODARAYA DHIMAHI. TANNO VISHNU PRACODAYAT. 9 times*

BIBLE VERSES: (Proverbs)
16:18. Pride goeth before destruction: and the spirit is lifted up before a fall.

READ PSALMS #'s: 4, 13, 31 ,40, 49, 58, 76, 103, 121

APRIL 1, 2015

| 04/01/2015 WED | | This is considered a POSITIVE day for you | | | | | | | Shiva |

Moving	Shopping	Health	Investing	Gambling	Love is	Wedding	Travel	Work/Job	Planet
Good	Good	Excellent	Excellent	Good	Good	Good	Good	Excellent	Venus

KEYWORDS ARE: Abusive, Friendships, Fame - TV, High Pleasure, Business & money gains, Popularity, Death, Shopping, Investments

Lotto #'s	play 4 #s	play 3 #s	Ruling Angel:............	Color Sugestion:............	Ruling Deity
9,3,33,31,12,16	1975	817	Raziel	Red/Yellow/Pink	Durga

ADVICE & DETAILS	MANTRA FOR TODAY
Very good day for monetary transactions and investments. You will be able to achieve great things with the cooperation of others. There is a chance for promotion.	Kali Durge Namo Nama Om Durge aye nama swaha 108 times AUM TATPURUSAYA VIDMAHE VAKRATUNDAY DHIMAHI. TANNO DANTI PRACODAYAT.

BIBLE VERSES: (Proverbs)

16:17. The path of the just departeth from evils: he that keepeth his soul keepeth his way.

READ PSALMS #'s: 2, 11, 29 ,38, 47, 56, 74, 101, 119

9 times

APRIL 2, 2015

| 04/02/2015 THU | | This is considered a NEGATIVE day for you | | | | | | | Shiva |

Moving	Shopping	Health	Investing	Gambling	Love is	Wedding	Travel	Work/Job	Planet
Bad	Bad	Bad	Bad	Good	Bad	Good	Bad	Bad	Mercury

KEYWORDS ARE: Karmic debts, Teacher, IRS - Law, Denial - Doubt, Quarrels & lovers, Visitors, Sickness - cold, Social Functions, Abusive

Lotto #'s	play 4 #s	play 3 #s	Ruling Angel:............	Color Sugestion:............	Ruling Deity
10,4,33,31,12,17	3237	918	Zadkiel	Green/Sky Blue/White	Saraswaty

ADVICE & DETAILS	MANTRA FOR TODAY
This is a difficult day with anything related to children. There may be childrend denial, abortion, miscarriages, worry over children, arguments with children. Acting in a childish manner may also bring negative consequences for you.	Om Hareem Nama Swaha..Shri Maha Laxmi Aye Namah swaha 12 times Om maha laxmi cha vidmahe vishnu pataya dhi mahi tanno laxmi pracho dayat Om hareem namam swaha

BIBLE VERSES: (Proverbs)

16:19. It is better to be humbled with the meek, than to divide spoils with the proud.

READ PSALMS #'s: 3, 12, 30 ,39, 48, 57, 75, 102, 120

9 times

APRIL 3, 2015

| 04/03/2015 FRI | | This is considered a NEUTRAL day for you | | | | | | | Shiva |

Moving	Shopping	Health	Investing	Gambling	Love is	Wedding	Travel	Work/Job	Planet
Fair	Fair	Fair	Fair	Bad	Bad	Good	Fair	Bad	Pluto

KEYWORDS ARE: Commanding, Real Estate, Boastful, lonliness, Meditative, Shopping, Legal matter, High Temper, On Your Own

Lotto #'s	play 4 #s	play 3 #s	Ruling Angel:............	Color Sugestion:............	Ruling Deity
2,5,33,31,12,20	6539	119	Metatron	Dark Blue/ Purple/ Mauve	Ganesh

ADVICE & DETAILS	MANTRA FOR TODAY
This is slow and lazy day, but for your karma you are advised to work and to be industrious. Your accomplishments today will be important for your personal growth. You may be stressed out at work.	Om Ganga mataye nama swaha Om Varuna Devta aye Pahimam 11 times Om hareem mama sarva shatru janam vashee kuru kuru swaha om hareem ksham kasham kasheem kasheem swaha

BIBLE VERSES: (Proverbs)

16:21. The wise in heart shall be called prudent: and he that is sweet in words, shall attain to greater things.

READ PSALMS #'s: 4, 13, 31 ,40, 49, 58, 76, 103, 121

9 times

APRIL 4, 2015

04/04/2015 SAT		This is considered a POSITIVE day for you							Shiva
Moving	Shopping	Health	Investing	Gambling	Love is	Wedding	Travel	Work/Job	Planet
Good	Excellent	Good	Good	Good	Excellent	Good	Excelle	Good	Uranus

KEYWORDS ARE: Association, Beauty - Sex, Partnership, romamce, Spending, Food, Drinks, Abusive, Exercise, Affection

Lotto #'s	play 4 #s	play 3 #s	Ruling Angel:............	Color Sugestion:............	Ruling Deity
3,6,33,31,12,21	5221	2110	Camael	Orange/White/Light Green/ Beige	Krishna

ADVICE & DETAILS	MANTRA FOR TODAY
A very good day today. It will be filled with positive romance, dating, sexuality and friends. You may take short trips or have changes today. Take initiative in romance today.	*Om Namo Bhagawate Mukhtanandaya, 108 times AUM KRSNAYA VIDMAHE DAMODARAYA DHIMAHI. TANNO VISHNU PRACODAYAT. 9 times*

BIBLE VERSES: (Proverbs)
16:23. The heart of the wise shall instruct his mouth: and shall add grace to his lips.

READ PSALMS #'s: 5, 14, 32 ,41, 50, 59, 77, 104, 122

APRIL 5, 2015

04/05/2015 SUN		This is considered a POSITIVE day for you							Shiva
Moving	Shopping	Health	Investing	Gambling	Love is	Wedding	Travel	Work/Job	Planet
Good	Excellent	Excellent	Good	Fair	Good	Bad	Excelle	Good	Mars

KEYWORDS ARE: Communication, Anger - Ego, read, children, Social Functions, Co-operation, Karmic debts, Jealousy, Expression

Lotto #'s	play 4 #s	play 3 #s	Ruling Angel:............	Color Sugestion:............	Ruling Deity
4,7,34,32,12,15	3652	312	Raphael	Purple/DeepBlue/Rose	Hanuman

ADVICE & DETAILS	MANTRA FOR TODAY
There is a high chance of injury caused by childish, thoughtless behavior. There may be problems and rejection by children. Accidents or falls may cause injuries.	*Kali Durge Namo Nama Om Durge aye nama swaha 108 times AUM TATPURUSAYA VIDMAHE VAKRATUNDAY DHIMAHI. TANNO DANTI PRACODAYAT. 9 times*

BIBLE VERSES: (Proverbs)
16:25. There is a way that seemeth to a man right: and the ends thereof lead to death.

READ PSALMS #'s: 6, 15, 33 ,42, 51, 60, 78, 105, 123

APRIL 6, 2015

04/06/2015 MON		This is considered a NEUTRAL day for you							Shiva
Moving	Shopping	Health	Investing	Gambling	Love is	Wedding	Travel	Work/Job	Planet
Bad	Bad	Bad	Bad	Bad	Fair	Fair	Bad	Bad	Moon

KEYWORDS ARE: Tiredness, spiritual, career, building, Co-workers, Friendships, God - Karma, Slow Day, Industrial

Lotto #'s	play 4 #s	play 3 #s	Ruling Angel:............	Color Sugestion:............	Ruling Deity
5,8,34,32,12,16	8610	413	Zaphkiel	Light Blue/Purple/Peach	Ganga

ADVICE & DETAILS	MANTRA FOR TODAY
This day could bring some career progress. You will have to work hard. You will be stressed out about life and have many thoughts about your job. Pray for career advancement today. You may be sleepy and tired.	*Om hareem Kleem Hreem Aem Saraswataye namaha 21 times Om Guru bramha, Guru Vishnu Guru Deva mahaeshwara guru saksha paam bramha, tasmi shri guruve nama 9 times*

BIBLE VERSES: (Proverbs)
16:27. The wicked man diggeth evil, and in his lips is a burning fire.
0

READ PSALMS #'s: 7, 16, 34 ,43, 52, 61, 79, 106, 124

APRIL 7, 2015

| 04/07/2015 TUE | This is considered a POSITIVE day for you | | | | | | | | Shiva |

Moving	Shopping	Health	Investing	Gambling	Love is	Wedding	Travel	Work/Job	Planet
Excellent	Good	Excellent	Good	Excellent	Excellent	Excellent	Excelle	Good	Jupiter

KEYWORDS ARE: travel, investment, change, deception, Belief and faith, Affection, IRS - Law, High Pleasure, Short Trips

Lotto #'s	play 4 #s	play 3 #s	Ruling Angel:............	Color Sugestion:............	Ruling Deity
6,9,34,32,12,18	4659	514	Haniel	Yellow/White/Silver	Mahalaxmi

ADVICE & DETAILS	MANTRA FOR TODAY
It is a good day for gambling in either casinos or horse racing. You will receive visits from friends or take very enjoyable trips. You should see profits.	Om Jai Viganeshwaraya.. Lambodaraya Namo Namaha 21 times Om Sarva Mangal Mangalye, Shiva Sarvart Sadike, Sharan Tryambike Gowri, Narayane Namo asttute 9 times

BIBLE VERSES: (Proverbs)

16:29. An unjust man allureth his friend: and leadeth him into a way that is not good.

READ PSALMS #'s: 8, 17, 35 ,44, 53, 62, 80, 107, 125

APRIL 8, 2015

| 04/08/2015 WED | This is considered a NEGATIVE day for you | | | | | | | | Shiva |

Moving	Shopping	Health	Investing	Gambling	Love is	Wedding	Travel	Work/Job	Planet
Bad	Bad	Bad	Fair	Bad	Bad	Bad	Bad	Bad	Saturn

KEYWORDS ARE: frustration, finish, power, electricity, Money conflicts, Association, Accidents, Denial - Doubt, responsibility

Lotto #'s	play 4 #s	play 3 #s	Ruling Angel:............	Color Sugestion:............	Ruling Deity
7,1,33,32,12,11	10900	615	Mikael	Gold/Brown/Blue/Dark Green	Pitridev

ADVICE & DETAILS	MANTRA FOR TODAY
Your authoritative attitude mixed with arrogance and the need to feel superior may bring you difficulties with government or any of its agencies and may also make you feel lonely. Being humble today will be beneficial.	Om Graam Greem Graum Sa Gurave namah swaha 21 times AUM VAGDEVYAI CA VIDMAHE KAMARAJAYA DHIMAHI. TANNO DEVI PRACODAYAT. 9 times

BIBLE VERSES: (Proverbs)

16:31. Old age is a crown of dignity, when it is found in the ways of justice.
0

READ PSALMS #'s: 9, 18, 36 ,45, 54, 63, 81, 108, 126

APRIL 9, 2015

| 04/09/2015 THU | This is considered a NEUTRAL day for you | | | | | | | | Shiva |

Moving	Shopping	Health	Investing	Gambling	Love is	Wedding	Travel	Work/Job	Planet
Good	Fair	Fair	Bad	Fair	Good	Fair	Good	Fair	Sun

KEYWORDS ARE: finish, individuality, religion, priests, Slow Day with Tension, Music, Denial - Doubt, lonliness, sleepiness

Lotto #'s	play 4 #s	play 3 #s	Ruling Angel:............	Color Sugestion:............	Ruling Deity
8,3,34,32,12,13	2727	716	Gabriel	White/Yellow/ Peach	Gaitree

ADVICE & DETAILS	MANTRA FOR TODAY
You will feel connected to spirit today. Use your creative abilities to honor the universe and think that by honoring the universe you are honoring yourself. You are part of the universe.	Om Mana Swasti Shanti Kuru kuru Swaha Shivoham Shivoham 27 times om haring jawala mukhi mam sarva shatru bakshaya bakshaya hung phat swaha Om Nama shivaya pahimam 9 times

BIBLE VERSES: (Proverbs)

16:24. Well ordered words are as a honeycomb: sweet to the soul, and health to the bones.

READ PSALMS #'s: 1, 10, 28 ,37, 46, 55, 73, 100, 118

APRIL 10, 2015

04/10/2015 FRI			This is considered a POSITIVE day for you						Shiva
Moving	Shopping	Health	Investing	Gambling	Love is	Wedding	Travel	Work/Job	Planet
Good	Good	Excellent	Excellent	Good	Good	Good	Good	Excellent	Venus

KEYWORDS ARE: Abusive, Friendships, Fame - TV, High Pleasure, Business & money gains, Popularity, Death, Shopping, Investments

Lotto #'s	play 4 #s	play 3 #s	Ruling Angel:...........	Color Sugestion:...........	Ruling Deity
9,3,33,32,12,16	8867	817	Raziel	Red/Yellow/Pink	Durga

ADVICE & DETAILS	MANTRA FOR TODAY
Very good day for monetary transactions and investments. You will be able to achieve great things with the cooperation of others. There is a chance for promotion.	Jai Jai Shiva Shambo.(2) ...Mahadeva Shambo (2) 21 times Om Jayanti Mangala Kali Bhadrakali Kapalini Durga Kshama Shiva Dhatri Swaha Swadha Namostute 9 times
BIBLE VERSES: (Proverbs) 16:26. The soul of him that laboureth, laboureth for himself, because his mouth hath obliged him to it. **READ PSALMS #'s:** 2, 11, 29 ,38, 47, 56, 74, 101, 119	

APRIL 11, 2015

04/11/2015 SAT			This is considered a NEGATIVE day for you						Shiva
Moving	Shopping	Health	Investing	Gambling	Love is	Wedding	Travel	Work/Job	Planet
Bad	Bad	Bad	Bad	Good	Bad	Good	Bad	Bad	Mercury

KEYWORDS ARE: Karmic debts, Teacher, IRS - Law, Denial - Doubt, Quarrels & lovers, Visitors, Sickness - cold, Social Functions, Abusive

Lotto #'s	play 4 #s	play 3 #s	Ruling Angel:...........	Color Sugestion:...........	Ruling Deity
10,4,33,31,12,18	9337	918	Zadkiel	Green/Sky Blue/White	Saraswaty

ADVICE & DETAILS	MANTRA FOR TODAY
This is a difficult day with anything related to children. There may be childrend denial, abortion, miscarriages, worry over children, arguments with children. Acting in a childish manner may also bring negative consequences for you.	Om Hareem Nama Swaha..Shri Maha Laxmi Aye Namah swaha 12 times Om maha laxmi cha vidmahe vishnu pataya dhi mahi tanno laxmi pracho dayat Om hareem namam swaha 9 times
BIBLE VERSES: (Proverbs) 16:28. A perverse man stirreth up quarrels: and one full of words separateth princes. **READ PSALMS #'s:** 3, 12, 30 ,39, 48, 57, 75, 102, 120	

APRIL 12, 2015

04/12/2015 SUN			This is considered a NEUTRAL day for you						Shiva
Moving	Shopping	Health	Investing	Gambling	Love is	Wedding	Travel	Work/Job	Planet
Fair	Fair	Fair	Fair	Bad	Bad	Good	Fair	Bad	Pluto

KEYWORDS ARE: God - Karma, Real Estate, Accidents, death, Illnese, children, hypertension, Shopping, Legal matter, High Temper, Karmic debts

Lotto #'s	play 4 #s	play 3 #s	Ruling Angel:...........	Color Sugestion:...........	Ruling Deity
2,5,34,31,12,20	7926	119	Metatron	Dark Blue/ Purple/ Mauve	Ganesh

ADVICE & DETAILS	MANTRA FOR TODAY
This is slow and lazy day, but for your karma you are advised to work and to be industrious. Your accomplishments today will be important for your personal growth. You may be stressed out at work.	Om Ganga mataye nama swaha Om Varuna Devta aye Pahimam 11 times Om hareem mama sarva shatru janam vashee kuru kuru swaha om hareem ksham kasham kasheem kasheem swaha 9 times
BIBLE VERSES: (Proverbs) 16:30. He that with fixed eyes deviseth wicked things, biting his lips, bringeth evil to pass. **READ PSALMS #'s:** 4, 13, 31 ,40, 49, 58, 76, 103, 121	

APRIL 13, 2015

04/13/2015 MON		This is considered a POSITIVE day for you							Shiva
Moving	Shopping	Health	Investing	Gambling	Love is	Wedding	Travel	Work/Job	Planet
Good	Excellent	Good	Good	Good	Excellent	Good	Excelle	Good	Uranus

KEYWORDS ARE: Association, Beauty - Sex, Partnership, romamce, Spending, Food, Drinks, Abusive, Exercise, Affection

Lotto #'s	play 4 #s	play 3 #s	Ruling Angel:............	Color Sugestion:............	Ruling Deity
3,7,33,32,12,22	5869	2110	Camael	Orange/White/Light Green/ Beige	Krishna

ADVICE & DETAILS	MANTRA FOR TODAY
A very good day today. It will be filled with positive romance, dating, sexuality and friends. You may take short trips or have changes today. Take initiative in romance today.	*Om Namo Bhagawate Mukhtanandaya,* 108 times *AUM KRSNAYA VIDMAHE DAMODARAYA DHIMAHI. TANNO VISHNU PRACODAYAT.* 9 times

BIBLE VERSES: (Proverbs)

16:32. The patient man is better than the valiant: and he that ruleth his spirit, than he that taketh cities.

READ PSALMS #'s: 5, 14, 32 ,41, 50, 59, 77, 104, 122

APRIL 14, 2015

04/14/2015 TUE		This is considered a POSITIVE day for you							Shiva
Moving	Shopping	Health	Investing	Gambling	Love is	Wedding	Travel	Work/Job	Planet
Good	Excellent	Excellent	Good	Fair	Good	Bad	Excelle	Good	Mars

KEYWORDS ARE: Communication, Anger - Ego, read, children, Social Functions, Co-operation, Karmic debts, Jealousy, Expression

Lotto #'s	play 4 #s	play 3 #s	Ruling Angel:............	Color Sugestion:............	Ruling Deity
4,8,34,31,12,15	4757	312	Raphael	Purple/DeepBlue/Rose	Hanuman

ADVICE & DETAILS	MANTRA FOR TODAY
There is a high chance of injury caused by childish, thoughtless behavior. There may be problems and rejection by children. Accidents or falls may cause injuries.	*Kali Durge Namo Nama Om Durge aye nama swaha* 108 times *AUM TATPURUSAYA VIDMAHE VAKRATUNDAY DHIMAHI. TANNO DANTI PRACODAYAT.* 9 times

BIBLE VERSES: (Proverbs)

17:2. A wise servant shall rule over foolish sons, and shall divide the inheritance among the brethren.

READ PSALMS #'s: 6, 15, 33 ,42, 51, 60, 78, 105, 123

APRIL 15, 2015

04/15/2015 WED		This is considered a NEUTRAL day for you							Shiva
Moving	Shopping	Health	Investing	Gambling	Love is	Wedding	Travel	Work/Job	Planet
Bad	Bad	Bad	Bad	Bad	Fair	Fair	Bad	Bad	Moon

KEYWORDS ARE: Tiredness, spiritual, career, building, Co-workers, Friendships, God - Karma, Slow Day, Industrial

Lotto #'s	play 4 #s	play 3 #s	Ruling Angel:............	Color Sugestion:............	Ruling Deity
5,9,34,31,12,16	5415	413	Zaphkiel	Light Blue/Purple/Peach	Ganga

ADVICE & DETAILS	MANTRA FOR TODAY
This day could bring some career progress. You will have to work hard. You will be stressed out about life and have many thoughts about your job. Pray for career advancement today. You may be sleepy and tired.	*Om hareem Kleem Hreem Aem Saraswataye namaha* 21 times *Om Guru bramha, Guru Vishnu Guru Deva mahaeshwara guru saksha paam bramha, tasmi shri guruve nama* 9 times

BIBLE VERSES: (Proverbs)

17:4. The evil man obeyeth an unjust tongue: and the deceitful hearkeneth to lying lips.

READ PSALMS #'s: 7, 16, 34 ,43, 52, 61, 79, 106, 124

APRIL 16, 2015

04/16/2015	THU		This is considered a POSITIVE day for you							Shiva

Moving	Shopping	Health	Investing	Gambling	Love is	Wedding	Travel	Work/Job	Planet
Excellent	Good	Excellent	Good	Excellent	Excellent	Excellent	Excelle	Good	Jupiter

KEYWORDS ARE: travel, investment, change, deception, Belief and faith, Affection, IRS - Law, High Pleasure, Short Trips

Lotto #'s	play 4 #s	play 3 #s	Ruling Angel:............	Color Sugestion:............	Ruling Deity
6,10,33,31,12,19	7781	514	Haniel	Yellow/White/Silver	Mahalaxmi

ADVICE & DETAILS

It is a good day for gambling in either casinos or horse racing. You will receive visits from friends or take very enjoyable trips. You should see profits.

MANTRA FOR TODAY

Om Jai Viganeshwaraya..
Lambodaraya Namo Namaha
21 times
Om Sarva Mangal Mangalye,
Shiva Sarvart Sadike, Sharan
Tryambike Gowri, Narayane
Namo asttute
9 times

BIBLE VERSES: (Proverbs)

17:6. Children's children are the crown of old men: and the glory of children are their fathers.

READ PSALMS #'s: 8, 17, 35 ,44, 53, 62, 80, 107, 125

APRIL 17, 2015

04/17/2015	FRI		This is considered a NEGATIVE day for you							Shiva

Moving	Shopping	Health	Investing	Gambling	Love is	Wedding	Travel	Work/Job	Planet
Bad	Bad	Bad	Fair	Bad	Bad	Bad	Bad	Bad	Saturn

KEYWORDS ARE: frustration, finish, power, electricity, Money conflicts, Association, Accidents, Denial - Doubt, responsibility

Lotto #'s	play 4 #s	play 3 #s	Ruling Angel:............	Color Sugestion:............	Ruling Deity
7,1,34,31,12,11	3003	615	Mikael	Gold/Brown/Blue/Dark Green	Pitridev

ADVICE & DETAILS

Your authoritative attitude mixed with arrogance and the need to feel superior may bring you difficulties with government or any of its agencies and may also make you feel lonely. Being humble today will be beneficial.

MANTRA FOR TODAY

Om Graam Greem Graum Sa
Gurave namah swaha
21 times
AUM VAGDEVYAI CA
VIDMAHE KAMARAJAYA
DHIMAHI. TANNO DEVI
PRACODAYAT.
9 times

BIBLE VERSES: (Proverbs)

17:8. The expectation of him that expecteth is a most acceptable jewel: whithersoever he turneth himself, he understandeth wisely.

READ PSALMS #'s: 9, 18, 36 ,45, 54, 63, 81, 108, 126

APRIL 18, 2015

04/18/2015	SAT		This is considered a NEUTRAL day for you							Shiva

Moving	Shopping	Health	Investing	Gambling	Love is	Wedding	Travel	Work/Job	Planet
Good	Fair	Fair	Bad	Fair	Good	Fair	Good	Fair	Sun

KEYWORDS ARE: finish, individuality, religion, priests, Slow Day with Tension, Music, Denial - Doubt, lonliness, sleepiness

Lotto #'s	play 4 #s	play 3 #s	Ruling Angel:............	Color Sugestion:............	Ruling Deity
8,3,34,32,12,13	10960	716	Gabriel	White/Yellow/ Peach	Gaitree

ADVICE & DETAILS

You will feel connected to spirit today.   Use your creative abilities to honor the universe and think that by honoring the universe you are honoring yourself. You are part of the universe.

MANTRA FOR TODAY

Om Mana Swasti Shanti Kuru
kuru Swaha Shivoham Shivoham
27 times
om haring jawala mukhi mam
sarva shatru bakshaya bakshaya
hung phat swaha
Om Nama shivaya pahimam
9 times

BIBLE VERSES: (Proverbs)

17:1. Better is a dry morsel with joy, than a house full of victims with strife.
0

READ PSALMS #'s: 1, 10, 28 ,37, 46, 55, 73, 100, 118

APRIL 19, 2015

04/19/2015 SUN		This is considered a POSITIVE day for you							Shiva
Moving	Shopping	Health	Investing	Gambling	Love is	Wedding	Travel	Work/Job	Planet
Good	Good	Excellent	Excellent	Good	Good	Good	Good	Excellent	Venus

KEYWORDS ARE: Abusive, Friendships, Fame - TV, High Pleasure, Business & money gains, Popularity, Death, Shopping, Investments

Lotto #'s	play 4 #s	play 3 #s	Ruling Angel:............	Color Sugestion:............	Ruling Deity
9,4,33,32,12,16	7243	817	Raziel	Red/Yellow/Pink	Durga

ADVICE & DETAILS	MANTRA FOR TODAY
Very good day for monetary transactions and investments. You will be able to achieve great things with the cooperation of others. There is a chance for promotion.	Jai Jai Shiva Shambo.(2) ...Mahadeva Shambo (2) 21 times Om Jayanti Mangala Kali Bhadrakali Kapalini Durga Kshama Shiva Dhatri Swaha Swadha Namostute 9 times
BIBLE VERSES: (Proverbs)	
17:3. As silver is tried by fire, and gold in the furnace: so the Lord trieth the hearts.	
READ PSALMS #'s: 2, 11, 29 ,38, 47, 56, 74, 101, 119	

APRIL 20, 2015

04/20/2015 MON		This is considered a NEGATIVE day for you							Shiva
Moving	Shopping	Health	Investing	Gambling	Love is	Wedding	Travel	Work/Job	Planet
Bad	Bad	Bad	Bad	Good	Bad	Good	Bad	Bad	Mercury

KEYWORDS ARE: Karmic debts, Teacher, IRS - Law, Denial - Doubt, Quarrels & lovers, Visitors, Sickness - cold, Social Functions, Abusive

Lotto #'s	play 4 #s	play 3 #s	Ruling Angel:............	Color Sugestion:............	Ruling Deity
10,5,33,31,12,17	6271	918	Zadkiel	Green/Sky Blue/White	Saraswaty

ADVICE & DETAILS	MANTRA FOR TODAY
This is a difficult day with anything related to children. There may be childrend denial, abortion, miscarriages, worry over children, arguments with children. Acting in a childish manner may also bring negative consequences for you.	Om Hareem Nama Swaha..Shri Maha Laxmi Aye Namah swaha 12 times Om maha laxmi cha vidmahe vishnu pataya dhi mahi tanno laxmi pracho dayat Om hareem namam swaha 9 times
BIBLE VERSES: (Proverbs)	
17:5. He that despiseth the poor, reproacheth his maker: and he that rejoiceth at another man's ruin, shall not be unpunished.	
READ PSALMS #'s: 3, 12, 30 ,39, 48, 57, 75, 102, 120	

APRIL 21, 2015

04/21/2015 TUE		This is considered a NEUTRAL day for you							Shiva
Moving	Shopping	Health	Investing	Gambling	Love is	Wedding	Travel	Work/Job	Planet
Fair	Fair	Fair	Fair	Bad	Bad	Good	Fair	Bad	Pluto

KEYWORDS ARE: God - Karma, Real Estate, Accidents, death, Illnese, children, hypertension, Shopping, Legal matter, High Temper, Karmic debts

Lotto #'s	play 4 #s	play 3 #s	Ruling Angel:............	Color Sugestion:............	Ruling Deity
2,5,33,31,12,20	6741	119	Metatron	Dark Blue/ Purple/ Mauve	Ganesh

ADVICE & DETAILS	MANTRA FOR TODAY
This is slow and lazy day, but for your karma you are advised to work and to be industrious. Your accomplishments today will be important for your personal growth. You may be stressed out at work.	Om Ganga mataye nama swaha Om Varuna Devta aye Pahimam 11 times Om hareem mama sarva shatru janam vashee kuru kuru swaha om hareem ksham kasham kasheem kasheem swaha 9 times
BIBLE VERSES: (Proverbs)	
17:7. Eloquent words do not become a fool, nor lying lips a prince.	
0	
READ PSALMS #'s: 4, 13, 31 ,40, 49, 58, 76, 103, 121	

APRIL 22, 2015

| 04/22/2015 | WED | | This is considered a POSITIVE day for you | | | | | | | Shiva |

Moving	Shopping	Health	Investing	Gambling	Love is	Wedding	Travel	Work/Job	Planet
Good	Excellent	Good	Good	Good	Excellent	Good	Excelle	Good	Uranus

KEYWORDS ARE: IRS - Law, Beauty - Sex, Denial - Doubt, losses, Stress with Bosses, Food, Drinks, Abusive, Exercise, God - Karma

Lotto #'s	play 4 #s	play 3 #s	Ruling Angel:............	Color Sugestion:............	Ruling Deity
3,7,33,31,12,22	4134	2110	Camael	Orange/White/Light Green/ Beige	Krishna

ADVICE & DETAILS	MANTRA FOR TODAY
A very good day today. It will be filled with positive romance, dating, sexuality and friends. You may take short trips or have changes today. Take initiative in romance today.	*Om Namo Bhagawate Mukhtanandaya, 108 times AUM KRSNAYA VIDMAHE DAMODARAYA DHIMAHI. TANNO VISHNU PRACODAYAT. 9 times*

BIBLE VERSES: (Proverbs)
17:9. He that concealeth a transgression, seeketh friendships: he that repeateth it again, separateth friends.

READ PSALMS #'s: 5, 14, 32 ,41, 50, 59, 77, 104, 122

APRIL 23, 2015

| 04/23/2015 | THU | | This is considered a POSITIVE day for you | | | | | | | Shiva |

Moving	Shopping	Health	Investing	Gambling	Love is	Wedding	Travel	Work/Job	Planet
Good	Excellent	Excellent	Good	Fair	Good	Bad	Excelle	Good	Mars

KEYWORDS ARE: Communication, Anger - Ego, read, children, Social Functions, Co-operation, Karmic debts, Jealousy, Expression

Lotto #'s	play 4 #s	play 3 #s	Ruling Angel:............	Color Sugestion:............	Ruling Deity
4,8,33,31,12,14	2902	312	Raphael	Purple/DeepBlue/Rose	Hanuman

ADVICE & DETAILS	MANTRA FOR TODAY
There is a high chance of injury caused by childish, thoughtless behavior. There may be problems and rejection by children. Accidents or falls may cause injuries.	*Kali Durge Namo Nama Om Durge aye nama swaha 108 times AUM TATPURUSAYA VIDMAHE VAKRATUNDAY DHIMAHI. TANNO DANTI PRACODAYAT. 9 times*

BIBLE VERSES: (Proverbs)
17:11. An evil man always seeketh quarrels: but a cruel angel shall be sent against him.

READ PSALMS #'s: 6, 15, 33 ,42, 51, 60, 78, 105, 123

APRIL 24, 2015

| 04/24/2015 | FRI | | This is considered a NEUTRAL day for you | | | | | | | Shiva |

Moving	Shopping	Health	Investing	Gambling	Love is	Wedding	Travel	Work/Job	Planet
Bad	Bad	Bad	Bad	Bad	Fair	Fair	Bad	Bad	Moon

KEYWORDS ARE: Tiredness, spiritual, career, building, Co-workers, Friendships, God - Karma, Slow Day, Industrial

Lotto #'s	play 4 #s	play 3 #s	Ruling Angel:............	Color Sugestion:............	Ruling Deity
5,8,34,31,12,16	10484	413	Zaphkiel	Light Blue/Purple/Peach	Ganga

ADVICE & DETAILS	MANTRA FOR TODAY
This day could bring some career progress. You will have to work hard. You will be stressed out about life and have many thoughts about your job. Pray for career advancement today. You may be sleepy and tired.	*Om hareem Kleem Hreem Aem Saraswataye namaha 21 times Om Guru bramha, Guru Vishnu Guru Deva mahaeshwara guru saksha paam bramha, tasmi shri guruve nama 9 times*

BIBLE VERSES: (Proverbs)
17:13. He that rendereth evil for good, evil shall not depart from his house.
0

READ PSALMS #'s: 7, 16, 34 ,43, 52, 61, 79, 106, 124

APRIL 25, 2015

04/25/2015 SAT		This is considered a POSITIVE day for you							Shiva
Moving	Shopping	Health	Investing	Gambling	Love is	Wedding	Travel	Work/Job	Planet
Excellent	Good	Excellent	Good	Excellent	Excellent	Excellent	Excelle	Good	Jupiter

KEYWORDS ARE: travel, investment, change, deception, Belief and faith, Affection, IRS - Law, High Pleasure, Short Trips

Lotto #'s	play 4 #s	play 3 #s	Ruling Angel:...........	Color Sugestion:...........	Ruling Deity
6,10,34,32,12,19	8368	514	Haniel	Yellow/White/Silver	Mahalaxmi

ADVICE & DETAILS

It is a good day for gambling in either casinos or horse racing. You will receive visits from friends or take very enjoyable trips. You should see profits.

BIBLE VERSES: (Proverbs)

17:15. He that justifieth the wicked, and he that condemneth the just, both are abominable before God.

READ PSALMS #'s: 8, 17, 35 ,44, 53, 62, 80, 107, 125

MANTRA FOR TODAY

Om Jai Viganeshwaraya..
Lambodaraya Namo Namaha
21 times
Om Sarva Mangal Mangalye,
Shiva Sarvart Sadike, Sharan
Tryambike Gowri, Narayane
Namo asttute
9 times

APRIL 26, 2015

04/26/2015 SUN		This is considered a NEGATIVE day for you							Shiva
Moving	Shopping	Health	Investing	Gambling	Love is	Wedding	Travel	Work/Job	Planet
Bad	Bad	Bad	Fair	Bad	Bad	Bad	Bad	Bad	Saturn

KEYWORDS ARE: frustration, finish, power, electricity, Money conflicts, Association, Accidents, Denial - Doubt, responsibility

Lotto #'s	play 4 #s	play 3 #s	Ruling Angel:...........	Color Sugestion:...........	Ruling Deity
7,1,34,32,12,11	1427	615	Mikael	Gold/Brown/Blue/Dark Green	Pitridev

ADVICE & DETAILS

Your authoritative attitude mixed with arrogance and the need to feel superior may bring you difficulties with government or any of its agencies and may also make you feel lonely. Being humble today will be beneficial.

BIBLE VERSES: (Proverbs)

17:17. He that is a friend loveth at all times: and a brother is proved in distress.

READ PSALMS #'s: 9, 18, 36 ,45, 54, 63, 81, 108, 126

MANTRA FOR TODAY

Om Graam Greem Graum Sa
Gurave namah swaha
21 times
AUM VAGDEVYAI CA
VIDMAHE KAMARAJAYA
DHIMAHI. TANNO DEVI
PRACODAYAT.
9 times

APRIL 27, 2015

04/27/2015 MON		This is considered a NEUTRAL day for you							Shiva
Moving	Shopping	Health	Investing	Gambling	Love is	Wedding	Travel	Work/Job	Planet
Good	Fair	Fair	Bad	Fair	Good	Fair	Good	Fair	Sun

KEYWORDS ARE: finish, individuality, religion, priests, Slow Day with Tension, Music, Denial - Doubt, lonliness, sleepiness

Lotto #'s	play 4 #s	play 3 #s	Ruling Angel:...........	Color Sugestion:...........	Ruling Deity
8,2,34,32,12,13	2214	716	Gabriel	White/Yellow/ Peach	Gaitree

ADVICE & DETAILS

You will feel connected to spirit today. Use your creative abilities to honor the universe and think that by honoring the universe you are honoring yourself. You are part of the universe.

BIBLE VERSES: (Proverbs)

17:10. A reproof availeth more with a wise man, than a hundred stripes with a fool.

READ PSALMS #'s: 1, 10, 28 ,37, 46, 55, 73, 100, 118

MANTRA FOR TODAY

Om Mana Swasti Shanti Kuru
kuru Swaha Shivoham Shivoham
27 times
om haring jawala mukhi mam
sarva shatru bakshaya bakshaya
hung phat swaha
Om Nama shivaya pahimam
9 times

APRIL 28, 2015

04/28/2015	TUE		This is considered a POSITIVE day for you						Shiva	
Moving	*Shopping*	*Health*	*Investing*	*Gambling*	*Love is*	*Wedding*	*Travel*	*Work/Job*		*Planet*
Good	Good	Excellent	Excellent	Good	Good	Good	Good	Excellent		Venus

KEYWORDS ARE: Abusive, Friendships, Fame - TV, High Pleasure, Business & money gains, Popularity, Death, Shopping, Investments

Lotto #'s	*play 4 #s*	*play 3 #s*	Ruling Angel:............	Color Sugestion:............	*Ruling Deity*
9,3,33,32,12,16	1110	817	**Raziel**	**Red/Yellow/Pink**	**Durga**

ADVICE & DETAILS

Very good day for monetary transactions and investments. You will be able to achieve great things with the cooperation of others. There is a chance for promotion.

BIBLE VERSES: (Proverbs)

17:12. It is better to meet a bear robbed of her whelps, than a fool trusting in his own folly.

READ PSALMS #'s: 2, 11, 29 ,38, 47, 56, 74, 101, 119

MANTRA FOR TODAY

Jai Jai Shiva Shambo.(2)
...Mahadeva Shambo (2)
21 times
Om Jayanti Mangala Kali
Bhadrakali Kapalini Durga
Kshama Shiva Dhatri Swaha
Swadha Namostute
9 times

APRIL 29, 2015

04/29/2015	WED		This is considered a NEGATIVE day for you						Shiva	
Moving	*Shopping*	*Health*	*Investing*	*Gambling*	*Love is*	*Wedding*	*Travel*	*Work/Job*		*Planet*
Bad	Bad	Bad	Bad	Good	Bad	Good	Bad	Bad		Mercury

KEYWORDS ARE: Karmic debts, Teacher, IRS - Law, Denial - Doubt, Quarrels & lovers, Visitors, Sickness - cold, Social Functions, Abusive

Lotto #'s	*play 4 #s*	*play 3 #s*	Ruling Angel:............	Color Sugestion:............	*Ruling Deity*
10,5,33,31,12,18	8323	918	**Zadkiel**	**Green/Sky Blue/White**	**Saraswaty**

ADVICE & DETAILS

This is a difficult day with anything related to children. There may be childrend denial, abortion, miscarriages, worry over children, arguments with children. Acting in a childish manner may also bring negative consequences for you.

BIBLE VERSES: (Proverbs)

17:14. The beginning of quarrels is as when one letteth out water: and before he suffereth reproach, he forsaketh judgment.

READ PSALMS #'s: 3, 12, 30 ,39, 48, 57, 75, 102, 120

MANTRA FOR TODAY

Om Hareem Nama Swaha..Shri
Maha Laxmi Aye Namah swaha
12 times
Om maha laxmi cha vidmahe
vishnu pataya dhi mahi tanno
laxmi pracho dayat
Om hareem namam swaha
9 times

APRIL 30, 2015

04/30/2015	THU		This is considered a NEUTRAL day for you						Shiva	
Moving	*Shopping*	*Health*	*Investing*	*Gambling*	*Love is*	*Wedding*	*Travel*	*Work/Job*		*Planet*
Fair	Fair	Fair	Fair	Bad	Bad	Good	Fair	Bad		Pluto

KEYWORDS ARE: God - Karma, Real Estate, Accidents, death, Illnese, children, hypertension, Shopping, Legal matter, High Temper, Karmic debts

Lotto #'s	*play 4 #s*	*play 3 #s*	Ruling Angel:............	Color Sugestion:............	*Ruling Deity*
2,6,34,32,12,20	4637	119	**Metatron**	**Dark Blue/ Purple/ Mauve**	**Ganesh**

ADVICE & DETAILS

This is slow and lazy day, but for your karma you are advised to work and to be industrious. Your accomplishments today will be important for your personal growth. You may be stressed out at work.

BIBLE VERSES: (Proverbs)

17:16. What doth it avail a fool to have riches, seeing he cannot buy wisdom? He that maketh his house high, seeketh a downfall: and he that

READ PSALMS #'s: 4, 13, 31 ,40, 49, 58, 76, 103, 121

MANTRA FOR TODAY

Om Ganga mataye nama swaha
Om Varuna Devta aye Pahimam
11 times
Om hareem mama sarva shatru
janam vashee kuru kuru swaha
om hareem ksham kasham
kasheem kasheem swaha
9 times

MAY 1, 2015

05/01/2015 FRI			This is considered a POSITIVE day for you						Shiva
Moving	*Shopping*	*Health*	*Investing*	*Gambling*	*Love is*	*Wedding*	*Travel*	*Work/Job*	*Planet*
Good	Good	Excellent	Excellent	Good	Good	Good	Good	Excellent	Mercury

KEYWORDS ARE: IRS - Law, Communication, Big Expense, investment, Income is low and expenses, Social Functions, Abusive, Groups - Parties, Fame - TV

Lotto #'s	*play 4 #s*	*play 3 #s*	Ruling Angel:............	Color Sugestion:............	*Ruling Deity*
9,5,33,31,13,17	2526	827	Zadkiel	Green/Sky Blue/White	Saraswaty

ADVICE & DETAILS	MANTRA FOR TODAY
You will receive money today, it could be winnings from the lotto or profits from investments. The market is high. You will be surrounded by beauty and others will cooperate with you today.	*Om Namo Bhagawate Mukhtanandaya,* 108 times *AUM KRSNAYA VIDMAHE DAMODARAYA DHIMAHI. TANNO VISHNU PRACODAYAT.* 9 times

BIBLE VERSES: (Proverbs)
17:16. What doth it avail a fool to have riches, seeing he cannot buy wisdom? He that maketh his house high, seeketh a downfall: and he that

READ PSALMS #'s: 3, 12, 30 ,39, 48, 57, 75, 102, 120

MAY 2, 2015

05/02/2015 SAT			This is considered a NEGATIVE day for you						Shiva
Moving	*Shopping*	*Health*	*Investing*	*Gambling*	*Love is*	*Wedding*	*Travel*	*Work/Job*	*Planet*
Bad	Bad	Bad	Bad	Bad	Bad	Good	Bad	Bad	Pluto

KEYWORDS ARE: Accidents, Tiredness, death, finish, Traffic problems, Tickets, Childishness, Karmic debts, Laziness, IRS - Law

Lotto #'s	*play 4 #s*	*play 3 #s*	Ruling Angel:............	Color Sugestion:............	*Ruling Deity*
10,6,33,32,13,19	4390	928	Metatron	Dark Blue/ Purple/ Mauve	Ganesh

ADVICE & DETAILS	MANTRA FOR TODAY
You will have job stress and arguments today. You will have low energy, but you will have to do every task twice to complete it correctly. Try to relax with your lover and enjoy good food with them.	*Om Hareem Nama Swaha..Shri Maha Laxmi Aye Namah swaha* 12 times *Om maha laxmi cha vidmahe vishnu pataya dhi mahi tanno laxmi pracho dayat Om hareem namam swaha* 9 times

BIBLE VERSES: (Proverbs)
17:18. A foolish man will clap hands, when he is surety for his friend.
0

READ PSALMS #'s: 4, 13, 31 ,40, 49, 58, 76, 103, 121

MAY 3, 2015

05/03/2015 SUN			This is considered a NEUTRAL day for you						Shiva
Moving	*Shopping*	*Health*	*Investing*	*Gambling*	*Love is*	*Wedding*	*Travel*	*Work/Job*	*Planet*
Fair	Fair	Fair	Fair	Good	Bad	Good	Fair	Bad	Uranus

KEYWORDS ARE: Confined, travel, independence, individuality, Illness - Cold, Groups - Parties, God - Karma, Moving, Boastful

Lotto #'s	*play 4 #s*	*play 3 #s*	Ruling Angel:............	Color Sugestion:............	*Ruling Deity*
2,7,33,31,13,20	5165	129	Camael	Orange/White/Light Green/ Beige	Krishna

ADVICE & DETAILS	MANTRA FOR TODAY
You will either be missing your lover or have sexual enjoyment and romance with partner. You must watch your words and think of others.	*Om Ganga mataye nama swaha Om Varuna Devta aye Pahimam* 11 times *Om hareem mama sarva shatru janam vashee kuru kuru swaha om hareem ksham kasham kasheem kasheem swaha* 9 times

BIBLE VERSES: (Proverbs)
17:20. He that is of a perverse heart, shall not find good: and he that perverteth his tongue, shall fall into evil.

READ PSALMS #'s: 5, 14, 32 ,41, 50, 59, 77, 104, 122

MAY 4, 2015

05/04/2015 MON				This is considered a POSITIVE day for you						Shiva
Moving	*Shopping*	*Health*	*Investing*	*Gambling*	*Love is*	*Wedding*	*Travel*	*Work/Job*		*Planet*
Good	Excellent	Good	Good	Fair	Excellent	Bad	Excelle	Good		Mars

KEYWORDS ARE:	love, frustration, marriage, Talkative, Spritual meeting, Teacher, IRS - Law, Government, Partnership

Lotto #'s	*play 4 #s*	*play 3 #s*	Ruling Angel:............	Color Sugestion:............	*Ruling Deity*
3,8,34,32,13,22	3824	2210	Raphael	Purple/DeepBlue/Rose	Hanuman

ADVICE & DETAILS	MANTRA FOR TODAY
This will be a positive day if you can control your tongue and do not criticize anyone, particularly your loved ones and especially your partner. The influences are love and marriage. This is the opportunity to create a special surprise meal for your partner and share it with love in a romantic setting with soothing music as background.	*Om Namo Bhagawate Mukhtanandaya, 108 times AUM KRSNAYA VIDMAHE DAMODARAYA DHIMAHI. TANNO VISHNU PRACODAYAT. 9 times*

BIBLE VERSES: (Proverbs)
17:22. A joyful mind maketh age flourishing: a sorrowful spirit drieth up the bones.

READ PSALMS #'s: 6, 15, 33 ,42, 51, 60, 78, 105, 123

MAY 5, 2015

05/05/2015 TUE				This is considered a POSITIVE day for you						Shiva
Moving	*Shopping*	*Health*	*Investing*	*Gambling*	*Love is*	*Wedding*	*Travel*	*Work/Job*		*Planet*
Good	Excellent	Excellent	Good	Bad	Good	Fair	Excelle	Good		Moon

KEYWORDS ARE:	children, religion, publishing, telephone, Shopping & bargains, Expression, Accidents, Criticism, read

Lotto #'s	*play 4 #s*	*play 3 #s*	Ruling Angel:............	Color Sugestion:............	*Ruling Deity*
4,9,34,32,13,16	2606	322	Zaphkiel	Light Blue/Purple/Peach	Ganga

ADVICE & DETAILS	MANTRA FOR TODAY
It is important that you communicate clearly and concisely with children today. Do not try to cover or conceal information. The same type of communication will benefit partnerships. Read to acquire information or to children if possible.	*Kali Durge Namo Nama Om Durge aye nama swaha 108 times AUM TATPURUSAYA VIDMAHE VAKRATUNDAY DHIMAHI. TANNO DANTI PRACODAYAT. 9 times*

BIBLE VERSES: (Proverbs)
17:24. Wisdom shineth in the face of the wise: the eyes of fools are in the ends of the earth.

READ PSALMS #'s: 7, 16, 34 ,43, 52, 61, 79, 106, 124

MAY 6, 2015

05/06/2015 WED				This is considered a NEUTRAL day for you						Shiva
Moving	*Shopping*	*Health*	*Investing*	*Gambling*	*Love is*	*Wedding*	*Travel*	*Work/Job*		*Planet*
Bad	Bad	Bad	Bad	Excellent	Fair	Excellent	Bad	Bad		Jupiter

KEYWORDS ARE:	employment, luxury, stress, co-worker, Real Estate, Communication, Denial - Doubt, money, career

Lotto #'s	*play 4 #s*	*play 3 #s*	Ruling Angel:............	Color Sugestion:............	*Ruling Deity*
5,10,33,31,13,18	1422	423	Haniel	Yellow/White/Silver	Mahalaxmi

ADVICE & DETAILS	MANTRA FOR TODAY
Career is important today. You will have a lot of work to do, but you may be getting a raise from boss. Your coworkers are friendly and there may be a love spark or beginning of friendship at work as well.	*Om hareem Kleem Hreem Aem Saraswataye namaha 21 times Om Guru bramha, Guru Vishnu Guru Deva mahaeshwara guru saksha paam bramha, tasmi shri guruve nama 9 times*

BIBLE VERSES: (Proverbs)
17:26. It is no good thing to do hurt to the just: nor to strike the prince, who judgeth right.

READ PSALMS #'s: 8, 17, 35 ,44, 53, 62, 80, 107, 125

MAY 7, 2015

05/07/2015 THU		This is considered a POSITIVE day for you								Shiva
Moving	Shopping	Health	Investing	Gambling	Love is	Wedding	Travel	Work/Job		Planet
Excellent	Good	Excellent	Good	Bad	Excellent	Bad	Excelle	Good		Saturn

KEYWORDS ARE: Deception, Karmic debts, Illicit Affairs, Beauty - Sex, High sexuality, Education, Death, Sickness - cold, Travel delays

Lotto #'s	play 4 #s	play 3 #s	Ruling Angel:...........	Color Sugestion:...........	Ruling Deity
6,2,33,32,13,10	5400	524	Mikael	Gold/Brown/Blue/Dark Green	Pitridev

ADVICE & DETAILS	MANTRA FOR TODAY
Sexual energy will be high today. There will be room for misinterpretation of facts or misleading statements from others. You will need to be flexible as there will be many changes today. You will feel like observing your mental and emotional processes.	*Om Jai Viganeshwaraya.. Lambodaraya Namo Namaha 21 times Om Sarva Mangal Mangalye, Shiva Sarvart Sadike, Sharan Tryambike Gowri, Narayane Namo asttute 9 times*

BIBLE VERSES: (Proverbs)

17:28. Even a fool, if he will hold his peace, shall be counted wise: and if he close his lips, a man of understanding.

READ PSALMS #'s: 9, 18, 36 ,45, 54, 63, 81, 108, 126

MAY 8, 2015

05/08/2015 FRI		This is considered a NEGATIVE day for you								Shiva
Moving	Shopping	Health	Investing	Gambling	Love is	Wedding	Travel	Work/Job		Planet
Bad	Bad	Bad	Fair	Fair	Bad	Fair	Bad	Bad		Sun

KEYWORDS ARE: Quarrels, Commanding, Police, Anger - Ego, Disagreement in Love, Astrology, Sickness - cold, Dominating, Traffic Ticket

Lotto #'s	play 4 #s	play 3 #s	Ruling Angel:...........	Color Sugestion:...........	Ruling Deity
7,3,34,31,13,13	10894	625	Gabriel	White/Yellow/ Peach	Gaitree

ADVICE & DETAILS	MANTRA FOR TODAY
There will be frustration between lovers today. This frustration may result in rejection of lovers. The ego will be high and it will be difficult for you to be humble. You will enjoy love from family or relatives.	*Om Graam Greem Graum Sa Gurave namah swaha 21 times AUM VAGDEVYAI CA VIDMAHE KAMARAJAYA DHIMAHI. TANNO DEVI PRACODAYAT. 9 times*

BIBLE VERSES: (Proverbs)

17:21. A fool is born to his own disgrace: and even his father shall not rejoice in a fool.

READ PSALMS #'s: 1, 10, 28 ,37, 46, 55, 73, 100, 118

MAY 9, 2015

05/09/2015 SAT		This is considered a NEUTRAL day for you								Shiva
Moving	Shopping	Health	Investing	Gambling	Love is	Wedding	Travel	Work/Job		Planet
Good	Fair	Fair	Bad	Good	Good	Good	Good	Fair		Venus

KEYWORDS ARE: God - Karma, Association, Enemies, spiritual, Astrologers, Psychics, priests, Bargains, Legal matter, Co-operation, Advice given

Lotto #'s	play 4 #s	play 3 #s	Ruling Angel:...........	Color Sugestion:...........	Ruling Deity
8,4,33,32,13,15	6528	726	Raziel	Red/Yellow/Pink	Durga

ADVICE & DETAILS	MANTRA FOR TODAY
Instead of criticism, offer advice from the heart; not ego. It will be a slow day, but you will feel your connection to God. Do positive actions for good karma.	*Om Mana Swasti Shanti Kuru kuru Swaha Shivoham Shivoham 27 times om haring jawala mukhi mam sarva shatru bakshaya bakshaya hung phat swaha Om Nama shivaya pahimam 9 times*

BIBLE VERSES: (Proverbs)

17:23. The wicked man taketh gifts out of the bosom, that he may pervert the paths of judgment.

READ PSALMS #'s: 2, 11, 29 ,38, 47, 56, 74, 101, 119

MAY 10, 2015

05/10/2015 SUN		This is considered a POSITIVE day for you							Shiva
Moving	Shopping	Health	Investing	Gambling	Love is	Wedding	Travel	Work/Job	Planet
Good	Good	Excellent	Excellent	Good	Good	Good	Good	Excellent	Mercury

KEYWORDS ARE: IRS - Law, Communication, Big Expense, investment, Income is low and expenses, Social Functions, Abusive, Groups - Parties, Fame - TV

Lotto #'s	play 4 #s	play 3 #s	Ruling Angel:............	Color Sugestion:............	Ruling Deity
9,4,34,32,13,16	10030	827	Zadkiel	Green/Sky Blue/White	Saraswaty

ADVICE & DETAILS	MANTRA FOR TODAY
You will receive money today, it could be winnings from the lotto or profits from investments. The market is high. You will be surrounded by beauty and others will cooperate with you today.	Jai Jai Shiva Shambo.(2) ...Mahadeva Shambo (2) 21 times Om Jayanti Mangala Kali Bhadrakali Kapalini Durga Kshama Shiva Dhatri Swaha Swadha Namostute 9 times
BIBLE VERSES: (Proverbs) 17:25. A foolish son is the anger of the father: and the sorrow of the mother that bore him. **READ PSALMS #'s:** 3, 12, 30 ,39, 48, 57, 75, 102, 120	

MAY 11, 2015

05/11/2015 MON		This is considered a NEGATIVE day for you							Shiva
Moving	Shopping	Health	Investing	Gambling	Love is	Wedding	Travel	Work/Job	Planet
Bad	Bad	Bad	Bad	Bad	Bad	Good	Bad	Bad	Pluto

KEYWORDS ARE: Accidents, Tiredness, death, finish, Traffic problems, Tickets, Childishness, Karmic debts, Laziness, IRS - Law

Lotto #'s	play 4 #s	play 3 #s	Ruling Angel:............	Color Sugestion:............	Ruling Deity
10,5,34,31,13,19	9030	928	Metatron	Dark Blue/ Purple/ Mauve	Ganesh

ADVICE & DETAILS	MANTRA FOR TODAY
You will have job stress and arguments today. You will have low energy, but you will have to do every task twice to complete it correctly. Try to relax with your lover and enjoy good food with them.	Om Hareem Nama Swaha..Shri Maha Laxmi Aye Namah swaha 12 times Om maha laxmi cha vidmahe vishnu pataya dhi mahi tanno laxmi pracho dayat Om hareem namam swaha 9 times
BIBLE VERSES: (Proverbs) 17:27. He that setteth bounds to his words, is knowing and wise: and the man of understanding is of a precious spirit. **READ PSALMS #'s:** 4, 13, 31 ,40, 49, 58, 76, 103, 121	

MAY 12, 2015

05/12/2015 TUE		This is considered a NEUTRAL day for you							Shiva
Moving	Shopping	Health	Investing	Gambling	Love is	Wedding	Travel	Work/Job	Planet
Fair	Fair	Fair	Fair	Good	Bad	Good	Fair	Bad	Uranus

KEYWORDS ARE: Denial - Doubt, travel, losses, sadness, Family conflicts, Arguments, Groups - Parties, God - Karma, Moving, Accidents

Lotto #'s	play 4 #s	play 3 #s	Ruling Angel:............	Color Sugestion:............	Ruling Deity
2,6,33,32,13,21	4416	129	Camael	Orange/White/Light Green/ Beige	Krishna

ADVICE & DETAILS	MANTRA FOR TODAY
You will either be missing your lover or have sexual enjoyment and romance with partner. You must watch your words and think of others.	Om Ganga mataye nama swaha Om Varuna Devta aye Pahimam 11 times Om hareem mama sarva shatru janam vashee kuru kuru swaha om hareem ksham kasham kasheem kasheem swaha 9 times
BIBLE VERSES: (Proverbs) 18:1. He that hath a mind to depart from a friend, seeketh occasions: he shall ever be subject to reproach. **READ PSALMS #'s:** 5, 14, 32 ,41, 50, 59, 77, 104, 122	

MAY 13, 2015

| 05/13/2015 WED | This is considered a POSITIVE day for you | | | | | | | | Shiva |

Moving	Shopping	Health	Investing	Gambling	Love is	Wedding	Travel	Work/Job	Planet
Good	Excellent	Good	Good	Fair	Excellent	Bad	Excelle	Good	Mars

KEYWORDS ARE: love, frustration, marriage, Talkative, Spritual meeting, Teacher, IRS - Law, Government, Partnership

Lotto #'s	play 4 #s	play 3 #s	Ruling Angel:............	Color Sugestion:............	Ruling Deity
3,8,34,31,13,23	4530	2210	Raphael	Purple/DeepBlue/Rose	Hanuman

ADVICE & DETAILS	MANTRA FOR TODAY
This will be a positive day if you can control your tongue and do not criticize anyone, particularly your loved ones and especially your partner. The influences are love and marriage. This is the opportunity to create a special surprise meal for your partner and share it with love in a romantic setting with soothing music as background.	Om Namo Bhagawate Mukhtanandaya, 108 times AUM KRSNAYA VIDMAHE DAMODARAYA DHIMAHI. TANNO VISHNU PRACODAYAT. 9 times

BIBLE VERSES: (Proverbs)

18:3. The wicked man, when he is come into the depths of sins, contemneth: but ignominy and reproach follow him.

READ PSALMS #'s: 6, 15, 33 ,42, 51, 60, 78, 105, 123

MAY 14, 2015

| 05/14/2015 THU | This is considered a POSITIVE day for you | | | | | | | | Shiva |

Moving	Shopping	Health	Investing	Gambling	Love is	Wedding	Travel	Work/Job	Planet
Good	Excellent	Excellent	Good	Bad	Good	Fair	Excelle	Good	Moon

KEYWORDS ARE: children, religion, publishing, telephone, Shopping & bargains, Expression, Accidents, Criticism, read

Lotto #'s	play 4 #s	play 3 #s	Ruling Angel:............	Color Sugestion:............	Ruling Deity
4,8,33,32,13,15	1097	322	Zaphkiel	Light Blue/Purple/Peach	Ganga

ADVICE & DETAILS	MANTRA FOR TODAY
It is important that you communicate clearly and concisely with children today. Do not try to cover or conceal information. The same type of communication will benefit partnerships. Read to acquire information or to children if possible.	Kali Durge Namo Nama Om Durge aye nama swaha 108 times AUM TATPURUSAYA VIDMAHE VAKRATUNDAY DHIMAHI. TANNO DANTI PRACODAYAT. 9 times

BIBLE VERSES: (Proverbs)

18:5. It is not good to accept the person of the wicked, to decline from the truth of judgment.

READ PSALMS #'s: 7, 16, 34 ,43, 52, 61, 79, 106, 124

MAY 15, 2015

| 05/15/2015 FRI | This is considered a NEUTRAL day for you | | | | | | | | Shiva |

Moving	Shopping	Health	Investing	Gambling	Love is	Wedding	Travel	Work/Job	Planet
Bad	Bad	Bad	Bad	Excellent	Fair	Excellent	Bad	Bad	Jupiter

KEYWORDS ARE: employment, luxury, stress, co-worker, Real Estate, Communication, Denial - Doubt, money, career

Lotto #'s	play 4 #s	play 3 #s	Ruling Angel:............	Color Sugestion:............	Ruling Deity
5,9,34,32,13,18	5119	423	Haniel	Yellow/White/Silver	Mahalaxmi

ADVICE & DETAILS	MANTRA FOR TODAY
Career is important today. You will have a lot of work to do, but you may be getting a raise from boss. Your coworkers are friendly and there may be a love spark or beginning of friendship at work as well.	Om hareem Kleem Hreem Aem Saraswataye namaha 21 times Om Guru bramha, Guru Vishnu Guru Deva mahaeshwara guru saksha paam bramha, tasmi shri guruve nama 9 times

BIBLE VERSES: (Proverbs)

18:7. The mouth of a fool is his destruction: and his lips are the ruin of his soul.

READ PSALMS #'s: 8, 17, 35 ,44, 53, 62, 80, 107, 125

MAY 16, 2015

05/16/2015 SAT			This is considered a POSITIVE day for you						Shiva
Moving	Shopping	Health	Investing	Gambling	Love is	Wedding	Travel	Work/Job	Planet
Excellent	Good	Excellent	Good	Bad	Excellent	Bad	Excelle	Good	Saturn

KEYWORDS ARE: Deception, Karmic debts, Illicit Affairs, Beauty - Sex,
High sexuality, Education, Death, Sickness - cold, Travel delays

Lotto #'s	play 4 #s	play 3 #s	Ruling Angel:............	Color Sugestion:............	Ruling Deity
6,1,33,31,13,10	3234	524	Mikael	Gold/Brown/Blue/Dark Green	Pitridev

ADVICE & DETAILS	MANTRA FOR TODAY
Sexual energy will be high today. There will be room for misinterpretation of facts or misleading statements from others. You will need to be flexible as there will be many changes today. You will feel like observing your mental and emotional processes.	*Om Jai Viganeshwaraya.. Lambodaraya Namo Namaha 21 times Om Sarva Mangal Mangalye, Shiva Sarvart Sadike, Sharan Tryambike Gowri, Narayane Namo asttute 9 times*

BIBLE VERSES: (Proverbs)
18:9. He that is loose and slack in his work, is the brother of him that wasteth his own works.

READ PSALMS #'s: 9, 18, 36 ,45, 54, 63, 81, 108, 126

MAY 17, 2015

05/17/2015 SUN			This is considered a NEGATIVE day for you						Shiva
Moving	Shopping	Health	Investing	Gambling	Love is	Wedding	Travel	Work/Job	Planet
Bad	Bad	Bad	Fair	Fair	Bad	Fair	Bad	Bad	Sun

KEYWORDS ARE: Quarrels, Commanding, Police, Anger - Ego,
Disagreement in Love, Astrology, Sickness - cold, Dominating, Traffic Ticket

Lotto #'s	play 4 #s	play 3 #s	Ruling Angel:............	Color Sugestion:............	Ruling Deity
7,2,34,32,13,13	6827	625	Gabriel	White/Yellow/ Peach	Gaitree

ADVICE & DETAILS	MANTRA FOR TODAY
There will be frustration between lovers today. This frustration may result in rejection of lovers. The ego will be high and it will be difficult for you to be humble. You will enjoy love from family or relatives.	*Om Graam Greem Graum Sa Gurave namah swaha 21 times AUM VAGDEVYAI CA VIDMAHE KAMARAJAYA DHIMAHI. TANNO DEVI PRACODAYAT. 9 times*

BIBLE VERSES: (Proverbs)
18:2. A fool receiveth not the words of prudence: unless thou say those things which are in his heart.

READ PSALMS #'s: 1, 10, 28 ,37, 46, 55, 73, 100, 118

MAY 18, 2015

05/18/2015 MON			This is considered a NEUTRAL day for you						Shiva
Moving	Shopping	Health	Investing	Gambling	Love is	Wedding	Travel	Work/Job	Planet
Good	Fair	Fair	Bad	Good	Good	Good	Good	Fair	Venus

KEYWORDS ARE: God - Karma, Association, Enemies, spiritual,
Astrologers, Psychics, priests, Bargains, Legal matter, Co-operation, Advice given

Lotto #'s	play 4 #s	play 3 #s	Ruling Angel:............	Color Sugestion:............	Ruling Deity
8,3,33,32,13,15	6150	726	Raziel	Red/Yellow/Pink	Durga

ADVICE & DETAILS	MANTRA FOR TODAY
Instead of criticism, offer advice from the heart; not ego. It will be a slow day, but you will feel your connection to God. Do positive actions for good karma.	*Om Mana Swasti Shanti Kuru kuru Swaha Shivoham Shivoham 27 times om haring jawala mukhi mam sarva shatru bakshaya bakshaya hung phat swaha Om Nama shivaya pahimam 9 times*

BIBLE VERSES: (Proverbs)
18:4. Words from the mouth of a man are as deep water: and the fountain of wisdom is an overflowing stream.

READ PSALMS #'s: 2, 11, 29 ,38, 47, 56, 74, 101, 119

MAY 19, 2015

05/19/2015 TUE				This is considered a POSITIVE day for you					Shiva	
Moving	*Shopping*	*Health*	*Investing*	*Gambling*	*Love is*	*Wedding*	*Travel*	*Work/Job*	*Planet*	
Good	Good	Excellent	Excellent	Good	Good	Good	Good	Excellent	Mercury	

KEYWORDS ARE: IRS - Law, Communication, Big Expense, investment, Income is low and expenses, Social Functions, Abusive, Groups - Parties, Fame - TV

Lotto #'s	*play 4 #s*	*play 3 #s*	Ruling Angel:............	Color Sugestion:............	*Ruling Deity*
9,5,33,31,13,17	8766	827	Zadkiel	Green/Sky Blue/White	Saraswaty

ADVICE & DETAILS	MANTRA FOR TODAY
You will receive money today, it could be winnings from the lotto or profits from investments. The market is high. You will be surrounded by beauty and others will cooperate with you today.	*Jai Jai Shiva Shambo.(2) ...Mahadeva Shambo (2) 21 times Om Jayanti Mangala Kali Bhadrakali Kapalini Durga Kshama Shiva Dhatri Swaha Swadha Namostute 9 times*

BIBLE VERSES: (Proverbs)	
18:6. The lips of a fool intermeddle with strife: and his mouth provoketh quarrels.	
READ PSALMS #'s:	3, 12, 30 ,39, 48, 57, 75, 102, 120

MAY 20, 2015

05/20/2015 WED				This is considered a NEGATIVE day for you					Shiva	
Moving	*Shopping*	*Health*	*Investing*	*Gambling*	*Love is*	*Wedding*	*Travel*	*Work/Job*	*Planet*	
Bad	Bad	Bad	Bad	Bad	Bad	Good	Bad	Bad	Pluto	

KEYWORDS ARE: Accidents, Tiredness, death, finish, Traffic problems, Tickets, Childishness, Karmic debts, Laziness, IRS - Law

Lotto #'s	*play 4 #s*	*play 3 #s*	Ruling Angel:............	Color Sugestion:............	*Ruling Deity*
10,5,33,32,13,19	5338	928	Metatron	Dark Blue/ Purple/ Mauve	Ganesh

ADVICE & DETAILS	MANTRA FOR TODAY
You will have job stress and arguments today. You will have low energy, but you will have to do every task twice to complete it correctly. Try to relax with your lover and enjoy good food with them.	*Om Hareem Nama Swaha..Shri Maha Laxmi Aye Namah swaha 12 times Om maha laxmi cha vidmahe vishnu pataya dhi mahi tanno laxmi pracho dayat Om hareem namam swaha 9 times*

BIBLE VERSES: (Proverbs)	
18:8. The words of the double tongued are as if they were harmless: and they reach even to the inner parts of the bowels. Fear casteth down the	
READ PSALMS #'s:	4, 13, 31 ,40, 49, 58, 76, 103, 121

MAY 21, 2015

05/21/2015 THU				This is considered a NEUTRAL day for you					Shiva	
Moving	*Shopping*	*Health*	*Investing*	*Gambling*	*Love is*	*Wedding*	*Travel*	*Work/Job*	*Planet*	
Fair	Fair	Fair	Fair	Good	Bad	Good	Fair	Bad	Uranus	

KEYWORDS ARE: Denial - Doubt, travel, losses, sadness, Family conflicts, Arguments, Groups - Parties, God - Karma, Moving, Accidents

Lotto #'s	*play 4 #s*	*play 3 #s*	Ruling Angel:............	Color Sugestion:............	*Ruling Deity*
2,7,34,32,13,20	8628	129	Camael	Orange/White/Light Green/ Beige	Krishna

ADVICE & DETAILS	MANTRA FOR TODAY
You will either be missing your lover or have sexual enjoyment and romance with partner. You must watch your words and think of others.	*Om Ganga mataye nama swaha Om Varuna Devta aye Pahimam 11 times Om hareem mama sarva shatru janam vashee kuru kuru swaha om hareem ksham kasham kasheem kasheem swaha 9 times*

BIBLE VERSES: (Proverbs)	
18:10. The name of the Lord is a strong tower: the just runneth to it, and shall be exalted.	
READ PSALMS #'s:	5, 14, 32 ,41, 50, 59, 77, 104, 122

MAY 22, 2015

05/22/2015 FRI		This is considered a POSITIVE day for you								Shiva
Moving	*Shopping*	*Health*	*Investing*	*Gambling*	*Love is*	*Wedding*	*Travel*	*Work/Job*		*Planet*
Good	**Excellent**	**Good**	**Good**	**Fair**	**Excellent**	**Bad**	**Excelle**	**Good**		**Mars**

KEYWORDS ARE: death, frustration, finish, fame,
Tiredness, Low Energy, Sleepy, Teacher, IRS - Law, Government, Denial - Doubt

Lotto #'s	*play 4 #s*	*play 3 #s*	Ruling Angel:............	Color Sugestion:............	*Ruling Deity*
3,7,34,31,13,22	**8321**	**2210**	**Raphael**	**Purple/DeepBlue/Rose**	**Hanuman**

ADVICE & DETAILS	MANTRA FOR TODAY
This will be a positive day if you can control your tongue and do not criticize anyone, particularly your loved ones and especially your partner. The influences are love and marriage. This is the opportunity to create a special surprise meal for your partner and share it with love in a romantic setting with soothing music as background.	*Om Namo Bhagawate Mukhtanandaya,* *108 times* *AUM KRSNAYA VIDMAHE DAMODARAYA DHIMAHI. TANNO VISHNU PRACODAYAT.* *9 times*

BIBLE VERSES: (Proverbs)
18:12. Before destruction, the heart of a man is exalted: and before he be glorified, it is humbled.

READ PSALMS #'s: 6, 15, 33 ,42, 51, 60, 78, 105, 123

MAY 23, 2015

05/23/2015 SAT		This is considered a POSITIVE day for you								Shiva
Moving	*Shopping*	*Health*	*Investing*	*Gambling*	*Love is*	*Wedding*	*Travel*	*Work/Job*		*Planet*
Good	**Excellent**	**Excellent**	**Good**	**Bad**	**Good**	**Fair**	**Excelle**	**Good**		**Moon**

KEYWORDS ARE: children, religion, publishing, telephone,
Shopping & bargains, Expression, Accidents, Criticism, read

Lotto #'s	*play 4 #s*	*play 3 #s*	Ruling Angel:............	Color Sugestion:............	*Ruling Deity*
4,9,33,32,13,16	**5915**	**322**	**Zaphkiel**	**Light Blue/Purple/Peach**	**Ganga**

ADVICE & DETAILS	MANTRA FOR TODAY
It is important that you communicate clearly and concisely with children today. Do not try to cover or conceal information. The same type of communication will benefit partnerships. Read to acquire information or to children if possible.	*Kali Durge Namo Nama* *Om Durge aye nama swaha* *108 times* *AUM TATPURUSAYA VIDMAHE VAKRATUNDAY DHIMAHI. TANNO DANTI PRACODAYAT.* *9 times*

BIBLE VERSES: (Proverbs)
18:14. The spirit of a man upholdeth his infirmity: but a spirit that is easily angered, who can bear?

READ PSALMS #'s: 7, 16, 34 ,43, 52, 61, 79, 106, 124

MAY 24, 2015

05/24/2015 SUN		This is considered a NEUTRAL day for you								Shiva
Moving	*Shopping*	*Health*	*Investing*	*Gambling*	*Love is*	*Wedding*	*Travel*	*Work/Job*		*Planet*
Bad	**Bad**	**Bad**	**Bad**	**Excellent**	**Fair**	**Excellent**	**Bad**	**Bad**		**Jupiter**

KEYWORDS ARE: employment, luxury, stress, co-worker,
Real Estate, Communication, Denial - Doubt, money, career

Lotto #'s	*play 4 #s*	*play 3 #s*	Ruling Angel:............	Color Sugestion:............	*Ruling Deity*
5,9,33,31,13,18	**3860**	**423**	**Haniel**	**Yellow/White/Silver**	**Mahalaxmi**

ADVICE & DETAILS	MANTRA FOR TODAY
Career is important today. You will have a lot of work to do, but you may be getting a raise from boss. Your coworkers are friendly and there may be a love spark or beginning of friendship at work as well.	*Om hareem Kleem Hreem Aem Saraswataye namaha* *21 times* *Om Guru bramha, Guru Vishnu Guru Deva mahaeshwara guru saksha paam bramha, tasmi shri guruve nama* *9 times*

BIBLE VERSES: (Proverbs)
18:16. A man's gift enlargeth his way, and maketh him room before princes.

READ PSALMS #'s: 8, 17, 35 ,44, 53, 62, 80, 107, 125

MAY 25, 2015

05/25/2015	MON	This is considered a POSITIVE day for you							Shiva
Moving	Shopping	Health	Investing	Gambling	Love is	Wedding	Travel	Work/Job	Planet
Excellent	Good	Excellent	Good	Bad	Excellent	Bad	Excelle	Good	Saturn

KEYWORDS ARE: Deception, Karmic debts, Illicit Affairs, Beauty - Sex, High sexuality, Education, Death, Sickness - cold, Travel delays

Lotto #'s	play 4 #s	play 3 #s	Ruling Angel:............	Color Sugestion:............	Ruling Deity
6,1,34,31,13,11	3460	524	Mikael	Gold/Brown/Blue/Dark Green	Pitridev

ADVICE & DETAILS

Sexual energy will be high today. There will be room for misinterpretation of facts or misleading statements from others. You will need to be flexible as there will be many changes today. You will feel like observing your mental and emotional processes.

BIBLE VERSES: (Proverbs)

18:18. The lot suppresseth contentions, and determineth even between the mighty.

READ PSALMS #'s: 9, 18, 36 ,45, 54, 63, 81, 108, 126

MANTRA FOR TODAY

Om Jai Viganeshwaraya.. Lambodaraya Namo Namaha
21 times
Om Sarva Mangal Mangalye, Shiva Sarvart Sadike, Sharan Tryambike Gowri, Narayane Namo asttute
9 times

MAY 26, 2015

05/26/2015	TUE	This is considered a NEGATIVE day for you							Shiva
Moving	Shopping	Health	Investing	Gambling	Love is	Wedding	Travel	Work/Job	Planet
Bad	Bad	Bad	Fair	Fair	Bad	Fair	Bad	Bad	Sun

KEYWORDS ARE: Quarrels, Commanding, Police, Anger - Ego, Disagreement in Love, Astrology, Sickness - cold, Dominating, Traffic Ticket

Lotto #'s	play 4 #s	play 3 #s	Ruling Angel:............	Color Sugestion:............	Ruling Deity
7,3,33,31,13,12	2848	625	Gabriel	White/Yellow/ Peach	Gaitree

ADVICE & DETAILS

There will be frustration between lovers today. This frustration may result in rejection of lovers. The ego will be high and it will be difficult for you to be humble. You will enjoy love from family or relatives.

BIBLE VERSES: (Proverbs)

18:11. The substance of the rich man is the city of his strength, and as a strong wall compassing him about.

READ PSALMS #'s: 1, 10, 28 ,37, 46, 55, 73, 100, 118

MANTRA FOR TODAY

Om Graam Greem Graum Sa Gurave namah swaha
21 times
AUM VAGDEVYAI CA VIDMAHE KAMARAJAYA DHIMAHI. TANNO DEVI PRACODAYAT.
9 times

MAY 27, 2015

05/27/2015	WED	This is considered a NEUTRAL day for you							Shiva
Moving	Shopping	Health	Investing	Gambling	Love is	Wedding	Travel	Work/Job	Planet
Good	Fair	Fair	Bad	Good	Good	Good	Good	Fair	Venus

KEYWORDS ARE: God - Karma, Association, Enemies, spiritual, Astrologers, Psychics, priests, Bargains, Legal matter, Co-operation, Advice given

Lotto #'s	play 4 #s	play 3 #s	Ruling Angel:............	Color Sugestion:............	Ruling Deity
8,4,33,31,13,15	8456	726	Raziel	Red/Yellow/Pink	Durga

ADVICE & DETAILS

Instead of criticism, offer advice from the heart; not ego. It will be a slow day, but you will feel your connection to God. Do positive actions for good karma.

BIBLE VERSES: (Proverbs)

18:13. He that answereth before he heareth, sheweth himself to be a fool, and worthy of confusion.

READ PSALMS #'s: 2, 11, 29 ,38, 47, 56, 74, 101, 119

MANTRA FOR TODAY

Om Mana Swasti Shanti Kuru kuru Swaha Shivoham Shivoham
27 times
om haring jawala mukhi mam sarva shatru bakshaya bakshaya hung phat swaha
Om Nama shivaya pahimam
9 times

MAY 28, 2015

| 05/28/2015 THU | This is considered a POSITIVE day for you | | | | | | | | Shiva |

Moving	Shopping	Health	Investing	Gambling	Love is	Wedding	Travel	Work/Job	Planet
Good	Good	Excellent	Excellent	Good	Good	Good	Good	Excellent	Mercury

KEYWORDS ARE: IRS - Law, Communication, Big Expense, investment,
Income is low and expenses, Social Functions, Abusive, Groups - Parties, Fame - TV

Lotto #'s	play 4 #s	play 3 #s	Ruling Angel:............	Color Sugestion:............	Ruling Deity
9,4,33,32,13,16	7673	827	Zadkiel	Green/Sky Blue/White	Saraswaty

ADVICE & DETAILS

You will receive money today, it could be winnings from the lotto or profits from investments. The market is high. You will be surrounded by beauty and others will cooperate with you today.

BIBLE VERSES: (Proverbs)

18:15. A wise heart shall acquire knowledge: and the ear of the wise seeketh instruction.

READ PSALMS #'s: 3, 12, 30 ,39, 48, 57, 75, 102, 120

MANTRA FOR TODAY

Jai Jai Shiva Shambo.(2)
...Mahadeva Shambo (2)
21 times
Om Jayanti Mangala Kali
Bhadrakali Kapalini Durga
Kshama Shiva Dhatri Swaha
Swadha Namostute
9 times

MAY 29, 2015

| 05/29/2015 FRI | This is considered a NEGATIVE day for you | | | | | | | | Shiva |

Moving	Shopping	Health	Investing	Gambling	Love is	Wedding	Travel	Work/Job	Planet
Bad	Bad	Bad	Bad	Bad	Bad	Good	Bad	Bad	Pluto

KEYWORDS ARE: Accidents, Tiredness, death, finish,
Traffic problems, Tickets, Childishness, Karmic debts, Laziness, IRS - Law

Lotto #'s	play 4 #s	play 3 #s	Ruling Angel:............	Color Sugestion:............	Ruling Deity
10,5,34,31,13,19	7408	928	Metatron	Dark Blue/ Purple/ Mauve	Ganesh

ADVICE & DETAILS

You will have job stress and arguments today. You will have low energy, but you will have to do every task twice to complete it correctly. Try to relax with your lover and enjoy good food with them.

BIBLE VERSES: (Proverbs)

18:17. The just is first accuser of himself: his friend cometh, and shall search him.

READ PSALMS #'s: 4, 13, 31 ,40, 49, 58, 76, 103, 121

MANTRA FOR TODAY

Om Hareem Nama Swaha..Shri
Maha Laxmi Aye Namah swaha
12 times
Om maha laxmi cha vidmahe
vishnu pataya dhi mahi tanno
laxmi pracho dayat
Om hareem namam swaha
9 times

MAY 30, 2015

| 05/30/2015 SAT | This is considered a NEUTRAL day for you | | | | | | | | Shiva |

Moving	Shopping	Health	Investing	Gambling	Love is	Wedding	Travel	Work/Job	Planet
Fair	Fair	Fair	Fair	Good	Bad	Good	Fair	Bad	Uranus

KEYWORDS ARE: Denial - Doubt, travel, losses, sadness,
Family conflicts, Arguments, Groups - Parties, God - Karma, Moving, Accidents

Lotto #'s	play 4 #s	play 3 #s	Ruling Angel:............	Color Sugestion:............	Ruling Deity
2,6,34,31,13,21	5147	129	Camael	Orange/White/Light Green/ Beige	Krishna

ADVICE & DETAILS

You will either be missing your lover or have sexual enjoyment and romance with partner.
You must watch your words and think of others.

BIBLE VERSES: (Proverbs)

18:19. A brother that is helped by his brother, is like a strong city: and judgments are like the bars of cities.

READ PSALMS #'s: 5, 14, 32 ,41, 50, 59, 77, 104, 122

MANTRA FOR TODAY

Om Ganga mataye nama swaha
Om Varuna Devta aye Pahimam
11 times
Om hareem mama sarva shatru
janam vashee kuru kuru swaha
om hareem ksham kasham
kasheem kasheem swaha
9 times

MAY 31, 2015

05/31/2015 SUN			This is considered a POSITIVE day for you						Shiva
Moving	*Shopping*	*Health*	*Investing*	*Gambling*	*Love is*	*Wedding*	*Travel*	*Work/Job*	*Planet*
Good	Excellent	Good	Good	Fair	Excellent	Bad	Excelle	Good	Mars

KEYWORDS ARE: death, frustration, finish, fame, Tiredness, Low Energy, Sleepy, Teacher, IRS - Law, Government, Denial - Doubt

Lotto #'s	*play 4 #s*	*play 3 #s*	*Ruling Angel:*............	*Color Sugestion:*............	*Ruling Deity*
3,7,34,31,13,23	6672	2210	**Raphael**	**Purple/DeepBlue/Rose**	**Hanuman**

ADVICE & DETAILS

This will be a positive day if you can control your tongue and do not criticize anyone, particularly your loved ones and especially your partner. The influences are love and marriage. This is the opportunity to create a special surprise meal for your partner and share it with love in a romantic setting with soothing music as background.

BIBLE VERSES: (Proverbs)

18:21. Death and life are in the power of the tongue: they that love it, shall eat the fruits thereof.

READ PSALMS #'s: 6, 15, 33 ,42, 51, 60, 78, 105, 123

MANTRA FOR TODAY

Om Namo Bhagawate Mukhtanandaya, 108 times AUM KRSNAYA VIDMAHE DAMODARAYA DHIMAHI. TANNO VISHNU PRACODAYAT. 9 times

JUNE 1, 2015

06/01/2015 MON			This is considered a POSITIVE day for you						Shiva
Moving	*Shopping*	*Health*	*Investing*	*Gambling*	*Love is*	*Wedding*	*Travel*	*Work/Job*	*Planet*
Good	Good	Excellent	Excellent	Bad	Good	Good	Good	Excellent	Pluto

KEYWORDS ARE: losses, employment, luxury, beauty, Popularity & Reputation, Real Estate, Accidents, Tiredness, money

Lotto #'s	*play 4 #s*	*play 3 #s*	*Ruling Angel:*............	*Color Sugestion:*............	*Ruling Deity*
9,6,34,31,14,18	10849	837	**Metatron**	**Dark Blue/ Purple/ Mauve**	**Ganesh**

ADVICE & DETAILS

Your business will be slow today. Your incoming income will be equal to your outcoming expenses. Children will demand money for necessities of and for college payments or education.

BIBLE VERSES: (Proverbs)

18:20. Of the fruit of a man's mouth shall his belly be satisfied: and the offspring of his lips shall fill him.

READ PSALMS #'s: 4, 13, 31 ,40, 49, 58, 76, 103, 121

MANTRA FOR TODAY

Kali Durge Namo Nama Om Durge aye nama swaha 108 times AUM TATPURUSAYA VIDMAHE VAKRATUNDAY DHIMAHI. TANNO DANTI PRACODAYAT. 9 times

JUNE 2, 2015

06/02/2015 TUE			This is considered a NEGATIVE day for you						Shiva
Moving	*Shopping*	*Health*	*Investing*	*Gambling*	*Love is*	*Wedding*	*Travel*	*Work/Job*	*Planet*
Bad	Bad	Bad	Bad	Good	Bad	Good	Bad	Bad	Uranus

KEYWORDS ARE: finish, fraudulent, fame, pregnancy, Accidents, Illness, Alcoholism, Industrial, Denial - Doubt, travel, losses

Lotto #'s	*play 4 #s*	*play 3 #s*	*Ruling Angel:*............	*Color Sugestion:*............	*Ruling Deity*
10,7,34,32,14,20	4040	938	**Camael**	**Orange/White/Light Green/ Beige**	**Krishna**

ADVICE & DETAILS

This day marks the death or end of a period, a time, a person or a thought. The end may be related to your independence or fame or to the death of a famous person.

BIBLE VERSES: (Proverbs)

18:22. He that hath found a good wife, hath found a good thing, and shall receive a pleasure from the Lord. He that driveth away a good wife,

READ PSALMS #'s: 5, 14, 32 ,41, 50, 59, 77, 104, 122

MANTRA FOR TODAY

Om Hareem Nama Swaha...Shri Maha Laxmi Aye Namah swaha 12 times Om maha laxmi cha vidmahe vishnu pataya dhi mahi tanno laxmi pracho dayat Om hareem namam swaha 9 times

JUNE 3, 2015

06/03/2015 WED		This is considered a NEUTRAL day for you							Shiva
Moving	Shopping	Health	Investing	Gambling	Love is	Wedding	Travel	Work/Job	Planet
Fair	Fair	Fair	Fair	Fair	Bad	Bad	Fair	Bad	Mars

KEYWORDS ARE: Illness - Cold, Quarrels, Commanding, Boastful, Independence, Hard Work, Death, Back Pain, Dominating

Lotto #'s	play 4 #s	play 3 #s	Ruling Angel:............	Color Sugestion:............	Ruling Deity
2,7,34,32,14,22	1873	139	Raphael	Purple/DeepBlue/Rose	Hanuman

ADVICE & DETAILS

You will feel like you have high status today. Your ego will also be high. You would like to be in control and dominate the situation today. You will find satisfaction when others do what you tell them. You may be involved in tutoring or teaching.

BIBLE VERSES: (Proverbs)
18:24. A man amiable in society, shall be more friendly than a brother.

0

READ PSALMS #'s: 6, 15, 33 ,42, 51, 60, 78, 105, 123

MANTRA FOR TODAY

Om Ganga mataye nama swaha
Om Varuna Devta aye Pahimam
11 times
Om hareem mama sarva shatru
janam vashee kuru kuru swaha
om hareem ksham kasham
kasheem kasheem swaha
9 times

JUNE 4, 2015

06/04/2015 THU		This is considered a POSITIVE day for you							Shiva
Moving	Shopping	Health	Investing	Gambling	Love is	Wedding	Travel	Work/Job	Planet
Good	Excellent	Good	Good	Bad	Excellent	Fair	Excelle	Good	Moon

KEYWORDS ARE: Friendships, Alcohol - drugs, Association, Partnership, Popularity, Co-workers, Sickness - cold, Religious , Co-operation

Lotto #'s	play 4 #s	play 3 #s	Ruling Angel:............	Color Sugestion:............	Ruling Deity
3,9,34,31,14,24	3348	2310	Zaphkiel	Light Blue/Purple/Peach	Ganga

ADVICE & DETAILS

Your faith in God and the universe will be ver strong today. You will probably be going to religious places, shrines, temples or for a visit or phone call with the pastor or spiritual teacher.

BIBLE VERSES: (Proverbs)
19:2. Where there is no knowledge of the soul, there is no good: and he that is hasty with his feet shall stumble.

READ PSALMS #'s: 7, 16, 34 ,43, 52, 61, 79, 106, 124

MANTRA FOR TODAY

Om Namo Bhagawate
Mukhtanandaya,
108 times
AUM KRSNAYA VIDMAHE
DAMODARAYA DHIMAHI.
TANNO VISHNU
PRACODAYAT.
9 times

JUNE 5, 2015

06/05/2015 FRI		This is considered a POSITIVE day for you							Shiva
Moving	Shopping	Health	Investing	Gambling	Love is	Wedding	Travel	Work/Job	Planet
Good	Excellent	Excellent	Good	Excellent	Good	Excellent	Excelle	Good	Jupiter

KEYWORDS ARE: Teacher, Money Wasted, Communication, read, Social Groups, Low Payment, Legal matter, Power, Groups - Parties

Lotto #'s	play 4 #s	play 3 #s	Ruling Angel:............	Color Sugestion:............	Ruling Deity
4,9,33,31,14,16	9580	332	Haniel	Yellow/White/Silver	Mahalaxmi

ADVICE & DETAILS

This is definetely an excellent day to go out shopping looking for bargains. You will be saving money and have a chance to use coupons. It is also a good time to get a quote or quotes for a major project.

BIBLE VERSES: (Proverbs)
19:4. Riches make many friends: but from the poor man, even they whom he had, depart.

READ PSALMS #'s: 8, 17, 35 ,44, 53, 62, 80, 107, 125

MANTRA FOR TODAY

Kali Durge Namo Nama
Om Durge aye nama swaha
108 times
AUM TATPURUSAYA
VIDMAHE VAKRATUNDAY
DHIMAHI. TANNO DANTI
PRACODAYAT.
9 times

JUNE 6, 2015

06/06/2015 SAT			This is considered a NEUTRAL day for you						Shiva
Moving	Shopping	Health	Investing	Gambling	Love is	Wedding	Travel	Work/Job	Planet
Bad	Bad	Bad	Bad	Bad	Fair	Bad	Bad	Bad	Saturn

KEYWORDS ARE: Real Estate, Accidents, Tiredness, career, Money & stress, Job Problems, Abusive, Karmic debts, Laziness

Lotto #'s	play 4 #s	play 3 #s	Ruling Angel:............	Color Sugestion:............	Ruling Deity
5,1,33,31,14,10	1305	433	Mikael	Gold/Brown/Blue/Dark Green	Pitridev

ADVICE & DETAILS	MANTRA FOR TODAY
There will be delays and postponements at work place. You wil be denied comfort at your place of employment due to physical arrangements or psychological factors. There will be a lack of responsibility on your part. Your ego will be high.	Om hareem Kleem Hreem Aem Saraswataye namaha 21 times Om Guru bramha, Guru Vishnu Guru Deva mahaeshwara guru saksha paam bramha, tasmi shri guruve nama 9 times

BIBLE VERSES: (Proverbs)

19:6. Many honour the person of him that is mighty, and are friends of him that giveth gifts.

READ PSALMS #'s: 9, 18, 36 ,45, 54, 63, 81, 108, 126

JUNE 7, 2015

06/07/2015 SUN			This is considered a POSITIVE day for you						Shiva
Moving	Shopping	Health	Investing	Gambling	Love is	Wedding	Travel	Work/Job	Planet
Excellent	Good	Excellent	Good	Fair	Excellent	Fair	Excelle	Good	Sun

KEYWORDS ARE: Beauty - Sex, Confined, travel, change, Car & driving , High Temper, Karmic debts, Commanding, Moving

Lotto #'s	play 4 #s	play 3 #s	Ruling Angel:............	Color Sugestion:............	Ruling Deity
6,2,34,32,14,11	6385	534	Gabriel	White/Yellow/ Peach	Gaitree

ADVICE & DETAILS	MANTRA FOR TODAY
You will have to travel alone today. You will distrust children or they will distrust you. You will have a good day at work. There could be changes in plans associated with children and their needs.	Om Jai Viganeshwaraya.. Lambodaraya Namo Namaha 21 times Om Sarva Mangal Mangalye, Shiva Sarvart Sadike, Sharan Tryambike Gowri, Narayane Namo asttute 9 times

BIBLE VERSES: (Proverbs)

18:23. The poor will speak with supplications, and the rich will speak roughly.

READ PSALMS #'s: 1, 10, 28 ,37, 46, 55, 73, 100, 118

JUNE 8, 2015

06/08/2015 MON			This is considered a NEGATIVE day for you						Shiva
Moving	Shopping	Health	Investing	Gambling	Love is	Wedding	Travel	Work/Job	Planet
Bad	Bad	Bad	Fair	Good	Bad	Good	Bad	Bad	Venus

KEYWORDS ARE: Anger - Ego, love, frustration, power, Police and frustrations, Low Pay, God - Karma, Association, Government

Lotto #'s	play 4 #s	play 3 #s	Ruling Angel:............	Color Sugestion:............	Ruling Deity
7,3,33,32,14,13	1145	635	Raziel	Red/Yellow/Pink	Durga

ADVICE & DETAILS	MANTRA FOR TODAY
Today, you will have doubts and frustration over romance and children. You can expect delay in romance. You will have to watch your words and communication to ease the situation with lover and children.	Om Graam Greem Graum Sa Gurave namah swaha 21 times AUM VAGDEVYAI CA VIDMAHE KAMARAJAYA DHIMAHI. TANNO DEVI PRACODAYAT. 9 times

BIBLE VERSES: (Proverbs)

19:1. Better is the poor man, that walketh in his simplicity, than a rich man that is perverse in his lips and unwise.

READ PSALMS #'s: 2, 11, 29 ,38, 47, 56, 74, 101, 119

JUNE 9, 2015

06/09/2015 TUE			This is considered a NEUTRAL day for you						Shiva
Moving	*Shopping*	*Health*	*Investing*	*Gambling*	*Love is*	*Wedding*	*Travel*	*Work/Job*	*Planet*
Good	**Fair**	**Fair**	**Bad**	**Good**	**Good**	**Good**	**Good**	**Fair**	**Mercury**

KEYWORDS ARE: death, children, religion, religion, Alcohol - drugs , Laziness, IRS - Law, Communication, Criticism

Lotto #'s	*play 4 #s*	*play 3 #s*	Ruling Angel:............	Color Sugestion:............	*Ruling Deity*
8,5,34,32,14,16	8278	736	**Zadkiel**	**Green/Sky Blue/White**	**Saraswaty**

ADVICE & DETAILS	MANTRA FOR TODAY
You will receive and give powerful advice today if you are centered. You will have the opportunity of having pleasure and connection with fame and television.	*Om Mana Swasti Shanti Kuru kuru Swaha Shivoham Shivoham 27 times* *om haring jawala mukhi mam sarva shatru bakshaya bakshaya hung phat swaha* *Om Nama shivaya pahimam 9 times*

BIBLE VERSES: (Proverbs)
19:3. The folly of a man supplanteth his steps: and he fretteth in his mind against God.
READ PSALMS #'s: 3, 12, 30 ,39, 48, 57, 75, 102, 120

JUNE 10, 2015

06/10/2015 WED			This is considered a POSITIVE day for you						Shiva
Moving	*Shopping*	*Health*	*Investing*	*Gambling*	*Love is*	*Wedding*	*Travel*	*Work/Job*	*Planet*
Good	**Good**	**Excellent**	**Excellent**	**Bad**	**Good**	**Good**	**Good**	**Excellent**	**Pluto**

KEYWORDS ARE: losses, employment, luxury, beauty, Popularity & Reputation, Real Estate, Accidents, Tiredness, money

Lotto #'s	*play 4 #s*	*play 3 #s*	Ruling Angel:............	Color Sugestion:............	*Ruling Deity*
9,6,34,32,14,17	1687	837	**Metatron**	**Dark Blue/ Purple/ Mauve**	**Ganesh**

ADVICE & DETAILS	MANTRA FOR TODAY
Your business will be slow today. Your incoming income will be equal to your outcoming expenses. Children will demand money for necessities of and for college payments or education.	*Jai Jai Shiva Shambo.(2)* *...Mahadeva Shambo (2)* *21 times* *Om Jayanti Mangala Kali Bhadrakali Kapalini Durga Kshama Shiva Dhatri Swaha Swadha Namostute* *9 times*

BIBLE VERSES: (Proverbs)
19:5. A false witness shall not be unpunished: and he that speaketh lies, shall not escape.
READ PSALMS #'s: 4, 13, 31 ,40, 49, 58, 76, 103, 121

JUNE 11, 2015

06/11/2015 THU			This is considered a NEGATIVE day for you						Shiva
Moving	*Shopping*	*Health*	*Investing*	*Gambling*	*Love is*	*Wedding*	*Travel*	*Work/Job*	*Planet*
Bad	**Bad**	**Bad**	**Bad**	**Good**	**Bad**	**Good**	**Bad**	**Bad**	**Uranus**

KEYWORDS ARE: finish, fraudulent, fame, pregnancy, Accidents, Illness, Alcoholism, Industrial, Denial - Doubt, travel, losses

Lotto #'s	*play 4 #s*	*play 3 #s*	Ruling Angel:............	Color Sugestion:............	*Ruling Deity*
10,6,33,31,14,19	1969	938	**Camael**	**Orange/White/Light Green/ Beige**	**Krishna**

ADVICE & DETAILS	MANTRA FOR TODAY
This day marks the death or end of a period, a time, a person or a thought. The end may be related to your independence or fame or to the death of a famous person.	*Om Hareem Nama Swaha...Shri Maha Laxmi Aye Namah swaha 12 times* *Om maha laxmi cha vidmahe vishnu pataya dhi mahi tanno laxmi pracho dayat* *Om hareem namam swaha 9 times*

BIBLE VERSES: (Proverbs)
19:7. The brethren of the poor man hate him: moreover also his friends have departed far from him. He that followeth after words only, shall have
READ PSALMS #'s: 5, 14, 32 ,41, 50, 59, 77, 104, 122

JUNE 12, 2015

06/12/2015 FRI			This is considered a NEUTRAL day for you						Shiva
Moving	Shopping	Health	Investing	Gambling	Love is	Wedding	Travel	Work/Job	Planet
Fair	Fair	Fair	Fair	Fair	Bad	Bad	Fair	Bad	Mars

KEYWORDS ARE: Abusive, Quarrels, God - Karma, Accidents, Depression & Lonliness, Hard Work, Death, Back Pain, Legal matter

Lotto #'s	play 4 #s	play 3 #s	Ruling Angel:............	Color Sugestion:............	Ruling Deity
2,8,33,31,14,22	5020	139	Raphael	Purple/DeepBlue/Rose	Hanuman

ADVICE & DETAILS	MANTRA FOR TODAY
You will feel like you have high status today. Your ego will also be high. You would like to be in control and dominate the situation today. You will find satisfaction when others do what you tell them. You may be involved in tutoring or teaching.	*Om Ganga mataye nama swaha Om Varuna Devta aye Pahimam 11 times Om hareem mama sarva shatru janam vashee kuru kuru swaha om hareem ksham kasham kasheem kasheem swaha 9 times*

BIBLE VERSES: (Proverbs)
19:9. A false witness shall not be unpunished: and he that speaketh lies, shall perish.

READ PSALMS #'s: 6, 15, 33 ,42, 51, 60, 78, 105, 123

JUNE 13, 2015

06/13/2015 SAT			This is considered a POSITIVE day for you						Shiva
Moving	Shopping	Health	Investing	Gambling	Love is	Wedding	Travel	Work/Job	Planet
Good	Excellent	Good	Good	Bad	Excellent	Fair	Excelle	Good	Moon

KEYWORDS ARE: Friendships, Alcohol - drugs, Association, Partnership, Popularity, Co-workers, Sickness - cold, Religious , Co-operation

Lotto #'s	play 4 #s	play 3 #s	Ruling Angel:............	Color Sugestion:............	Ruling Deity
3,9,34,32,14,23	4500	2310	Zaphkiel	Light Blue/Purple/Peach	Ganga

ADVICE & DETAILS	MANTRA FOR TODAY
Your faith in God and the universe will be ver strong today. You will probably be going to religious places, shrines, temples or for a visit or phone call with the pastor or spiritual teacher.	*Om Namo Bhagawate Mukhtanandaya, 108 times AUM KRSNAYA VIDMAHE DAMODARAYA DHIMAHI. TANNO VISHNU PRACODAYAT. 9 times*

BIBLE VERSES: (Proverbs)
19:11. The learning of a man is known by patience: and his glory is to pass over wrongs.

READ PSALMS #'s: 7, 16, 34 ,43, 52, 61, 79, 106, 124

JUNE 14, 2015

06/14/2015 SUN			This is considered a POSITIVE day for you						Shiva
Moving	Shopping	Health	Investing	Gambling	Love is	Wedding	Travel	Work/Job	Planet
Good	Excellent	Excellent	Good	Excellent	Good	Excellent	Excelle	Good	Jupiter

KEYWORDS ARE: Teacher, Money Wasted, Communication, read, Social Groups, Low Payment, Legal matter, Power, Groups - Parties

Lotto #'s	play 4 #s	play 3 #s	Ruling Angel:............	Color Sugestion:............	Ruling Deity
4,10,33,32,14,16	10743	332	Haniel	Yellow/White/Silver	Mahalaxmi

ADVICE & DETAILS	MANTRA FOR TODAY
This is definetely an excellent day to go out shopping looking for bargains. You will be saving money and have a chance to use coupons. It is also a good time to get a quote or quotes for a major project.	*Kali Durge Namo Nama Om Durge aye nama swaha 108 times AUM TATPURUSAYA VIDMAHE VAKRATUNDAY DHIMAHI. TANNO DANTI PRACODAYAT. 9 times*

BIBLE VERSES: (Proverbs)
19:13. A foolish son is the grief of his father: and a wrangling wife is like a roof continually dropping through.

READ PSALMS #'s: 8, 17, 35 ,44, 53, 62, 80, 107, 125

JUNE 15, 2015

06/15/2015 MON			This is considered a NEUTRAL day for you						Shiva
Moving	Shopping	Health	Investing	Gambling	Love is	Wedding	Travel	Work/Job	Planet
Bad	Bad	Bad	Bad	Bad	Fair	Bad	Bad	Bad	Saturn

KEYWORDS ARE: Real Estate, Accidents, Tiredness, career,
Money & stress, Job Problems, Abusive, Karmic debts, Laziness

Lotto #'s	play 4 #s	play 3 #s	Ruling Angel:............	Color Sugestion:............	Ruling Deity
5,1,33,32,14,10	7191	433	Mikael	Gold/Brown/Blue/Dark Green	Pitridev

ADVICE & DETAILS	MANTRA FOR TODAY
There will be delays and postponements at work place. You wil be denied comfort at your place of employment due to physical arrangements or psychological factors. There will be a lack of responsibility on your part. Your ego will be high.	*Om hareem Kleem Hreem Aem Saraswataye namaha* *21 times* *Om Guru bramha, Guru Vishnu Guru Deva mahaeshwara guru saksha paam bramha, tasmi shri guruve nama* *9 times*

BIBLE VERSES: (Proverbs)
19:15. Slothfulness casteth into a deep sleep, and an idle soul shall suffer hunger.
READ PSALMS #'s: 9, 18, 36 ,45, 54, 63, 81, 108, 126

JUNE 16, 2015

06/16/2015 TUE			This is considered a POSITIVE day for you						Shiva
Moving	Shopping	Health	Investing	Gambling	Love is	Wedding	Travel	Work/Job	Planet
Excellent	Good	Excellent	Good	Fair	Excellent	Fair	Excelle	Good	Sun

KEYWORDS ARE: Beauty - Sex, Confined, travel, change,
Car & driving , High Temper, Karmic debts, Commanding, Moving

Lotto #'s	play 4 #s	play 3 #s	Ruling Angel:............	Color Sugestion:............	Ruling Deity
6,2,34,31,14,11	8225	534	Gabriel	White/Yellow/ Peach	Gaitree

ADVICE & DETAILS	MANTRA FOR TODAY
You will have to travel alone today. You will distrust children or they will distrust you. You will have a good day at work. There could be changes in plans associated with children and their needs.	*Om Jai Viganeshwaraya.. Lambodaraya Namo Namaha* *21 times* *Om Sarva Mangal Mangalye, Shiva Sarvart Sadike, Sharan Tryambike Gowri, Narayane Namo asttute* *9 times*

BIBLE VERSES: (Proverbs)
19:8. But he that possesseth a mind, loveth his own soul, and he that keepeth prudence, shall find good things.
READ PSALMS #'s: 1, 10, 28 ,37, 46, 55, 73, 100, 118

JUNE 17, 2015

06/17/2015 WED			This is considered a NEGATIVE day for you						Shiva
Moving	Shopping	Health	Investing	Gambling	Love is	Wedding	Travel	Work/Job	Planet
Bad	Bad	Bad	Fair	Good	Bad	Good	Bad	Bad	Venus

KEYWORDS ARE: Anger - Ego, love, frustration, power,
Police and frustrations, Low Pay, God - Karma, Association, Government

Lotto #'s	play 4 #s	play 3 #s	Ruling Angel:............	Color Sugestion:............	Ruling Deity
7,3,33,32,14,14	5205	635	Raziel	Red/Yellow/Pink	Durga

ADVICE & DETAILS	MANTRA FOR TODAY
Today, you will have doubts and frustration over romance and children. You can expect delay in romance. You will have to watch your words and communication to ease the situation with lover and children.	*Om Graam Greem Graum Sa Gurave namah swaha* *21 times* *AUM VAGDEVYAI CA VIDMAHE KAMARAJAYA DHIMAHI. TANNO DEVI PRACODAYAT.* *9 times*

BIBLE VERSES: (Proverbs)
19:10. Delicacies are not seemly for a fool: nor for a servant to have rule over princes.
READ PSALMS #'s: 2, 11, 29 ,38, 47, 56, 74, 101, 119

JUNE 18, 2015

06/18/2015 THU		This is considered a NEUTRAL day for you							Shiva
Moving	Shopping	Health	Investing	Gambling	Love is	Wedding	Travel	Work/Job	Planet
Good	Fair	Fair	Bad	Good	Good	Good	Good	Fair	Mercury

KEYWORDS ARE: death, children, religion, religion, Alcohol - drugs , Laziness, IRS - Law, Communication, Criticism

Lotto #'s	play 4 #s	play 3 #s	Ruling Angel:............	Color Sugestion:............	Ruling Deity
8,5,33,32,14,16	8376	736	Zadkiel	Green/Sky Blue/White	Saraswaty

ADVICE & DETAILS	MANTRA FOR TODAY
You will receive and give powerful advice today if you are centered. You will have the opportunity of having pleasure and connection with fame and television.	Om Mana Swasti Shanti Kuru kuru Swaha Shivoham Shivoham 27 times om haring jawala mukhi mam sarva shatru bakshaya bakshaya hung phat swaha Om Nama shivaya pahimam 9 times

BIBLE VERSES: (Proverbs)

19:12. As the roaring of a lion, so also is the anger of a king: and his cheerfulness as the dew upon the grass.

READ PSALMS #'s: 3, 12, 30 ,39, 48, 57, 75, 102, 120

JUNE 19, 2015

06/19/2015 FRI		This is considered a POSITIVE day for you							Shiva
Moving	Shopping	Health	Investing	Gambling	Love is	Wedding	Travel	Work/Job	Planet
Good	Good	Excellent	Excellent	Bad	Good	Good	Good	Excellent	Pluto

KEYWORDS ARE: losses, employment, luxury, beauty, Popularity & Reputation, Real Estate, Accidents, Tiredness, money

Lotto #'s	play 4 #s	play 3 #s	Ruling Angel:............	Color Sugestion:............	Ruling Deity
9,6,33,32,14,18	9616	837	Metatron	Dark Blue/ Purple/ Mauve	Ganesh

ADVICE & DETAILS	MANTRA FOR TODAY
Your business will be slow today. Your incoming income will be equal to your outcoming expenses. Children will demand money for necessities of and for college payments or education.	Jai Jai Shiva Shambo.(2) ...Mahadeva Shambo (2) 21 times Om Jayanti Mangala Kali Bhadrakali Kapalini Durga Kshama Shiva Dhatri Swaha Swadha Namostute 9 times

BIBLE VERSES: (Proverbs)

19:14. House and riches are given by parents: but a prudent wife is properly from the Lord.

READ PSALMS #'s: 4, 13, 31 ,40, 49, 58, 76, 103, 121

JUNE 20, 2015

06/20/2015 SAT		This is considered a NEGATIVE day for you							Shiva
Moving	Shopping	Health	Investing	Gambling	Love is	Wedding	Travel	Work/Job	Planet
Bad	Bad	Bad	Bad	Good	Bad	Good	Bad	Bad	Uranus

KEYWORDS ARE: finish, fraudulent, fame, pregnancy, Accidents, Illness, Alcoholism, Industrial, Denial - Doubt, travel, losses

Lotto #'s	play 4 #s	play 3 #s	Ruling Angel:............	Color Sugestion:............	Ruling Deity
10,7,33,32,14,19	3381	938	Camael	Orange/White/Light Green/ Beige	Krishna

ADVICE & DETAILS	MANTRA FOR TODAY
This day marks the death or end of a period, a time, a person or a thought. The end may be related to your independence or fame or to the death of a famous person.	Om Hareem Nama Swaha...Shri Maha Laxmi Aye Namah swaha 12 times Om maha laxmi cha vidmahe vishnu pataya dhi mahi tanno laxmi pracho dayat Om hareem namam swaha 9 times

BIBLE VERSES: (Proverbs)

19:16. He that keepeth the commandment, keepeth his own soul: but he that neglecteth his own way, shall die.

READ PSALMS #'s: 5, 14, 32 ,41, 50, 59, 77, 104, 122

JUNE 21, 2015

06/21/2015 SUN			This is considered a NEUTRAL day for you						Shiva
Moving	*Shopping*	*Health*	*Investing*	*Gambling*	*Love is*	*Wedding*	*Travel*	*Work/Job*	*Planet*
Fair	Fair	Fair	Fair	Fair	Bad	Bad	Fair	Bad	Mars

KEYWORDS ARE: Abusive, Quarrels, God - Karma, Accidents, Depression & Lonliness, Hard Work, Death, Back Pain, Legal matter

Lotto #'s	*play 4 #s*	*play 3 #s*	Ruling Angel:............	Color Sugestion:............	*Ruling Deity*
2,8,33,32,14,21	2010	139	Raphael	Purple/DeepBlue/Rose	Hanuman

ADVICE & DETAILS

You will feel like you have high status today. Your ego will also be high. You would like to be in control and dominate the situation today. You will find satisfaction when others do what you tell them. You may be involved in tutoring or teaching.

BIBLE VERSES: (Proverbs)

19:18. Chastise thy son, despair not: but to the killing of him set not thy soul.
0

READ PSALMS #'s: 6, 15, 33 ,42, 51, 60, 78, 105, 123

MANTRA FOR TODAY

Om Ganga mataye nama swaha
Om Varuna Devta aye Pahimam
11 times
Om hareem mama sarva shatru
janam vashee kuru kuru swaha
om hareem ksham kasham
kasheem kasheem swaha
9 times

JUNE 22, 2015

06/22/2015 MON			This is considered a POSITIVE day for you						Shiva
Moving	*Shopping*	*Health*	*Investing*	*Gambling*	*Love is*	*Wedding*	*Travel*	*Work/Job*	*Planet*
Good	Excellent	Good	Good	Bad	Excellent	Fair	Excelle	Good	Moon

KEYWORDS ARE: Karmic debts, Alcohol - drugs, IRS - Law, Denial - Doubt, Quarrels & lovers, Co-workers, Sickness - cold, Religious , Abusive

Lotto #'s	*play 4 #s*	*play 3 #s*	Ruling Angel:............	Color Sugestion:............	*Ruling Deity*
3,8,33,32,14,23	1130	2310	Zaphkiel	Light Blue/Purple/Peach	Ganga

ADVICE & DETAILS

Your faith in God and the universe will be ver strong today. You will probably be going to religious places, shrines, temples or for a visit or phone call with the pastor or spiritual teacher.

BIBLE VERSES: (Proverbs)

19:20. Hear counsel, and receive instruction, that thou mayst be wise in thy latter end.

READ PSALMS #'s: 7, 16, 34 ,43, 52, 61, 79, 106, 124

MANTRA FOR TODAY

Om Namo Bhagawate
Mukhtanandaya,
108 times
AUM KRSNAYA VIDMAHE
DAMODARAYA DHIMAHI.
TANNO VISHNU
PRACODAYAT.
9 times

JUNE 23, 2015

06/23/2015 TUE			This is considered a POSITIVE day for you						Shiva
Moving	*Shopping*	*Health*	*Investing*	*Gambling*	*Love is*	*Wedding*	*Travel*	*Work/Job*	*Planet*
Good	Excellent	Excellent	Good	Excellent	Good	Excellent	Excelle	Good	Jupiter

KEYWORDS ARE: Teacher, Money Wasted, Communication, read, Social Groups, Low Payment, Legal matter, Power, Groups - Parties

Lotto #'s	*play 4 #s*	*play 3 #s*	Ruling Angel:............	Color Sugestion:............	*Ruling Deity*
4,9,33,32,14,16	4486	332	Haniel	Yellow/White/Silver	Mahalaxmi

ADVICE & DETAILS

This is definetely an excellent day to go out shopping looking for bargains. You will be saving money and have a chance to use coupons. It is also a good time to get a quote or quotes for a major project.

BIBLE VERSES: (Proverbs)

19:22. A needy man is merciful: and better is the poor than the lying man.
0

READ PSALMS #'s: 8, 17, 35 ,44, 53, 62, 80, 107, 125

MANTRA FOR TODAY

Kali Durge Namo Nama
Om Durge aye nama swaha
108 times
AUM TATPURUSAYA
VIDMAHE VAKRATUNDAY
DHIMAHI. TANNO DANTI
PRACODAYAT.
9 times

JUNE 24, 2015

06/24/2015 WED		This is considered a NEUTRAL day for you							Shiva

Moving	Shopping	Health	Investing	Gambling	Love is	Wedding	Travel	Work/Job	Planet
Bad	Bad	Bad	Bad	Bad	Fair	Bad	Bad	Bad	Saturn

KEYWORDS ARE: Real Estate, Accidents, Tiredness, career, Money & stress, Job Problems, Abusive, Karmic debts, Laziness

Lotto #'s	play 4 #s	play 3 #s	Ruling Angel:............	Color Sugestion:............	Ruling Deity
5,2,33,32,14,10	9848	433	Mikael	Gold/Brown/Blue/Dark Green	Pitridev

ADVICE & DETAILS

There will be delays and postponements at work place. You wil be denied comfort at your place of employment due to physical arrangements or psychological factors. There will be a lack of responsibility on your part. Your ego will be high.

BIBLE VERSES: (Proverbs)

19:24. The slothful hideth his hand under his armpit, and will not so much as bring it to his mouth.

READ PSALMS #'s: 9, 18, 36 ,45, 54, 63, 81, 108, 126

MANTRA FOR TODAY

Om hareem Kleem Hreem Aem Saraswataye namaha
21 times
Om Guru bramha, Guru Vishnu Guru Deva mahaeshwara guru saksha paam bramha, tasmi shri guruve nama
9 times

JUNE 25, 2015

06/25/2015 THU		This is considered a POSITIVE day for you							Shiva

Moving	Shopping	Health	Investing	Gambling	Love is	Wedding	Travel	Work/Job	Planet
Excellent	Good	Excellent	Good	Fair	Excellent	Fair	Excelle	Good	Sun

KEYWORDS ARE: Beauty - Sex, Confined, travel, change, Car & driving , High Temper, Karmic debts, Commanding, Moving

Lotto #'s	play 4 #s	play 3 #s	Ruling Angel:............	Color Sugestion:............	Ruling Deity
6,3,33,32,14,12	3654	534	Gabriel	White/Yellow/ Peach	Gaitree

ADVICE & DETAILS

You will have to travel alone today. You will distrust children or they will distrust you. You will have a good day at work. There could be changes in plans associated with children and their needs.

BIBLE VERSES: (Proverbs)

19:17. He that hath mercy on the poor, lendeth to the Lord: and he will repay him.

READ PSALMS #'s: 1, 10, 28 ,37, 46, 55, 73, 100, 118

MANTRA FOR TODAY

Om Jai Viganeshwaraya.. Lambodaraya Namo Namaha
21 times
Om Sarva Mangal Mangalye, Shiva Sarvart Sadike, Sharan Tryambike Gowri, Narayane Namo asttute
9 times

JUNE 26, 2015

06/26/2015 FRI		This is considered a NEGATIVE day for you							Shiva

Moving	Shopping	Health	Investing	Gambling	Love is	Wedding	Travel	Work/Job	Planet
Bad	Bad	Bad	Fair	Good	Bad	Good	Bad	Bad	Venus

KEYWORDS ARE: Anger - Ego, love, frustration, power, Police and frustrations, Low Pay, God - Karma, Association, Government

Lotto #'s	play 4 #s	play 3 #s	Ruling Angel:............	Color Sugestion:............	Ruling Deity
7,3,33,31,14,14	5247	635	Raziel	Red/Yellow/Pink	Durga

ADVICE & DETAILS

Today, you will have doubts and frustration over romance and children. You can expect delay in romance. You will have to watch your words and communication to ease the situation with lover and children.

BIBLE VERSES: (Proverbs)

19:19. He that is impatient, shall suffer damage: and when he shall take away, he shall add another thing.

READ PSALMS #'s: 2, 11, 29 ,38, 47, 56, 74, 101, 119

MANTRA FOR TODAY

Om Graam Greem Graum Sa Gurave namah swaha
21 times
AUM VAGDEVYAI CA VIDMAHE KAMARAJAYA DHIMAHI. TANNO DEVI PRACODAYAT.
9 times

JUNE 27, 2015

06/27/2015 SAT		This is considered a NEUTRAL day for you							Shiva
Moving	*Shopping*	*Health*	*Investing*	*Gambling*	*Love is*	*Wedding*	*Travel*	*Work/Job*	*Planet*
Good	**Fair**	**Fair**	**Bad**	**Good**	**Good**	**Good**	**Good**	**Fair**	**Mercury**

KEYWORDS ARE: death, children, religion, religion, Alcohol - drugs , Laziness, IRS - Law, Communication, Criticism

Lotto #'s	*play 4 #s*	*play 3 #s*	Ruling Angel:...........	Color Sugestion:...........	*Ruling Deity*
8,4,33,31,14,15	2084	736	**Zadkiel**	**Green/Sky Blue/White**	**Saraswaty**

ADVICE & DETAILS	MANTRA FOR TODAY
You will receive and give powerful advice today if you are centered. You will have the opportunity of having pleasure and connection with fame and television.	*Om Mana Swasti Shanti Kuru kuru Swaha Shivoham Shivoham 27 times om haring jawala mukhi mam sarva shatru bakshaya bakshaya hung phat swaha Om Nama shivaya pahimam 9 times*

BIBLE VERSES: (Proverbs)
19:21. There are many thoughts in the heart of a man: but the will of the Lord shall stand firm.
READ PSALMS #'s: 3, 12, 30 ,39, 48, 57, 75, 102, 120

JUNE 28, 2015

06/28/2015 SUN		This is considered a POSITIVE day for you							Shiva
Moving	*Shopping*	*Health*	*Investing*	*Gambling*	*Love is*	*Wedding*	*Travel*	*Work/Job*	*Planet*
Good	**Good**	**Excellent**	**Excellent**	**Bad**	**Good**	**Good**	**Good**	**Excellent**	**Pluto**

KEYWORDS ARE: losses, employment, luxury, beauty, Popularity & Reputation, Real Estate, Accidents, Tiredness, money

Lotto #'s	*play 4 #s*	*play 3 #s*	Ruling Angel:...........	Color Sugestion:...........	*Ruling Deity*
9,5,34,31,14,18	2720	837	**Metatron**	**Dark Blue/ Purple/ Mauve**	**Ganesh**

ADVICE & DETAILS	MANTRA FOR TODAY
Your business will be slow today. Your incoming income will be equal to your outcoming expenses. Children will demand money for necessities of and for college payments or education.	*Jai Jai Shiva Shambo.(2) ...Mahadeva Shambo (2) 21 times Om Jayanti Mangala Kali Bhadrakali Kapalini Durga Kshama Shiva Dhatri Swaha Swadha Namostute 9 times*

BIBLE VERSES: (Proverbs)
19:23. The fear of the Lord is unto life: and he shall abide in the fulness without being visited with evil.
READ PSALMS #'s: 4, 13, 31 ,40, 49, 58, 76, 103, 121

JUNE 29, 2015

06/29/2015 MON		This is considered a NEGATIVE day for you							Shiva
Moving	*Shopping*	*Health*	*Investing*	*Gambling*	*Love is*	*Wedding*	*Travel*	*Work/Job*	*Planet*
Bad	**Bad**	**Bad**	**Bad**	**Good**	**Bad**	**Good**	**Bad**	**Bad**	**Uranus**

KEYWORDS ARE: finish, fraudulent, fame, pregnancy, Accidents, Illness, Alcoholism, Industrial, Denial - Doubt, travel, losses

Lotto #'s	*play 4 #s*	*play 3 #s*	Ruling Angel:...........	Color Sugestion:...........	*Ruling Deity*
10,7,34,32,14,19	3306	938	**Camael**	**Orange/White/Light Green/ Beige**	**Krishna**

ADVICE & DETAILS	MANTRA FOR TODAY
This day marks the death or end of a period, a time, a person or a thought. The end may be related to your independence or fame or to the death of a famous person.	*Om Hareem Nama Swaha...Shri Maha Laxmi Aye Namah swaha 12 times Om maha laxmi cha vidmahe vishnu pataya dhi mahi tanno laxmi pracho dayat Om hareem namam swaha 9 times*

BIBLE VERSES: (Proverbs)
19:25. The wicked man being scourged, the fool shall be wiser: but if thou rebuke a wise man, he will understand discipline.
READ PSALMS #'s: 5, 14, 32 ,41, 50, 59, 77, 104, 122

JUNE 30, 2015

06/30/2015 TUE		This is considered a NEUTRAL day for you							Shiva
Moving	Shopping	Health	Investing	Gambling	Love is	Wedding	Travel	Work/Job	Planet
Fair	Fair	Fair	Fair	Fair	Bad	Bad	Fair	Bad	Mars

KEYWORDS ARE: Abusive, Quarrels, God - Karma, Accidents, Depression & Lonliness, Hard Work, Death, Back Pain, Legal matter

Lotto #'s	play 4 #s	play 3 #s	Ruling Angel:............	Color Sugestion:............	Ruling Deity
2,8,33,32,14,22	7044	139	Raphael	Purple/DeepBlue/Rose	Hanuman

ADVICE & DETAILS
You will feel like you have high status today. Your ego will also be high. You would like to be in control and dominate the situation today. You will find satisfaction when others do what you tell them. You may be involved in tutoring or teaching.

BIBLE VERSES: (Proverbs)
19:27. Cease not, O my son, to hear instruction, and be not ignorant of the words of knowledge.

READ PSALMS #'s: 6, 15, 33 ,42, 51, 60, 78, 105, 123

MANTRA FOR TODAY
Om Ganga mataye nama swaha
Om Varuna Devta aye Pahimam
11 times
Om hareem mama sarva shatru janam vashee kuru kuru swaha
om hareem ksham kasham kasheem kasheem swaha
9 times

JULY 1, 2015

07/01/2015 WED		This is considered a POSITIVE day for you							Shiva
Moving	Shopping	Health	Investing	Gambling	Love is	Wedding	Travel	Work/Job	Planet
Good	Good	Excellent	Excellent	Good	Good	Good	Good	Excellent	Uranus

KEYWORDS ARE: Karmic debts, Illicit Affairs, Money Wasted, Big Expense, Romantic day for love, Change, Sickness - cold, Travel delays, Power

Lotto #'s	play 4 #s	play 3 #s	Ruling Angel:............	Color Sugestion:............	Ruling Deity
9,7,33,32,15,18	5321	847	Camael	Orange/White/Light Green/ Beige	Krishna

ADVICE & DETAILS
Change of pay scale or salary for you is expected todays or perhaps a change of position; all these changes are positive. There is a possibility that you will be refinancing your home or purchasing a new home.

BIBLE VERSES: (Proverbs)
19:27. Cease not, O my son, to hear instruction, and be not ignorant of the words of knowledge.

READ PSALMS #'s: 5, 14, 32 ,41, 50, 59, 77, 104, 122

MANTRA FOR TODAY
Om Namo Bhagawate Mukhtanandaya,
108 times
AUM KRSNAYA VIDMAHE DAMODARAYA DHIMAHI. TANNO VISHNU PRACODAYAT.
9 times

JULY 2, 2015

07/02/2015 THU		This is considered a NEGATIVE day for you							Shiva
Moving	Shopping	Health	Investing	Gambling	Love is	Wedding	Travel	Work/Job	Planet
Bad	Bad	Bad	Bad	Fair	Bad	Bad	Bad	Bad	Mars

KEYWORDS ARE: God - Karma, Police, Accidents, death, Illnese, children, hypertension, Distant, far, Legal matter, Traffic Ticket, Karmic debts

Lotto #'s	play 4 #s	play 3 #s	Ruling Angel:............	Color Sugestion:............	Ruling Deity
10,7,34,31,15,21	1933	948	Raphael	Purple/DeepBlue/Rose	Hanuman

ADVICE & DETAILS
You may have to confront today some problems at work and tension with bosses. Today there is the possibility of illness or accident at work. You must be very careful with machinery.

BIBLE VERSES: (Proverbs)
19:29. Judgments are prepared for scorners: and striking hammers for the bodies of fools.

READ PSALMS #'s: 6, 15, 33 ,42, 51, 60, 78, 105, 123

MANTRA FOR TODAY
Om Hareem Nama Swaha..Shri Maha Laxmi Aye Namah swaha
12 times
Om maha laxmi cha vidmahe vishnu pataya dhi mahi tanno laxmi pracho dayat
Om hareem namam swaha
9 times

JULY 3, 2015

| 07/03/2015 FRI | | | This is considered a NEUTRAL day for you | | | | | | Shiva |

Moving	Shopping	Health	Investing	Gambling	Love is	Wedding	Travel	Work/Job	Planet
Fair	Fair	Fair	Fair	Bad	Bad	Fair	Fair	Bad	Moon

KEYWORDS ARE: Home Alone, Enemies, Confined, independence, Worry, Travel delays, Abusive, Advice given, Commanding

Lotto #'s	play 4 #s	play 3 #s	Ruling Angel:............	Color Sugestion:............	Ruling Deity
2,9,34,32,15,23	4756	149	Zaphkiel	Light Blue/Purple/Peach	Ganga

ADVICE & DETAILS	MANTRA FOR TODAY
All duties fall on your shoulders today, you will have to do everything alone today. Do not expect any cooperation from others, there will be job pressure.	Om Ganga mataye nama swaha Om Varuna Devta aye Pahimam 11 times Om hareem mama sarva shatru janam vashee kuru kuru swaha om hareem ksham kasham kasheem kasheem swaha 9 times

BIBLE VERSES: (Proverbs)

20:2. As the roaring of a lion, so also is the dread of a king: he that provoketh him, sinneth against his own soul.

READ PSALMS #'s: 7, 16, 34 ,43, 52, 61, 79, 106, 124

JULY 4, 2015

| 07/04/2015 SAT | | | This is considered a POSITIVE day for you | | | | | | Shiva |

Moving	Shopping	Health	Investing	Gambling	Love is	Wedding	Travel	Work/Job	Planet
Good	Excellent	Good	Good	Excellent	Excellent	Excellent	Excelle	Good	Jupiter

KEYWORDS ARE: Music, Big Expense, love, marriage, Travel partner, Deception, Karmic debts, Fame - TV, Association

Lotto #'s	play 4 #s	play 3 #s	Ruling Angel:............	Color Sugestion:............	Ruling Deity
3,9,34,31,15,24	9492	2410	Haniel	Yellow/White/Silver	Mahalaxmi

ADVICE & DETAILS	MANTRA FOR TODAY
You will receive visitors at work. Meetings and gatherings will be profitable. You will receive cooperation at work and you will be likely to receive money today.	Om Namo Bhagawate Mukhtanandaya, 108 times AUM KRSNAYA VIDMAHE DAMODARAYA DHIMAHI. TANNO VISHNU PRACODAYAT. 9 times

BIBLE VERSES: (Proverbs)

20:4. Because of the cold the sluggard would not plough: he shall beg therefore in the summer, and it shall not be given him.

READ PSALMS #'s: 8, 17, 35 ,44, 53, 62, 80, 107, 125

JULY 5, 2015

| 07/05/2015 SUN | | | This is considered a POSITIVE day for you | | | | | | Shiva |

Moving	Shopping	Health	Investing	Gambling	Love is	Wedding	Travel	Work/Job	Planet
Good	Excellent	Excellent	Good	Bad	Good	Bad	Excelle	Good	Saturn

KEYWORDS ARE: Publishing, death, children, publishing, Childishness, Excercise, God - Karma, IRS - Law, Communication

Lotto #'s	play 4 #s	play 3 #s	Ruling Angel:............	Color Sugestion:............	Ruling Deity
4,1,34,31,15,9	5690	342	Mikael	Gold/Brown/Blue/Dark Green	Pitridev

ADVICE & DETAILS	MANTRA FOR TODAY
There will be a great deal of disturbances and stress with children or younger people. You must watch your speech or communication because it could turn back on you at work.	Kali Durge Namo Nama Om Durge aye nama swaha 108 times AUM TATPURUSAYA VIDMAHE VAKRATUNDAY DHIMAHI. TANNO DANTI PRACODAYAT. 9 times

BIBLE VERSES: (Proverbs)

20:6. Many men are called merciful: but who shall find a faithful man?

0

READ PSALMS #'s: 9, 18, 36 ,45, 54, 63, 81, 108, 126

JULY 6, 2015

07/06/2015 MON		This is considered a NEUTRAL day for you							Shiva
Moving	*Shopping*	*Health*	*Investing*	*Gambling*	*Love is*	*Wedding*	*Travel*	*Work/Job*	*Planet*
Bad	Bad	Bad	Bad	Fair	Fair	Fair	Bad	Bad	Sun

KEYWORDS ARE: work, independence, employment, stress, Low Pay, Illicit Affairs, IRS - Law, Boastful, Tiredness

Lotto #'s	*play 4 #s*	*play 3 #s*	Ruling Angel:............	Color Sugestion:............	*Ruling Deity*
5,3,33,32,15,10	2859	443	Gabriel	White/Yellow/ Peach	Gaitree

ADVICE & DETAILS	MANTRA FOR TODAY
You are going to feel very lazy today, but you must push through this feeling and devote your day to work with others and work diligently.	*Om hareem Kleem Hreem Aem Saraswataye namaha* *21 times* *Om Guru bramha, Guru Vishnu Guru Deva mahaeshwara guru saksha paam bramha, tasmi shri guruve nama* *9 times*

BIBLE VERSES: (Proverbs)

19:28. An unjust witness scorneth judgment: and the mouth of the wicked devoureth iniquity.

READ PSALMS #'s: 1, 10, 28 ,37, 46, 55, 73, 100, 118

JULY 7, 2015

07/07/2015 TUE		This is considered a POSITIVE day for you							Shiva
Moving	*Shopping*	*Health*	*Investing*	*Gambling*	*Love is*	*Wedding*	*Travel*	*Work/Job*	*Planet*
Excellent	Good	Excellent	Good	Good	Excellent	Good	Excelle	Good	Venus

KEYWORDS ARE: short trips, marriage, fraudulent, move, Affairs with oppoite sex, Moving, Accidents, Partnership, travel

Lotto #'s	*play 4 #s*	*play 3 #s*	Ruling Angel:............	Color Sugestion:............	*Ruling Deity*
6,4,33,32,15,12	3218	544	Raziel	Red/Yellow/Pink	Durga

ADVICE & DETAILS	MANTRA FOR TODAY
This will be a very lucky day for travel. There will be many, but very good changes at work. There may also be changes in your relationships. You will have to endure some stress over sex and love.	*Om Jai Viganeshwaraya.. Lambodaraya Namo Namaha* *21 times* *Om Sarva Mangal Mangalye, Shiva Sarvart Sadike, Sharan Tryambike Gowri, Narayane Namo asttute* *9 times*

BIBLE VERSES: (Proverbs)

20:1. Wine is a luxurious thing, and drunkenness riotous: whosoever is delighted therewith, shall not be wise.

READ PSALMS #'s: 2, 11, 29 ,38, 47, 56, 74, 101, 119

JULY 8, 2015

07/08/2015 WED		This is considered a NEGATIVE day for you							Shiva
Moving	*Shopping*	*Health*	*Investing*	*Gambling*	*Love is*	*Wedding*	*Travel*	*Work/Job*	*Planet*
Bad	Bad	Bad	Fair	Good	Bad	Good	Bad	Bad	Mercury

KEYWORDS ARE: family, publishing, quarell, disagreements , Police,courts, tickets, Beauty - Sex, Denial - Doubt, read, frustration

Lotto #'s	*play 4 #s*	*play 3 #s*	Ruling Angel:............	Color Sugestion:............	*Ruling Deity*
7,4,34,31,15,15	2079	645	Zadkiel	Green/Sky Blue/White	Saraswaty

ADVICE & DETAILS	MANTRA FOR TODAY
You will have lots of responsibilities with children today. Your duties will be largely increase at both work and with children. You will have stress with education.	*Om Graam Greem Graum Sa Gurave namah swaha* *21 times* *AUM VAGDEVYAI CA VIDMAHE KAMARAJAYA DHIMAHI. TANNO DEVI PRACODAYAT.* *9 times*

BIBLE VERSES: (Proverbs)

20:3. It is an honour for a man to separate himself from quarrels: but all fools are meddling with reproaches.

READ PSALMS #'s: 3, 12, 30 ,39, 48, 57, 75, 102, 120

JULY 9, 2015

07/09/2015 THU		This is considered a NEUTRAL day for you							Shiva
Moving	Shopping	Health	Investing	Gambling	Love is	Wedding	Travel	Work/Job	Planet
Good	Fair	Fair	Bad	Bad	Good	Good	Good	Fair	Pluto

KEYWORDS ARE: Abusive, Low Pay, Alcohol - drugs, Enemies, Spirituality & belief, Travel, Death, Low Payment, Religious

Lotto #'s	play 4 #s	play 3 #s	Ruling Angel:............	Color Sugestion:............	Ruling Deity
8,5,34,31,15,17	9734	746	Metatron	Dark Blue/ Purple/ Mauve	Ganesh

ADVICE & DETAILS
You will feel distress over your job. You need to try to relax since stress is very high and could affect your health. You may be depressed over job issues and have thoughts about leaving the job.

BIBLE VERSES: (Proverbs)
20:5. Counsel in the heart of a man is like deep water: but a wise man will draw it out.

READ PSALMS #'s: 4, 13, 31 ,40, 49, 58, 76, 103, 121

MANTRA FOR TODAY
Om Mana Swasti Shanti Kuru kuru Swaha Shivoham Shivoham
27 times
om haring jawala mukhi mam sarva shatru bakshaya bakshaya hung phat swaha
Om Nama shivaya pahimam
9 times

JULY 10, 2015

07/10/2015 FRI		This is considered a POSITIVE day for you							Shiva
Moving	Shopping	Health	Investing	Gambling	Love is	Wedding	Travel	Work/Job	Planet
Good	Good	Excellent	Excellent	Good	Good	Good	Good	Excellent	Uranus

KEYWORDS ARE: Karmic debts, Illicit Affairs, Money Wasted, Big Expense, Romantic day for love, Change, Sickness - cold, Travel delays, Power

Lotto #'s	play 4 #s	play 3 #s	Ruling Angel:............	Color Sugestion:............	Ruling Deity
9,7,34,31,15,18	10123	847	Camael	Orange/White/Light Green/ Beige	Krishna

ADVICE & DETAILS
Change of pay scale or salary for you is expected todays or perhaps a change of position; all these changes are positive. There is a possibility that you will be refinancing your home or purchasing a new home.

BIBLE VERSES: (Proverbs)
20:7. The just that walketh in his simplicity, shall leave behind him blessed children.

READ PSALMS #'s: 5, 14, 32 ,41, 50, 59, 77, 104, 122

MANTRA FOR TODAY
Jai Jai Shiva Shambo.(2)
...Mahadeva Shambo (2)
21 times
Om Jayanti Mangala Kali Bhadrakali Kapalini Durga Kshama Shiva Dhatri Swaha Swadha Namostute
9 times

JULY 11, 2015

07/11/2015 SAT		This is considered a NEGATIVE day for you							Shiva
Moving	Shopping	Health	Investing	Gambling	Love is	Wedding	Travel	Work/Job	Planet
Bad	Bad	Bad	Bad	Fair	Bad	Bad	Bad	Bad	Mars

KEYWORDS ARE: God - Karma, Police, Accidents, death, Illnese, children, hypertension, Distant, far, Legal matter, Traffic Ticket, Karmic debts

Lotto #'s	play 4 #s	play 3 #s	Ruling Angel:............	Color Sugestion:............	Ruling Deity
10,7,33,32,15,21	2673	948	Raphael	Purple/DeepBlue/Rose	Hanuman

ADVICE & DETAILS
You may have to confront today some problems at work and tension with bosses. Today there is the possibility of illness or accident at work. You must be very careful with machinery.

BIBLE VERSES: (Proverbs)
20:9. Who can say: My heart is clean, I am pure from sin?

0

READ PSALMS #'s: 6, 15, 33 ,42, 51, 60, 78, 105, 123

MANTRA FOR TODAY
Om Hareem Nama Swaha..Shri Maha Laxmi Aye Namah swaha
12 times
Om maha laxmi cha vidmahe vishnu pataya dhi mahi tanno laxmi pracho dayat
Om hareem namam swaha
9 times

JULY 12, 2015

07/12/2015 SUN		This is considered a NEUTRAL day for you							Shiva
Moving	Shopping	Health	Investing	Gambling	Love is	Wedding	Travel	Work/Job	Planet
Fair	Fair	Fair	Fair	Bad	Bad	Fair	Fair	Bad	Moon

KEYWORDS ARE: IRS - Law, Enemies, Denial - Doubt, losses, Stress with Bosses, Travel delays, Abusive, Advice given, God - Karma

Lotto #'s	play 4 #s	play 3 #s	Ruling Angel:............	Color Sugestion:............	Ruling Deity
2,8,34,32,15,23	3755	149	Zaphkiel	Light Blue/Purple/Peach	Ganga

ADVICE & DETAILS	MANTRA FOR TODAY
All duties fall on your shoulders today, you will have to do everything alone today. Do not expect any cooperation from others, there will be job pressure.	Om Ganga mataye nama swaha Om Varuna Devta aye Pahimam 11 times Om hareem mama sarva shatru janam vashee kuru kuru swaha om hareem ksham kasham kasheem kasheem swaha 9 times

BIBLE VERSES: (Proverbs)

20:11. By his inclinations a child is known, if his works be clean and right.
0

READ PSALMS #'s: 7, 16, 34 ,43, 52, 61, 79, 106, 124

JULY 13, 2015

07/13/2015 MON		This is considered a POSITIVE day for you							Shiva
Moving	Shopping	Health	Investing	Gambling	Love is	Wedding	Travel	Work/Job	Planet
Good	Excellent	Good	Good	Excellent	Excellent	Excellent	Excelle	Good	Jupiter

KEYWORDS ARE: Music, Big Expense, love, marriage, Travel partner, Deception, Karmic debts, Fame - TV, Association

Lotto #'s	play 4 #s	play 3 #s	Ruling Angel:............	Color Sugestion:............	Ruling Deity
3,9,34,32,15,25	9321	2410	Haniel	Yellow/White/Silver	Mahalaxmi

ADVICE & DETAILS	MANTRA FOR TODAY
You will receive visitors at work. Meetings and gatherings will be profitable. You will receive cooperation at work and you will be likely to receive money today.	Om Namo Bhagawate Mukhtanandaya, 108 times AUM KRSNAYA VIDMAHE DAMODARAYA DHIMAHI. TANNO VISHNU PRACODAYAT. 9 times

BIBLE VERSES: (Proverbs)

20:13. Love not sleep, lest poverty oppress thee: open thy eyes, and be filled with bread.

READ PSALMS #'s: 8, 17, 35 ,44, 53, 62, 80, 107, 125

JULY 14, 2015

07/14/2015 TUE		This is considered a POSITIVE day for you							Shiva
Moving	Shopping	Health	Investing	Gambling	Love is	Wedding	Travel	Work/Job	Planet
Good	Excellent	Excellent	Good	Bad	Good	Bad	Excelle	Good	Saturn

KEYWORDS ARE: Publishing, death, children, publishing, Childishness, Excercise, God - Karma, IRS - Law, Communication

Lotto #'s	play 4 #s	play 3 #s	Ruling Angel:............	Color Sugestion:............	Ruling Deity
4,1,34,32,15,9	9538	342	Mikael	Gold/Brown/Blue/Dark Green	Pitridev

ADVICE & DETAILS	MANTRA FOR TODAY
There will be a great deal of disturbances and stress with children or younger people. You must watch your speech or communication because it could turn back on you at work.	Kali Durge Namo Nama Om Durge aye nama swaha 108 times AUM TATPURUSAYA VIDMAHE VAKRATUNDAY DHIMAHI. TANNO DANTI PRACODAYAT. 9 times

BIBLE VERSES: (Proverbs)

20:15. There is gold and a multitude of jewels: but the lips of knowledge are a precious vessel.

READ PSALMS #'s: 9, 18, 36 ,45, 54, 63, 81, 108, 126

JULY 15, 2015

07/15/2015 WED		This is considered a NEUTRAL day for you							Shiva
Moving	Shopping	Health	Investing	Gambling	Love is	Wedding	Travel	Work/Job	Planet
Bad	Bad	Bad	Bad	Fair	Fair	Fair	Bad	Bad	Sun

KEYWORDS ARE: work, independence, employment, stress, Low Pay, Illicit Affairs, IRS - Law, Boastful, Tiredness

Lotto #'s	play 4 #s	play 3 #s	Ruling Angel:............	Color Sugestion:............	Ruling Deity
5,3,34,31,15,10	8029	443	Gabriel	White/Yellow/ Peach	Gaitree

ADVICE & DETAILS

You are going to feel very lazy today, but you must push through this feeling and devote your day to work with others and work diligently.

BIBLE VERSES: (Proverbs)

20:8. The king, that sitteth on the throne of judgment, scattereth away all evil with his look.

READ PSALMS #'s: 1, 10, 28 ,37, 46, 55, 73, 100, 118

MANTRA FOR TODAY

Om hareem Kleem Hreem Aem Saraswataye namaha
21 times
Om Guru bramha, Guru Vishnu Guru Deva mahaeshwara guru saksha paam bramha, tasmi shri guruve nama
9 times

JULY 16, 2015

07/16/2015 THU		This is considered a POSITIVE day for you							Shiva
Moving	Shopping	Health	Investing	Gambling	Love is	Wedding	Travel	Work/Job	Planet
Excellent	Good	Excellent	Good	Good	Excellent	Good	Excelle	Good	Venus

KEYWORDS ARE: short trips, marriage, fraudulent, move, Affairs with oppoite sex, Moving, Accidents, Partnership, travel

Lotto #'s	play 4 #s	play 3 #s	Ruling Angel:............	Color Sugestion:............	Ruling Deity
6,4,34,31,15,13	6413	544	Raziel	Red/Yellow/Pink	Durga

ADVICE & DETAILS

This will be a very lucky day for travel. There will be many, but very good changes at work. There may also be changes in your relationships. You will have to endure some stress over sex and love.

BIBLE VERSES: (Proverbs)

20:10. Diverse weights and diverse measures, both are abominable before God.

READ PSALMS #'s: 2, 11, 29 ,38, 47, 56, 74, 101, 119

MANTRA FOR TODAY

Om Jai Viganeshwaraya..
Lambodaraya Namo Namaha
21 times
Om Sarva Mangal Mangalye, Shiva Sarvart Sadike, Sharan Tryambike Gowri, Narayane Namo asttute
9 times

JULY 17, 2015

07/17/2015 FRI		This is considered a NEGATIVE day for you							Shiva
Moving	Shopping	Health	Investing	Gambling	Love is	Wedding	Travel	Work/Job	Planet
Bad	Bad	Bad	Fair	Good	Bad	Good	Bad	Bad	Mercury

KEYWORDS ARE: family, publishing, quarell, disagreements , Police,courts, tickets, Beauty - Sex, Denial - Doubt, read, frustration

Lotto #'s	play 4 #s	play 3 #s	Ruling Angel:............	Color Sugestion:............	Ruling Deity
7,5,33,32,15,15	3908	645	Zadkiel	Green/Sky Blue/White	Saraswaty

ADVICE & DETAILS

You will have lots of responsibilities with children today. Your duties will be largely increase at both work and with children. You will have stress with education.

BIBLE VERSES: (Proverbs)

20:12. The hearing ear, and the seeing eye, the Lord hath made them both.

READ PSALMS #'s: 3, 12, 30 ,39, 48, 57, 75, 102, 120

MANTRA FOR TODAY

Om Graam Greem Graum Sa Gurave namah swaha
21 times
AUM VAGDEVYAI CA VIDMAHE KAMARAJAYA DHIMAHI. TANNO DEVI PRACODAYAT.
9 times

JULY 18, 2015

07/18/2015 SAT		This is considered a NEUTRAL day for you							Shiva
Moving	*Shopping*	*Health*	*Investing*	*Gambling*	*Love is*	*Wedding*	*Travel*	*Work/Job*	*Planet*
Good	Fair	Fair	Bad	Bad	Good	Good	Good	Fair	Pluto

KEYWORDS ARE: Abusive, Low Pay, Alcohol - drugs, Enemies, Spirituality & belief, Travel, Death, Low Payment, Religious

Lotto #'s	*play 4 #s*	*play 3 #s*	Ruling Angel:............	Color Sugestion:............	*Ruling Deity*
8,5,34,32,15,17	3990	746	Metatron	Dark Blue/ Purple/ Mauve	Ganesh

ADVICE & DETAILS	MANTRA FOR TODAY
You will feel distress over your job. You need to try to relax since stress is very high and could affect your health. You may be depressed over job issues and have thoughts about leaving the job.	*Om Mana Swasti Shanti Kuru kuru Swaha Shivoham Shivoham 27 times om haring jawala mukhi mam sarva shatru bakshaya bakshaya hung phat swaha Om Nama shivaya pahimam 9 times*

BIBLE VERSES: (Proverbs)

20:14. It is naught, it is naught, saith every buyer: and when he is gone away, then he will boast.

READ PSALMS #'s: 4, 13, 31 ,40, 49, 58, 76, 103, 121

JULY 19, 2015

07/19/2015 SUN		This is considered a POSITIVE day for you							Shiva
Moving	*Shopping*	*Health*	*Investing*	*Gambling*	*Love is*	*Wedding*	*Travel*	*Work/Job*	*Planet*
Good	Good	Excellent	Excellent	Good	Good	Good	Good	Excellent	Uranus

KEYWORDS ARE: Karmic debts, Illicit Affairs, Money Wasted, Big Expense, Romantic day for love, Change, Sickness - cold, Travel delays, Power

Lotto #'s	*play 4 #s*	*play 3 #s*	Ruling Angel:............	Color Sugestion:............	*Ruling Deity*
9,7,33,31,15,18	8666	847	Camael	Orange/White/Light Green/ Beige	Krishna

ADVICE & DETAILS	MANTRA FOR TODAY
Change of pay scale or salary for you is expected todays or perhaps a change of position; all these changes are positive. There is a possibility that you will be refinancing your home or purchasing a new home.	*Jai Jai Shiva Shambo.(2) ...Mahadeva Shambo (2) 21 times Om Jayanti Mangala Kali Bhadrakali Kapalini Durga Kshama Shiva Dhatri Swaha Swadha Namostute 9 times*

BIBLE VERSES: (Proverbs)

20:16. Take away the garment of him that is surety for a stranger, and take a pledge from him for strangers.

READ PSALMS #'s: 5, 14, 32 ,41, 50, 59, 77, 104, 122

JULY 20, 2015

07/20/2015 MON		This is considered a NEGATIVE day for you							Shiva
Moving	*Shopping*	*Health*	*Investing*	*Gambling*	*Love is*	*Wedding*	*Travel*	*Work/Job*	*Planet*
Bad	Bad	Bad	Bad	Fair	Bad	Bad	Bad	Bad	Mars

KEYWORDS ARE: God - Karma, Police, Accidents, death, Illnese, children, hypertension, Distant, far, Legal matter, Traffic Ticket, Karmic debts

Lotto #'s	*play 4 #s*	*play 3 #s*	Ruling Angel:............	Color Sugestion:............	*Ruling Deity*
10,7,33,32,15,21	2387	948	Raphael	Purple/DeepBlue/Rose	Hanuman

ADVICE & DETAILS	MANTRA FOR TODAY
You may have to confront today some problems at work and tension with bosses. Today there is the possibility of illness or accident at work. You must be very careful with machinery.	*Om Hareem Nama Swaha..Shri Maha Laxmi Aye Namah swaha 12 times Om maha laxmi cha vidmahe vishnu pataya dhi mahi tanno laxmi pracho dayat Om hareem namam swaha 9 times*

BIBLE VERSES: (Proverbs)

20:18. Designs are strengthened by counsels: and wars are to be managed by governments.

READ PSALMS #'s: 6, 15, 33 ,42, 51, 60, 78, 105, 123

JULY 21, 2015

07/21/2015	TUE		This is considered a NEUTRAL day for you						Shiva
Moving	Shopping	Health	Investing	Gambling	Love is	Wedding	Travel	Work/Job	Planet
Fair	Fair	Fair	Fair	Bad	Bad	Fair	Fair	Bad	Moon

KEYWORDS ARE: IRS - Law, Enemies, Denial - Doubt, losses, Stress with Bosses, Travel delays, Abusive, Advice given, God - Karma

Lotto #'s	play 4 #s	play 3 #s	Ruling Angel:............	Color Sugestion:............	Ruling Deity
2,8,34,31,15,23	5348	149	Zaphkiel	Light Blue/Purple/Peach	Ganga

ADVICE & DETAILS	MANTRA FOR TODAY
All duties fall on your shoulders today, you will have to do everything alone today. Do not expect any cooperation from others, there will be job pressure.	Om Ganga mataye nama swaha
Om Varuna Devta aye Pahimam
11 times
Om hareem mama sarva shatru janam vashee kuru kuru swaha
om hareem ksham kasham kaseem kasheem swaha
9 times

BIBLE VERSES: (Proverbs)

20:20. He that curseth his father, and mother, his lamp shall be put out in the midst of darkness.

READ PSALMS #'s: 7, 16, 34 ,43, 52, 61, 79, 106, 124

JULY 22, 2015

07/22/2015	WED		This is considered a POSITIVE day for you						Shiva
Moving	Shopping	Health	Investing	Gambling	Love is	Wedding	Travel	Work/Job	Planet
Good	Excellent	Good	Good	Excellent	Excellent	Excellent	Excelle	Good	Jupiter

KEYWORDS ARE: Accidents, Big Expense, death, finish, Traffic problems, Tickets, Deception, Karmic debts, Fame - TV, IRS - Law

Lotto #'s	play 4 #s	play 3 #s	Ruling Angel:............	Color Sugestion:............	Ruling Deity
3,10,34,32,15,25	2751	2410	Haniel	Yellow/White/Silver	Mahalaxmi

ADVICE & DETAILS	MANTRA FOR TODAY
You will receive visitors at work. Meetings and gatherings will be profitable. You will receive cooperation at work and you will be likely to receive money today.	Om Namo Bhagawate Mukhtanandaya,
108 times
AUM KRSNAYA VIDMAHE DAMODARAYA DHIMAHI. TANNO VISHNU PRACODAYAT.
9 times

BIBLE VERSES: (Proverbs)

20:22. Say not: I will return evil: wait for the Lord, and he will deliver thee.
0

READ PSALMS #'s: 8, 17, 35 ,44, 53, 62, 80, 107, 125

JULY 23, 2015

07/23/2015	THU		This is considered a POSITIVE day for you						Shiva
Moving	Shopping	Health	Investing	Gambling	Love is	Wedding	Travel	Work/Job	Planet
Good	Excellent	Excellent	Good	Bad	Good	Bad	Excelle	Good	Saturn

KEYWORDS ARE: Publishing, death, children, publishing, Childishness, Excercise, God - Karma, IRS - Law, Communication

Lotto #'s	play 4 #s	play 3 #s	Ruling Angel:............	Color Sugestion:............	Ruling Deity
4,2,33,31,15,8	4692	342	Mikael	Gold/Brown/Blue/Dark Green	Pitridev

ADVICE & DETAILS	MANTRA FOR TODAY
There will be a great deal of disturbances and stress with children or younger people. You must watch your speech or communication because it could turn back on you at work.	Kali Durge Namo Nama
Om Durge aye nama swaha
108 times
AUM TATPURUSAYA VIDMAHE VAKRATUNDAY DHIMAHI. TANNO DANTI PRACODAYAT.
9 times

BIBLE VERSES: (Proverbs)

20:24. The steps of men are guided by the Lord: but who is the man that can understand his own way?

READ PSALMS #'s: 9, 18, 36 ,45, 54, 63, 81, 108, 126

JULY 24, 2015

07/24/2015 FRI			This is considered a NEUTRAL day for you						Shiva
Moving	Shopping	Health	Investing	Gambling	Love is	Wedding	Travel	Work/Job	Planet
Bad	Bad	Bad	Bad	Fair	Fair	Fair	Bad	Bad	Sun

KEYWORDS ARE: work, independence, employment, stress, Low Pay, Illicit Affairs, IRS - Law, Boastful, Tiredness

Lotto #'s	play 4 #s	play 3 #s	Ruling Angel:............	Color Sugestion:............	Ruling Deity
5,2,34,31,15,10	9060	443	Gabriel	White/Yellow/ Peach	Gaitree

ADVICE & DETAILS	MANTRA FOR TODAY
You are going to feel very lazy today, but you must push through this feeling and devote your day to work with others and work diligently.	Om hareem Kleem Hreem Aem Saraswataye namaha 21 times Om Guru bramha, Guru Vishnu Guru Deva mahaeshwara guru saksha paam bramha, tasmi shri guruve nama 9 times

BIBLE VERSES: (Proverbs)
20:17. The bread of lying is sweet to a man: but afterwards his mouth shall be filled with gravel.

READ PSALMS #'s: 1, 10, 28 ,37, 46, 55, 73, 100, 118

JULY 25, 2015

07/25/2015 SAT			This is considered a POSITIVE day for you						Shiva
Moving	Shopping	Health	Investing	Gambling	Love is	Wedding	Travel	Work/Job	Planet
Excellent	Good	Excellent	Good	Good	Excellent	Good	Excelle	Good	Venus

KEYWORDS ARE: short trips, marriage, fraudulent, move, Affairs with oppoite sex, Moving, Accidents, Partnership, travel

Lotto #'s	play 4 #s	play 3 #s	Ruling Angel:............	Color Sugestion:............	Ruling Deity
6,3,33,31,15,12	2463	544	Raziel	Red/Yellow/Pink	Durga

ADVICE & DETAILS	MANTRA FOR TODAY
This will be a very lucky day for travel. There will be many, but very good changes at work. There may also be changes in your relationships. You will have to endure some stress over sex and love.	Om Jai Viganeshwaraya.. Lambodaraya Namo Namaha 21 times Om Sarva Mangal Mangalye, Shiva Sarvart Sadike, Sharan Tryambike Gowri, Narayane Namo asttute 9 times

BIBLE VERSES: (Proverbs)
20:19. Meddle not with him that revealeth secrets, and walketh deceitfully, and openeth wide his lips.

READ PSALMS #'s: 2, 11, 29 ,38, 47, 56, 74, 101, 119

JULY 26, 2015

07/26/2015 SUN			This is considered a NEGATIVE day for you						Shiva
Moving	Shopping	Health	Investing	Gambling	Love is	Wedding	Travel	Work/Job	Planet
Bad	Bad	Bad	Fair	Good	Bad	Good	Bad	Bad	Mercury

KEYWORDS ARE: family, publishing, quarell, disagreements , Police,courts, tickets, Beauty - Sex, Denial - Doubt, read, frustration

Lotto #'s	play 4 #s	play 3 #s	Ruling Angel:............	Color Sugestion:............	Ruling Deity
7,4,33,32,15,15	3595	645	Zadkiel	Green/Sky Blue/White	Saraswaty

ADVICE & DETAILS	MANTRA FOR TODAY
You will have lots of responsibilities with children today. Your duties will be largely increase at both work and with children. You will have stress with education.	Om Graam Greem Graum Sa Gurave namah swaha 21 times AUM VAGDEVYAI CA VIDMAHE KAMARAJAYA DHIMAHI. TANNO DEVI PRACODAYAT. 9 times

BIBLE VERSES: (Proverbs)
20:21. The inheritance gotten hastily in the beginning, in the end shall be without a blessing.

READ PSALMS #'s: 3, 12, 30 ,39, 48, 57, 75, 102, 120

JULY 27, 2015

| 07/27/2015 MON | This is considered a NEUTRAL day for you | | | | | | | Shiva |

Moving	Shopping	Health	Investing	Gambling	Love is	Wedding	Travel	Work/Job	Planet
Good	Fair	Fair	Bad	Bad	Good	Good	Good	Fair	Pluto

KEYWORDS ARE: Abusive, Low Pay, Alcohol - drugs, Enemies, Spirituality & belief, Travel, Death, Low Payment, Religious

Lotto #'s	play 4 #s	play 3 #s	Ruling Angel:............	Color Sugestion:............	Ruling Deity
8,6,33,32,15,16	7531	746	Metatron	Dark Blue/ Purple/ Mauve	Ganesh

ADVICE & DETAILS

You will feel distress over your job. You need to try to relax since stress is very high and could affect your health. You may be depressed over job issues and have thoughts about leaving the job.

MANTRA FOR TODAY

Om Mana Swasti Shanti Kuru kuru Swaha Shivoham Shivoham 27 times
om haring jawala mukhi mam sarva shatru bakshaya bakshaya hung phat swaha
Om Nama shivaya pahimam 9 times

BIBLE VERSES: (Proverbs)

20:23. Diverse weights are an abomination before the Lord: a deceitful balance is not good.

READ PSALMS #'s: 4, 13, 31 ,40, 49, 58, 76, 103, 121

JULY 28, 2015

| 07/28/2015 TUE | This is considered a POSITIVE day for you | | | | | | | Shiva |

Moving	Shopping	Health	Investing	Gambling	Love is	Wedding	Travel	Work/Job	Planet
Good	Good	Excellent	Excellent	Good	Good	Good	Good	Excellent	Uranus

KEYWORDS ARE: Karmic debts, Illicit Affairs, Money Wasted, Big Expense, Romantic day for love, Change, Sickness - cold, Travel delays, Power

Lotto #'s	play 4 #s	play 3 #s	Ruling Angel:............	Color Sugestion:............	Ruling Deity
9,7,33,32,15,19	1997	847	Camael	Orange/White/Light Green/ Beige	Krishna

ADVICE & DETAILS

Change of pay scale or salary for you is expected todays or perhaps a change of position; all these changes are positive. There is a possibility that you will be refinancing your home or purchasing a new home.

MANTRA FOR TODAY

Jai Jai Shiva Shambo.(2)
...Mahadeva Shambo (2)
21 times
Om Jayanti Mangala Kali Bhadrakali Kapalini Durga Kshama Shiva Dhatri Swaha Swadha Namostute
9 times

BIBLE VERSES: (Proverbs)

20:25. It is ruin to a man to devour holy ones, and after vows to retract.
0

READ PSALMS #'s: 5, 14, 32 ,41, 50, 59, 77, 104, 122

JULY 29, 2015

| 07/29/2015 WED | This is considered a NEGATIVE day for you | | | | | | | Shiva |

Moving	Shopping	Health	Investing	Gambling	Love is	Wedding	Travel	Work/Job	Planet
Bad	Bad	Bad	Bad	Fair	Bad	Bad	Bad	Bad	Mars

KEYWORDS ARE: God - Karma, Police, Accidents, death, Illnese, children, hypertension, Distant, far, Legal matter, Traffic Ticket, Karmic debts

Lotto #'s	play 4 #s	play 3 #s	Ruling Angel:............	Color Sugestion:............	Ruling Deity
10,7,34,31,15,21	10893	948	Raphael	Purple/DeepBlue/Rose	Hanuman

ADVICE & DETAILS

You may have to confront today some problems at work and tension with bosses. Today there is the possibility of illness or accident at work. You must be very careful with machinery.

MANTRA FOR TODAY

Om Hareem Nama Swaha..Shri Maha Laxmi Aye Namah swaha 12 times
Om maha laxmi cha vidmahe vishnu pataya dhi mahi tanno laxmi pracho dayat
Om hareem namam swaha 9 times

BIBLE VERSES: (Proverbs)

20:27. The spirit of a man is the lamp of the Lord, which searcheth all the hidden things of the bowels.

READ PSALMS #'s: 6, 15, 33 ,42, 51, 60, 78, 105, 123

JULY 30, 2015

07/30/2015 THU			This is considered a NEUTRAL day for you						Shiva

Moving	Shopping	Health	Investing	Gambling	Love is	Wedding	Travel	Work/Job	Planet
Fair	Fair	Fair	Fair	Bad	Bad	Fair	Fair	Bad	Moon

KEYWORDS ARE: IRS - Law, Enemies, Denial - Doubt, losses, Stress with Bosses, Travel delays, Abusive, Advice given, God - Karma

Lotto #'s	play 4 #s	play 3 #s	Ruling Angel:............	Color Sugestion:............	Ruling Deity
2,8,33,32,15,22	1385	149	Zaphkiel	Light Blue/Purple/Peach	Ganga

ADVICE & DETAILS	MANTRA FOR TODAY
All duties fall on your shoulders today, you will have to do everything alone today. Do not expect any cooperation from others, there will be job pressure.	*Om Ganga mataye nama swaha Om Varuna Devta aye Pahimam 11 times Om hareem mama sarva shatru janam vashee kuru kuru swaha om hareem ksham kasham kasheem kasheem swaha 9 times*

BIBLE VERSES: (Proverbs)

20:29. The joy of young men is their strength: and the dignity of old men, their grey hairs.

READ PSALMS #'s: 7, 16, 34 ,43, 52, 61, 79, 106, 124

JULY 31, 2015

07/31/2015 FRI			This is considered a POSITIVE day for you						Shiva

Moving	Shopping	Health	Investing	Gambling	Love is	Wedding	Travel	Work/Job	Planet
Good	Excellent	Good	Good	Excellent	Excellent	Excellent	Excelle	Good	Jupiter

KEYWORDS ARE: Accidents, Big Expense, death, finish, Traffic problems, Tickets, Deception, Karmic debts, Fame - TV, IRS - Law

Lotto #'s	play 4 #s	play 3 #s	Ruling Angel:............	Color Sugestion:............	Ruling Deity
3,10,34,32,15,25	5198	2410	Haniel	Yellow/White/Silver	Mahalaxmi

ADVICE & DETAILS	MANTRA FOR TODAY
You will receive visitors at work. Meetings and gatherings will be profitable. You will receive cooperation at work and you will be likely to receive money today.	*Om Namo Bhagawate Mukhtanandaya, 108 times AUM KRSNAYA VIDMAHE DAMODARAYA DHIMAHI. TANNO VISHNU PRACODAYAT. 9 times*

BIBLE VERSES: (Proverbs)

21:1. As the divisions of waters, so the heart of the king is in the hand of the Lord: whithersoever he will, he shall turn it.

READ PSALMS #'s: 8, 17, 35 ,44, 53, 62, 80, 107, 125

AUGUST 1, 2015

08/01/2015 SAT			This is considered a POSITIVE day for you						Shiva

Moving	Shopping	Health	Investing	Gambling	Love is	Wedding	Travel	Work/Job	Planet
Good	Good	Excellent	Excellent	Fair	Good	Bad	Good	Excellent	Mars

KEYWORDS ARE: Denial - Doubt, responsibility, investment, luxury, Loans and Mortgages, Quarrels, God - Karma, Police, High Pleasure

Lotto #'s	play 4 #s	play 3 #s	Ruling Angel:............	Color Sugestion:............	Ruling Deity
9,8,34,31,16,20	2683	857	Raphael	Purple/DeepBlue/Rose	Hanuman

ADVICE & DETAILS	MANTRA FOR TODAY
You will have to deal with bills and creditors harrassing you today. You will feel extremely frustrated over expenses. You need to try and solve your money problems.	*Kali Durge Namo Nama Om Durge aye nama swaha 108 times AUM TATPURUSAYA VIDMAHE VAKRATUNDAY DHIMAHI. TANNO DANTI PRACODAYAT. 9 times*

BIBLE VERSES: (Proverbs)

20:30. The blueness of a wound shall wipe away evils: and stripes in the more inward parts of the belly.

READ PSALMS #'s: 6, 15, 33 ,42, 51, 60, 78, 105, 123

AUGUST 2, 2015

08/02/2015 SUN	This is considered a NEGATIVE day for you								Shiva

Moving	Shopping	Health	Investing	Gambling	Love is	Wedding	Travel	Work/Job	Planet
Bad	Bad	Bad	Bad	Bad	Bad	Fair	Bad	Bad	Moon

KEYWORDS ARE: death, sleepiness, finish, fame,
Tiredness, Low Energy, Sleepy, Jealousy, IRS - Law, Enemies, Denial - Doubt

Lotto #'s	play 4 #s	play 3 #s	Ruling Angel:............	Color Sugestion:............	Ruling Deity
10,8,33,32,16,22	3466	958	Zaphkiel	Light Blue/Purple/Peach	Ganga

ADVICE & DETAILS	MANTRA FOR TODAY
There will be disturbances and tensions in travel plans. You will hear bad news that come from far away. You should drink a lot of water because you could be dehydrated easily. You should visit the beach today.	Om Hareem Nama Swaha..Shri Maha Laxmi Aye Namah swaha 12 times Om maha laxmi cha vidmahe vishnu pataya dhi mahi tanno laxmi pracho dayat Om hareem namam swaha 9 times

BIBLE VERSES: (Proverbs)
21:2. Every way of a man seemeth right to himself: but the Lord weigheth the hearts.
READ PSALMS #'s: 7, 16, 34 ,43, 52, 61, 79, 106, 124

AUGUST 3, 2015

08/03/2015 MON	This is considered a NEUTRAL day for you								Shiva

Moving	Shopping	Health	Investing	Gambling	Love is	Wedding	Travel	Work/Job	Planet
Fair	Fair	Fair	Fair	Excellent	Bad	Excellent	Fair	Bad	Jupiter

KEYWORDS ARE: independence, profits, individuality, unique,
Commanding, Police, Accidents, Big Expense, lonliness

Lotto #'s	play 4 #s	play 3 #s	Ruling Angel:............	Color Sugestion:............	Ruling Deity
2,9,34,31,16,23	3374	159	Haniel	Yellow/White/Silver	Mahalaxmi

ADVICE & DETAILS	MANTRA FOR TODAY
Today is a positive day to spend with others. You will be surrounded by partners, friends, associates and teachers. The exchange is beneficial, even if it is not what you expect.	Om Ganga mataye nama swaha Om Varuna Devta aye Pahimam 11 times Om hareem mama sarva shatru janam vashee kuru kuru swaha om hareem ksham kasham kasheem kasheem swaha 9 times

BIBLE VERSES: (Proverbs)
21:4. Haughtiness of the eyes is the enlarging of the heart: the lamp of the wicked is sin.
READ PSALMS #'s: 8, 17, 35 ,44, 53, 62, 80, 107, 125

AUGUST 4, 2015

08/04/2015 TUE	This is considered a POSITIVE day for you								Shiva

Moving	Shopping	Health	Investing	Gambling	Love is	Wedding	Travel	Work/Job	Planet
Good	Excellent	Good	Good	Bad	Excellent	Bad	Excelle	Good	Saturn

KEYWORDS ARE: marriage, sadness, Talkative, food,
Love quarrels, Government, Denial - Doubt, death, romamce

Lotto #'s	play 4 #s	play 3 #s	Ruling Angel:............	Color Sugestion:............	Ruling Deity
3,1,33,32,16,16	2255	2510	Mikael	Gold/Brown/Blue/Dark Green	Pitridev

ADVICE & DETAILS	MANTRA FOR TODAY
The influences of today are about losses and doubts. Encounters with government agencies or representatives may not be beneficial. You will feel like denying the actions that have brought you to this place, but if you do so you will not be able to learn the lesson and you may have to do it again. Music today will have a soothing and relaxing effect.	Om Namo Bhagawate Mukhtanandaya, 108 times AUM KRSNAYA VIDMAHE DAMODARAYA DHIMAHI. TANNO VISHNU PRACODAYAT. 9 times

BIBLE VERSES: (Proverbs)
21:6. He that gathereth treasures by a lying tongue, is vain and foolish, and shall stumble upon the snares of death.
READ PSALMS #'s: 9, 18, 36 ,45, 54, 63, 81, 108, 126

AUGUST 5, 2015

08/05/2015 WED				This is considered a POSITIVE day for you					Shiva

Moving	Shopping	Health	Investing	Gambling	Love is	Wedding	Travel	Work/Job	Planet
Good	Excellent	Excellent	Good	Fair	Good	Fair	Excelle	Good	Sun

KEYWORDS ARE: Childishness, On Your Own, Teacher, Communication, Feeling playful, Disagreement, Death, Worry, Social Functions

Lotto #'s	play 4 #s	play 3 #s	Ruling Angel:............	Color Sugestion:............	Ruling Deity
4,3,34,31,16,9	5221	352	Gabriel	White/Yellow/ Peach	Gaitree

ADVICE & DETAILS	MANTRA FOR TODAY
Children will need attention from you today. You are advised to spend time with them. You should also take a short trip and if possible go to the movies. Shop for bargains today, you will find them!	*Kali Durge Namo Nama* *Om Durge aye nama swaha* *108 times* *AUM TATPURUSAYA VIDMAHE VAKRATUNDAY DHIMAHI. TANNO DANTI PRACODAYAT.* *9 times*

BIBLE VERSES: (Proverbs)

20:29. The joy of young men is their strength: and the dignity of old men, their grey hairs.

READ PSALMS #'s: 1, 10, 28 ,37, 46, 55, 73, 100, 118

AUGUST 6, 2015

08/06/2015 THU				This is considered a NEUTRAL day for you					Shiva

Moving	Shopping	Health	Investing	Gambling	Love is	Wedding	Travel	Work/Job	Planet
Bad	Bad	Bad	Bad	Good	Fair	Good	Bad	Bad	Venus

KEYWORDS ARE: Low Pay, Affection, Real Estate, Tiredness, Job enjoyment, Family, Sickness - cold, Food, Drinks, High Temper

Lotto #'s	play 4 #s	play 3 #s	Ruling Angel:............	Color Sugestion:............	Ruling Deity
5,3,33,32,16,12	5229	453	Raziel	Red/Yellow/Pink	Durga

ADVICE & DETAILS	MANTRA FOR TODAY
You will be stressed out over relationships or partnerships. You may be involved in short travels. You should avoid all types of alcohol, drugs or smoking today.	*Om hareem Kleem Hreem Aem Saraswataye namaha* *21 times* *Om Guru bramha, Guru Vishnu Guru Deva mahaeshwara guru saksha paam bramha, tasmi shri guruve nama* *9 times*

BIBLE VERSES: (Proverbs)

21:1. As the divisions of waters, so the heart of the king is in the hand of the Lord: whithersoever he will, he shall turn it.

READ PSALMS #'s: 2, 11, 29 ,38, 47, 56, 74, 101, 119

AUGUST 7, 2015

08/07/2015 FRI				This is considered a POSITIVE day for you					Shiva

Moving	Shopping	Health	Investing	Gambling	Love is	Wedding	Travel	Work/Job	Planet
Excellent	Good	Excellent	Good	Good	Excellent	Good	Excelle	Good	Mercury

KEYWORDS ARE: Illicit Affairs, Expression, Beauty - Sex, travel, Comfort & Jokes, Back Pain, Legal matter, Childishness, Excercise

Lotto #'s	play 4 #s	play 3 #s	Ruling Angel:............	Color Sugestion:............	Ruling Deity
6,4,33,31,16,13	4113	554	Zadkiel	Green/Sky Blue/White	Saraswaty

ADVICE & DETAILS	MANTRA FOR TODAY
This is an excellent day to make a trip to any vacation location or to do any type of air travel. The energy today will be very high. You will be able to get everything you want to get accomplished today.	*Om Jai Viganeshwaraya..* *Lambodaraya Namo Namaha* *21 times* *Om Sarva Mangal Mangalye, Shiva Sarvart Sadike, Sharan Tryambike Gowri, Narayane Namo asttute* *9 times*

BIBLE VERSES: (Proverbs)

21:3. To do mercy and judgment, pleaseth the Lord more than victims.

0

READ PSALMS #'s: 3, 12, 30 ,39, 48, 57, 75, 102, 120

AUGUST 8, 2015

08/08/2015 SAT		This is considered a NEGATIVE day for you							Shiva
Moving	Shopping	Health	Investing	Gambling	Love is	Wedding	Travel	Work/Job	Planet
Bad	Bad	Bad	Fair	Bad	Bad	Good	Bad	Bad	Pluto

KEYWORDS ARE: Police, Industrial, Anger - Ego, frustration, Back Pain and job stress, Family Conflicts, Abusive, Low Pay, Jealousy

Lotto #'s	play 4 #s	play 3 #s	Ruling Angel:............	Color Sugestion:............	Ruling Deity
7,6,33,32,16,16	5218	655	Metatron	Dark Blue/ Purple/ Mauve	Ganesh

ADVICE & DETAILS	MANTRA FOR TODAY
There is a great deal of frustration with coworkers. You will disagree with coworkers and bosses at your job. You may also be frustrated with your sexual or romantic advances today, wait for a better day.	*Om Graam Greem Graum Sa Gurave namah swaha* *21 times* *AUM VAGDEVYAI CA VIDMAHE KAMARAJAYA DHIMAHI. TANNO DEVI PRACODAYAT.* *9 times*

BIBLE VERSES: (Proverbs)
21:5. The thoughts of the industrious always bring forth abundance: but every sluggard is always in want.

READ PSALMS #'s: 4, 13, 31 ,40, 49, 58, 76, 103, 121

AUGUST 9, 2015

08/09/2015 SUN		This is considered a NEUTRAL day for you							Shiva
Moving	Shopping	Health	Investing	Gambling	Love is	Wedding	Travel	Work/Job	Planet
Good	Fair	Fair	Bad	Good	Good	Good	Good	Fair	Uranus

KEYWORDS ARE: Accidents, Short Trips, spiritual, religion, Religious miracle, Traffic Ticket, Karmic debts, Illicit Affairs, Slow Day

Lotto #'s	play 4 #s	play 3 #s	Ruling Angel:............	Color Sugestion:............	Ruling Deity
8,7,34,32,16,18	9374	756	Camael	Orange/White/Light Green/ Beige	Krishna

ADVICE & DETAILS	MANTRA FOR TODAY
It is important to follow God-like ways in order to receive protection from deceitful people that may want to take advantage of you today. Today you should expect short trips or some movement of some sort either places, people or things.	*Om Mana Swasti Shanti Kuru kuru Swaha Shivoham Shivoham* *27 times* *om haring jawala mukhi mam sarva shatru bakshaya bakshaya hung phat swaha* *Om Nama shivaya pahimam* *9 times*

BIBLE VERSES: (Proverbs)
21:7. The robberies of the wicked shall be their downfall, because they would not do judgment.

READ PSALMS #'s: 5, 14, 32 ,41, 50, 59, 77, 104, 122

AUGUST 10, 2015

08/10/2015 MON		This is considered a POSITIVE day for you							Shiva
Moving	Shopping	Health	Investing	Gambling	Love is	Wedding	Travel	Work/Job	Planet
Good	Good	Excellent	Excellent	Fair	Good	Bad	Good	Excellent	Mars

KEYWORDS ARE: Denial - Doubt, responsibility, investment, luxury, Loans and Mortgages, Quarrels, God - Karma, Police, High Pleasure

Lotto #'s	play 4 #s	play 3 #s	Ruling Angel:............	Color Sugestion:............	Ruling Deity
9,7,34,32,16,20	9829	857	Raphael	Purple/DeepBlue/Rose	Hanuman

ADVICE & DETAILS	MANTRA FOR TODAY
You will have to deal with bills and creditors harrassing you today. You will feel extremely frustrated over expenses. You need to try and solve your money problems.	*Jai Jai Shiva Shambo.(2)* *...Mahadeva Shambo (2)* *21 times* *Om Jayanti Mangala Kali Bhadrakali Kapalini Durga Kshama Shiva Dhatri Swaha Swadha Namostute* *9 times*

BIBLE VERSES: (Proverbs)
21:9. It is better to sit in a corner of the housetop, than with a brawling woman, and in a common house.

READ PSALMS #'s: 6, 15, 33 ,42, 51, 60, 78, 105, 123

AUGUST 11, 2015

| 08/11/2015 | TUE | This is considered a NEGATIVE day for you | | | | | | | Shiva |

Moving	Shopping	Health	Investing	Gambling	Love is	Wedding	Travel	Work/Job	Planet
Bad	Bad	Bad	Bad	Bad	Bad	Fair	Bad	Bad	Moon

KEYWORDS ARE: death, sleepiness, finish, fame, Tiredness, Low Energy, Sleepy, Jealousy, IRS - Law, Enemies, Denial - Doubt

Lotto #'s	play 4 #s	play 3 #s	Ruling Angel:............	Color Sugestion:............	Ruling Deity
10,9,34,31,16,22	7796	958	Zaphkiel	Light Blue/Purple/Peach	Ganga

ADVICE & DETAILS

There will be disturbances and tensions in travel plans. You will hear bad news that come from far away. You should drink a lot of water because you could be dehydrated easily. You should visit the beach today.

BIBLE VERSES: (Proverbs)

21:11. When a pestilent man is punished, the little one will be wiser: and if he follow the wise, he will receive knowledge.

READ PSALMS #'s: 7, 16, 34 ,43, 52, 61, 79, 106, 124

MANTRA FOR TODAY

Om Hareem Nama Swaha..Shri Maha Laxmi Aye Namah swaha 12 times
Om maha laxmi cha vidmahe vishnu pataya dhi mahi tanno laxmi pracho dayat
Om hareem namam swaha 9 times

AUGUST 12, 2015

| 08/12/2015 | WED | This is considered a NEUTRAL day for you | | | | | | | Shiva |

Moving	Shopping	Health	Investing	Gambling	Love is	Wedding	Travel	Work/Job	Planet
Fair	Fair	Fair	Fair	Excellent	Bad	Excellent	Fair	Bad	Jupiter

KEYWORDS ARE: losses, profits, sadness, sickness, Financial losses & expenses, Police, Accidents, Big Expense, death

Lotto #'s	play 4 #s	play 3 #s	Ruling Angel:............	Color Sugestion:............	Ruling Deity
2,10,33,31,16,24	10542	159	Haniel	Yellow/White/Silver	Mahalaxmi

ADVICE & DETAILS

Today is a positive day to spend with others. You will be surrounded by partners, friends, associates and teachers. The exchange is beneficial, even if it is not what you expect.

BIBLE VERSES: (Proverbs)

21:13. He that stoppeth his ear against the cry of the poor, shall also cry himself, and shall not be heard.

READ PSALMS #'s: 8, 17, 35 ,44, 53, 62, 80, 107, 125

MANTRA FOR TODAY

Om Ganga mataye nama swaha
Om Varuna Devta aye Pahimam 11 times
Om hareem mama sarva shatru janam vashee kuru kuru swaha
om hareem ksham kasham kasheem kasheem swaha 9 times

AUGUST 13, 2015

| 08/13/2015 | THU | This is considered a POSITIVE day for you | | | | | | | Shiva |

Moving	Shopping	Health	Investing	Gambling	Love is	Wedding	Travel	Work/Job	Planet
Good	Excellent	Good	Good	Bad	Excellent	Bad	Excelle	Good	Saturn

KEYWORDS ARE: marriage, sadness, Talkative, food, Love quarrels, Government, Denial - Doubt, death, romamce

Lotto #'s	play 4 #s	play 3 #s	Ruling Angel:............	Color Sugestion:............	Ruling Deity
3,2,34,31,16,17	6025	2510	Mikael	Gold/Brown/Blue/Dark Green	Pitridev

ADVICE & DETAILS

The influences of today are about losses and doubts. Encounters with government agencies or representatives may not be beneficial. You will feel like denying the actions that have brought you to this place, but if you do so you will not be able to learn the lesson and you may have to do it again. Music today will have a soothing and relaxing effect.

BIBLE VERSES: (Proverbs)

21:15. It is joy to the just to do judgment: and dread to them that work iniquity.

READ PSALMS #'s: 9, 18, 36 ,45, 54, 63, 81, 108, 126

MANTRA FOR TODAY

Om Namo Bhagawate Mukhtanandaya, 108 times
AUM KRSNAYA VIDMAHE DAMODARAYA DHIMAHI. TANNO VISHNU PRACODAYAT. 9 times

AUGUST 14, 2015

08/14/2015	FRI		This is considered a POSITIVE day for you						Shiva	
Moving	Shopping	Health	Investing	Gambling	Love is	Wedding	Travel	Work/Job	Planet	
Good	Excellent	Excellent	Good	Fair	Good	Fair	Excelle	Good	Sun	

KEYWORDS ARE: Childishness, On Your Own, Teacher, Communication, Feeling playful, Disagreement, Death, Worry, Social Functions

Lotto #'s	play 4 #s	play 3 #s	Ruling Angel:............	Color Sugestion:...........	Ruling Deity
4,3,34,32,16,9	6829	352	Gabriel	White/Yellow/ Peach	Gaitree

ADVICE & DETAILS

Children will need attention from you today. You are advised to spend time with them. You should also take a short trip and if possible go to the movies. Shop for bargains today, you will find them!

BIBLE VERSES: (Proverbs)

21:8. The perverse way of a man is strange: but as for him that is pure, his work is right.

READ PSALMS #'s: 1, 10, 28 ,37, 46, 55, 73, 100, 118

MANTRA FOR TODAY

Kali Durge Namo Nama
Om Durge aye nama swaha
108 times
AUM TATPURUSAYA
VIDMAHE VAKRATUNDAY
DHIMAHI. TANNO DANTI
PRACODAYAT.
9 times

AUGUST 15, 2015

08/15/2015	SAT		This is considered a NEUTRAL day for you						Shiva	
Moving	Shopping	Health	Investing	Gambling	Love is	Wedding	Travel	Work/Job	Planet	
Bad	Bad	Bad	Bad	Good	Fair	Good	Bad	Bad	Venus	

KEYWORDS ARE: Low Pay, Affection, Real Estate, Tiredness, Job enjoyment, Family, Sickness - cold, Food, Drinks, High Temper

Lotto #'s	play 4 #s	play 3 #s	Ruling Angel:............	Color Sugestion:...........	Ruling Deity
5,4,33,31,16,12	6576	453	Raziel	Red/Yellow/Pink	Durga

ADVICE & DETAILS

You will be stressed out over relationships or partnerships. You may be involved in short travels. You should avoid all types of alcohol, drugs or smoking today.

BIBLE VERSES: (Proverbs)

21:10. The soul of the wicked desireth evil, he will not have pity on his neighbour.

READ PSALMS #'s: 2, 11, 29 ,38, 47, 56, 74, 101, 119

MANTRA FOR TODAY

Om hareem Kleem Hreem Aem
Saraswataye namaha
21 times
Om Guru bramha, Guru Vishnu
Guru Deva mahaeshwara guru
saksha paam bramha, tasmi shri
guruve nama
9 times

AUGUST 16, 2015

08/16/2015	SUN		This is considered a POSITIVE day for you						Shiva	
Moving	Shopping	Health	Investing	Gambling	Love is	Wedding	Travel	Work/Job	Planet	
Excellent	Good	Excellent	Good	Good	Excellent	Good	Excelle	Good	Mercury	

KEYWORDS ARE: Illicit Affairs, Expression, Beauty - Sex, travel, Comfort & Jokes, Back Pain, Legal matter, Childishness, Excercise

Lotto #'s	play 4 #s	play 3 #s	Ruling Angel:............	Color Sugestion:...........	Ruling Deity
6,4,34,32,16,13	10079	554	Zadkiel	Green/Sky Blue/White	Saraswaty

ADVICE & DETAILS

This is an excellent day to make a trip to any vacation location or to do any type of air travel. The energy today will be very high. You will be able to get everything you want to get accomplished today.

BIBLE VERSES: (Proverbs)

21:12. The just considereth seriously the house of the wicked, that he may withdraw the wicked from evil.

READ PSALMS #'s: 3, 12, 30 ,39, 48, 57, 75, 102, 120

MANTRA FOR TODAY

Om Jai Viganeshwaraya..
Lambodaraya Namo Namaha
21 times
Om Sarva Mangal Mangalye,
Shiva Sarvart Sadike, Sharan
Tryambike Gowri, Narayane
Namo asttute
9 times

AUGUST 17, 2015

08/17/2015	MON	This is considered a NEGATIVE day for you							Shiva

Moving	Shopping	Health	Investing	Gambling	Love is	Wedding	Travel	Work/Job	Planet
Bad	Bad	Bad	Fair	Bad	Bad	Good	Bad	Bad	Pluto

KEYWORDS ARE: Police, Industrial, Anger - Ego, frustration, Back Pain and job stress, Family Conflicts, Abusive, Low Pay, Jealousy

Lotto #'s	play 4 #s	play 3 #s	Ruling Angel:............	Color Sugestion:............	Ruling Deity
7,6,33,32,16,15	7844	655	Metatron	Dark Blue/ Purple/ Mauve	Ganesh

ADVICE & DETAILS	MANTRA FOR TODAY
There is a great deal of frustration with coworkers. You will disagree with coworkers and bosses at your job. You may also be frustrated with your sexual or romantic advances today, wait for a better day.	Om Graam Greem Graum Sa Gurave namah swaha 21 times AUM VAGDEVYAI CA VIDMAHE KAMARAJAYA DHIMAHI. TANNO DEVI PRACODAYAT. 9 times

BIBLE VERSES: (Proverbs)

21:14. A secret present quencheth anger: and a gift in the bosom, the greatest wrath.

READ PSALMS #'s: 4, 13, 31 ,40, 49, 58, 76, 103, 121

AUGUST 18, 2015

08/18/2015	TUE	This is considered a NEUTRAL day for you							Shiva

Moving	Shopping	Health	Investing	Gambling	Love is	Wedding	Travel	Work/Job	Planet
Good	Fair	Fair	Bad	Good	Good	Good	Good	Fair	Uranus

KEYWORDS ARE: Accidents, Short Trips, spiritual, religion, Religious miracle, Traffic Ticket, Karmic debts, Illicit Affairs, Slow Day

Lotto #'s	play 4 #s	play 3 #s	Ruling Angel:............	Color Sugestion:............	Ruling Deity
8,7,33,32,16,17	9366	756	Camael	Orange/White/Light Green/ Beige	Krishna

ADVICE & DETAILS	MANTRA FOR TODAY
It is important to follow God-like ways in order to receive protection from deceitful people that may want to take advantage of you today. Today you should expect short trips or some movement of some sort either places, people or things.	Om Mana Swasti Shanti Kuru kuru Swaha Shivoham Shivoham 27 times om haring jawala mukhi mam sarva shatru bakshaya bakshaya hung phat swaha Om Nama shivaya pahimam 9 times

BIBLE VERSES: (Proverbs)

21:16. A man that shall wander out of the way of doctrine, shall abide in the company of the giants.

READ PSALMS #'s: 5, 14, 32 ,41, 50, 59, 77, 104, 122

AUGUST 19, 2015

08/19/2015	WED	This is considered a POSITIVE day for you							Shiva

Moving	Shopping	Health	Investing	Gambling	Love is	Wedding	Travel	Work/Job	Planet
Good	Good	Excellent	Excellent	Fair	Good	Bad	Good	Excellent	Mars

KEYWORDS ARE: Denial - Doubt, responsibility, investment, luxury, Loans and Mortgages, Quarrels, God - Karma, Police, High Pleasure

Lotto #'s	play 4 #s	play 3 #s	Ruling Angel:............	Color Sugestion:............	Ruling Deity
9,7,34,32,16,19	10986	857	Raphael	Purple/DeepBlue/Rose	Hanuman

ADVICE & DETAILS	MANTRA FOR TODAY
You will have to deal with bills and creditors harrassing you today. You will feel extremely frustrated over expenses. You need to try and solve your money problems.	Jai Jai Shiva Shambo.(2) ...Mahadeva Shambo (2) 21 times Om Jayanti Mangala Kali Bhadrakali Kapalini Durga Kshama Shiva Dhatri Swaha Swadha Namostute 9 times

BIBLE VERSES: (Proverbs)

21:18. The wicked is delivered up for the just: and the unjust for the righteous.

READ PSALMS #'s: 6, 15, 33 ,42, 51, 60, 78, 105, 123

AUGUST 20, 2015

08/20/2015 THU	This is considered a NEGATIVE day for you								Shiva

Moving	Shopping	Health	Investing	Gambling	Love is	Wedding	Travel	Work/Job	Planet
Bad	Bad	Bad	Bad	Bad	Bad	Fair	Bad	Bad	Moon

KEYWORDS ARE: death, sleepiness, finish, fame,
Tiredness, Low Energy, Sleepy, Jealousy, IRS - Law, Enemies, Denial - Doubt

Lotto #'s	play 4 #s	play 3 #s	Ruling Angel:............	Color Sugestion:............	Ruling Deity
10,8,34,32,16,21	8164	958	Zaphkiel	Light Blue/Purple/Peach	Ganga

ADVICE & DETAILS	MANTRA FOR TODAY
There will be disturbances and tensions in travel plans. You will hear bad news that come from far away. You should drink a lot of water because you could be dehydrated easily. You should visit the beach today.	*Om Hareem Nama Swaha..Shri Maha Laxmi Aye Namah swaha 12 times Om maha laxmi cha vidmahe vishnu pataya dhi mahi tanno laxmi pracho dayat Om hareem namam swaha 9 times*

BIBLE VERSES: (Proverbs)
21:20. There is a treasure to be desired, and oil in the dwelling of the just: and the foolish man shall spend it.

READ PSALMS #'s: 7, 16, 34 ,43, 52, 61, 79, 106, 124

AUGUST 21, 2015

08/21/2015 FRI	This is considered a NEUTRAL day for you								Shiva

Moving	Shopping	Health	Investing	Gambling	Love is	Wedding	Travel	Work/Job	Planet
Fair	Fair	Fair	Fair	Excellent	Bad	Excellent	Fair	Bad	Jupiter

KEYWORDS ARE: losses, profits, sadness, sickness,
Financial losses & expenses, Police, Accidents, Big Expense, death

Lotto #'s	play 4 #s	play 3 #s	Ruling Angel:............	Color Sugestion:............	Ruling Deity
2,9,33,32,16,24	5253	159	Haniel	Yellow/White/Silver	Mahalaxmi

ADVICE & DETAILS	MANTRA FOR TODAY
Today is a positive day to spend with others. You will be surrounded by partners, friends, associates and teachers. The exchange is beneficial, even if it is not what you expect.	*Om Ganga mataye nama swaha Om Varuna Devta aye Pahimam 11 times Om hareem mama sarva shatru janam vashee kuru kuru swaha om hareem ksham kasham kasheem kasheem swaha 9 times*

BIBLE VERSES: (Proverbs)
21:22. The wise man hath scaled the city of the strong, and hath cast down the strength of the confidence thereof.

READ PSALMS #'s: 8, 17, 35 ,44, 53, 62, 80, 107, 125

AUGUST 22, 2015

08/22/2015 SAT	This is considered a POSITIVE day for you								Shiva

Moving	Shopping	Health	Investing	Gambling	Love is	Wedding	Travel	Work/Job	Planet
Good	Excellent	Good	Good	Bad	Excellent	Bad	Excelle	Good	Saturn

KEYWORDS ARE: finish, sadness, fame, pregnancy,
Accidents, Illness, Alcoholism, Government, Denial - Doubt, death, losses

Lotto #'s	play 4 #s	play 3 #s	Ruling Angel:............	Color Sugestion:............	Ruling Deity
3,1,33,32,16,17	3970	2510	Mikael	Gold/Brown/Blue/Dark Green	Pitridev

ADVICE & DETAILS	MANTRA FOR TODAY
The influences of today are about losses and doubts. Encounters with government agencies or representatives may not be beneficial. You will feel like denying the actions that have brought you to this place, but if you do so you will not be able to learn the lesson and you may have to do it again. Music today will have a soothing and relaxing effect.	*Om Namo Bhagawate Mukhtanandaya, 108 times AUM KRSNAYA VIDMAHE DAMODARAYA DHIMAHI. TANNO VISHNU PRACODAYAT. 9 times*

BIBLE VERSES: (Proverbs)
21:24. The proud and the arrogant is called ignorant, who in anger worketh pride.

READ PSALMS #'s: 9, 18, 36 ,45, 54, 63, 81, 108, 126

AUGUST 23, 2015

08/23/2015 SUN		This is considered a POSITIVE day for you							Shiva
Moving	Shopping	Health	Investing	Gambling	Love is	Wedding	Travel	Work/Job	Planet
Good	Excellent	Excellent	Good	Fair	Good	Fair	Excelle	Good	Sun

KEYWORDS ARE: Childishness, On Your Own, Teacher, Communication, Feeling playful, Disagreement, Death, Worry, Social Functions

Lotto #'s	play 4 #s	play 3 #s	Ruling Angel:............	Color Sugestion:............	Ruling Deity
4,2,33,32,16,10	7803	352	Gabriel	White/Yellow/ Peach	Gaitree

ADVICE & DETAILS	MANTRA FOR TODAY
Children will need attention from you today. You are advised to spend time with them. You should also take a short trip and if possible go to the movies. Shop for bargains today, you will find them!	Kali Durge Namo Nama Om Durge aye nama swaha 108 times AUM TATPURUSAYA VIDMAHE VAKRATUNDAY DHIMAHI. TANNO DANTI PRACODAYAT.
BIBLE VERSES: (Proverbs) 21:17. He that loveth good cheer, shall be in want: he that loveth wine, and fat things, shall not be rich.	
READ PSALMS #'s: 1, 10, 28 ,37, 46, 55, 73, 100, 118	9 times

AUGUST 24, 2015

08/24/2015 MON		This is considered a NEUTRAL day for you							Shiva
Moving	Shopping	Health	Investing	Gambling	Love is	Wedding	Travel	Work/Job	Planet
Bad	Bad	Bad	Bad	Good	Fair	Good	Bad	Bad	Venus

KEYWORDS ARE: Low Pay, Affection, Real Estate, Tiredness, Job enjoyment, Family, Sickness - cold, Food, Drinks, High Temper

Lotto #'s	play 4 #s	play 3 #s	Ruling Angel:............	Color Sugestion:............	Ruling Deity
5,3,34,31,16,12	8384	453	Raziel	Red/Yellow/Pink	Durga

ADVICE & DETAILS	MANTRA FOR TODAY
You will be stressed out over relationships or partnerships. You may be involved in short travels. You should avoid all types of alcohol, drugs or smoking today.	Om hareem Kleem Hreem Aem Saraswataye namaha 21 times Om Guru bramha, Guru Vishnu Guru Deva mahaeshwara guru saksha paam bramha, tasmi shri guruve nama
BIBLE VERSES: (Proverbs) 21:19. It is better to dwell in a wilderness, than with a quarrelsome and passionate woman.	
READ PSALMS #'s: 2, 11, 29 ,38, 47, 56, 74, 101, 119	9 times

AUGUST 25, 2015

08/25/2015 TUE		This is considered a POSITIVE day for you							Shiva
Moving	Shopping	Health	Investing	Gambling	Love is	Wedding	Travel	Work/Job	Planet
Excellent	Good	Excellent	Good	Good	Excellent	Good	Excelle	Good	Mercury

KEYWORDS ARE: Illicit Affairs, Expression, Beauty - Sex, travel, Comfort & Jokes, Back Pain, Legal matter, Childishness, Excercise

Lotto #'s	play 4 #s	play 3 #s	Ruling Angel:............	Color Sugestion:............	Ruling Deity
6,5,34,32,16,13	9937	554	Zadkiel	Green/Sky Blue/White	Saraswaty

ADVICE & DETAILS	MANTRA FOR TODAY
This is an excellent day to make a trip to any vacation location or to do any type of air travel. The energy today will be very high. You will be able to get everything you want to get accomplished today.	Om Jai Viganeshwaraya.. Lambodaraya Namo Namaha 21 times Om Sarva Mangal Mangalye, Shiva Sarvart Sadike, Sharan Tryambike Gowri, Narayane Namo asttute
BIBLE VERSES: (Proverbs) 21:21. He that followeth justice and mercy, shall find life, justice, and glory. 0	
READ PSALMS #'s: 3, 12, 30 ,39, 48, 57, 75, 102, 120	9 times

AUGUST 26, 2015

08/26/2015 WED		This is considered a NEGATIVE day for you							Shiva
Moving	Shopping	Health	Investing	Gambling	Love is	Wedding	Travel	Work/Job	Planet
Bad	Bad	Bad	Fair	Bad	Bad	Good	Bad	Bad	Pluto

KEYWORDS ARE: Police, Industrial, Anger - Ego, frustration, Back Pain and job stress, Family Conflicts, Abusive, Low Pay, Jealousy

Lotto #'s	play 4 #s	play 3 #s	Ruling Angel:............	Color Sugestion:............	Ruling Deity
7,6,33,32,16,16	9917	655	Metatron	Dark Blue/ Purple/ Mauve	Ganesh

ADVICE & DETAILS	MANTRA FOR TODAY
There is a great deal of frustration with coworkers. You will disagree with coworkers and bosses at your job. You may also be frustrated with your sexual or romantic advances today, wait for a better day.	*Om Graam Greem Graum Sa Gurave namah swaha* *21 times* *AUM VAGDEVYAI CA VIDMAHE KAMARAJAYA DHIMAHI. TANNO DEVI PRACODAYAT.* *9 times*

BIBLE VERSES: (Proverbs)
21:23. He that keepeth his mouth and his tongue, keepeth his soul from distress.

READ PSALMS #'s: 4, 13, 31 ,40, 49, 58, 76, 103, 121

AUGUST 27, 2015

08/27/2015 THU		This is considered a NEUTRAL day for you							Shiva
Moving	Shopping	Health	Investing	Gambling	Love is	Wedding	Travel	Work/Job	Planet
Good	Fair	Fair	Bad	Good	Good	Good	Good	Fair	Uranus

KEYWORDS ARE: Accidents, Short Trips, spiritual, religion, Religious miracle, Traffic Ticket, Karmic debts, Illicit Affairs, Slow Day

Lotto #'s	play 4 #s	play 3 #s	Ruling Angel:............	Color Sugestion:............	Ruling Deity
8,6,34,32,16,17	10009	756	Camael	Orange/White/Light Green/ Beige	Krishna

ADVICE & DETAILS	MANTRA FOR TODAY
It is important to follow God-like ways in order to receive protection from deceitful people that may want to take advantage of you today. Today you should expect short trips or some movement of some sort either places, people or things.	*Om Mana Swasti Shanti Kuru kuru Swaha Shivoham Shivoham* *27 times* *om haring jawala mukhi mam sarva shatru bakshaya bakshaya hung phat swaha* *Om Nama shivaya pahimam* *9 times*

BIBLE VERSES: (Proverbs)
21:25. Desires kill the slothful: for his hands have refused to work at all.
0

READ PSALMS #'s: 5, 14, 32 ,41, 50, 59, 77, 104, 122

AUGUST 28, 2015

08/28/2015 FRI		This is considered a POSITIVE day for you							Shiva
Moving	Shopping	Health	Investing	Gambling	Love is	Wedding	Travel	Work/Job	Planet
Good	Good	Excellent	Excellent	Fair	Good	Bad	Good	Excellent	Mars

KEYWORDS ARE: Denial - Doubt, responsibility, investment, luxury, Loans and Mortgages, Quarrels, God - Karma, Police, High Pleasure

Lotto #'s	play 4 #s	play 3 #s	Ruling Angel:............	Color Sugestion:............	Ruling Deity
9,8,33,32,16,20	2910	857	Raphael	Purple/DeepBlue/Rose	Hanuman

ADVICE & DETAILS	MANTRA FOR TODAY
You will have to deal with bills and creditors harrassing you today. You will feel extremely frustrated over expenses. You need to try and solve your money problems.	*Jai Jai Shiva Shambo.(2)* *...Mahadeva Shambo (2)* *21 times* *Om Jayanti Mangala Kali Bhadrakali Kapalini Durga Kshama Shiva Dhatri Swaha Swadha Namostute* *9 times*

BIBLE VERSES: (Proverbs)
21:27. The sacrifices of the wicked are abominable, because they are offered of wickedness.

READ PSALMS #'s: 6, 15, 33 ,42, 51, 60, 78, 105, 123

AUGUST 29, 2015

08/29/2015 SAT		This is considered a NEGATIVE day for you							Shiva
Moving	*Shopping*	*Health*	*Investing*	*Gambling*	*Love is*	*Wedding*	*Travel*	*Work/Job*	*Planet*
Bad	Bad	Bad	Bad	Bad	Bad	Fair	Bad	Bad	**Moon**

KEYWORDS ARE: death, sleepiness, finish, fame, Tiredness, Low Energy, Sleepy, Jealousy, IRS - Law, Enemies, Denial - Doubt

Lotto #'s	*play 4 #s*	*play 3 #s*	*Ruling Angel:............*	*Color Sugestion:...........*	*Ruling Deity*
10,8,33,31,16,21	8235	958	**Zaphkiel**	**Light Blue/Purple/Peach**	**Ganga**

ADVICE & DETAILS	MANTRA FOR TODAY
There will be disturbances and tensions in travel plans. You will hear bad news that come from far away. You should drink a lot of water because you could be dehydrated easily. You should visit the beach today.	*Om Hareem Nama Swaha..Shri Maha Laxmi Aye Namah swaha 12 times Om maha laxmi cha vidmahe vishnu pataya dhi mahi tanno laxmi pracho dayat Om hareem namam swaha 9 times*

BIBLE VERSES: (Proverbs)

21:29. The wicked man impudently hardeneth his face: but he that is righteous, correcteth his way.

READ PSALMS #'s: 7, 16, 34 ,43, 52, 61, 79, 106, 124

AUGUST 30, 2015

08/30/2015 SUN		This is considered a NEUTRAL day for you							Shiva
Moving	*Shopping*	*Health*	*Investing*	*Gambling*	*Love is*	*Wedding*	*Travel*	*Work/Job*	*Planet*
Fair	Fair	Fair	Fair	Excellent	Bad	Excellent	Fair	Bad	**Jupiter**

KEYWORDS ARE: losses, profits, sadness, sickness, Financial losses & expenses, Police, Accidents, Big Expense, death

Lotto #'s	*play 4 #s*	*play 3 #s*	*Ruling Angel:............*	*Color Sugestion:...........*	*Ruling Deity*
2,9,34,32,16,24	10751	159	**Haniel**	**Yellow/White/Silver**	**Mahalaxmi**

ADVICE & DETAILS	MANTRA FOR TODAY
Today is a positive day to spend with others. You will be surrounded by partners, friends, associates and teachers. The exchange is beneficial, even if it is not what you expect.	*Om Ganga mataye nama swaha Om Varuna Devta aye Pahimam 11 times Om hareem mama sarva shatru janam vashee kuru kuru swaha om hareem ksham kasham kasheem kasheem swaha 9 times*

BIBLE VERSES: (Proverbs)

21:31. The horse is prepared for the day of battle: but the Lord giveth safety.

READ PSALMS #'s: 8, 17, 35 ,44, 53, 62, 80, 107, 125

AUGUST 31, 2015

08/31/2015 MON		This is considered a POSITIVE day for you							Shiva
Moving	*Shopping*	*Health*	*Investing*	*Gambling*	*Love is*	*Wedding*	*Travel*	*Work/Job*	*Planet*
Good	Excellent	Good	Good	Bad	Excellent	Bad	Excelle	Good	**Saturn**

KEYWORDS ARE: finish, sadness, fame, pregnancy, Accidents, Illness, Alcoholism, Government, Denial - Doubt, death, losses

Lotto #'s	*play 4 #s*	*play 3 #s*	*Ruling Angel:............*	*Color Sugestion:...........*	*Ruling Deity*
3,1,34,31,16,17	1244	2510	**Mikael**	**Gold/Brown/Blue/Dark Green**	**Pitridev**

ADVICE & DETAILS	MANTRA FOR TODAY
The influences of today are about losses and doubts. Encounters with government agencies or representatives may not be beneficial. You will feel like denying the actions that have brought you to this place, but if you do so you will not be able to learn the lesson and you may have to do it again. Music today will have a soothing and relaxing effect.	*Om Namo Bhagawate Mukhtanandaya, 108 times AUM KRSNAYA VIDMAHE DAMODARAYA DHIMAHI. TANNO VISHNU PRACODAYAT. 9 times*

BIBLE VERSES: (Proverbs)

22:2. The rich and poor have met one another: the Lord is the maker of them both.

READ PSALMS #'s: 9, 18, 36 ,45, 54, 63, 81, 108, 126

SEPTEMBER 1, 2015

| 09/01/2015 | TUE | This is considered a POSITIVE day for you | | | | | | | Shiva |

Moving	Shopping	Health	Investing	Gambling	Love is	Wedding	Travel	Work/Job	Planet
Good	Good	Excellent	Excellent	Bad	Good	Fair	Good	Excellent	Moon

KEYWORDS ARE: Abusive, Advice given, Fame - TV, High Pleasure, Business & money gains, Religious, Death, Inner Conflicts, Investments

Lotto #'s	play 4 #s	play 3 #s	Ruling Angel:............	Color Sugestion:............	Ruling Deity
9,8,33,31,17,20	6031	867	Zaphkiel	Light Blue/Purple/Peach	Ganga

ADVICE & DETAILS	MANTRA FOR TODAY
There is a great deal of worries about your investments or financial affairs. You may feel depressed over money. You will have to deal with unwanted expenses.	Kali Durge Namo Nama Om Durge aye nama swaha 108 times AUM TATPURUSAYA VIDMAHE VAKRATUNDAY DHIMAHI. TANNO DANTI PRACODAYAT. 9 times

BIBLE VERSES: (Proverbs)
22:1. A good name is better than great riches: and good favour is above silver and gold.

READ PSALMS #'s: 7, 16, 34 ,43, 52, 61, 79, 106, 124

SEPTEMBER 2, 2015

| 09/02/2015 | WED | This is considered a NEGATIVE day for you | | | | | | | Shiva |

Moving	Shopping	Health	Investing	Gambling	Love is	Wedding	Travel	Work/Job	Planet
Bad	Bad	Bad	Bad	Excellent	Bad	Excellent	Bad	Bad	Jupiter

KEYWORDS ARE: Karmic debts, Fame - TV, IRS - Law, Denial - Doubt, Quarrels & lovers, Astrology, Sickness - cold, Investments, Abusive

Lotto #'s	play 4 #s	play 3 #s	Ruling Angel:............	Color Sugestion:............	Ruling Deity
10,9,34,31,17,23	5139	968	Haniel	Yellow/White/Silver	Mahalaxmi

ADVICE & DETAILS	MANTRA FOR TODAY
There is a great deal of tension about money and family. You may lose money today. There will be conflict with family members. You must control your ego. IRS and taxes could affect you today.	Om Hareem Nama Swaha..Shri Maha Laxmi Aye Namah swaha 12 times Om maha laxmi cha vidmahe vishnu pataya dhi mahi tanno laxmi pracho dayat Om hareem namam swaha 9 times

BIBLE VERSES: (Proverbs)
22:3. The prudent man saw the evil, and hid himself: the simple passed on, and suffered loss.

READ PSALMS #'s: 8, 17, 35 ,44, 53, 62, 80, 107, 125

SEPTEMBER 3, 2015

| 09/03/2015 | THU | This is considered a NEUTRAL day for you | | | | | | | Shiva |

Moving	Shopping	Health	Investing	Gambling	Love is	Wedding	Travel	Work/Job	Planet
Fair	Fair	Fair	Fair	Bad	Bad	Bad	Fair	Bad	Saturn

KEYWORDS ARE: Commanding, IRS - Law, Boastful, lonliness, Meditative, Inner Conflicts, Legal matter, Abusive, On Your Own

Lotto #'s	play 4 #s	play 3 #s	Ruling Angel:............	Color Sugestion:............	Ruling Deity
2,1,34,32,17,15	3059	169	Mikael	Gold/Brown/Blue/Dark Green	Pitridev

ADVICE & DETAILS	MANTRA FOR TODAY
You will feel sad today. There will be a sense of loss perhaps due to a death, divorce or project or idea that no longer has vitality. Instinctually you will want to deny that this change could bring any positive change, but time will show you valuable lessons you have learned from this experience. Regardless, you will be plagued with doubts about everythin	Om Ganga mataye nama swaha Om Varuna Devta aye Pahimam 11 times Om hareem mama sarva shatru janam vashee kuru kuru swaha om hareem ksham kasham kasheem kasheem swaha 9 times

BIBLE VERSES: (Proverbs)
22:5. Arms and swords are in the way of the perverse: but he that keepeth his own soul, departeth far from them.

READ PSALMS #'s: 9, 18, 36 ,45, 54, 63, 81, 108, 126

SEPTEMBER 4, 2015

09/04/2015 FRI		This is considered a POSITIVE day for you							Shiva

Moving	Shopping	Health	Investing	Gambling	Love is	Wedding	Travel	Work/Job	Planet
Good	Excellent	Good	Good	Fair	Excellent	Fair	Excelle	Good	Sun

KEYWORDS ARE: Association, Boastful, Partnership, romamce, Spending, Religious , Abusive, On Your Own, Affection

Lotto #'s	play 4 #s	play 3 #s	Ruling Angel:............	Color Sugestion:............	Ruling Deity
3,2,33,31,17,18	8646	2610	Gabriel	White/Yellow/ Peach	Gaitree

ADVICE & DETAILS	MANTRA FOR TODAY
It is a bad day for love, romance and companionship. You will be very frustrated with friends, lovers or just about anyone. You must avoid being too bossy or demanding with your loved ones.	Om Namo Bhagawate Mukhtanandaya, 108 times AUM KRSNAYA VIDMAHE DAMODARAYA DHIMAHI. TANNO VISHNU PRACODAYAT. 9 times

BIBLE VERSES: (Proverbs)

21:29. The wicked man impudently hardeneth his face: but he that is righteous, correcteth his way.

READ PSALMS #'s: 1, 10, 28 ,37, 46, 55, 73, 100, 118

SEPTEMBER 5, 2015

09/05/2015 SAT		This is considered a POSITIVE day for you							Shiva

Moving	Shopping	Health	Investing	Gambling	Love is	Wedding	Travel	Work/Job	Planet
Good	Excellent	Excellent	Good	Good	Good	Good	Excelle	Good	Venus

KEYWORDS ARE: Communication, Partnership, read, children, Social Functions, Sleepiness, Karmic debts, Affection, Expression

Lotto #'s	play 4 #s	play 3 #s	Ruling Angel:............	Color Sugestion:............	Ruling Deity
4,3,34,31,17,10	9515	362	Raziel	Red/Yellow/Pink	Durga

ADVICE & DETAILS	MANTRA FOR TODAY
You will have children and family members that are cooperative today. They will also demand much attention. There may be arguments between lovers.	Kali Durge Namo Nama Om Durge aye nama swaha 108 times AUM TATPURUSAYA VIDMAHE VAKRATUNDAY DHIMAHI. TANNO DANTI PRACODAYAT. 9 times

BIBLE VERSES: (Proverbs)

21:31. The horse is prepared for the day of battle: but the Lord giveth safety.

READ PSALMS #'s: 2, 11, 29 ,38, 47, 56, 74, 101, 119

SEPTEMBER 6, 2015

09/06/2015 SUN		This is considered a NEUTRAL day for you							Shiva

Moving	Shopping	Health	Investing	Gambling	Love is	Wedding	Travel	Work/Job	Planet
Bad	Bad	Bad	Bad	Good	Fair	Good	Bad	Bad	Mercury

KEYWORDS ARE: Tiredness, read, career, building, Co-workers, Advice given, God - Karma, Expression, Industrial

Lotto #'s	play 4 #s	play 3 #s	Ruling Angel:............	Color Sugestion:............	Ruling Deity
5,5,34,31,17,12	5920	463	Zadkiel	Green/Sky Blue/White	Saraswaty

ADVICE & DETAILS	MANTRA FOR TODAY
This is a good day to chant your mantras as there will be tension, stress and many challenges at work. Avoid going to any meetings or joining any groups in this day. Children will also be difficult.	Om hareem Kleem Hreem Aem Saraswataye namaha 21 times Om Guru bramha, Guru Vishnu Guru Deva mahaeshwara guru saksha paam bramha, tasmi shri guruve nama 9 times

BIBLE VERSES: (Proverbs)

22:2. The rich and poor have met one another: the Lord is the maker of them both.

READ PSALMS #'s: 3, 12, 30 ,39, 48, 57, 75, 102, 120

SEPTEMBER 7, 2015

09/07/2015	MON		This is considered a POSITIVE day for you							Shiva
Moving	Shopping	Health	Investing	Gambling	Love is	Wedding	Travel	Work/Job		Planet
Excellent	Good	Excellent	Good	Bad	Excellent	Good	Excelle	Good		Pluto

KEYWORDS ARE: travel, career, change, deception,
Belief and faith, Alcohol - drugs, IRS - Law, Industrial, Short Trips

Lotto #'s	play 4 #s	play 3 #s	Ruling Angel:...........	Color Sugestion:...........	Ruling Deity
6,6,33,32,17,14	9257	564	Metatron	Dark Blue/ Purple/ Mauve	Ganesh

ADVICE & DETAILS	MANTRA FOR TODAY
Travel will be difficult today, you may get into an accident if you drive. So you must watch out for traffic tickets and follow all rules of the road. There may be positive social gatherings.	Om Jai Viganeshwaraya.. Lambodaraya Namo Namaha 21 times Om Sarva Mangal Mangalye, Shiva Sarvart Sadike, Sharan Tryambike Gowri, Narayane Namo asttute 9 times
BIBLE VERSES: (Proverbs)	
22:4. The fruit of humility is the fear of the Lord, riches and glory and life. 0	
READ PSALMS #'s: 4, 13, 31 ,40, 49, 58, 76, 103, 121	

SEPTEMBER 8, 2015

09/08/2015	TUE		This is considered a NEGATIVE day for you							Shiva
Moving	Shopping	Health	Investing	Gambling	Love is	Wedding	Travel	Work/Job		Planet
Bad	Bad	Bad	Fair	Good	Bad	Good	Bad	Bad		Uranus

KEYWORDS ARE: frustration, change, power, electricity,
Money conflicts, Slow Day, Accidents, Short Trips, responsibility

Lotto #'s	play 4 #s	play 3 #s	Ruling Angel:...........	Color Sugestion:...........	Ruling Deity
7,7,34,32,17,16	2947	665	Camael	Orange/White/Light Green/ Beige	Krishna

ADVICE & DETAILS	MANTRA FOR TODAY
You will have a great deal of frustration and anxiety with changes that are hard for you to accept. There will be an uncomfortable move or separation. You will be frustrated over living conditions.	Om Graam Greem Graum Sa Gurave namah swaha 21 times AUM VAGDEVYAI CA VIDMAHE KAMARAJAYA DHIMAHI. TANNO DEVI PRACODAYAT. 9 times
BIBLE VERSES: (Proverbs)	
22:6. It is a proverb: A young man according to his way, even when he is old, he will not depart from it.	
READ PSALMS #'s: 5, 14, 32 ,41, 50, 59, 77, 104, 122	

SEPTEMBER 9, 2015

09/09/2015	WED		This is considered a NEUTRAL day for you							Shiva
Moving	Shopping	Health	Investing	Gambling	Love is	Wedding	Travel	Work/Job		Planet
Good	Fair	Fair	Bad	Fair	Good	Bad	Good	Fair		Mars

KEYWORDS ARE: finish, power, religion, priests,
Slow Day with Tension, Enemies, Denial - Doubt, responsibility, sleepiness

Lotto #'s	play 4 #s	play 3 #s	Ruling Angel:...........	Color Sugestion:...........	Ruling Deity
8,8,33,32,17,18	10876	766	Raphael	Purple/DeepBlue/Rose	Hanuman

ADVICE & DETAILS	MANTRA FOR TODAY
You will feel distress over life goal and objectives. You will have the feeling that life is moving too slow for you. You may be bored or be disturbed. Government agencies will affect you today. Follow rules.	Om Mana Swasti Shanti Kuru kuru Swaha Shivoham Shivoham 27 times om haring jawala mukhi mam sarva shatru bakshaya bakshaya hung phat swaha Om Nama shivaya pahimam 9 times
BIBLE VERSES: (Proverbs)	
22:8. He that soweth iniquity, shall reap evils, and with the rod of his anger he shall be consumed.	
READ PSALMS #'s: 6, 15, 33 ,42, 51, 60, 78, 105, 123	

SEPTEMBER 10, 2015

| 09/10/2015 THU | This is considered a POSITIVE day for you | | | | | | | | Shiva |

Moving	Shopping	Health	Investing	Gambling	Love is	Wedding	Travel	Work/Job	Planet
Good	Good	Excellent	Excellent	Bad	Good	Fair	Good	Excellent	Moon

KEYWORDS ARE: Abusive, Advice given, Fame - TV, High Pleasure, Business & money gains, Religious, Death, Inner Conflicts, Investments

Lotto #'s	play 4 #s	play 3 #s	Ruling Angel:............	Color Sugestion:............	Ruling Deity
9,8,34,31,17,20	3090	867	Zaphkiel	Light Blue/Purple/Peach	Ganga

ADVICE & DETAILS

There is a great deal of worries about your investments or financial affairs. You may feel depressed over money. You will have to deal with unwanted expenses.

BIBLE VERSES: (Proverbs)

22:10. Cast out the scoffer, and contention shall go out with him, and quarrels and reproaches shall cease.

READ PSALMS #'s: 7, 16, 34 ,43, 52, 61, 79, 106, 124

MANTRA FOR TODAY

Jai Jai Shiva Shambo.(2)
...Mahadeva Shambo (2)
21 times
Om Jayanti Mangala Kali
Bhadrakali Kapalini Durga
Kshama Shiva Dhatri Swaha
Swadha Namostute
9 times

SEPTEMBER 11, 2015

| 09/11/2015 FRI | This is considered a NEGATIVE day for you | | | | | | | | Shiva |

Moving	Shopping	Health	Investing	Gambling	Love is	Wedding	Travel	Work/Job	Planet
Bad	Bad	Bad	Bad	Excellent	Bad	Excellent	Bad	Bad	Jupiter

KEYWORDS ARE: Karmic debts, Fame - TV, IRS - Law, Denial - Doubt, Quarrels & lovers, Astrology, Sickness - cold, Investments, Abusive

Lotto #'s	play 4 #s	play 3 #s	Ruling Angel:............	Color Sugestion:............	Ruling Deity
10,10,33,31,17,23	3299	968	Haniel	Yellow/White/Silver	Mahalaxmi

ADVICE & DETAILS

There is a great deal of tension about money and family. You may lose money today. There will be conflict with family members. You must control your ego. IRS and taxes could affect you today.

BIBLE VERSES: (Proverbs)

22:12. The eyes of the Lord preserve knowledge: and the words of the unjust are overthrown.

READ PSALMS #'s: 8, 17, 35 ,44, 53, 62, 80, 107, 125

MANTRA FOR TODAY

Om Hareem Nama Swaha..Shri
Maha Laxmi Aye Namah swaha
12 times
Om maha laxmi cha vidmahe
vishnu pataya dhi mahi tanno
laxmi pracho dayat
Om hareem namam swaha
9 times

SEPTEMBER 12, 2015

| 09/12/2015 SAT | This is considered a NEUTRAL day for you | | | | | | | | Shiva |

Moving	Shopping	Health	Investing	Gambling	Love is	Wedding	Travel	Work/Job	Planet
Fair	Fair	Fair	Fair	Bad	Bad	Bad	Fair	Bad	Saturn

KEYWORDS ARE: God - Karma, IRS - Law, Accidents, death, Illnese, children, hypertension, Inner Conflicts, Legal matter, Abusive, Karmic debts

Lotto #'s	play 4 #s	play 3 #s	Ruling Angel:............	Color Sugestion:............	Ruling Deity
2,2,34,31,17,16	3065	169	Mikael	Gold/Brown/Blue/Dark Green	Pitridev

ADVICE & DETAILS

You will feel sad today. There will be a sense of loss perhaps due to a death, divorce or project or idea that no longer has vitality. Instinctually you will want to deny that this change could bring any positive change, but time will show you valuable lessons you have learned from this experience. Regardless, you will be plagued with doubts about everythin

BIBLE VERSES: (Proverbs)

22:14. The mouth of a strange woman is a deep pit: he whom the Lord is angry with, shall fall into it.

READ PSALMS #'s: 9, 18, 36 ,45, 54, 63, 81, 108, 126

MANTRA FOR TODAY

Om Ganga mataye nama swaha
Om Varuna Devta aye Pahimam
11 times
Om hareem mama sarva shatru
janam vashee kuru kuru swaha
om hareem ksham kasham
kasheem kasheem swaha
9 times

SEPTEMBER 13, 2015

09/13/2015 SUN			This is considered a POSITIVE day for you						Shiva

Moving	Shopping	Health	Investing	Gambling	Love is	Wedding	Travel	Work/Job	Planet
Good	Excellent	Good	Good	Fair	Excellent	Fair	Excelle	Good	Sun

KEYWORDS ARE: Association, Boastful, Partnership, romamce, Spending, Religious , Abusive, On Your Own, Affection

Lotto #'s	play 4 #s	play 3 #s	Ruling Angel:............	Color Sugestion:............	Ruling Deity
3,3,34,31,17,18	1875	2610	Gabriel	White/Yellow/ Peach	Gaitree

ADVICE & DETAILS	MANTRA FOR TODAY
It is a bad day for love, romance and companionship. You will be very frustrated with friends, lovers or just about anyone. You must avoid being too bossy or demanding with your loved ones.	*Om Namo Bhagawate Mukhtanandaya, 108 times AUM KRSNAYA VIDMAHE DAMODARAYA DHIMAHI. TANNO VISHNU PRACODAYAT. 9 times*

BIBLE VERSES: (Proverbs)

22:7. The rich ruleth over the poor: and the borrower is servant to him that lendeth.

READ PSALMS #'s: 1, 10, 28 ,37, 46, 55, 73, 100, 118

SEPTEMBER 14, 2015

09/14/2015 MON			This is considered a POSITIVE day for you						Shiva

Moving	Shopping	Health	Investing	Gambling	Love is	Wedding	Travel	Work/Job	Planet
Good	Excellent	Excellent	Good	Good	Good	Good	Excelle	Good	Venus

KEYWORDS ARE: Communication, Partnership, read, children, Social Functions, Sleepiness, Karmic debts, Affection, Expression

Lotto #'s	play 4 #s	play 3 #s	Ruling Angel:............	Color Sugestion:............	Ruling Deity
4,4,33,32,17,10	4195	362	Raziel	Red/Yellow/Pink	Durga

ADVICE & DETAILS	MANTRA FOR TODAY
You will have children and family members that are cooperative today. They will also demand much attention. There may be arguments between lovers.	*Kali Durge Namo Nama Om Durge aye nama swaha 108 times AUM TATPURUSAYA VIDMAHE VAKRATUNDAY DHIMAHI. TANNO DANTI PRACODAYAT. 9 times*

BIBLE VERSES: (Proverbs)

22:9. He that is inclined to mercy, shall be blessed: for of his bread he hath given to the poor. He that maketh presents, shall purchase victory

READ PSALMS #'s: 2, 11, 29 ,38, 47, 56, 74, 101, 119

SEPTEMBER 15, 2015

09/15/2015 TUE			This is considered a NEUTRAL day for you						Shiva

Moving	Shopping	Health	Investing	Gambling	Love is	Wedding	Travel	Work/Job	Planet
Bad	Bad	Bad	Bad	Good	Fair	Good	Bad	Bad	Mercury

KEYWORDS ARE: Tiredness, read, career, building, Co-workers, Advice given, God - Karma, Expression, Industrial

Lotto #'s	play 4 #s	play 3 #s	Ruling Angel:............	Color Sugestion:............	Ruling Deity
5,5,34,32,17,13	4057	463	Zadkiel	Green/Sky Blue/White	Saraswaty

ADVICE & DETAILS	MANTRA FOR TODAY
This is a good day to chant your mantras as there will be tension, stress and many challenges at work. Avoid going to any meetings or joining any groups in this day. Children will also be difficult.	*Om hareem Kleem Hreem Aem Saraswataye namaha 21 times Om Guru bramha, Guru Vishnu Guru Deva mahaeshwara guru saksha paam bramha, tasmi shri guruve nama 9 times*

BIBLE VERSES: (Proverbs)

22:11. He that loveth cleanness of heart, for the grace of his lips shall have the king for his friend.

READ PSALMS #'s: 3, 12, 30 ,39, 48, 57, 75, 102, 120

SEPTEMBER 16, 2015

09/16/2015 WED		This is considered a POSITIVE day for you							Shiva
Moving	*Shopping*	*Health*	*Investing*	*Gambling*	*Love is*	*Wedding*	*Travel*	*Work/Job*	*Planet*
Excellent	Good	Excellent	Good	Bad	Excellent	Good	Excelle	Good	**Pluto**

KEYWORDS ARE: travel, career, change, deception, Belief and faith, Alcohol - drugs, IRS - Law, Industrial, Short Trips

Lotto #'s	*play 4 #s*	*play 3 #s*	*Ruling Angel:...........*	*Color Sugestion:............*	*Ruling Deity*
6,6,34,31,17,14	7426	564	**Metatron**	**Dark Blue/ Purple/ Mauve**	**Ganesh**

ADVICE & DETAILS	MANTRA FOR TODAY
Travel will be difficult today, you may get into an accident if you drive. So you must watch out for traffic tickets and follow all rules of the road. There may be positive social gatherings.	*Om Jai Viganeshwaraya.. Lambodaraya Namo Namaha 21 times Om Sarva Mangal Mangalye, Shiva Sarvart Sadike, Sharan Tryambike Gowri, Narayane Namo asttute 9 times*

BIBLE VERSES: (Proverbs)
22:13. The slothful man saith: There is a lion without, I shall be slain in the midst of the streets.

READ PSALMS #'s: 4, 13, 31 ,40, 49, 58, 76, 103, 121

SEPTEMBER 17, 2015

09/17/2015 THU		This is considered a NEGATIVE day for you							Shiva
Moving	*Shopping*	*Health*	*Investing*	*Gambling*	*Love is*	*Wedding*	*Travel*	*Work/Job*	*Planet*
Bad	Bad	Bad	Fair	Good	Bad	Good	Bad	Bad	**Uranus**

KEYWORDS ARE: frustration, change, power, electricity, Money conflicts, Slow Day, Accidents, Short Trips, responsibility

Lotto #'s	*play 4 #s*	*play 3 #s*	*Ruling Angel:...........*	*Color Sugestion:............*	*Ruling Deity*
7,6,34,31,17,16	2119	665	**Camael**	**Orange/White/Light Green/ Beige**	**Krishna**

ADVICE & DETAILS	MANTRA FOR TODAY
You will have a great deal of frustration and anxiety with changes that are hard for you to accept. There will be an uncomfortable move or separation. You will be frustrated over living conditions.	*Om Graam Greem Graum Sa Gurave namah swaha 21 times AUM VAGDEVYAI CA VIDMAHE KAMARAJAYA DHIMAHI. TANNO DEVI PRACODAYAT. 9 times*

BIBLE VERSES: (Proverbs)
22:15. Folly is bound up in the heart of a child, and the rod of correction shall drive it away.

READ PSALMS #'s: 5, 14, 32 ,41, 50, 59, 77, 104, 122

SEPTEMBER 18, 2015

09/18/2015 FRI		This is considered a NEUTRAL day for you							Shiva
Moving	*Shopping*	*Health*	*Investing*	*Gambling*	*Love is*	*Wedding*	*Travel*	*Work/Job*	*Planet*
Good	Fair	Fair	Bad	Fair	Good	Bad	Good	Fair	**Mars**

KEYWORDS ARE: finish, power, religion, priests, Slow Day with Tension, Enemies, Denial - Doubt, responsibility, sleepiness

Lotto #'s	*play 4 #s*	*play 3 #s*	*Ruling Angel:...........*	*Color Sugestion:............*	*Ruling Deity*
8,8,34,31,17,18	2938	766	**Raphael**	**Purple/DeepBlue/Rose**	**Hanuman**

ADVICE & DETAILS	MANTRA FOR TODAY
You will feel distress over life goal and objectives. You will have the feeling that life is moving too slow for you. You may be bored or be disturbed. Government agencies will affect you today. Follow rules.	*Om Mana Swasti Shanti Kuru kuru Swaha Shivoham Shivoham 27 times om haring jawala mukhi mam sarva shatru bakshaya bakshaya hung phat swaha Om Nama shivaya pahimam 9 times*

BIBLE VERSES: (Proverbs)
22:17. Incline thy ear, and hear the words of the wise: and apply thy heart to my doctrine:

READ PSALMS #'s: 6, 15, 33 ,42, 51, 60, 78, 105, 123

SEPTEMBER 19, 2015

09/19/2015 SAT		This is considered a POSITIVE day for you							Shiva
Moving	Shopping	Health	Investing	Gambling	Love is	Wedding	Travel	Work/Job	Planet
Good	Good	Excellent	Excellent	Bad	Good	Fair	Good	Excellent	Moon

KEYWORDS ARE: Abusive, Advice given, Fame - TV, High Pleasure, Business & money gains, Religious, Death, Inner Conflicts, Investments

Lotto #'s	play 4 #s	play 3 #s	Ruling Angel:............	Color Sugestion:............	Ruling Deity
9,9,33,32,17,21	3329	867	Zaphkiel	Light Blue/Purple/Peach	Ganga

ADVICE & DETAILS	MANTRA FOR TODAY
There is a great deal of worries about your investments or financial affairs. You may feel depressed over money. You will have to deal with unwanted expenses.	Jai Jai Shiva Shambo.(2) ...Mahadeva Shambo (2) 21 times Om Jayanti Mangala Kali Bhadrakali Kapalini Durga Kshama Shiva Dhatri Swaha Swadha Namostute 9 times

BIBLE VERSES: (Proverbs)
22:19. That thy trust may be in the Lord, wherefore I have also shewn it to thee this day.
READ PSALMS #'s: 7, 16, 34 ,43, 52, 61, 79, 106, 124

SEPTEMBER 20, 2015

09/20/2015 SUN		This is considered a NEGATIVE day for you							Shiva
Moving	Shopping	Health	Investing	Gambling	Love is	Wedding	Travel	Work/Job	Planet
Bad	Bad	Bad	Bad	Excellent	Bad	Excellent	Bad	Bad	Jupiter

KEYWORDS ARE: Karmic debts, Fame - TV, IRS - Law, Denial - Doubt, Quarrels & lovers, Astrology, Sickness - cold, Investments, Abusive

Lotto #'s	play 4 #s	play 3 #s	Ruling Angel:............	Color Sugestion:............	Ruling Deity
10,10,34,32,17,23	8843	968	Haniel	Yellow/White/Silver	Mahalaxmi

ADVICE & DETAILS	MANTRA FOR TODAY
There is a great deal of tension about money and family. You may lose money today. There will be conflict with family members. You must control your ego. IRS and taxes could affect you today.	Om Hareem Nama Swaha..Shri Maha Laxmi Aye Namah swaha 12 times Om maha laxmi cha vidmahe vishnu pataya dhi mahi tanno laxmi pracho dayat Om hareem namam swaha 9 times

BIBLE VERSES: (Proverbs)
22:21. That I might shew thee the certainty, and the words of truth, to answer out of these to them that sent thee.
READ PSALMS #'s: 8, 17, 35 ,44, 53, 62, 80, 107, 125

SEPTEMBER 21, 2015

09/21/2015 MON		This is considered a NEUTRAL day for you							Shiva
Moving	Shopping	Health	Investing	Gambling	Love is	Wedding	Travel	Work/Job	Planet
Fair	Fair	Fair	Fair	Bad	Bad	Bad	Fair	Bad	Saturn

KEYWORDS ARE: God - Karma, IRS - Law, Accidents, death, Illnese, children, hypertension, Inner Conflicts, Legal matter, Abusive, Karmic debts

Lotto #'s	play 4 #s	play 3 #s	Ruling Angel:............	Color Sugestion:............	Ruling Deity
2,2,34,31,17,15	4617	169	Mikael	Gold/Brown/Blue/Dark Green	Pitridev

ADVICE & DETAILS	MANTRA FOR TODAY
You will feel sad today. There will be a sense of loss perhaps due to a death, divorce or project or idea that no longer has vitality. Instinctually you will want to deny that this change could bring any positive change, but time will show you valuable lessons you have learned from this experience. Regardless, you will be plagued with doubts about everythin	Om Ganga mataye nama swaha Om Varuna Devta aye Pahimam 11 times Om hareem mama sarva shatru janam vashee kuru kuru swaha om hareem ksham kasham kasheem kasheem swaha 9 times

BIBLE VERSES: (Proverbs)
22:23. Because the Lord will judge his cause: and will afflict them that have afflicted his soul.
READ PSALMS #'s: 9, 18, 36 ,45, 54, 63, 81, 108, 126

SEPTEMBER 22, 2015

| 09/22/2015 TUE | | | This is considered a POSITIVE day for you | | | | | | Shiva |

Moving	Shopping	Health	Investing	Gambling	Love is	Wedding	Travel	Work/Job	Planet
Good	Excellent	Good	Good	Fair	Excellent	Fair	Excelle	Good	Sun

KEYWORDS ARE: IRS - Law, Boastful, Denial - Doubt, losses, Stress with Bosses, Religious , Abusive, On Your Own, God - Karma

Lotto #'s	play 4 #s	play 3 #s	Ruling Angel:............	Color Sugestion:............	Ruling Deity
3,3,33,31,17,17	2069	2610	Gabriel	White/Yellow/ Peach	Gaitree

ADVICE & DETAILS	MANTRA FOR TODAY
It is a bad day for love, romance and companionship. You will be very frustrated with friends, lovers or just about anyone. You must avoid being too bossy or demanding with your loved ones.	Om Namo Bhagawate Mukhtanandaya, 108 times AUM KRSNAYA VIDMAHE DAMODARAYA DHIMAHI. TANNO VISHNU PRACODAYAT. 9 times

BIBLE VERSES: (Proverbs)
22:16. He that oppresseth the poor, to increase his own riches, shall himself give to one that is richer, and shall be in need.

READ PSALMS #'s: 1, 10, 28 ,37, 46, 55, 73, 100, 118

SEPTEMBER 23, 2015

| 09/23/2015 WED | | | This is considered a POSITIVE day for you | | | | | | Shiva |

Moving	Shopping	Health	Investing	Gambling	Love is	Wedding	Travel	Work/Job	Planet
Good	Excellent	Excellent	Good	Good	Good	Good	Excelle	Good	Venus

KEYWORDS ARE: Communication, Partnership, read, children, Social Functions, Sleepiness, Karmic debts, Affection, Expression

Lotto #'s	play 4 #s	play 3 #s	Ruling Angel:............	Color Sugestion:............	Ruling Deity
4,4,34,31,17,10	10127	362	Raziel	Red/Yellow/Pink	Durga

ADVICE & DETAILS	MANTRA FOR TODAY
You will have children and family members that are cooperative today. They will also demand much attention. There may be arguments between lovers.	Kali Durge Namo Nama Om Durge aye nama swaha 108 times AUM TATPURUSAYA VIDMAHE VAKRATUNDAY DHIMAHI. TANNO DANTI PRACODAYAT. 9 times

BIBLE VERSES: (Proverbs)
22:18. Which shall be beautiful for thee, if thou keep it in thy bowels, and it shall flow in thy lips:

READ PSALMS #'s: 2, 11, 29 ,38, 47, 56, 74, 101, 119

SEPTEMBER 24, 2015

| 09/24/2015 THU | | | This is considered a NEUTRAL day for you | | | | | | Shiva |

Moving	Shopping	Health	Investing	Gambling	Love is	Wedding	Travel	Work/Job	Planet
Bad	Bad	Bad	Bad	Good	Fair	Good	Bad	Bad	Mercury

KEYWORDS ARE: Tiredness, read, career, building, Co-workers, Advice given, God - Karma, Expression, Industrial

Lotto #'s	play 4 #s	play 3 #s	Ruling Angel:............	Color Sugestion:............	Ruling Deity
5,5,33,31,17,12	8887	463	Zadkiel	Green/Sky Blue/White	Saraswaty

ADVICE & DETAILS	MANTRA FOR TODAY
This is a good day to chant your mantras as there will be tension, stress and many challenges at work. Avoid going to any meetings or joining any groups in this day. Children will also be difficult.	Om hareem Kleem Hreem Aem Saraswataye namaha 21 times Om Guru bramha, Guru Vishnu Guru Deva mahaeshwara guru saksha paam bramha, tasmi shri guruve nama 9 times

BIBLE VERSES: (Proverbs)
22:20. Behold I have described it to thee three manner of ways, in thoughts and knowledge:

READ PSALMS #'s: 3, 12, 30 ,39, 48, 57, 75, 102, 120

SEPTEMBER 25, 2015

| 09/25/2015 | FRI | | This is considered a POSITIVE day for you | | | | | | | Shiva |

Moving	Shopping	Health	Investing	Gambling	Love is	Wedding	Travel	Work/Job	Planet
Excellent	Good	Excellent	Good	Bad	Excellent	Good	Excelle	Good	Pluto

KEYWORDS ARE: travel, career, change, deception, Belief and faith, Alcohol - drugs, IRS - Law, Industrial, Short Trips

Lotto #'s	play 4 #s	play 3 #s	Ruling Angel:............	Color Sugestion:............	Ruling Deity
6,5,34,32,17,14	3702	564	Metatron	Dark Blue/ Purple/ Mauve	Ganesh

ADVICE & DETAILS

Travel will be difficult today, you may get into an accident if you drive. So you must watch out for traffic tickets and follow all rules of the road. There may be positive social gatherings.

MANTRA FOR TODAY

Om Jai Viganeshwaraya..
Lambodaraya Namo Namaha
21 times
Om Sarva Mangal Mangalye,
Shiva Sarvart Sadike, Sharan
Tryambike Gowri, Narayane
Namo asttute
9 times

BIBLE VERSES: (Proverbs)

22:22. Do no violence to the poor, because he is poor: and do not oppress the needy in the gate:

READ PSALMS #'s: 4, 13, 31 ,40, 49, 58, 76, 103, 121

SEPTEMBER 26, 2015

| 09/26/2015 | SAT | | This is considered a NEGATIVE day for you | | | | | | | Shiva |

Moving	Shopping	Health	Investing	Gambling	Love is	Wedding	Travel	Work/Job	Planet
Bad	Bad	Bad	Fair	Good	Bad	Good	Bad	Bad	Uranus

KEYWORDS ARE: frustration, change, power, electricity, Money conflicts, Slow Day, Accidents, Short Trips, responsibility

Lotto #'s	play 4 #s	play 3 #s	Ruling Angel:............	Color Sugestion:............	Ruling Deity
7,7,34,32,17,17	6856	665	Camael	Orange/White/Light Green/ Beige	Krishna

ADVICE & DETAILS

You will have a great deal of frustration and anxiety with changes that are hard for you to accept. There will be an uncomfortable move or separation. You will be frustrated over living conditions.

MANTRA FOR TODAY

Om Graam Greem Graum Sa
Gurave namah swaha
21 times
AUM VAGDEVYAI CA
VIDMAHE KAMARAJAYA
DHIMAHI. TANNO DEVI
PRACODAYAT.
9 times

BIBLE VERSES: (Proverbs)

22:24. Be not a friend to an angry man, and do not walk with a furious man:
0

READ PSALMS #'s: 5, 14, 32 ,41, 50, 59, 77, 104, 122

SEPTEMBER 27, 2015

| 09/27/2015 | SUN | | This is considered a NEUTRAL day for you | | | | | | | Shiva |

Moving	Shopping	Health	Investing	Gambling	Love is	Wedding	Travel	Work/Job	Planet
Good	Fair	Fair	Bad	Fair	Good	Bad	Good	Fair	Mars

KEYWORDS ARE: finish, power, religion, priests, Slow Day with Tension, Enemies, Denial - Doubt, responsibility, sleepiness

Lotto #'s	play 4 #s	play 3 #s	Ruling Angel:............	Color Sugestion:............	Ruling Deity
8,8,33,32,17,19	10781	766	Raphael	Purple/DeepBlue/Rose	Hanuman

ADVICE & DETAILS

You will feel distress over life goal and objectives. You will have the feeling that life is moving too slow for you. You may be bored or be disturbed. Government agencies will affect you today. Follow rules.

MANTRA FOR TODAY

Om Mana Swasti Shanti Kuru
kuru Swaha Shivoham Shivoham
27 times
om haring jawala mukhi mam
sarva shatru bakshaya bakshaya
hung phat swaha
Om Nama shivaya pahimam
9 times

BIBLE VERSES: (Proverbs)

22:26. Be not with them that fasten down their hands, and that offer themselves sureties for debts:

READ PSALMS #'s: 6, 15, 33 ,42, 51, 60, 78, 105, 123

SEPTEMBER 28, 2015

09/28/2015 MON		This is considered a POSITIVE day for you							Shiva

Moving	Shopping	Health	Investing	Gambling	Love is	Wedding	Travel	Work/Job	Planet
Good	Good	Excellent	Excellent	Bad	Good	Fair	Good	Excellent	Moon

KEYWORDS ARE: Abusive, Advice given, Fame - TV, High Pleasure, Business & money gains, Religious, Death, Inner Conflicts, Investments

Lotto #'s	play 4 #s	play 3 #s	Ruling Angel:............	Color Sugestion:............	Ruling Deity
9,9,33,32,17,20	10760	867	Zaphkiel	Light Blue/Purple/Peach	Ganga

ADVICE & DETAILS	MANTRA FOR TODAY
There is a great deal of worries about your investments or financial affairs. You may feel depressed over money. You will have to deal with unwanted expenses.	Jai Jai Shiva Shambo.(2) ...Mahadeva Shambo (2) 21 times Om Jayanti Mangala Kali Bhadrakali Kapalini Durga Kshama Shiva Dhatri Swaha Swadha Namostute 9 times

BIBLE VERSES: (Proverbs)
22:28. Pass not beyond the ancient bounds which thy fathers have set.
0
READ PSALMS #'s: 7, 16, 34 ,43, 52, 61, 79, 106, 124

SEPTEMBER 29, 2015

09/29/2015 TUE		This is considered a NEGATIVE day for you							Shiva

Moving	Shopping	Health	Investing	Gambling	Love is	Wedding	Travel	Work/Job	Planet
Bad	Bad	Bad	Bad	Excellent	Bad	Excellent	Bad	Bad	Jupiter

KEYWORDS ARE: Karmic debts, Fame - TV, IRS - Law, Denial - Doubt, Quarrels & lovers, Astrology, Sickness - cold, Investments, Abusive

Lotto #'s	play 4 #s	play 3 #s	Ruling Angel:............	Color Sugestion:............	Ruling Deity
10,9,33,32,17,23	4243	968	Haniel	Yellow/White/Silver	Mahalaxmi

ADVICE & DETAILS	MANTRA FOR TODAY
There is a great deal of tension about money and family. You may lose money today. There will be conflict with family members. You must control your ego. IRS and taxes could affect you today.	Om Hareem Nama Swaha..Shri Maha Laxmi Aye Namah swaha 12 times Om maha laxmi cha vidmahe vishnu pataya dhi mahi tanno laxmi pracho dayat Om hareem namam swaha 9 times

BIBLE VERSES: (Proverbs)
23:1. When thou shalt sit to eat with a prince, consider diligently what is set before thy face:
READ PSALMS #'s: 8, 17, 35 ,44, 53, 62, 80, 107, 125

SEPTEMBER 30, 2015

09/30/2015 WED		This is considered a NEUTRAL day for you							Shiva

Moving	Shopping	Health	Investing	Gambling	Love is	Wedding	Travel	Work/Job	Planet
Fair	Fair	Fair	Fair	Bad	Bad	Bad	Fair	Bad	Saturn

KEYWORDS ARE: God - Karma, IRS - Law, Accidents, death, Illnese, children, hypertension, Inner Conflicts, Legal matter, Abusive, Karmic debts

Lotto #'s	play 4 #s	play 3 #s	Ruling Angel:............	Color Sugestion:............	Ruling Deity
2,1,34,32,17,15	4520	169	Mikael	Gold/Brown/Blue/Dark Green	Pitridev

ADVICE & DETAILS	MANTRA FOR TODAY
You will feel sad today. There will be a sense of loss perhaps due to a death, divorce or project or idea that no longer has vitality. Instinctually you will want to deny that this change could bring any positive change, but time will show you valuable lessons you have learned from this experience. Regardless, you will be plagued with doubts about everythin	Om Ganga mataye nama swaha Om Varuna Devta aye Pahimam 11 times Om hareem mama sarva shatru janam vashee kuru kuru swaha om hareem ksham kasham kasheem kasheem swaha 9 times

BIBLE VERSES: (Proverbs)
23:3. Be not desirous of his meats, in which is the bread of deceit.
0
READ PSALMS #'s: 9, 18, 36 ,45, 54, 63, 81, 108, 126

OCTOBER 1, 2015

10/01/2015 THU			This is considered a POSITIVE day for you						Shiva
Moving	Shopping	Health	Investing	Gambling	Love is	Wedding	Travel	Work/Job	Planet
Good	Good	Excellent	Excellent	Excellent	Good	Excellent	Good	Excellent	Jupiter

KEYWORDS ARE: IRS - Law, High Pleasure, Big Expense, investment,
Income is low and expenses, Investments, Abusive, Promotion, Fame - TV

Lotto #'s	play 4 #s	play 3 #s	Ruling Angel:............	Color Sugestion:............	Ruling Deity
9,10,33,31,18,21	4599	877	Haniel	Yellow/White/Silver	Mahalaxmi

ADVICE & DETAILS	MANTRA FOR TODAY
You will be having a good feeling about your income and expenses. It is a good day to purchase and make investments in the market. It is also a good day to look for a new home.	Om Namo Bhagawate Mukhtanandaya, 108 times AUM KRSNAYA VIDMAHE DAMODARAYA DHIMAHI. TANNO VISHNU PRACODAYAT. 9 times

BIBLE VERSES: (Proverbs)
23:3. Be not desirous of his meats, in which is the bread of deceit.
0
READ PSALMS #'s: 8, 17, 35 ,44, 53, 62, 80, 107, 125

OCTOBER 2, 2015

10/02/2015 FRI			This is considered a NEGATIVE day for you						Shiva
Moving	Shopping	Health	Investing	Gambling	Love is	Wedding	Travel	Work/Job	Planet
Bad	Bad	Bad	Bad	Bad	Bad	Bad	Bad	Bad	Saturn

KEYWORDS ARE: Accidents, Denial - Doubt, death, finish,
Traffic problems, Tickets, Power, Karmic debts, God - Karma, IRS - Law

Lotto #'s	play 4 #s	play 3 #s	Ruling Angel:............	Color Sugestion:............	Ruling Deity
10,2,34,32,18,15	4386	978	Mikael	Gold/Brown/Blue/Dark Green	Pitridev

ADVICE & DETAILS	MANTRA FOR TODAY
Death is the influence of today. This may be a physical death, the end of a project, idea, habit or thought. You must remember that death is necessary for life and that the end of something, brings new beginnings. This day is also influenced by accidents, so be aware of of your surroundings, do not text while driving or get involved in any kind of risky behavi	Om Hareem Nama Swaha..Shri Maha Laxmi Aye Namah swaha 12 times Om maha laxmi cha vidmahe vishnu pataya dhi mahi tanno laxmi pracho dayat Om hareem namam swaha 9 times

BIBLE VERSES: (Proverbs)
23:5. Lift not up thy eyes to riches which thou canst not have: because they shall make themselves wings like those of an eagle, and shall fly towards
READ PSALMS #'s: 9, 18, 36 ,45, 54, 63, 81, 108, 126

OCTOBER 3, 2015

10/03/2015 SAT			This is considered a NEUTRAL day for you						Shiva
Moving	Shopping	Health	Investing	Gambling	Love is	Wedding	Travel	Work/Job	Planet
Fair	Fair	Fair	Fair	Fair	Bad	Fair	Fair	Bad	Sun

KEYWORDS ARE: Confined, lonliness, independence, individuality,
Illness - Cold, Promotion, God - Karma, Home Alone, Boastful

Lotto #'s	play 4 #s	play 3 #s	Ruling Angel:............	Color Sugestion:............	Ruling Deity
2,3,33,32,18,17	2877	179	Gabriel	White/Yellow/ Peach	Gaitree

ADVICE & DETAILS	MANTRA FOR TODAY
You can connect with the real power within you, the universal consciousness that inhabits in you. Dedicate time to meditation, prayer, religious acts of devotion and if possible visit priests, Gurus or spiritual guides.	Om Ganga mataye nama swaha Om Varuna Devta aye Pahimam 11 times Om hareem mama sarva shatru janam vashee kuru kuru swaha om hareem ksham kasham kasheem kasheem swaha 9 times

BIBLE VERSES: (Proverbs)
22:27. For if thou have not wherewith to restore, what cause is there that he should take the covering from thy bed?
READ PSALMS #'s: 1, 10, 28 ,37, 46, 55, 73, 100, 118

OCTOBER 4, 2015

10/04/2015	SUN	This is considered a POSITIVE day for you							Shiva

Moving	Shopping	Health	Investing	Gambling	Love is	Wedding	Travel	Work/Job	Planet
Good	Excellent	Good	Good	Good	Excellent	Good	Excelle	Good	Venus

KEYWORDS ARE: love, romamce, marriage, Talkative, Spriritual meeting, Fame - TV, IRS - Law, Music, Partnership

Lotto #'s	play 4 #s	play 3 #s	Ruling Angel:............	Color Sugestion:............	Ruling Deity
3,3,34,31,18,19	8049	2710	Raziel	Red/Yellow/Pink	Durga

ADVICE & DETAILS	MANTRA FOR TODAY
Love will return to you this day. You will be able to make up back with your lover. You will be feeling very sleepy today. You will want to enjoy good food and have a quiet date.	Om Namo Bhagawate Mukhtanandaya, 108 times AUM KRSNAYA VIDMAHE DAMODARAYA DHIMAHI. TANNO VISHNU PRACODAYAT. 9 times

BIBLE VERSES: (Proverbs)
22:29. Hast thou seen a man swift in his work? he shall stand before kings, and shall not be before those that are obscure.

READ PSALMS #'s: 2, 11, 29 ,38, 47, 56, 74, 101, 119

OCTOBER 5, 2015

10/05/2015	MON	This is considered a POSITIVE day for you							Shiva

Moving	Shopping	Health	Investing	Gambling	Love is	Wedding	Travel	Work/Job	Planet
Good	Excellent	Excellent	Good	Good	Good	Good	Excelle	Good	Mercury

KEYWORDS ARE: children, children, publishing, telephone, Shopping & bargains, Money Wasted, Accidents, Publishing, read

Lotto #'s	play 4 #s	play 3 #s	Ruling Angel:............	Color Sugestion:............	Ruling Deity
4,5,33,32,18,12	8356	372	Zadkiel	Green/Sky Blue/White	Saraswaty

ADVICE & DETAILS	MANTRA FOR TODAY
The thought of watching TV is very appealing today. Spending time with children will benefit your creativity, but you must refrain from allowing immaturity to control your actions today.	Kali Durge Namo Nama Om Durge aye nama swaha 108 times AUM TATPURUSAYA VIDMAHE VAKRATUNDAY DHIMAHI. TANNO DANTI PRACODAYAT. 9 times

BIBLE VERSES: (Proverbs)
23:2. And put a knife to thy throat, if it be so that thou have thy soul in thy own power.

READ PSALMS #'s: 3, 12, 30 ,39, 48, 57, 75, 102, 120

OCTOBER 6, 2015

10/06/2015	TUE	This is considered a NEUTRAL day for you							Shiva

Moving	Shopping	Health	Investing	Gambling	Love is	Wedding	Travel	Work/Job	Planet
Bad	Bad	Bad	Bad	Bad	Fair	Good	Bad	Bad	Pluto

KEYWORDS ARE: employment, building, stress, co-worker, Real Estate, High Pleasure, Denial - Doubt, work, career

Lotto #'s	play 4 #s	play 3 #s	Ruling Angel:............	Color Sugestion:............	Ruling Deity
5,6,33,32,18,13	5220	473	Metatron	Dark Blue/ Purple/ Mauve	Ganesh

ADVICE & DETAILS	MANTRA FOR TODAY
You may have to deal with problems at your job today. Deal with these difficulties keeping in mind your long-term goals and ambitons. You will have to work very hard today.	Om hareem Kleem Hreem Aem Saraswataye namaha 21 times Om Guru bramha, Guru Vishnu Guru Deva mahaeshwara guru saksha paam bramha, tasmi shri guruve nama 9 times

BIBLE VERSES: (Proverbs)
23:4. Labour not to be rich: but set bounds to thy prudence.

0

READ PSALMS #'s: 4, 13, 31 ,40, 49, 58, 76, 103, 121

OCTOBER 7, 2015

| 10/07/2015 WED | This is considered a POSITIVE day for you | | | | | | | | Shiva |

Moving	Shopping	Health	Investing	Gambling	Love is	Wedding	Travel	Work/Job	Planet
Excellent	Good	Excellent	Good	Good	Excellent	Good	Excelle	Good	Uranus

KEYWORDS ARE: Deception, Exercise, Illicit Affairs, Beauty - Sex, High sexuality, Major Expense, Death, Distant, far, Travel delays

Lotto #'s	play 4 #s	play 3 #s	Ruling Angel:............	Color Sugestion:............	Ruling Deity
6,6,34,32,18,16	5290	574	Camael	Orange/White/Light Green/ Beige	Krishna

ADVICE & DETAILS	MANTRA FOR TODAY
The greatest influence ot this day is that of moving, taking short trips and changes. Following the divine laws of the universe will provide protection while you travel and will also protect you from deceit and trickery that others may use to gain an unfair and dishonest advantage.	*Om Jai Viganeshwaraya.. Lambodaraya Namo Namaha* *21 times* *Om Sarva Mangal Mangalye, Shiva Sarvart Sadike, Sharan Tryambike Gowri, Narayane Namo asttute* *9 times*

BIBLE VERSES: (Proverbs)

23:6. Eat not with an envious man, and desire not his meats:

0

READ PSALMS #'s: 5, 14, 32 ,41, 50, 59, 77, 104, 122

OCTOBER 8, 2015

| 10/08/2015 THU | This is considered a NEGATIVE day for you | | | | | | | | Shiva |

Moving	Shopping	Health	Investing	Gambling	Love is	Wedding	Travel	Work/Job	Planet
Bad	Bad	Bad	Fair	Fair	Bad	Bad	Bad	Bad	Mars

KEYWORDS ARE: Quarrels, Jealousy, Police, Anger - Ego, Disagreement in Love, Money - Profits, Sickness - cold, Family Conflicts, Traffic Ticket

Lotto #'s	play 4 #s	play 3 #s	Ruling Angel:............	Color Sugestion:............	Ruling Deity
7,8,33,31,18,17	4039	675	Raphael	Purple/DeepBlue/Rose	Hanuman

ADVICE & DETAILS	MANTRA FOR TODAY
Today your enemies will oppose you. Enemies are not only people, but also situations and addictions. You must avoid today alcohol and drugs because they may bring very negative consequences into your life. You will be invited to socialize and share with others, but make sure you do it in a balanced manner and leave as soon as you feel sleepy or tired.	*Om Graam Greem Graum Sa Gurave namah swaha* *21 times* *AUM VAGDEVYAI CA VIDMAHE KAMARAJAYA DHIMAHI. TANNO DEVI PRACODAYAT.* *9 times*

BIBLE VERSES: (Proverbs)

23:8. The meats which thou hadst eaten, thou shalt vomit up: and shalt lose thy beautiful words.

READ PSALMS #'s: 6, 15, 33 ,42, 51, 60, 78, 105, 123

OCTOBER 9, 2015

| 10/09/2015 FRI | This is considered a NEUTRAL day for you | | | | | | | | Shiva |

Moving	Shopping	Health	Investing	Gambling	Love is	Wedding	Travel	Work/Job	Planet
Good	Fair	Fair	Bad	Bad	Good	Fair	Good	Fair	Moon

KEYWORDS ARE: God - Karma, Slow Day, Enemies, spiritual, Astrologers, Psychics, priests, Income, Legal matter, Sleepiness, Advice given

Lotto #'s	play 4 #s	play 3 #s	Ruling Angel:............	Color Sugestion:............	Ruling Deity
8,8,33,32,18,19	3912	776	Zaphkiel	Light Blue/Purple/Peach	Ganga

ADVICE & DETAILS	MANTRA FOR TODAY
This day requires that you devote your internal power to the power of the Divine. This is a day where you are required to spend time in religious or spiritual pursuits, meditating, praying or visiting priests or holy people.	*Om Mana Swasti Shanti Kuru kuru Swaha Shivoham Shivoham* *27 times* *om haring jawala mukhi mam sarva shatru bakshaya bakshaya hung phat swaha* *Om Nama shivaya pahimam* *9 times*

BIBLE VERSES: (Proverbs)

23:10. Touch not the bounds of little ones: and enter not into the field of the fatherless:

READ PSALMS #'s: 7, 16, 34 ,43, 52, 61, 79, 106, 124

OCTOBER 10, 2015

10/10/2015 SAT		This is considered a POSITIVE day for you							Shiva
Moving	Shopping	Health	Investing	Gambling	Love is	Wedding	Travel	Work/Job	Planet
Good	Good	Excellent	Excellent	Excellent	Good	Excellent	Good	Excellent	Jupiter

KEYWORDS ARE: IRS - Law, High Pleasure, Big Expense, investment, Income is low and expenses, Investments, Abusive, Promotion, Fame - TV

Lotto #'s	play 4 #s	play 3 #s	Ruling Angel:............	Color Sugestion:............	Ruling Deity
9,10,33,31,18,21	10378	877	Haniel	Yellow/White/Silver	Mahalaxmi

ADVICE & DETAILS

You will be having a good feeling about your income and expenses. It is a good day to purchase and make investments in the market. It is also a good day to look for a new home.

MANTRA FOR TODAY

Jai Jai Shiva Shambo.(2)
...Mahadeva Shambo (2)
21 times
Om Jayanti Mangala Kali
Bhadrakali Kapalini Durga
Kshama Shiva Dhatri Swaha
Swadha Namostute
9 times

BIBLE VERSES: (Proverbs)

23:12. Let thy heart apply itself to instruction and thy ears to words of knowledge.

READ PSALMS #'s: 8, 17, 35 ,44, 53, 62, 80, 107, 125

OCTOBER 11, 2015

10/11/2015 SUN		This is considered a NEGATIVE day for you							Shiva
Moving	Shopping	Health	Investing	Gambling	Love is	Wedding	Travel	Work/Job	Planet
Bad	Bad	Bad	Bad	Bad	Bad	Bad	Bad	Bad	Saturn

KEYWORDS ARE: Accidents, Denial - Doubt, death, finish, Traffic problems, Tickets, Power, Karmic debts, God - Karma, IRS - Law

Lotto #'s	play 4 #s	play 3 #s	Ruling Angel:............	Color Sugestion:............	Ruling Deity
10,2,33,32,18,14	2239	978	Mikael	Gold/Brown/Blue/Dark Green	Pitridev

ADVICE & DETAILS

Death is the influence of today. This may be a physical death, the end of a project, idea, habit or thought. You must remember that death is necessary for life and that the end of something, brings new beginnings. This day is also influenced by accidents, so be aware of of your surroundings, do not text while driving or get involved in any kind of risky behavi

MANTRA FOR TODAY

Om Hareem Nama Swaha..Shri
Maha Laxmi Aye Namah swaha
12 times
Om maha laxmi cha vidmahe
vishnu pataya dhi mahi tanno
laxmi pracho dayat
Om hareem namam swaha
9 times

BIBLE VERSES: (Proverbs)

23:14. Thou shalt beat him with the rod, and deliver his soul from hell.

0

READ PSALMS #'s: 9, 18, 36 ,45, 54, 63, 81, 108, 126

OCTOBER 12, 2015

10/12/2015 MON		This is considered a NEUTRAL day for you							Shiva
Moving	Shopping	Health	Investing	Gambling	Love is	Wedding	Travel	Work/Job	Planet
Fair	Fair	Fair	Fair	Fair	Bad	Fair	Fair	Bad	Sun

KEYWORDS ARE: Denial - Doubt, lonliness, losses, sadness, Family conflicts, Arguments, Promotion, God - Karma, Home Alone, Accidents

Lotto #'s	play 4 #s	play 3 #s	Ruling Angel:............	Color Sugestion:............	Ruling Deity
2,2,34,32,18,17	8828	179	Gabriel	White/Yellow/ Peach	Gaitree

ADVICE & DETAILS

You can connect with the real power within you, the universal consciousness that inhabits in you. Dedicate time to meditation, prayer, religious acts of devotion and if possible visit priests, Gurus or spiritual guides.

MANTRA FOR TODAY

Om Ganga mataye nama swaha
Om Varuna Devta aye Pahimam
11 times
Om hareem mama sarva shatru
janam vashee kuru kuru swaha
om hareem ksham kasham
kasheem kasheem swaha
9 times

BIBLE VERSES: (Proverbs)

23:7. Because, like a soothsayer, and diviner, he thinketh that which he knoweth not. Eat and drink, will he say to thee: and his mind is not with

READ PSALMS #'s: 1, 10, 28 ,37, 46, 55, 73, 100, 118

OCTOBER 13, 2015

| 10/13/2015 TUE | | This is considered a POSITIVE day for you | | | | | | | Shiva |

Moving	Shopping	Health	Investing	Gambling	Love is	Wedding	Travel	Work/Job	Planet
Good	Excellent	Good	Good	Good	Excellent	Good	Excelle	Good	Venus

KEYWORDS ARE: love, romamce, marriage, Talkative, Spritual meeting, Fame - TV, IRS - Law, Music, Partnership

Lotto #'s	play 4 #s	play 3 #s	Ruling Angel:............	Color Sugestion:............	Ruling Deity
3,4,34,31,18,18	6278	2710	Raziel	Red/Yellow/Pink	Durga

ADVICE & DETAILS	MANTRA FOR TODAY
Love will return to you this day. You will be able to make up back with your lover. You will be feeling very sleepy today. You will want to enjoy good food and have a quiet date.	Om Namo Bhagawate Mukhtanandaya, 108 times AUM KRSNAYA VIDMAHE DAMODARAYA DHIMAHI. TANNO VISHNU PRACODAYAT. 9 times

BIBLE VERSES: (Proverbs)

23:9. Speak not in the ears of fools: because they will despise the instruction of thy speech.

READ PSALMS #'s: 2, 11, 29 ,38, 47, 56, 74, 101, 119

OCTOBER 14, 2015

| 10/14/2015 WED | | This is considered a POSITIVE day for you | | | | | | | Shiva |

Moving	Shopping	Health	Investing	Gambling	Love is	Wedding	Travel	Work/Job	Planet
Good	Excellent	Excellent	Good	Good	Good	Good	Excelle	Good	Mercury

KEYWORDS ARE: children, children, publishing, telephone, Shopping & bargains, Money Wasted, Accidents, Publishing, read

Lotto #'s	play 4 #s	play 3 #s	Ruling Angel:............	Color Sugestion:............	Ruling Deity
4,4,34,32,18,12	8991	372	Zadkiel	Green/Sky Blue/White	Saraswaty

ADVICE & DETAILS	MANTRA FOR TODAY
The thought of watching TV is very appealing today. Spending time with children will benefit your creativity, but you must refrain from allowing immaturity to control your actions today.	Kali Durge Namo Nama Om Durge aye nama swaha 108 times AUM TATPURUSAYA VIDMAHE VAKRATUNDAY DHIMAHI. TANNO DANTI PRACODAYAT. 9 times

BIBLE VERSES: (Proverbs)

23:11. For their near kinsman is strong: and he will judge their cause against thee.

READ PSALMS #'s: 3, 12, 30 ,39, 48, 57, 75, 102, 120

OCTOBER 15, 2015

| 10/15/2015 THU | | This is considered a NEUTRAL day for you | | | | | | | Shiva |

Moving	Shopping	Health	Investing	Gambling	Love is	Wedding	Travel	Work/Job	Planet
Bad	Bad	Bad	Bad	Bad	Fair	Good	Bad	Bad	Pluto

KEYWORDS ARE: employment, building, stress, co-worker, Real Estate, High Pleasure, Denial - Doubt, work, career

Lotto #'s	play 4 #s	play 3 #s	Ruling Angel:............	Color Sugestion:............	Ruling Deity
5,6,33,31,18,13	5987	473	Metatron	Dark Blue/ Purple/ Mauve	Ganesh

ADVICE & DETAILS	MANTRA FOR TODAY
You may have to deal with problems at your job today. Deal with these difficulties keeping in mind your long-term goals and ambitons. You will have to work very hard today.	Om hareem Kleem Hreem Aem Saraswataye namaha 21 times Om Guru bramha, Guru Vishnu Guru Deva mahaeshwara guru saksha paam bramha, tasmi shri guruve nama 9 times

BIBLE VERSES: (Proverbs)

23:13. Withhold not correction from a child: for if thou strike him with the rod, he shall not die.

READ PSALMS #'s: 4, 13, 31 ,40, 49, 58, 76, 103, 121

OCTOBER 16, 2015

10/16/2015 FRI		This is considered a POSITIVE day for you							Shiva
Moving	*Shopping*	*Health*	*Investing*	*Gambling*	*Love is*	*Wedding*	*Travel*	*Work/Job*	*Planet*
Excellent	Good	Excellent	Good	Good	Excellent	Good	Excelle	Good	Uranus

KEYWORDS ARE: Deception, Exercise, Illicit Affairs, Beauty - Sex,
High sexuality, Major Expense, Death, Distant, far, Travel delays

Lotto #'s	*play 4 #s*	*play 3 #s*	Ruling Angel:............	Color Sugestion:............	*Ruling Deity*
6,7,34,31,18,15	3611	574	Camael	Orange/White/Light Green/ Beige	Krishna

ADVICE & DETAILS	MANTRA FOR TODAY
The greatest influence ot this day is that of moving, taking short trips and changes. Following the divine laws of the universe will provide protection while you travel and will also protect you from deceit and trickery that others may use to gain an unfair and dishonest advantage.	*Om Jai Viganeshwaraya..* *Lambodaraya Namo Namaha* *21 times* *Om Sarva Mangal Mangalye,* *Shiva Sarvart Sadike, Sharan Tryambike Gowri, Narayane Namo asttute* *9 times*

BIBLE VERSES: (Proverbs)

23:15. My son, if thy mind be wise, my heart shall rejoice with thee:

0

READ PSALMS #'s: 5, 14, 32 ,41, 50, 59, 77, 104, 122

OCTOBER 17, 2015

10/17/2015 SAT		This is considered a NEGATIVE day for you							Shiva
Moving	*Shopping*	*Health*	*Investing*	*Gambling*	*Love is*	*Wedding*	*Travel*	*Work/Job*	*Planet*
Bad	Bad	Bad	Fair	Fair	Bad	Bad	Bad	Bad	Mars

KEYWORDS ARE: Quarrels, Jealousy, Police, Anger - Ego,
Disagreement in Love, Money - Profits, Sickness - cold, Family Conflicts, Traffic Ticket

Lotto #'s	*play 4 #s*	*play 3 #s*	Ruling Angel:............	Color Sugestion:............	*Ruling Deity*
7,8,34,31,18,17	2984	675	Raphael	Purple/DeepBlue/Rose	Hanuman

ADVICE & DETAILS	MANTRA FOR TODAY
Today your enemies will oppose you. Enemies are not only people, but also situations and addictions. You must avoid today alcohol and drugs because they may bring very negative consequences into your life. You will be invited to socialize and share with others, but make sure you do it in a balanced manner and leave as soon as you feel sleepy or tired.	*Om Graam Greem Graum Sa Gurave namah swaha* *21 times* *AUM VAGDEVYAI CA VIDMAHE KAMARAJAYA DHIMAHI. TANNO DEVI PRACODAYAT.* *9 times*

BIBLE VERSES: (Proverbs)

23:17. Let not thy heart envy sinners: but be thou in the fear of the Lord all the day long:

READ PSALMS #'s: 6, 15, 33 ,42, 51, 60, 78, 105, 123

OCTOBER 18, 2015

10/18/2015 SUN		This is considered a NEUTRAL day for you							Shiva
Moving	*Shopping*	*Health*	*Investing*	*Gambling*	*Love is*	*Wedding*	*Travel*	*Work/Job*	*Planet*
Good	Fair	Fair	Bad	Bad	Good	Fair	Good	Fair	Moon

KEYWORDS ARE: God - Karma, Slow Day, Enemies, spiritual,
Astrologers, Psychics, priests, Income, Legal matter, Sleepiness, Advice given

Lotto #'s	*play 4 #s*	*play 3 #s*	Ruling Angel:............	Color Sugestion:............	*Ruling Deity*
8,8,33,32,18,19	4512	776	Zaphkiel	Light Blue/Purple/Peach	Ganga

ADVICE & DETAILS	MANTRA FOR TODAY
This day requires that you devote your internal power to the power of the Divine. This is a day where you are required to spend time in religious or spiritual pursuits, meditating, praying or visiting priests or holy people.	*Om Mana Swasti Shanti Kuru kuru Swaha Shivoham Shivoham* *27 times* *om haring jawala mukhi mam sarva shatru bakshaya bakshaya hung phat swaha* *Om Nama shivaya pahimam* *9 times*

BIBLE VERSES: (Proverbs)

23:19. Hear thou, my son, and be wise: and guide thy mind in the way.

0

READ PSALMS #'s: 7, 16, 34 ,43, 52, 61, 79, 106, 124

OCTOBER 19, 2015

| 10/19/2015 MON | | This is considered a POSITIVE day for you | | | | | | | Shiva |

Moving	Shopping	Health	Investing	Gambling	Love is	Wedding	Travel	Work/Job	Planet
Good	Good	Excellent	Excellent	Excellent	Good	Excellent	Good	Excellent	Jupiter

KEYWORDS ARE: IRS - Law, High Pleasure, Big Expense, investment, Income is low and expenses, Investments, Abusive, Promotion, Fame - TV

Lotto #'s	play 4 #s	play 3 #s	Ruling Angel:............	Color Sugestion:............	Ruling Deity
9,10,34,31,18,21	3135	877	Haniel	Yellow/White/Silver	Mahalaxmi

ADVICE & DETAILS

You will be having a good feeling about your income and expenses. It is a good day to purchase and make investments in the market. It is also a good day to look for a new home.

BIBLE VERSES: (Proverbs)

23:21. Because they that give themselves to drinking, and that club together, shall be consumed: and drowsiness shall be clothed with rags.

READ PSALMS #'s: 8, 17, 35 ,44, 53, 62, 80, 107, 125

MANTRA FOR TODAY

Jai Jai Shiva Shambo.(2)
...Mahadeva Shambo (2)
21 times
Om Jayanti Mangala Kali
Bhadrakali Kapalini Durga
Kshama Shiva Dhatri Swaha
Swadha Namostute
9 times

OCTOBER 20, 2015

| 10/20/2015 TUE | | This is considered a NEGATIVE day for you | | | | | | | Shiva |

Moving	Shopping	Health	Investing	Gambling	Love is	Wedding	Travel	Work/Job	Planet
Bad	Bad	Bad	Bad	Bad	Bad	Bad	Bad	Bad	Saturn

KEYWORDS ARE: Accidents, Denial - Doubt, death, finish, Traffic problems, Tickets, Power, Karmic debts, God - Karma, IRS - Law

Lotto #'s	play 4 #s	play 3 #s	Ruling Angel:............	Color Sugestion:............	Ruling Deity
10,1,34,32,18,15	6095	978	Mikael	Gold/Brown/Blue/Dark Green	Pitridev

ADVICE & DETAILS

Death is the influence of today. This may be a physical death, the end of a project, idea, habit or thought. You must remember that death is necessary for life and that the end of something, brings new beginnings. This day is also influenced by accidents, so be aware of of your surroundings, do not text while driving or get involved in any kind of risky behavi

BIBLE VERSES: (Proverbs)

23:23. Buy truth, and do not sell wisdom, and instruction, and understanding.

READ PSALMS #'s: 9, 18, 36 ,45, 54, 63, 81, 108, 126

MANTRA FOR TODAY

Om Hareem Nama Swaha..Shri Maha Laxmi Aye Namah swaha
12 times
Om maha laxmi cha vidmahe vishnu pataya dhi mahi tanno laxmi pracho dayat
Om hareem namam swaha
9 times

OCTOBER 21, 2015

| 10/21/2015 WED | | This is considered a NEUTRAL day for you | | | | | | | Shiva |

Moving	Shopping	Health	Investing	Gambling	Love is	Wedding	Travel	Work/Job	Planet
Fair	Fair	Fair	Fair	Fair	Bad	Fair	Fair	Bad	Sun

KEYWORDS ARE: Denial - Doubt, lonliness, losses, sadness, Family conflicts, Arguments, Promotion, God - Karma, Home Alone, Accidents

Lotto #'s	play 4 #s	play 3 #s	Ruling Angel:............	Color Sugestion:............	Ruling Deity
2,3,34,31,18,16	6898	179	Gabriel	White/Yellow/ Peach	Gaitree

ADVICE & DETAILS

You can connect with the real power within you, the universal consciousness that inhabits in you. Dedicate time to meditation, prayer, religious acts of devotion and if possible visit priests, Gurus or spiritual guides.

BIBLE VERSES: (Proverbs)

23:16. And my reins shall rejoice, when thy lips shall speak what is right.
0

READ PSALMS #'s: 1, 10, 28 ,37, 46, 55, 73, 100, 118

MANTRA FOR TODAY

Om Ganga mataye nama swaha
Om Varuna Devta aye Pahimam
11 times
Om hareem mama sarva shatru janam vashee kuru kuru swaha
om hareem ksham kasham kasheem kasheem swaha
9 times

OCTOBER 22, 2015

10/22/2015 THU		This is considered a POSITIVE day for you							Shiva

Moving	Shopping	Health	Investing	Gambling	Love is	Wedding	Travel	Work/Job	Planet
Good	Excellent	Good	Good	Good	Excellent	Good	Excelle	Good	Venus

KEYWORDS ARE: death, romamce, finish, fame,
Tiredness, Low Energy, Sleepy, Fame - TV, IRS - Law, Music, Denial - Doubt

Lotto #'s	play 4 #s	play 3 #s	Ruling Angel:............	Color Sugestion:............	Ruling Deity
3,4,34,31,18,18	8561	2710	Raziel	Red/Yellow/Pink	Durga

ADVICE & DETAILS	MANTRA FOR TODAY
Love will return to you this day. You will be able to make up back with your lover. You will be feeling very sleepy today. You will want to enjoy good food and have a quiet date.	Om Namo Bhagawate Mukhtanandaya, 108 times AUM KRSNAYA VIDMAHE DAMODARAYA DHIMAHI. TANNO VISHNU PRACODAYAT. 9 times
BIBLE VERSES: (Proverbs)	
23:18. Because thou shalt have hope in the latter end, and thy expectation shall not be taken away.	
READ PSALMS #'s: 2, 11, 29 ,38, 47, 56, 74, 101, 119	

OCTOBER 23, 2015

10/23/2015 FRI		This is considered a POSITIVE day for you							Shiva

Moving	Shopping	Health	Investing	Gambling	Love is	Wedding	Travel	Work/Job	Planet
Good	Excellent	Excellent	Good	Good	Good	Good	Excelle	Good	Mercury

KEYWORDS ARE: children, children, publishing, telephone,
Shopping & bargains, Money Wasted, Accidents, Publishing, read

Lotto #'s	play 4 #s	play 3 #s	Ruling Angel:............	Color Sugestion:............	Ruling Deity
4,4,34,31,18,11	6138	372	Zadkiel	Green/Sky Blue/White	Saraswaty

ADVICE & DETAILS	MANTRA FOR TODAY
The thought of watching TV is very appealing today. Spending time with children will benefit your creativity, but you must refrain from allowing immaturity to control your actions today.	Kali Durge Namo Nama Om Durge aye nama swaha 108 times AUM TATPURUSAYA VIDMAHE VAKRATUNDAY DHIMAHI. TANNO DANTI PRACODAYAT. 9 times
BIBLE VERSES: (Proverbs)	
23:20. Be not in the feasts of great drinkers, nor in their revellings, who contribute flesh to eat:	
READ PSALMS #'s: 3, 12, 30 ,39, 48, 57, 75, 102, 120	

OCTOBER 24, 2015

10/24/2015 SAT		This is considered a NEUTRAL day for you							Shiva

Moving	Shopping	Health	Investing	Gambling	Love is	Wedding	Travel	Work/Job	Planet
Bad	Bad	Bad	Bad	Bad	Fair	Good	Bad	Bad	Pluto

KEYWORDS ARE: employment, building, stress, co-worker,
Real Estate, High Pleasure, Denial - Doubt, work, career

Lotto #'s	play 4 #s	play 3 #s	Ruling Angel:............	Color Sugestion:............	Ruling Deity
5,5,33,31,18,14	1952	473	Metatron	Dark Blue/ Purple/ Mauve	Ganesh

ADVICE & DETAILS	MANTRA FOR TODAY
You may have to deal with problems at your job today. Deal with these difficulties keeping in mind your long-term goals and ambitons. You will have to work very hard today.	Om hareem Kleem Hreem Aem Saraswataye namaha 21 times Om Guru bramha, Guru Vishnu Guru Deva mahaeshwara guru saksha paam bramha, tasmi shri guruve nama 9 times
BIBLE VERSES: (Proverbs)	
23:22. Hearken to thy father, that begot thee: and despise not thy mother when she is old.	
READ PSALMS #'s: 4, 13, 31 ,40, 49, 58, 76, 103, 121	

OCTOBER 25, 2015

| 10/25/2015 SUN | This is considered a POSITIVE day for you | | | | | | | | Shiva |

Moving	Shopping	Health	Investing	Gambling	Love is	Wedding	Travel	Work/Job	Planet
Excellent	Good	Excellent	Good	Good	Excellent	Good	Excelle	Good	Uranus

KEYWORDS ARE: Deception, Exercise, Illicit Affairs, Beauty - Sex, High sexuality, Major Expense, Death, Distant, far, Travel delays

Lotto #'s	play 4 #s	play 3 #s	Ruling Angel:...........	Color Sugestion:...........	Ruling Deity
6,7,34,31,18,16	2545	574	Camael	Orange/White/Light Green/ Beige	Krishna

ADVICE & DETAILS	MANTRA FOR TODAY
The greatest influence ot this day is that of moving, taking short trips and changes. Following the divine laws of the universe will provide protection while you travel and will also protect you from deceit and trickery that others may use to gain an unfair and dishonest advantage.	*Om Jai Viganeshwaraya.. Lambodaraya Namo Namaha 21 times Om Sarva Mangal Mangalye, Shiva Sarvart Sadike, Sharan Tryambike Gowri, Narayane Namo asttute 9 times*

BIBLE VERSES: (Proverbs)

23:24. The father of the just rejoiceth greatly: he that hath begotten a wise son, shall have joy in him.

READ PSALMS #'s: 5, 14, 32 ,41, 50, 59, 77, 104, 122

OCTOBER 26, 2015

| 10/26/2015 MON | This is considered a NEGATIVE day for you | | | | | | | | Shiva |

Moving	Shopping	Health	Investing	Gambling	Love is	Wedding	Travel	Work/Job	Planet
Bad	Bad	Bad	Fair	Fair	Bad	Bad	Bad	Bad	Mars

KEYWORDS ARE: Quarrels, Jealousy, Police, Anger - Ego, Disagreement in Love, Money - Profits, Sickness - cold, Family Conflicts, Traffic Ticket

Lotto #'s	play 4 #s	play 3 #s	Ruling Angel:...........	Color Sugestion:...........	Ruling Deity
7,8,34,32,18,18	7874	675	Raphael	Purple/DeepBlue/Rose	Hanuman

ADVICE & DETAILS	MANTRA FOR TODAY
Today your enemies will oppose you. Enemies are not only people, but also situations and addictions. You must avoid today alcohol and drugs because they may bring very negative consequences into your life. You will be invited to socialize and share with others, but make sure you do it in a balanced manner and leave as soon as you feel sleepy or tired.	*Om Graam Greem Graum Sa Gurave namah swaha 21 times AUM VAGDEVYAI CA VIDMAHE KAMARAJAYA DHIMAHI. TANNO DEVI PRACODAYAT. 9 times*

BIBLE VERSES: (Proverbs)

23:26. My son, give me thy heart: and let thy eyes keep my ways.

0

READ PSALMS #'s: 6, 15, 33 ,42, 51, 60, 78, 105, 123

OCTOBER 27, 2015

| 10/27/2015 TUE | This is considered a NEUTRAL day for you | | | | | | | | Shiva |

Moving	Shopping	Health	Investing	Gambling	Love is	Wedding	Travel	Work/Job	Planet
Good	Fair	Fair	Bad	Bad	Good	Fair	Good	Fair	Moon

KEYWORDS ARE: God - Karma, Slow Day, Enemies, spiritual, Astrologers, Psychics, priests, Income, Legal matter, Sleepiness, Advice given

Lotto #'s	play 4 #s	play 3 #s	Ruling Angel:...........	Color Sugestion:...........	Ruling Deity
8,9,34,31,18,20	9234	776	Zaphkiel	Light Blue/Purple/Peach	Ganga

ADVICE & DETAILS	MANTRA FOR TODAY
This day requires that you devote your internal power to the power of the Divine. This is a day where you are required to spend time in religious or spiritual pursuits, meditating, praying or visiting priests or holy people.	*Om Mana Swasti Shanti Kuru kuru Swaha Shivoham Shivoham 27 times om haring jawala mukhi mam sarva shatru bakshaya bakshaya hung phat swaha Om Nama shivaya pahimam 9 times*

BIBLE VERSES: (Proverbs)

23:28. She lieth in wait in the way as a robber, and him whom she shall see unwary, she will kill.

READ PSALMS #'s: 7, 16, 34 ,43, 52, 61, 79, 106, 124

OCTOBER 28, 2015

| 10/28/2015 WED | This is considered a POSITIVE day for you | | | | | | | | Shiva |

Moving	Shopping	Health	Investing	Gambling	Love is	Wedding	Travel	Work/Job	Planet
Good	Good	Excellent	Excellent	Excellent	Good	Excellent	Good	Excellent	Jupiter

KEYWORDS ARE: IRS - Law, High Pleasure, Big Expense, investment, Income is low and expenses, Investments, Abusive, Promotion, Fame - TV

Lotto #'s	play 4 #s	play 3 #s	Ruling Angel:............	Color Sugestion:............	Ruling Deity
9,9,34,32,18,22	2943	877	Haniel	Yellow/White/Silver	Mahalaxmi

ADVICE & DETAILS

You will be having a good feeling about your income and expenses. It is a good day to purchase and make investments in the market. It is also a good day to look for a new home.

MANTRA FOR TODAY

Jai Jai Shiva Shambo.(2)
...Mahadeva Shambo (2)
21 times
Om Jayanti Mangala Kali
Bhadrakali Kapalini Durga
Kshama Shiva Dhatri Swaha
Swadha Namostute
9 times

BIBLE VERSES: (Proverbs)

23:30. Surely they that pass their time in wine, and study to drink off their cups.

READ PSALMS #'s: 8, 17, 35 ,44, 53, 62, 80, 107, 125

OCTOBER 29, 2015

| 10/29/2015 THU | This is considered a NEGATIVE day for you | | | | | | | | Shiva |

Moving	Shopping	Health	Investing	Gambling	Love is	Wedding	Travel	Work/Job	Planet
Bad	Bad	Bad	Bad	Bad	Bad	Bad	Bad	Bad	Saturn

KEYWORDS ARE: Accidents, Denial - Doubt, death, finish, Traffic problems, Tickets, Power, Karmic debts, God - Karma, IRS - Law

Lotto #'s	play 4 #s	play 3 #s	Ruling Angel:............	Color Sugestion:............	Ruling Deity
10,2,33,31,18,14	2691	978	Mikael	Gold/Brown/Blue/Dark Green	Pitridev

ADVICE & DETAILS

Death is the influence of today. This may be a physical death, the end of a project, idea, habit or thought. You must remember that death is necessary for life and that the end of something, brings new beginnings. This day is also influenced by accidents, so be aware of of your surroundings, do not text while driving or get involved in any kind of risky behavi

MANTRA FOR TODAY

Om Hareem Nama Swaha..Shri
Maha Laxmi Aye Namah swaha
12 times
Om maha laxmi cha vidmahe
vishnu pataya dhi mahi tanno
laxmi pracho dayat
Om hareem namam swaha
9 times

BIBLE VERSES: (Proverbs)

23:32. But in the end, it will bite like a snake, and will spread abroad poison like a basilisk.

READ PSALMS #'s: 9, 18, 36 ,45, 54, 63, 81, 108, 126

OCTOBER 30, 2015

| 10/30/2015 FRI | This is considered a NEUTRAL day for you | | | | | | | | Shiva |

Moving	Shopping	Health	Investing	Gambling	Love is	Wedding	Travel	Work/Job	Planet
Fair	Fair	Fair	Fair	Fair	Bad	Fair	Fair	Bad	Sun

KEYWORDS ARE: Denial - Doubt, lonliness, losses, sadness, Family conflicts, Arguments, Promotion, God - Karma, Home Alone, Accidents

Lotto #'s	play 4 #s	play 3 #s	Ruling Angel:............	Color Sugestion:............	Ruling Deity
2,3,33,31,18,16	3235	179	Gabriel	White/Yellow/ Peach	Gaitree

ADVICE & DETAILS

You can connect with the real power within you, the universal consciousness that inhabits in you. Dedicate time to meditation, prayer, religious acts of devotion and if possible visit priests, Gurus or spiritual guides.

MANTRA FOR TODAY

Om Ganga mataye nama swaha
Om Varuna Devta aye Pahimam
11 times
Om hareem mama sarva shatru
janam vashee kuru kuru swaha
om hareem ksham kasham
kasheem kasheem swaha
9 times

BIBLE VERSES: (Proverbs)

23:25. Let thy father and thy mother be joyful, and let her rejoice that bore thee.

READ PSALMS #'s: 1, 10, 28 ,37, 46, 55, 73, 100, 118

OCTOBER 31, 2015

10/31/2015 SAT	This is considered a POSITIVE day for you								Shiva

Moving	Shopping	Health	Investing	Gambling	Love is	Wedding	Travel	Work/Job	Planet
Good	Excellent	Good	Good	Good	Excellent	Good	Excelle	Good	Venus

KEYWORDS ARE: death, romamce, finish, fame,
Tiredness, Low Energy, Sleepy, Fame - TV, IRS - Law, Music, Denial - Doubt

Lotto #'s	play 4 #s	play 3 #s	Ruling Angel:............	Color Sugestion:............	Ruling Deity
3,3,34,32,18,18	10641	2710	Raziel	Red/Yellow/Pink	Durga

ADVICE & DETAILS	MANTRA FOR TODAY
Love will return to you this day. You will be able to make up back with your lover. You will be feeling very sleepy today. You will want to enjoy good food and have a quiet date.	Om Namo Bhagawate Mukhtanandaya, 108 times AUM KRSNAYA VIDMAHE DAMODARAYA DHIMAHI. TANNO VISHNU PRACODAYAT. 9 times

BIBLE VERSES: (Proverbs)
23:27. For a harlot is a deep ditch: and a strange woman is a narrow pit.
0
READ PSALMS #'s: 2, 11, 29 ,38, 47, 56, 74, 101, 119

NOVEMBER 1, 2015

11/01/2015 SUN	This is considered a POSITIVE day for you								Shiva

Moving	Shopping	Health	Investing	Gambling	Love is	Wedding	Travel	Work/Job	Planet
Good	Good	Excellent	Excellent	Bad	Good	Bad	Good	Excellent	Saturn

KEYWORDS ARE: losses, finish, luxury, beauty,
Popularity & Reputation, IRS - Law, Accidents, Denial - Doubt, money

Lotto #'s	play 4 #s	play 3 #s	Ruling Angel:............	Color Sugestion:............	Ruling Deity
9,2,33,32,19,14	7281	887	Mikael	Gold/Brown/Blue/Dark Green	Pitridev

ADVICE & DETAILS	MANTRA FOR TODAY
Today money comes in, money goes out. You will make profits, but at the same time you will have big expenses and you will enjoy high pleasure.	Kali Durge Namo Nama Om Durge aye nama swaha 108 times AUM TATPURUSAYA VIDMAHE VAKRATUNDAY DHIMAHI. TANNO DANTI PRACODAYAT. 9 times

BIBLE VERSES: (Proverbs)
23:35. And thou shalt say: They have beaten me, but I was not sensible of pain: they drew me, and I felt not: when shall I awake and find wine again?
READ PSALMS #'s: 9, 18, 36 ,45, 54, 63, 81, 108, 126

NOVEMBER 2, 2015

11/02/2015 MON	This is considered a NEGATIVE day for you								Shiva

Moving	Shopping	Health	Investing	Gambling	Love is	Wedding	Travel	Work/Job	Planet
Bad	Bad	Bad	Bad	Fair	Bad	Fair	Bad	Bad	Sun

KEYWORDS ARE: finish, individuality, fame, pregnancy,
Accidents, Illness, Alcoholism, Accidents, Denial - Doubt, lonliness, losses

Lotto #'s	play 4 #s	play 3 #s	Ruling Angel:............	Color Sugestion:............	Ruling Deity
10,2,34,31,19,15	7544	988	Gabriel	White/Yellow/ Peach	Gaitree

ADVICE & DETAILS	MANTRA FOR TODAY
There will be a great deal of confusion today. There will be many bills and expenses and you may not have enough money to cover them. There could be delays in court cases. You may have to pay for something you do not want.	Om Hareem Nama Swaha..Shri Maha Laxmi Aye Namah swaha 12 times Om maha laxmi cha vidmahe vishnu pataya dhi mahi tanno laxmi pracho dayat Om hareem namam swaha 9 times

BIBLE VERSES: (Proverbs)
23:28. She lieth in wait in the way as a robber, and him whom she shall see unwary, she will kill.
READ PSALMS #'s: 1, 10, 28 ,37, 46, 55, 73, 100, 118

NOVEMBER 3, 2015

11/03/2015 TUE		This is considered a NEUTRAL day for you							Shiva
Moving	Shopping	Health	Investing	Gambling	Love is	Wedding	Travel	Work/Job	Planet
Fair	Fair	Fair	Fair	Good	Bad	Good	Fair	Bad	Venus

KEYWORDS ARE: Illness - Cold, Friendships, Commanding, Boastful, Independence, Losses, Death, Shopping, Dominating

Lotto #'s	play 4 #s	play 3 #s	Ruling Angel:............	Color Sugestion:............	Ruling Deity
2,4,33,31,19,17	10743	189	Raziel	Red/Yellow/Pink	Durga

ADVICE & DETAILS	MANTRA FOR TODAY
This is one of those days that you want to have over and over again if you are connected with the gods. You should expect promotion, money and romance.	Om Ganga mataye nama swaha Om Varuna Devta aye Pahimam 11 times Om hareem mama sarva shatru janam vashee kuru kuru swaha om hareem ksham kasham kasheem kasheem swaha 9 times
BIBLE VERSES: (Proverbs)	
23:30. Surely they that pass their time in wine, and study to drink off their cups.	
READ PSALMS #'s: 2, 11, 29 ,38, 47, 56, 74, 101, 119	

NOVEMBER 4, 2015

11/04/2015 WED		This is considered a POSITIVE day for you							Shiva
Moving	Shopping	Health	Investing	Gambling	Love is	Wedding	Travel	Work/Job	Planet
Good	Excellent	Good	Good	Good	Excellent	Good	Excelle	Good	Mercury

KEYWORDS ARE: Friendships, Teacher, Association, Partnership, Popularity, Death, Sickness - cold, Social Functions, Co-operation

Lotto #'s	play 4 #s	play 3 #s	Ruling Angel:............	Color Sugestion:............	Ruling Deity
3,5,34,31,19,19	10403	2810	Zadkiel	Green/Sky Blue/White	Saraswaty

ADVICE & DETAILS	MANTRA FOR TODAY
Enjoy this day! If you fill it with sweet words and with kindness, you will encounter romance, good partnerships and to top it all off money.	Om Namo Bhagawate Mukhtanandaya, 108 times AUM KRSNAYA VIDMAHE DAMODARAYA DHIMAHI. TANNO VISHNU PRACODAYAT. 9 times
BIBLE VERSES: (Proverbs)	
23:32. But in the end, it will bite like a snake, and will spread abroad poison like a basilisk.	
READ PSALMS #'s: 3, 12, 30 ,39, 48, 57, 75, 102, 120	

NOVEMBER 5, 2015

11/05/2015 THU		This is considered a POSITIVE day for you							Shiva
Moving	Shopping	Health	Investing	Gambling	Love is	Wedding	Travel	Work/Job	Planet
Good	Excellent	Excellent	Good	Bad	Good	Good	Excelle	Good	Pluto

KEYWORDS ARE: Teacher, Real Estate, Communication, read, Social Groups, Sickness - cold, Legal matter, High Temper, Groups - Parties

Lotto #'s	play 4 #s	play 3 #s	Ruling Angel:............	Color Sugestion:............	Ruling Deity
4,5,33,32,19,12	4709	382	Metatron	Dark Blue/ Purple/ Mauve	Ganesh

ADVICE & DETAILS	MANTRA FOR TODAY
Today, it will feel very comfortable at your work place, at your job. Opportunities to advance may present themselves. Financial situation improves.	Kali Durge Namo Nama Om Durge aye nama swaha 108 times AUM TATPURUSAYA VIDMAHE VAKRATUNDAY DHIMAHI. TANNO DANTI PRACODAYAT. 9 times
BIBLE VERSES: (Proverbs)	
23:34. And thou shalt be as one sleeping in the midst of the sea, and as a pilot fast asleep when the stern is lost.	
READ PSALMS #'s: 4, 13, 31 ,40, 49, 58, 76, 103, 121	

NOVEMBER 6, 2015

11/06/2015 FRI		This is considered a NEUTRAL day for you							Shiva

Moving	Shopping	Health	Investing	Gambling	Love is	Wedding	Travel	Work/Job	Planet
Bad	Bad	Bad	Bad	Good	Fair	Good	Bad	Bad	Uranus

KEYWORDS ARE: Real Estate, Beauty - Sex, Tiredness, career, Money & stress, Legal matter, Abusive, Exercise, Laziness

Lotto #'s	play 4 #s	play 3 #s	Ruling Angel:............	Color Sugestion:...........	Ruling Deity
5,6,33,31,19,14	6915	483	Camael	Orange/White/Light Green/ Beige	Krishna

ADVICE & DETAILS

There will be changes at the job, and these will be in your favor. You will enjoy engaging in new projects. Coworkers may be friendly, but you must be careful with whom you trust.

MANTRA FOR TODAY

Om hareem Kleem Hreem Aem Saraswataye namaha
21 times
Om Guru bramha, Guru Vishnu Guru Deva mahaeshwara guru saksha paam bramha, tasmi shri guruve nama
9 times

BIBLE VERSES: (Proverbs)

24:1. Seek not to be like evil men, neither desire to be with them:
0

READ PSALMS #'s: 5, 14, 32 ,41, 50, 59, 77, 104, 122

NOVEMBER 7, 2015

11/07/2015 SAT		This is considered a POSITIVE day for you							Shiva

Moving	Shopping	Health	Investing	Gambling	Love is	Wedding	Travel	Work/Job	Planet
Excellent	Good	Excellent	Good	Fair	Excellent	Bad	Excelle	Good	Mars

KEYWORDS ARE: Beauty - Sex, Anger - Ego, travel, change, Car & driving , Abusive, Karmic debts, Jealousy, Moving

Lotto #'s	play 4 #s	play 3 #s	Ruling Angel:............	Color Sugestion:............	Ruling Deity
6,8,34,32,19,16	8073	584	Raphael	Purple/DeepBlue/Rose	Hanuman

ADVICE & DETAILS

You will have delays in travel. Your business sales will be low. You need to watch out for accidents or health problems. You may experience some constipation or bad digestion from bad meals.

MANTRA FOR TODAY

Om Jai Viganeshwaraya..
Lambodaraya Namo Namaha
21 times
Om Sarva Mangal Mangalye, Shiva Sarvart Sadike, Sharan Tryambike Gowri, Narayane Namo asttute
9 times

BIBLE VERSES: (Proverbs)

24:3. By wisdom the house shall be built, and by prudence it shall be strengthened.

READ PSALMS #'s: 6, 15, 33 ,42, 51, 60, 78, 105, 123

NOVEMBER 8, 2015

11/08/2015 SUN		This is considered a NEGATIVE day for you							Shiva

Moving	Shopping	Health	Investing	Gambling	Love is	Wedding	Travel	Work/Job	Planet
Bad	Bad	Bad	Fair	Bad	Bad	Fair	Bad	Bad	Moon

KEYWORDS ARE: Anger - Ego, spiritual, frustration, power, Police and frustrations, Karmic debts, God - Karma, Slow Day, Government

Lotto #'s	play 4 #s	play 3 #s	Ruling Angel:............	Color Sugestion:............	Ruling Deity
7,8,33,32,19,18	2619	685	Zaphkiel	Light Blue/Purple/Peach	Ganga

ADVICE & DETAILS

You will have disagreemets and frustration over your financial situation today. You will be worried about losing your position. The jealousy of coworkers may affect your performance at work. Do not be rude to bosses.

MANTRA FOR TODAY

Om Graam Greem Graum Sa Gurave namah swaha
21 times
AUM VAGDEVYAI CA VIDMAHE KAMARAJAYA DHIMAHI. TANNO DEVI PRACODAYAT.
9 times

BIBLE VERSES: (Proverbs)

24:5. A wise man is strong: and a knowing man, stout and valiant.
0

READ PSALMS #'s: 7, 16, 34 ,43, 52, 61, 79, 106, 124

NOVEMBER 9, 2015

11/09/2015 MON		This is considered a NEUTRAL day for you							Shiva
Moving	*Shopping*	*Health*	*Investing*	*Gambling*	*Love is*	*Wedding*	*Travel*	*Work/Job*	*Planet*
Good	Fair	Fair	Bad	Excellent	Good	Excellent	Good	Fair	**Jupiter**

KEYWORDS ARE: death, investment, religion, religion, Alcohol - drugs , God - Karma, IRS - Law, High Pleasure, Criticism

Lotto #'s	*play 4 #s*	*play 3 #s*	*Ruling Angel:...........*	*Color Sugestion:...........*	*Ruling Deity*
8,10,33,32,19,20	4462	786	**Haniel**	**Yellow/White/Silver**	**Mahalaxmi**

ADVICE & DETAILS

You may receive an unexpected financial windfall today. It is a good day to save money and to plan your financial future. Set up a retirement plan. Donate to charity today.

BIBLE VERSES: (Proverbs)

24:7. Wisdom is too high for a fool; in the gate he shall not open his mouth.
0

READ PSALMS #'s: 8, 17, 35 ,44, 53, 62, 80, 107, 125

MANTRA FOR TODAY

Om Mana Swasti Shanti Kuru kuru Swaha Shivoham Shivoham 27 times
om haring jawala mukhi mam sarva shatru bakshaya bakshaya hung phat swaha
Om Nama shivaya pahimam 9 times

NOVEMBER 10, 2015

11/10/2015 TUE		This is considered a POSITIVE day for you							Shiva
Moving	*Shopping*	*Health*	*Investing*	*Gambling*	*Love is*	*Wedding*	*Travel*	*Work/Job*	*Planet*
Good	Good	Excellent	Excellent	Bad	Good	Bad	Good	Excellent	**Saturn**

KEYWORDS ARE: losses, finish, luxury, beauty, Popularity & Reputation, IRS - Law, Accidents, Denial - Doubt, money

Lotto #'s	*play 4 #s*	*play 3 #s*	*Ruling Angel:...........*	*Color Sugestion:...........*	*Ruling Deity*
9,1,33,31,19,13	3169	887	**Mikael**	**Gold/Brown/Blue/Dark Green**	**Pitridev**

ADVICE & DETAILS

Today money comes in, money goes out. You will make profits, but at the same time you will have big expenses and you will enjoy high pleasure.

BIBLE VERSES: (Proverbs)

24:9. The thought of a fool is sin: and the detractor is the abomination of men.

READ PSALMS #'s: 9, 18, 36 ,45, 54, 63, 81, 108, 126

MANTRA FOR TODAY

Jai Jai Shiva Shambo.(2) ...Mahadeva Shambo (2) 21 times
Om Jayanti Mangala Kali Bhadrakali Kapalini Durga Kshama Shiva Dhatri Swaha Swadha Namostute 9 times

NOVEMBER 11, 2015

11/11/2015 WED		This is considered a NEGATIVE day for you							Shiva
Moving	*Shopping*	*Health*	*Investing*	*Gambling*	*Love is*	*Wedding*	*Travel*	*Work/Job*	*Planet*
Bad	Bad	Bad	Bad	Fair	Bad	Fair	Bad	Bad	**Sun**

KEYWORDS ARE: finish, individuality, fame, pregnancy, Accidents, Illness, Alcoholism, Accidents, Denial - Doubt, lonliness, losses

Lotto #'s	*play 4 #s*	*play 3 #s*	*Ruling Angel:...........*	*Color Sugestion:...........*	*Ruling Deity*
10,2,33,31,19,16	6242	988	**Gabriel**	**White/Yellow/ Peach**	**Gaitree**

ADVICE & DETAILS

There will be a great deal of confusion today. There will be many bills and expenses and you may not have enough money to cover them. There could be delays in court cases. You may have to pay for something you do not want.

BIBLE VERSES: (Proverbs)

24:2. Because their mind studieth robberies, and their lips speak deceits.
0

READ PSALMS #'s: 1, 10, 28 ,37, 46, 55, 73, 100, 118

MANTRA FOR TODAY

Om Hareem Nama Swaha..Shri Maha Laxmi Aye Namah swaha 12 times
Om maha laxmi cha vidmahe vishnu pataya dhi mahi tanno laxmi pracho dayat
Om hareem namam swaha 9 times

NOVEMBER 12, 2015

11/12/2015 THU				This is considered a NEUTRAL day for you					Shiva

Moving	Shopping	Health	Investing	Gambling	Love is	Wedding	Travel	Work/Job	Planet
Fair	Fair	Fair	Fair	Good	Bad	Good	Fair	Bad	Venus

KEYWORDS ARE: Abusive, Friendships, God - Karma, Accidents, Depression & Lonliness, Losses, Death, Shopping, Legal matter

Lotto #'s	play 4 #s	play 3 #s	Ruling Angel:............	Color Sugestion:............	Ruling Deity
2,4,33,32,19,18	7714	189	Raziel	Red/Yellow/Pink	Durga

ADVICE & DETAILS

This is one of those days that you want to have over and over again if you are connected with the gods. You should expect promotion, money and romance.

BIBLE VERSES: (Proverbs)
24:4. By instruction the storerooms shall be filled with all precious and most beautiful wealth.

READ PSALMS #'s: 2, 11, 29 ,38, 47, 56, 74, 101, 119

MANTRA FOR TODAY

Om Ganga mataye nama swaha
Om Varuna Devta aye Pahimam
11 times
Om hareem mama sarva shatru
janam vashee kuru kuru swaha
om hareem ksham kasham
kasheem kasheem swaha
9 times

NOVEMBER 13, 2015

11/13/2015 FRI				This is considered a POSITIVE day for you					Shiva

Moving	Shopping	Health	Investing	Gambling	Love is	Wedding	Travel	Work/Job	Planet
Good	Excellent	Good	Good	Good	Excellent	Good	Excelle	Good	Mercury

KEYWORDS ARE: Friendships, Teacher, Association, Partnership, Popularity, Death, Sickness - cold, Social Functions, Co-operation

Lotto #'s	play 4 #s	play 3 #s	Ruling Angel:............	Color Sugestion:............	Ruling Deity
3,5,33,31,19,20	7777	2810	Zadkiel	Green/Sky Blue/White	Saraswaty

ADVICE & DETAILS

Enjoy this day! If you fill it with sweet words and with kindness, you will encounter romance, good partnerships and to top it all off money.

BIBLE VERSES: (Proverbs)
24:6. Because war is managed by due ordering: and there shall be safety where there are many counsels.

READ PSALMS #'s: 3, 12, 30 ,39, 48, 57, 75, 102, 120

MANTRA FOR TODAY

Om Namo Bhagawate
Mukhtanandaya,
108 times
AUM KRSNAYA VIDMAHE
DAMODARAYA DHIMAHI.
TANNO VISHNU
PRACODAYAT.
9 times

NOVEMBER 14, 2015

11/14/2015 SAT				This is considered a POSITIVE day for you					Shiva

Moving	Shopping	Health	Investing	Gambling	Love is	Wedding	Travel	Work/Job	Planet
Good	Excellent	Excellent	Good	Bad	Good	Good	Excelle	Good	Pluto

KEYWORDS ARE: Teacher, Real Estate, Communication, read, Social Groups, Sickness - cold, Legal matter, High Temper, Groups - Parties

Lotto #'s	play 4 #s	play 3 #s	Ruling Angel:............	Color Sugestion:............	Ruling Deity
4,6,33,32,19,12	4613	382	Metatron	Dark Blue/ Purple/ Mauve	Ganesh

ADVICE & DETAILS

Today, it will feel very comfortable at your work place, at your job. Opportunities to advance may present themselves. Financial situation improves.

BIBLE VERSES: (Proverbs)
24:8. He that deviseth to do evils, shall be called a fool.

0

READ PSALMS #'s: 4, 13, 31 ,40, 49, 58, 76, 103, 121

MANTRA FOR TODAY

Kali Durge Namo Nama
Om Durge aye nama swaha
108 times
AUM TATPURUSAYA
VIDMAHE VAKRATUNDAY
DHIMAHI. TANNO DANTI
PRACODAYAT.
9 times

NOVEMBER 15, 2015

11/15/2015 SUN		This is considered a NEUTRAL day for you							Shiva
Moving	Shopping	Health	Investing	Gambling	Love is	Wedding	Travel	Work/Job	Planet
Bad	Bad	Bad	Bad	Good	Fair	Good	Bad	Bad	Uranus

KEYWORDS ARE: Real Estate, Beauty - Sex, Tiredness, career, Money & stress, Legal matter, Abusive, Exercise, Laziness

Lotto #'s	play 4 #s	play 3 #s	Ruling Angel:............	Color Sugestion:............	Ruling Deity
5,6,33,31,19,14	10704	483	Camael	Orange/White/Light Green/ Beige	Krishna

ADVICE & DETAILS

There will be changes at the job, and these will be in your favor. You will enjoy engaging in new projects. Coworkers may be friendly, but you must be careful with whom you trust.

BIBLE VERSES: (Proverbs)

24:10. If thou lose hope, being weary in the day of distress, thy strength shall be diminished.

READ PSALMS #'s: 5, 14, 32 ,41, 50, 59, 77, 104, 122

MANTRA FOR TODAY

Om hareem Kleem Hreem Aem Saraswataye namaha
21 times
Om Guru bramha, Guru Vishnu Guru Deva mahaeshwara guru saksha paam bramha, tasmi shri guruve nama
9 times

NOVEMBER 16, 2015

11/16/2015 MON		This is considered a POSITIVE day for you							Shiva
Moving	Shopping	Health	Investing	Gambling	Love is	Wedding	Travel	Work/Job	Planet
Excellent	Good	Excellent	Good	Fair	Excellent	Bad	Excelle	Good	Mars

KEYWORDS ARE: Beauty - Sex, Anger - Ego, travel, change, Car & driving , Abusive, Karmic debts, Jealousy, Moving

Lotto #'s	play 4 #s	play 3 #s	Ruling Angel:............	Color Sugestion:............	Ruling Deity
6,7,34,32,19,17	5168	584	Raphael	Purple/DeepBlue/Rose	Hanuman

ADVICE & DETAILS

You will have delays in travel. Your business sales will be low. You need to watch out for accidents or health problems. You may experience some constipation or bad digestion from bad meals.

BIBLE VERSES: (Proverbs)

24:12. If thou say: I have not strength enough: he that seeth into the heart, he understandeth, and nothing deceiveth the keeper of thy soul, and he

READ PSALMS #'s: 6, 15, 33 ,42, 51, 60, 78, 105, 123

MANTRA FOR TODAY

Om Jai Viganeshwaraya..
Lambodaraya Namo Namaha
21 times
Om Sarva Mangal Mangalye, Shiva Sarvart Sadike, Sharan Tryambike Gowri, Narayane Namo asttute
9 times

NOVEMBER 17, 2015

11/17/2015 TUE		This is considered a NEGATIVE day for you							Shiva
Moving	Shopping	Health	Investing	Gambling	Love is	Wedding	Travel	Work/Job	Planet
Bad	Bad	Bad	Fair	Bad	Bad	Fair	Bad	Bad	Moon

KEYWORDS ARE: Anger - Ego, spiritual, frustration, power, Police and frustrations, Karmic debts, God - Karma, Slow Day, Government

Lotto #'s	play 4 #s	play 3 #s	Ruling Angel:............	Color Sugestion:............	Ruling Deity
7,8,33,31,19,19	10046	685	Zaphkiel	Light Blue/Purple/Peach	Ganga

ADVICE & DETAILS

You will have disagreemets and frustration over your financial situation today. You will be worried about losing your position. The jealousy of coworkers may affect your performance at work. Do not be rude to bosses.

BIBLE VERSES: (Proverbs)

24:14. So also is the doctrine of wisdom to thy soul: which when thou hast found, thou shalt have hope in the end, and thy hope shall not perish.

READ PSALMS #'s: 7, 16, 34 ,43, 52, 61, 79, 106, 124

MANTRA FOR TODAY

Om Graam Greem Graum Sa Gurave namah swaha
21 times
AUM VAGDEVYAI CA VIDMAHE KAMARAJAYA DHIMAHI. TANNO DEVI PRACODAYAT.
9 times

NOVEMBER 18, 2015

| 11/18/2015 WED | | | This is considered a NEUTRAL day for you | | | | | | Shiva |

Moving	Shopping	Health	Investing	Gambling	Love is	Wedding	Travel	Work/Job	Planet
Good	Fair	Fair	Bad	Excellent	Good	Excellent	Good	Fair	Jupiter

KEYWORDS ARE: death, investment, religion, religion, Alcohol - drugs , God - Karma, IRS - Law, High Pleasure, Criticism

Lotto #'s	play 4 #s	play 3 #s	Ruling Angel:............	Color Sugestion:............	Ruling Deity
8,9,33,32,19,20	8027	786	Haniel	Yellow/White/Silver	Mahalaxmi

ADVICE & DETAILS	MANTRA FOR TODAY
You may receive an unexpected financial windfall today. It is a good day to save money and to plan your financial future. Set up a retirement plan. Donate to charity today.	Om Mana Swasti Shanti Kuru kuru Swaha Shivoham Shivoham 27 times om haring jawala mukhi mam sarva shatru bakshaya bakshaya hung phat swaha Om Nama shivaya pahimam 9 times

BIBLE VERSES: (Proverbs)

24:16. For a just man shall fall seven times, and shall rise again: but the wicked shall fall down into evil.

READ PSALMS #'s: 8, 17, 35 ,44, 53, 62, 80, 107, 125

NOVEMBER 19, 2015

| 11/19/2015 THU | | | This is considered a POSITIVE day for you | | | | | | Shiva |

Moving	Shopping	Health	Investing	Gambling	Love is	Wedding	Travel	Work/Job	Planet
Good	Good	Excellent	Excellent	Bad	Good	Bad	Good	Excellent	Saturn

KEYWORDS ARE: losses, finish, luxury, beauty, Popularity & Reputation, IRS - Law, Accidents, Denial - Doubt, money

Lotto #'s	play 4 #s	play 3 #s	Ruling Angel:............	Color Sugestion:............	Ruling Deity
9,1,34,31,19,14	4116	887	Mikael	Gold/Brown/Blue/Dark Green	Pitridev

ADVICE & DETAILS	MANTRA FOR TODAY
Today money comes in, money goes out. You will make profits, but at the same time you will have big expenses and you will enjoy high pleasure.	Jai Jai Shiva Shambo.(2) ...Mahadeva Shambo (2) 21 times Om Jayanti Mangala Kali Bhadrakali Kapalini Durga Kshama Shiva Dhatri Swaha Swadha Namostute 9 times

BIBLE VERSES: (Proverbs)

24:18. Lest the Lord see, and it displease him, and he turn away his wrath from him.

READ PSALMS #'s: 9, 18, 36 ,45, 54, 63, 81, 108, 126

NOVEMBER 20, 2015

| 11/20/2015 FRI | | | This is considered a NEGATIVE day for you | | | | | | Shiva |

Moving	Shopping	Health	Investing	Gambling	Love is	Wedding	Travel	Work/Job	Planet
Bad	Bad	Bad	Bad	Fair	Bad	Fair	Bad	Bad	Sun

KEYWORDS ARE: finish, individuality, fame, pregnancy, Accidents, Illness, Alcoholism, Accidents, Denial - Doubt, lonliness, losses

Lotto #'s	play 4 #s	play 3 #s	Ruling Angel:............	Color Sugestion:............	Ruling Deity
10,2,33,32,19,16	5110	988	Gabriel	White/Yellow/ Peach	Gaitree

ADVICE & DETAILS	MANTRA FOR TODAY
There will be a great deal of confusion today. There will be many bills and expenses and you may not have enough money to cover them. There could be delays in court cases. You may have to pay for something you do not want.	Om Hareem Nama Swaha..Shri Maha Laxmi Aye Namah swaha 12 times Om maha laxmi cha vidmahe vishnu pataya dhi mahi tanno laxmi pracho dayat Om hareem namam swaha 9 times

BIBLE VERSES: (Proverbs)

24:11. Deliver them that are led to death: and those that are drawn to death, forbear not to deliver.

READ PSALMS #'s: 1, 10, 28 ,37, 46, 55, 73, 100, 118

NOVEMBER 21, 2015

11/21/2015 SAT	This is considered a NEUTRAL day for you								Shiva
Moving	Shopping	Health	Investing	Gambling	Love is	Wedding	Travel	Work/Job	Planet
Fair	Fair	Fair	Fair	Good	Bad	Good	Fair	Bad	Venus

KEYWORDS ARE: Abusive, Friendships, God - Karma, Accidents, Depression & Lonliness, Losses, Death, Shopping, Legal matter

Lotto #'s	play 4 #s	play 3 #s	Ruling Angel:............	Color Sugestion:............	Ruling Deity
2,4,33,32,19,18	9266	189	Raziel	Red/Yellow/Pink	Durga

ADVICE & DETAILS	MANTRA FOR TODAY
This is one of those days that you want to have over and over again if you are connected with the gods. You should expect promotion, money and romance.	*Om Ganga mataye nama swaha* *Om Varuna Devta aye Pahimam* *11 times* *Om hareem mama sarva shatru janam vashee kuru kuru swaha* *om hareem ksham kasham kasheem kaseem swaha* *9 times*
BIBLE VERSES: (Proverbs)	
24:13. Eat honey, my son, because it is good, and the honeycomb most sweet to thy throat.	
READ PSALMS #'s: 2, 11, 29 ,38, 47, 56, 74, 101, 119	

NOVEMBER 22, 2015

11/22/2015 SUN	This is considered a POSITIVE day for you								Shiva
Moving	Shopping	Health	Investing	Gambling	Love is	Wedding	Travel	Work/Job	Planet
Good	Excellent	Good	Good	Good	Excellent	Good	Excelle	Good	Mercury

KEYWORDS ARE: Karmic debts, Teacher, IRS - Law, Denial - Doubt, Quarrels & lovers, Death, Sickness - cold, Social Functions, Abusive

Lotto #'s	play 4 #s	play 3 #s	Ruling Angel:............	Color Sugestion:............	Ruling Deity
3,5,33,31,19,20	2465	2810	Zadkiel	Green/Sky Blue/White	Saraswaty

ADVICE & DETAILS	MANTRA FOR TODAY
Enjoy this day! If you fill it with sweet words and with kindness, you will encounter romance, good partnerships and to top it all off money.	*Om Namo Bhagawate Mukhtanandaya,* *108 times* *AUM KRSNAYA VIDMAHE DAMODARAYA DHIMAHI.* *TANNO VISHNU PRACODAYAT.* *9 times*
BIBLE VERSES: (Proverbs)	
24:15. Lie not in wait, nor seek after wickedness in the house of the just, nor spoil his rest.	
READ PSALMS #'s: 3, 12, 30 ,39, 48, 57, 75, 102, 120	

NOVEMBER 23, 2015

11/23/2015 MON	This is considered a POSITIVE day for you								Shiva
Moving	Shopping	Health	Investing	Gambling	Love is	Wedding	Travel	Work/Job	Planet
Good	Excellent	Excellent	Good	Bad	Good	Good	Excelle	Good	Pluto

KEYWORDS ARE: Teacher, Real Estate, Communication, read, Social Groups, Sickness - cold, Legal matter, High Temper, Groups - Parties

Lotto #'s	play 4 #s	play 3 #s	Ruling Angel:............	Color Sugestion:............	Ruling Deity
4,6,34,31,19,12	2732	382	Metatron	Dark Blue/ Purple/ Mauve	Ganesh

ADVICE & DETAILS	MANTRA FOR TODAY
Today, it will feel very comfortable at your work place, at your job. Opportunities to advance may present themselves. Financial situation improves.	*Kali Durge Namo Nama* *Om Durge aye nama swaha* *108 times* *AUM TATPURUSAYA VIDMAHE VAKRATUNDAY DHIMAHI. TANNO DANTI PRACODAYAT.* *9 times*
BIBLE VERSES: (Proverbs)	
24:17. When thy enemy shall fall, be not glad, and in his ruin let not thy heart rejoice:	
READ PSALMS #'s: 4, 13, 31 ,40, 49, 58, 76, 103, 121	

NOVEMBER 24, 2015

11/24/2015 TUE		This is considered a NEUTRAL day for you							Shiva
Moving	Shopping	Health	Investing	Gambling	Love is	Wedding	Travel	Work/Job	Planet
Bad	Bad	Bad	Bad	Good	Fair	Good	Bad	Bad	Uranus

KEYWORDS ARE: Real Estate, Beauty - Sex, Tiredness, career, Money & stress, Legal matter, Abusive, Exercise, Laziness

Lotto #'s	play 4 #s	play 3 #s	Ruling Angel:............	Color Sugestion:............	Ruling Deity
5,6,34,32,19,15	5964	483	Camael	Orange/White/Light Green/ Beige	Krishna

ADVICE & DETAILS

There will be changes at the job, and these will be in your favor. You will enjoy engaging in new projects. Coworkers may be friendly, but you must be careful with whom you trust.

MANTRA FOR TODAY

Om hareem Kleem Hreem Aem Saraswataye namaha
21 times
Om Guru bramha, Guru Vishnu Guru Deva mahaeshwara guru saksha paam bramha, tasmi shri guruve nama
9 times

BIBLE VERSES: (Proverbs)

24:19. Contend not with the wicked, nor seek to be like the ungodly.
0

READ PSALMS #'s: 5, 14, 32 ,41, 50, 59, 77, 104, 122

NOVEMBER 25, 2015

11/25/2015 WED		This is considered a POSITIVE day for you							Shiva
Moving	Shopping	Health	Investing	Gambling	Love is	Wedding	Travel	Work/Job	Planet
Excellent	Good	Excellent	Good	Fair	Excellent	Bad	Excelle	Good	Mars

KEYWORDS ARE: Beauty - Sex, Anger - Ego, travel, change, Car & driving , Abusive, Karmic debts, Jealousy, Moving

Lotto #'s	play 4 #s	play 3 #s	Ruling Angel:............	Color Sugestion:............	Ruling Deity
6,7,33,32,19,16	3262	584	Raphael	Purple/DeepBlue/Rose	Hanuman

ADVICE & DETAILS

You will have delays in travel. Your business sales will be low. You need to watch out for accidents or health problems. You may experience some constipation or bad digestion from bad meals.

MANTRA FOR TODAY

Om Jai Viganeshwaraya..
Lambodaraya Namo Namaha
21 times
Om Sarva Mangal Mangalye, Shiva Sarvart Sadike, Sharan Tryambike Gowri, Narayane Namo asttute
9 times

BIBLE VERSES: (Proverbs)

24:21. My son, fear the Lord, and the king: and have nothing to do with detractors.

READ PSALMS #'s: 6, 15, 33 ,42, 51, 60, 78, 105, 123

NOVEMBER 26, 2015

11/26/2015 THU		This is considered a NEGATIVE day for you							Shiva
Moving	Shopping	Health	Investing	Gambling	Love is	Wedding	Travel	Work/Job	Planet
Bad	Bad	Bad	Fair	Bad	Bad	Fair	Bad	Bad	Moon

KEYWORDS ARE: Anger - Ego, spiritual, frustration, power, Police and frustrations, Karmic debts, God - Karma, Slow Day, Government

Lotto #'s	play 4 #s	play 3 #s	Ruling Angel:............	Color Sugestion:............	Ruling Deity
7,9,33,32,19,19	6511	685	Zaphkiel	Light Blue/Purple/Peach	Ganga

ADVICE & DETAILS

You will have disagreemets and frustration over your financial situation today. You will be worried about losing your position. The jealousy of coworkers may affect your performance at work. Do not be rude to bosses.

MANTRA FOR TODAY

Om Graam Greem Graum Sa Gurave namah swaha
21 times
AUM VAGDEVYAI CA VIDMAHE KAMARAJAYA DHIMAHI. TANNO DEVI PRACODAYAT.
9 times

BIBLE VERSES: (Proverbs)

24:23. These things also to the wise: It is not good to have respect to persons in judgment.

READ PSALMS #'s: 7, 16, 34 ,43, 52, 61, 79, 106, 124

NOVEMBER 27, 2015

11/27/2015 FRI		This is considered a NEUTRAL day for you							Shiva
Moving	*Shopping*	*Health*	*Investing*	*Gambling*	*Love is*	*Wedding*	*Travel*	*Work/Job*	*Planet*
Good	Fair	Fair	Bad	Excellent	Good	Excellent	Good	Fair	**Jupiter**

KEYWORDS ARE: death, investment, religion, religion, Alcohol - drugs , God - Karma, IRS - Law, High Pleasure, Criticism

Lotto #'s	*play 4 #s*	*play 3 #s*	Ruling Angel:............	Color Sugestion:............	*Ruling Deity*
8,9,33,31,19,21	8344	786	**Haniel**	**Yellow/White/Silver**	**Mahalaxmi**

ADVICE & DETAILS

You may receive an unexpected financial windfall today. It is a good day to save money and to plan your financial future. Set up a retirement plan. Donate to charity today.

BIBLE VERSES: (Proverbs)

24:25. They that rebuke him shall be praised: and a blessing shall come upon them.

READ PSALMS #'s: 8, 17, 35 ,44, 53, 62, 80, 107, 125

MANTRA FOR TODAY

Om Mana Swasti Shanti Kuru kuru Swaha Shivoham Shivoham 27 times
om haring jawala mukhi mam sarva shatru bakshaya bakshaya hung phat swaha
Om Nama shivaya pahimam 9 times

NOVEMBER 28, 2015

11/28/2015 SAT		This is considered a POSITIVE day for you							Shiva
Moving	*Shopping*	*Health*	*Investing*	*Gambling*	*Love is*	*Wedding*	*Travel*	*Work/Job*	*Planet*
Good	Good	Excellent	Excellent	Bad	Good	Bad	Good	Excellent	**Saturn**

KEYWORDS ARE: losses, finish, luxury, beauty, Popularity & Reputation, IRS - Law, Accidents, Denial - Doubt, money

Lotto #'s	*play 4 #s*	*play 3 #s*	Ruling Angel:............	Color Sugestion:............	*Ruling Deity*
9,1,34,31,19,14	3525	887	**Mikael**	**Gold/Brown/Blue/Dark Green**	**Pitridev**

ADVICE & DETAILS

Today money comes in, money goes out. You will make profits, but at the same time you will have big expenses and you will enjoy high pleasure.

BIBLE VERSES: (Proverbs)

24:27. Prepare thy work without, and diligently till thy ground: that afterward thou mayst build thy house.

READ PSALMS #'s: 9, 18, 36 ,45, 54, 63, 81, 108, 126

MANTRA FOR TODAY

Jai Jai Shiva Shambo.(2)
...Mahadeva Shambo (2)
21 times
Om Jayanti Mangala Kali Bhadrakali Kapalini Durga Kshama Shiva Dhatri Swaha Swadha Namostute 9 times

NOVEMBER 29, 2015

11/29/2015 SUN		This is considered a NEGATIVE day for you							Shiva
Moving	*Shopping*	*Health*	*Investing*	*Gambling*	*Love is*	*Wedding*	*Travel*	*Work/Job*	*Planet*
Bad	Bad	Bad	Bad	Fair	Bad	Fair	Bad	Bad	**Sun**

KEYWORDS ARE: finish, individuality, fame, pregnancy, Accidents, Illness, Alcoholism, Accidents, Denial - Doubt, lonliness, losses

Lotto #'s	*play 4 #s*	*play 3 #s*	Ruling Angel:............	Color Sugestion:............	*Ruling Deity*
10,3,33,32,19,16	6119	988	**Gabriel**	**White/Yellow/ Peach**	**Gaitree**

ADVICE & DETAILS

There will be a great deal of confusion today. There will be many bills and expenses and you may not have enough money to cover them. There could be delays in court cases. You may have to pay for something you do not want.

BIBLE VERSES: (Proverbs)

24:20. For evil men have no hope of things to come, and the lamp of the wicked shall be put out.

READ PSALMS #'s: 1, 10, 28 ,37, 46, 55, 73, 100, 118

MANTRA FOR TODAY

Om Hareem Nama Swaha..Shri Maha Laxmi Aye Namah swaha 12 times
Om maha laxmi cha vidmahe vishnu pataya dhi mahi tanno laxmi pracho dayat
Om hareem namam swaha 9 times

NOVEMBER 30, 2015

11/30/2015 MON		This is considered a NEUTRAL day for you							Shiva
Moving	*Shopping*	*Health*	*Investing*	*Gambling*	*Love is*	*Wedding*	*Travel*	*Work/Job*	*Planet*
Fair	Fair	Fair	Fair	Good	Bad	Good	Fair	Bad	Venus

KEYWORDS ARE: Abusive, Friendships, God - Karma, Accidents, Depression & Lonliness, Losses, Death, Shopping, Legal matter

Lotto #'s	*play 4 #s*	*play 3 #s*	Ruling Angel:............	Color Sugestion:............	*Ruling Deity*
2,3,33,31,19,17	5897	189	Raziel	Red/Yellow/Pink	Durga

ADVICE & DETAILS	MANTRA FOR TODAY
This is one of those days that you want to have over and over again if you are connected with the gods. You should expect promotion, money and romance.	*Om Ganga mataye nama swaha Om Varuna Devta aye Pahimam 11 times Om hareem mama sarva shatru janam vashee kuru kuru swaha om hareem ksham kasham kasheem kasheem swaha 9 times*

BIBLE VERSES: (Proverbs)

24:22. For their destruction shall rise suddenly: and who knoweth the ruin of both?

READ PSALMS #'s: 2, 11, 29 ,38, 47, 56, 74, 101, 119

DECEMBER 1, 2015

12/01/2015 TUE		This is considered a POSITIVE day for you							Shiva
Moving	*Shopping*	*Health*	*Investing*	*Gambling*	*Love is*	*Wedding*	*Travel*	*Work/Job*	*Planet*
Good	Good	Excellent	Excellent	Fair	Good	Fair	Good	Excellent	Sun

KEYWORDS ARE: Karmic debts, Commanding, Money Wasted, Big Expense, Romantic day for love, Death, Sickness - cold, Dominating, Power

Lotto #'s	*play 4 #s*	*play 3 #s*	Ruling Angel:............	Color Sugestion:............	*Ruling Deity*
9,2,33,32,20,15	8378	897	Gabriel	White/Yellow/ Peach	Gaitree

ADVICE & DETAILS	MANTRA FOR TODAY
Be very careful of wasting money today, particularly in a big ticket item. The influences of today if you are positive may help you with a promotion, but if you are negative you will feel lazy and inactive, you must overcome this tendency and accomplish your tasks.	*Om Namo Bhagawate Mukhtanandaya, 108 times AUM KRSNAYA VIDMAHE DAMODARAYA DHIMAHI. TANNO VISHNU PRACODAYAT. 9 times*

BIBLE VERSES: (Proverbs)

24:22. For their destruction shall rise suddenly: and who knoweth the ruin of both?

READ PSALMS #'s: 1, 10, 28 ,37, 46, 55, 73, 100, 118

DECEMBER 2, 2015

12/02/2015 WED		This is considered a NEGATIVE day for you							Shiva
Moving	*Shopping*	*Health*	*Investing*	*Gambling*	*Love is*	*Wedding*	*Travel*	*Work/Job*	*Planet*
Bad	Bad	Bad	Bad	Good	Bad	Good	Bad	Bad	Venus

KEYWORDS ARE: God - Karma, Association, Accidents, death, Illnese, children, hypertension, Sickness - cold, Legal matter, Co-operation, Karmic debts

Lotto #'s	*play 4 #s*	*play 3 #s*	Ruling Angel:............	Color Sugestion:............	*Ruling Deity*
10,3,34,31,20,17	7835	998	Raziel	Red/Yellow/Pink	Durga

ADVICE & DETAILS	MANTRA FOR TODAY
Today is a great day to enjoy friends, associates, to venture into partnerships and to listen to and honor teachers. You could also lose or end a relationship with a lover.	*Om Hareem Nama Swaha..Shri Maha Laxmi Aye Namah swaha 12 times Om maha laxmi cha vidmahe vishnu pataya dhi mahi tanno laxmi pracho dayat Om hareem namam swaha 9 times*

BIBLE VERSES: (Proverbs)

24:24. They that say to the wicked man: Thou art just: shall be cursed by the people, and the tribes shall abhor them.

READ PSALMS #'s: 2, 11, 29 ,38, 47, 56, 74, 101, 119

DECEMBER 3, 2015

12/03/2015 THU	This is considered a NEUTRAL day for you								Shiva
Moving	Shopping	Health	Investing	Gambling	Love is	Wedding	Travel	Work/Job	Planet
Fair	Fair	Fair	Fair	Good	Bad	Good	Fair	Bad	Mercury

KEYWORDS ARE: Home Alone, Communication, Confined, independence, Worry, Legal matter, Abusive, Groups - Parties, Commanding

Lotto #'s	play 4 #s	play 3 #s	Ruling Angel:............	Color Sugestion:............	Ruling Deity
2,5,33,31,20,19	8227	199	Zadkiel	Green/Sky Blue/White	Saraswaty

ADVICE & DETAILS	MANTRA FOR TODAY
You may hear news of possible pregnancy of birth of a baby. Tension over children or younger people. You must watch your health today. You will be stressed.	Om Ganga mataye nama swaha Om Varuna Devta aye Pahimam 11 times Om hareem mama sarva shatru janam vashee kuru kuru swaha om hareem ksham kasham kasheem kasheem swaha 9 times

BIBLE VERSES: (Proverbs)
24:26. He shall kiss the lips, who answereth right words.
0

READ PSALMS #'s: 3, 12, 30 ,39, 48, 57, 75, 102, 120

DECEMBER 4, 2015

12/04/2015 FRI	This is considered a POSITIVE day for you								Shiva
Moving	Shopping	Health	Investing	Gambling	Love is	Wedding	Travel	Work/Job	Planet
Good	Excellent	Good	Good	Bad	Excellent	Good	Excelle	Good	Pluto

KEYWORDS ARE: Music, Tiredness, love, marriage, Travel partner, Abusive, Karmic debts, Laziness, Association

Lotto #'s	play 4 #s	play 3 #s	Ruling Angel:............	Color Sugestion:............	Ruling Deity
3,6,34,32,20,20	9356	2910	Metatron	Dark Blue/ Purple/ Mauve	Ganesh

ADVICE & DETAILS	MANTRA FOR TODAY
There is the possibility of tension at work with coworkers. You may have group projects that may create conflict. Coworkers are friendly but tense.	Om Namo Bhagawate Mukhtanandaya, 108 times AUM KRSNAYA VIDMAHE DAMODARAYA DHIMAHI. TANNO VISHNU PRACODAYAT. 9 times

BIBLE VERSES: (Proverbs)
24:28. Be not witness without cause against thy neighbour: and deceive not any man with thy lips.

READ PSALMS #'s: 4, 13, 31 ,40, 49, 58, 76, 103, 121

DECEMBER 5, 2015

12/05/2015 SAT	This is considered a POSITIVE day for you								Shiva
Moving	Shopping	Health	Investing	Gambling	Love is	Wedding	Travel	Work/Job	Planet
Good	Excellent	Excellent	Good	Good	Good	Good	Excelle	Good	Uranus

KEYWORDS ARE: Publishing, travel, children, publishing, Childishness, Karmic debts, God - Karma, Moving, Communication

Lotto #'s	play 4 #s	play 3 #s	Ruling Angel:............	Color Sugestion:............	Ruling Deity
4,6,33,31,20,13	6152	392	Camael	Orange/White/Light Green/ Beige	Krishna

ADVICE & DETAILS	MANTRA FOR TODAY
You will receive news of becoming pregnant or hear about someone else being pregnant or receive news about children. You will have the opportunity to buy or be somewhere related to luxury and fame. Do not begin any project today; today is a day to culminate projects of any type.	Kali Durge Namo Nama Om Durge aye nama swaha 108 times AUM TATPURUSAYA VIDMAHE VAKRATUNDAY DHIMAHI. TANNO DANTI PRACODAYAT. 9 times

BIBLE VERSES: (Proverbs)
24:30. I passed by the field of the slothful man, and by the vineyard of the foolish man:

READ PSALMS #'s: 5, 14, 32 ,41, 50, 59, 77, 104, 122

DECEMBER 6, 2015

12/06/2015 SUN	This is considered a NEUTRAL day for you								Shiva

Moving	Shopping	Health	Investing	Gambling	Love is	Wedding	Travel	Work/Job	Planet
Bad	Bad	Bad	Bad	Fair	Fair	Bad	Bad	Bad	Mars

KEYWORDS ARE: work, frustration, employment, stress, Low Pay, God - Karma, IRS - Law, Government, Tiredness

Lotto #'s	play 4 #s	play 3 #s	Ruling Angel:............	Color Sugestion:............	Ruling Deity
5,7,33,32,20,16	7760	493	Raphael	Purple/DeepBlue/Rose	Hanuman

ADVICE & DETAILS

You may have to deal with coworker problems today. You will also have conflicts and tensions with bosses. You should keep a low profile today. Keep your nose to the grindstone and do your duty without complaining. Avoid contact with coworkers.

BIBLE VERSES: (Proverbs)

24:32. Which when I had seen, I laid it up in my heart, and by the example I received instruction.

READ PSALMS #'s: 6, 15, 33 ,42, 51, 60, 78, 105, 123

MANTRA FOR TODAY

Om hareem Kleem Hreem Aem Saraswataye namaha
21 times
Om Guru bramha, Guru Vishnu Guru Deva mahaeshwara guru saksha paam bramha, tasmi shri guruve nama
9 times

DECEMBER 7, 2015

12/07/2015 MON	This is considered a POSITIVE day for you								Shiva

Moving	Shopping	Health	Investing	Gambling	Love is	Wedding	Travel	Work/Job	Planet
Excellent	Good	Excellent	Good	Bad	Excellent	Fair	Excelle	Good	Moon

KEYWORDS ARE: short trips, religion, fraudulent, move, Affairs with oppoite sex, IRS - Law, Accidents, Criticism, travel

Lotto #'s	play 4 #s	play 3 #s	Ruling Angel:............	Color Sugestion:............	Ruling Deity
6,9,34,32,20,18	5508	594	Zaphkiel	Light Blue/Purple/Peach	Ganga

ADVICE & DETAILS

This day is influenced by changes, moves and trips to close by locations. You will change your mind often and this lack of focus may cause you to get into an accident. Try to stay focused on your goals and minimize the multitasking especially when driving from one place to another.

BIBLE VERSES: (Proverbs)

24:34. And poverty shall come to thee as a runner, and beggary as an armed man.

READ PSALMS #'s: 7, 16, 34 ,43, 52, 61, 79, 106, 124

MANTRA FOR TODAY

Om Jai Viganeshwaraya..
Lambodaraya Namo Namaha
21 times
Om Sarva Mangal Mangalye, Shiva Sarvart Sadike, Sharan Tryambike Gowri, Narayane Namo asttute
9 times

DECEMBER 8, 2015

12/08/2015 TUE	This is considered a NEGATIVE day for you								Shiva

Moving	Shopping	Health	Investing	Gambling	Love is	Wedding	Travel	Work/Job	Planet
Bad	Bad	Bad	Fair	Excellent	Bad	Excellent	Bad	Bad	Jupiter

KEYWORDS ARE: family, luxury, quarell, disagreements , Police,courts, tickets, Accidents, Denial - Doubt, money, frustration

Lotto #'s	play 4 #s	play 3 #s	Ruling Angel:............	Color Sugestion:............	Ruling Deity
7,10,33,31,20,20	8482	695	Haniel	Yellow/White/Silver	Mahalaxmi

ADVICE & DETAILS

You will hear news of profit or gains or inheritance from far away. You will have a wealthy relative contact you or visit you. Avoid taking risks with money or signing contracts for purchases.

BIBLE VERSES: (Proverbs)

25:2. It is the glory of God to conceal the word, and the glory of kings to search out the speech.

READ PSALMS #'s: 8, 17, 35 ,44, 53, 62, 80, 107, 125

MANTRA FOR TODAY

Om Graam Greem Graum Sa Gurave namah swaha
21 times
AUM VAGDEVYAI CA VIDMAHE KAMARAJAYA DHIMAHI. TANNO DEVI PRACODAYAT.
9 times

DECEMBER 9, 2015

12/09/2015 WED		This is considered a NEUTRAL day for you							Shiva
Moving	*Shopping*	*Health*	*Investing*	*Gambling*	*Love is*	*Wedding*	*Travel*	*Work/Job*	*Planet*
Good	Fair	Fair	Bad	Bad	Good	Bad	Good	Fair	Saturn

KEYWORDS ARE: Abusive, Karmic debts, Alcohol - drugs, Enemies, Spirituality & belief, Losses, Death, Sickness - cold, Religious

Lotto #'s	*play 4 #s*	*play 3 #s*	Ruling Angel:............	Color Sugestion:............	*Ruling Deity*
8,1,33,32,20,12	5188	796	Mikael	Gold/Brown/Blue/Dark Green	Pitridev

ADVICE & DETAILS	MANTRA FOR TODAY
It will be difficult, but possible to overcome your sadness today. Your mind will tend to veer towards thoughts of losses, doubts, denial and death; if you cannot control it you will be creating this in your life. Pray, meditate and place your trust in the Higher Power.	*Om Mana Swasti Shanti Kuru kuru Swaha Shivoham Shivoham 27 times om haring jawala mukhi mam sarva shatru bakshaya bakshaya hung phat swaha Om Nama shivaya pahimam 9 times*

BIBLE VERSES: (Proverbs)
25:4. Take away the rust from silver, and there shall come forth a most pure vessel:

READ PSALMS #'s: 9, 18, 36 ,45, 54, 63, 81, 108, 126

DECEMBER 10, 2015

12/10/2015 THU		This is considered a POSITIVE day for you							Shiva
Moving	*Shopping*	*Health*	*Investing*	*Gambling*	*Love is*	*Wedding*	*Travel*	*Work/Job*	*Planet*
Good	Good	Excellent	Excellent	Fair	Good	Fair	Good	Excellent	Sun

KEYWORDS ARE: Karmic debts, Commanding, Money Wasted, Big Expense, Romantic day for love, Death, Sickness - cold, Dominating, Power

Lotto #'s	*play 4 #s*	*play 3 #s*	Ruling Angel:............	Color Sugestion:............	*Ruling Deity*
9,2,33,32,20,15	6300	897	Gabriel	White/Yellow/ Peach	Gaitree

ADVICE & DETAILS	MANTRA FOR TODAY
Be very careful of wasting money today, particularly in a big ticket item. The influences of today if you are positive may help you with a promotion, but if you are negative you will feel lazy and inactive, you must overcome this tendency and accomplish your tasks.	*Jai Jai Shiva Shambo.(2) ...Mahadeva Shambo (2) 21 times Om Jayanti Mangala Kali Bhadrakali Kapalini Durga Kshama Shiva Dhatri Swaha Swadha Namostute 9 times*

BIBLE VERSES: (Proverbs)
24:31. And behold it was all filled with nettles, and thorns had covered the face thereof, and the stone wall was broken down.

READ PSALMS #'s: 1, 10, 28 ,37, 46, 55, 73, 100, 118

DECEMBER 11, 2015

12/11/2015 FRI		This is considered a NEGATIVE day for you							Shiva
Moving	*Shopping*	*Health*	*Investing*	*Gambling*	*Love is*	*Wedding*	*Travel*	*Work/Job*	*Planet*
Bad	Bad	Bad	Bad	Good	Bad	Good	Bad	Bad	Venus

KEYWORDS ARE: God - Karma, Association, Accidents, death, Illnese, children, hypertension, Sickness - cold, Legal matter, Co-operation, Karmic debts

Lotto #'s	*play 4 #s*	*play 3 #s*	Ruling Angel:............	Color Sugestion:............	*Ruling Deity*
10,3,33,32,20,17	7807	998	Raziel	Red/Yellow/Pink	Durga

ADVICE & DETAILS	MANTRA FOR TODAY
Today is a great day to enjoy friends, associates, to venture into partnerships and to listen to and honor teachers. You could also lose or end a relationship with a lover.	*Om Hareem Nama Swaha..Shri Maha Laxmi Aye Namah swaha 12 times Om maha laxmi cha vidmahe vishnu pataya dhi mahi tanno laxmi pracho dayat Om hareem namam swaha 9 times*

BIBLE VERSES: (Proverbs)
24:33. Thou wilt sleep a little, said I, thou wilt slumber a little, thou wilt fold thy hands a little to rest.

READ PSALMS #'s: 2, 11, 29 ,38, 47, 56, 74, 101, 119

DECEMBER 12, 2015

12/12/2015 SAT	This is considered a NEUTRAL day for you								Shiva

Moving	Shopping	Health	Investing	Gambling	Love is		Wedding	Travel	Work/Job	Planet
Fair	Fair	Fair	Fair	Good	Bad		Good	Fair	Bad	Mercury

KEYWORDS ARE: IRS - Law, Communication, Denial - Doubt, losses, Stress with Bosses, Legal matter, Abusive, Groups - Parties, God - Karma

Lotto #'s	play 4 #s	play 3 #s	Ruling Angel:............	Color Sugestion:...........	Ruling Deity
2,5,33,31,20,19	3599	199	Zadkiel	Green/Sky Blue/White	Saraswaty

ADVICE & DETAILS

You may hear news of possible pregnancy of birth of a baby. Tension over children or younger people. You must watch your health today. You will be stressed.

BIBLE VERSES: (Proverbs)

25:1. These are also parables of Solomon, which the men of Ezechias, king of Juda, copied out.

READ PSALMS #'s: 3, 12, 30 ,39, 48, 57, 75, 102, 120

MANTRA FOR TODAY

Om Ganga mataye nama swaha
Om Varuna Devta aye Pahimam
11 times
Om hareem mama sarva shatru
janam vashee kuru kuru swaha
om hareem ksham kasham
kasheem kasheem swaha
9 times

DECEMBER 13, 2015

12/13/2015 SUN	This is considered a POSITIVE day for you								Shiva

Moving	Shopping	Health	Investing	Gambling	Love is		Wedding	Travel	Work/Job	Planet
Good	Excellent	Good	Good	Bad	Excellent		Good	Excelle	Good	Pluto

KEYWORDS ARE: Music, Tiredness, love, marriage, Travel partner, Abusive, Karmic debts, Laziness, Association

Lotto #'s	play 4 #s	play 3 #s	Ruling Angel:............	Color Sugestion:...........	Ruling Deity
3,5,34,32,20,20	4021	2910	Metatron	Dark Blue/ Purple/ Mauve	Ganesh

ADVICE & DETAILS

There is the possibility of tension at work with coworkers. You may have group projects that may create conflict. Coworkers are friendly but tense.

BIBLE VERSES: (Proverbs)

25:3. The heaven above and the earth beneath, and the heart of kings is unsearchable.

READ PSALMS #'s: 4, 13, 31 ,40, 49, 58, 76, 103, 121

MANTRA FOR TODAY

Om Namo Bhagawate
Mukhtanandaya,
108 times
AUM KRSNAYA VIDMAHE
DAMODARAYA DHIMAHI.
TANNO VISHNU
PRACODAYAT.
9 times

DECEMBER 14, 2015

12/14/2015 MON	This is considered a POSITIVE day for you								Shiva

Moving	Shopping	Health	Investing	Gambling	Love is		Wedding	Travel	Work/Job	Planet
Good	Excellent	Excellent	Good	Good	Good		Good	Excelle	Good	Uranus

KEYWORDS ARE: Publishing, travel, children, publishing, Childishness, Karmic debts, God - Karma, Moving, Communication

Lotto #'s	play 4 #s	play 3 #s	Ruling Angel:............	Color Sugestion:...........	Ruling Deity
4,7,34,31,20,13	4661	392	Camael	Orange/White/Light Green/ Beige	Krishna

ADVICE & DETAILS

You will receive news of becoming pregnant or hear about someone else being pregnant or receive news about children. You will have the opportunity to buy or be somewhere related to luxury and fame. Do not begin any project today; today is a day to culminate projects of any type.

BIBLE VERSES: (Proverbs)

25:5. Take away wickedness from the face of the king, and his throne shall be established with justice.

READ PSALMS #'s: 5, 14, 32 ,41, 50, 59, 77, 104, 122

MANTRA FOR TODAY

Kali Durge Namo Nama
Om Durge aye nama swaha
108 times
AUM TATPURUSAYA
VIDMAHE VAKRATUNDAY
DHIMAHI. TANNO DANTI
PRACODAYAT.
9 times

DECEMBER 15, 2015

12/15/2015 TUE	This is considered a NEUTRAL day for you									Shiva
Moving	Shopping	Health	Investing	Gambling	Love is	Wedding	Travel	Work/Job		Planet
Bad	Bad	Bad	Bad	Fair	Fair	Bad	Bad	Bad		Mars

KEYWORDS ARE: work, frustration, employment, stress, Low Pay, God - Karma, IRS - Law, Government, Tiredness

Lotto #'s	play 4 #s	play 3 #s	Ruling Angel:............	Color Sugestion:............	Ruling Deity
5,7,34,31,20,16	10809	493	Raphael	Purple/DeepBlue/Rose	Hanuman

ADVICE & DETAILS

You may have to deal with coworker problems today. You will also have conflicts and tensions with bosses. You should keep a low profile today. Keep your nose to the grindstone and do your duty without complaining. Avoid contact with coworkers.

MANTRA FOR TODAY

Om hareem Kleem Hreem Aem Saraswataye namaha
21 times
Om Guru bramha, Guru Vishnu Guru Deva mahaeshwara guru saksha paam bramha, tasmi shri guruve nama
9 times

BIBLE VERSES: (Proverbs)

25:7. For it is better that it should be said to thee: Come up hither; than that thou shouldst be humbled before the prince.

READ PSALMS #'s: 6, 15, 33 ,42, 51, 60, 78, 105, 123

DECEMBER 16, 2015

12/16/2015 WED	This is considered a POSITIVE day for you									Shiva
Moving	Shopping	Health	Investing	Gambling	Love is	Wedding	Travel	Work/Job		Planet
Excellent	Good	Excellent	Good	Bad	Excellent	Fair	Excelle	Good		Moon

KEYWORDS ARE: short trips, religion, fraudulent, move, Affairs with oppoite sex, IRS - Law, Accidents, Criticism, travel

Lotto #'s	play 4 #s	play 3 #s	Ruling Angel:............	Color Sugestion:............	Ruling Deity
6,8,33,31,20,18	8239	594	Zaphkiel	Light Blue/Purple/Peach	Ganga

ADVICE & DETAILS

This day is influenced by changes, moves and trips to close by locations. You will change your mind often and this lack of focus may cause you to get into an accident. Try to stay focused on your goals and minimize the multitasking especially when driving from one place to another.

MANTRA FOR TODAY

Om Jai Viganeshwaraya..
Lambodaraya Namo Namaha
21 times
Om Sarva Mangal Mangalye, Shiva Sarvart Sadike, Sharan Tryambike Gowri, Narayane Namo asttute
9 times

BIBLE VERSES: (Proverbs)

25:9. Treat thy cause with thy friend, and discover not the secret to a stranger:

READ PSALMS #'s: 7, 16, 34 ,43, 52, 61, 79, 106, 124

DECEMBER 17, 2015

12/17/2015 THU	This is considered a NEGATIVE day for you									Shiva
Moving	Shopping	Health	Investing	Gambling	Love is	Wedding	Travel	Work/Job		Planet
Bad	Bad	Bad	Fair	Excellent	Bad	Excellent	Bad	Bad		Jupiter

KEYWORDS ARE: family, luxury, quarell, disagreements , Police,courts, tickets, Accidents, Denial - Doubt, money, frustration

Lotto #'s	play 4 #s	play 3 #s	Ruling Angel:............	Color Sugestion:............	Ruling Deity
7,10,34,31,20,19	8972	695	Haniel	Yellow/White/Silver	Mahalaxmi

ADVICE & DETAILS

You will hear news of profit or gains or inheritance from far away. You will have a wealthy relative contact you or visit you. Avoid taking risks with money or signing contracts for purchases.

MANTRA FOR TODAY

Om Graam Greem Graum Sa Gurave namah swaha
21 times
AUM VAGDEVYAI CA VIDMAHE KAMARAJAYA DHIMAHI. TANNO DEVI PRACODAYAT.
9 times

BIBLE VERSES: (Proverbs)

25:11. To speak a word in due time, is like apples of gold on beds of silver.

READ PSALMS #'s: 8, 17, 35 ,44, 53, 62, 80, 107, 125

DECEMBER 18, 2015

12/18/2015 FRI	This is considered a NEUTRAL day for you									Shiva
Moving	Shopping	Health	Investing	Gambling	Love is	Wedding	Travel	Work/Job		Planet
Good	Fair	Fair	Bad	Bad	Good	Bad	Good	Fair		Saturn

KEYWORDS ARE: Abusive, Karmic debts, Alcohol - drugs, Enemies, Spirituality & belief, Losses, Death, Sickness - cold, Religious

Lotto #'s	play 4 #s	play 3 #s	Ruling Angel:............	Color Sugestion:............	Ruling Deity
8,1,33,32,20,12	8265	796	Mikael	Gold/Brown/Blue/Dark Green	Pitridev

ADVICE & DETAILS	MANTRA FOR TODAY
It will be difficult, but possible to overcome your sadness today. Your mind will tend to veer towards thoughts of losses, doubts, denial and death; if you cannot control it you will be creating this in your life. Pray, meditate and place your trust in the Higher Power.	Om Mana Swasti Shanti Kuru kuru Swaha Shivoham Shivoham 27 times om haring jawala mukhi mam sarva shatru bakshaya bakshaya hung phat swaha Om Nama shivaya pahimam 9 times

BIBLE VERSES: (Proverbs)

25:13. As the cold of snow in the time of harvest, so is a faithful messenger to him that sent him, for he refresheth his soul.

READ PSALMS #'s: 9, 18, 36 ,45, 54, 63, 81, 108, 126

DECEMBER 19, 2015

12/19/2015 SAT	This is considered a POSITIVE day for you									Shiva
Moving	Shopping	Health	Investing	Gambling	Love is	Wedding	Travel	Work/Job		Planet
Good	Good	Excellent	Excellent	Fair	Good	Fair	Good	Excellent		Sun

KEYWORDS ARE: Karmic debts, Commanding, Money Wasted, Big Expense, Romantic day for love, Death, Sickness - cold, Dominating, Power

Lotto #'s	play 4 #s	play 3 #s	Ruling Angel:............	Color Sugestion:............	Ruling Deity
9,2,34,31,20,14	10041	897	Gabriel	White/Yellow/ Peach	Gaitree

ADVICE & DETAILS	MANTRA FOR TODAY
Be very careful of wasting money today, particularly in a big ticket item. The influences of today if you are positive may help you with a promotion, but if you are negative you will feel lazy and inactive, you must overcome this tendency and accomplish your tasks.	Jai Jai Shiva Shambo.(2) ...Mahadeva Shambo (2) 21 times Om Jayanti Mangala Kali Bhadrakali Kapalini Durga Kshama Shiva Dhatri Swaha Swadha Namostute 9 times

BIBLE VERSES: (Proverbs)

25:6. Appear not glorious before the king, and stand not in the place of great men.

READ PSALMS #'s: 1, 10, 28 ,37, 46, 55, 73, 100, 118

DECEMBER 20, 2015

12/20/2015 SUN	This is considered a NEGATIVE day for you									Shiva
Moving	Shopping	Health	Investing	Gambling	Love is	Wedding	Travel	Work/Job		Planet
Bad	Bad	Bad	Bad	Good	Bad	Good	Bad	Bad		Venus

KEYWORDS ARE: God - Karma, Association, Accidents, death, Illnese, children, hypertension, Sickness - cold, Legal matter, Co-operation, Karmic debts

Lotto #'s	play 4 #s	play 3 #s	Ruling Angel:............	Color Sugestion:............	Ruling Deity
10,3,33,31,20,17	2891	998	Raziel	Red/Yellow/Pink	Durga

ADVICE & DETAILS	MANTRA FOR TODAY
Today is a great day to enjoy friends, associates, to venture into partnerships and to listen to and honor teachers. You could also lose or end a relationship with a lover.	Om Hareem Nama Swaha..Shri Maha Laxmi Aye Namah swaha 12 times Om maha laxmi cha vidmahe vishnu pataya dhi mahi tanno laxmi pracho dayat Om hareem namam swaha 9 times

BIBLE VERSES: (Proverbs)

25:8. The things which thy eyes have seen, utter not hastily in a quarrel: lest afterward thou mayst not be able to make amends, when thou hast

READ PSALMS #'s: 2, 11, 29 ,38, 47, 56, 74, 101, 119

DECEMBER 21, 2015

12/21/2015 MON		This is considered a NEUTRAL day for you							Shiva
Moving	Shopping	Health	Investing	Gambling	Love is	Wedding	Travel	Work/Job	Planet
Fair	Fair	Fair	Fair	Good	Bad	Good	Fair	Bad	Mercury

KEYWORDS ARE: IRS - Law, Communication, Denial - Doubt, losses, Stress with Bosses, Legal matter, Abusive, Groups - Parties, God - Karma

Lotto #'s	play 4 #s	play 3 #s	Ruling Angel:............	Color Sugestion:............	Ruling Deity
2,4,33,32,20,19	3929	199	Zadkiel	Green/Sky Blue/White	Saraswaty

ADVICE & DETAILS	MANTRA FOR TODAY
You may hear news of possible pregnancy of birth of a baby. Tension over children or younger people. You must watch your health today. You will be stressed.	Om Ganga mataye nama swaha Om Varuna Devta aye Pahimam 11 times Om hareem mama sarva shatru janam vashee kuru kuru swaha om hareem ksham kasham kasheem kasheem swaha 9 times

BIBLE VERSES: (Proverbs)
25:10. Lest he insult over thee, when he hath heard it, and cease not to upbraid thee. Grace and friendship deliver a man: keep these for thyself,

READ PSALMS #'s: 3, 12, 30 ,39, 48, 57, 75, 102, 120

DECEMBER 22, 2015

12/22/2015 TUE		This is considered a POSITIVE day for you							Shiva
Moving	Shopping	Health	Investing	Gambling	Love is	Wedding	Travel	Work/Job	Planet
Good	Excellent	Good	Good	Bad	Excellent	Good	Excelle	Good	Pluto

KEYWORDS ARE: Accidents, Tiredness, death, finish, Traffic problems, Tickets, Abusive, Karmic debts, Laziness, IRS - Law

Lotto #'s	play 4 #s	play 3 #s	Ruling Angel:............	Color Sugestion:............	Ruling Deity
3,5,33,32,20,21	8137	2910	Metatron	Dark Blue/ Purple/ Mauve	Ganesh

ADVICE & DETAILS	MANTRA FOR TODAY
There is the possibility of tension at work with coworkers. You may have group projects that may create conflict. Coworkers are friendly but tense.	Om Namo Bhagawate Mukhtanandaya, 108 times AUM KRSNAYA VIDMAHE DAMODARAYA DHIMAHI. TANNO VISHNU PRACODAYAT. 9 times

BIBLE VERSES: (Proverbs)
25:12. As an earring of gold and a bright pearl, so is he that reproveth the wise, and the obedient ear.

READ PSALMS #'s: 4, 13, 31 ,40, 49, 58, 76, 103, 121

DECEMBER 23, 2015

12/23/2015 WED		This is considered a POSITIVE day for you							Shiva
Moving	Shopping	Health	Investing	Gambling	Love is	Wedding	Travel	Work/Job	Planet
Good	Excellent	Excellent	Good	Good	Good	Good	Excelle	Good	Uranus

KEYWORDS ARE: Publishing, travel, children, publishing, Childishness, Karmic debts, God - Karma, Moving, Communication

Lotto #'s	play 4 #s	play 3 #s	Ruling Angel:............	Color Sugestion:............	Ruling Deity
4,6,34,31,20,13	5864	392	Camael	Orange/White/Light Green/ Beige	Krishna

ADVICE & DETAILS	MANTRA FOR TODAY
You will receive news of becoming pregnant or hear about someone else being pregnant or receive news about children. You will have the opportunity to buy or be somewhere related to luxury and fame. Do not begin any project today; today is a day to culminate projects of any type.	Kali Durge Namo Nama Om Durge aye nama swaha 108 times AUM TATPURUSAYA VIDMAHE VAKRATUNDAY DHIMAHI. TANNO DANTI PRACODAYAT. 9 times

BIBLE VERSES: (Proverbs)
25:14. As clouds, and wind, when no rain followeth, so is the man that boasteth, and doth not fulfil his promises.

READ PSALMS #'s: 5, 14, 32 ,41, 50, 59, 77, 104, 122

DECEMBER 24, 2015

12/24/2015 THU		This is considered a NEUTRAL day for you							Shiva
Moving	Shopping	Health	Investing	Gambling	Love is	Wedding	Travel	Work/Job	Planet
Bad	Bad	Bad	Bad	Fair	Fair	Bad	Bad	Bad	Mars

KEYWORDS ARE: work, frustration, employment, stress, Low Pay, God - Karma, IRS - Law, Government, Tiredness

Lotto #'s	play 4 #s	play 3 #s	Ruling Angel:............	Color Sugestion:............	Ruling Deity
5,7,33,32,20,16	1602	493	Raphael	Purple/DeepBlue/Rose	Hanuman

ADVICE & DETAILS

You may have to deal with coworker problems today. You will also have conflicts and tensions with bosses. You should keep a low profile today. Keep your nose to the grindstone and do your duty without complaining. Avoid contact with coworkers.

BIBLE VERSES: (Proverbs)

25:16. Thou hast found honey, eat what is sufficient for thee, lest being glutted therewith thou vomit it up.

READ PSALMS #'s: 6, 15, 33 ,42, 51, 60, 78, 105, 123

MANTRA FOR TODAY

Om hareem Kleem Hreem Aem Saraswataye namaha
21 times
Om Guru bramha, Guru Vishnu Guru Deva mahaeshwara guru saksha paam bramha, tasmi shri guruve nama
9 times

DECEMBER 25, 2015

12/25/2015 FRI		This is considered a POSITIVE day for you							Shiva
Moving	Shopping	Health	Investing	Gambling	Love is	Wedding	Travel	Work/Job	Planet
Excellent	Good	Excellent	Good	Bad	Excellent	Fair	Excelle	Good	Moon

KEYWORDS ARE: short trips, religion, fraudulent, move, Affairs with oppoite sex, IRS - Law, Accidents, Criticism, travel

Lotto #'s	play 4 #s	play 3 #s	Ruling Angel:............	Color Sugestion:............	Ruling Deity
6,9,33,32,20,17	4373	594	Zaphkiel	Light Blue/Purple/Peach	Ganga

ADVICE & DETAILS

This day is influenced by changes, moves and trips to close by locations. You will change your mind often and this lack of focus may cause you to get into an accident. Try to stay focused on your goals and minimize the multitasking especially when driving from one place to another.

BIBLE VERSES: (Proverbs)

25:18. A man that beareth false witness against his neighbour, is like a dart and a sword and a sharp arrow.

READ PSALMS #'s: 7, 16, 34 ,43, 52, 61, 79, 106, 124

MANTRA FOR TODAY

Om Jai Viganeshwaraya..
Lambodaraya Namo Namaha
21 times
Om Sarva Mangal Mangalye, Shiva Sarvart Sadike, Sharan Tryambike Gowri, Narayane Namo asttute
9 times

DECEMBER 26, 2015

12/26/2015 SAT		This is considered a NEGATIVE day for you							Shiva
Moving	Shopping	Health	Investing	Gambling	Love is	Wedding	Travel	Work/Job	Planet
Bad	Bad	Bad	Fair	Excellent	Bad	Excellent	Bad	Bad	Jupiter

KEYWORDS ARE: family, luxury, quarell, disagreements , Police,courts, tickets, Accidents, Denial - Doubt, money, frustration

Lotto #'s	play 4 #s	play 3 #s	Ruling Angel:............	Color Sugestion:............	Ruling Deity
7,10,33,31,20,20	4007	695	Haniel	Yellow/White/Silver	Mahalaxmi

ADVICE & DETAILS

You will hear news of profit or gains or inheritance from far away. You will have a wealthy relative contact you or visit you. Avoid taking risks with money or signing contracts for purchases.

BIBLE VERSES: (Proverbs)

25:20. And one that looseth his garment in cold weather. As vinegar upon nitre, so is he that singeth songs to a very evil heart. As a moth doth by a

READ PSALMS #'s: 8, 17, 35 ,44, 53, 62, 80, 107, 125

MANTRA FOR TODAY

Om Graam Greem Graum Sa Gurave namah swaha
21 times
AUM VAGDEVYAI CA VIDMAHE KAMARAJAYA DHIMAHI. TANNO DEVI PRACODAYAT.
9 times

DECEMBER 27, 2015

12/27/2015 SUN			This is considered a NEUTRAL day for you						Shiva
Moving	*Shopping*	*Health*	*Investing*	*Gambling*	*Love is*	*Wedding*	*Travel*	*Work/Job*	*Planet*
Good	Fair	Fair	Bad	Bad	Good	Bad	Good	Fair	Saturn

KEYWORDS ARE: Abusive, Karmic debts, Alcohol - drugs, Enemies, Spirituality & belief, Losses, Death, Sickness - cold, Religious

Lotto #'s	*play 4 #s*	*play 3 #s*	*Ruling Angel:*............	*Color Sugestion:*............	*Ruling Deity*
8,1,33,32,20,12	4933	796	Mikael	Gold/Brown/Blue/Dark Green	Pitridev

ADVICE & DETAILS	MANTRA FOR TODAY
It will be difficult, but possible to overcome your sadness today. Your mind will tend to veer towards thoughts of losses, doubts, denial and death; if you cannot control it you will be creating this in your life. Pray, meditate and place your trust in the Higher Power.	*Om Mana Swasti Shanti Kuru kuru Swaha Shivoham Shivoham 27 times om haring jawala mukhi mam sarva shatru bakshaya bakshaya hung phat swaha Om Nama shivaya pahimam 9 times*

BIBLE VERSES: (Proverbs)

25:22. For thou shalt heap hot coals upon his head, and the Lord will reward thee.

READ PSALMS #'s: 9, 18, 36 ,45, 54, 63, 81, 108, 126

DECEMBER 28, 2015

12/28/2015 MON			This is considered a POSITIVE day for you						Shiva
Moving	*Shopping*	*Health*	*Investing*	*Gambling*	*Love is*	*Wedding*	*Travel*	*Work/Job*	*Planet*
Good	Good	Excellent	Excellent	Fair	Good	Fair	Good	Excellent	Sun

KEYWORDS ARE: Karmic debts, Commanding, Money Wasted, Big Expense, Romantic day for love, Death, Sickness - cold, Dominating, Power

Lotto #'s	*play 4 #s*	*play 3 #s*	*Ruling Angel:*............	*Color Sugestion:*............	*Ruling Deity*
9,3,33,32,20,15	7883	897	Gabriel	White/Yellow/ Peach	Gaitree

ADVICE & DETAILS	MANTRA FOR TODAY
Be very careful of wasting money today, particularly in a big ticket item. The influences of today if you are positive may help you with a promotion, but if you are negative you will feel lazy and inactive, you must overcome this tendency and accomplish your tasks.	*Jai Jai Shiva Shambo.(2) ...Mahadeva Shambo (2) 21 times Om Jayanti Mangala Kali Bhadrakali Kapalini Durga Kshama Shiva Dhatri Swaha Swadha Namostute 9 times*

BIBLE VERSES: (Proverbs)

25:15. By patience a prince shall be appeased, and a soft tongue shall break hardness.

READ PSALMS #'s: 1, 10, 28 ,37, 46, 55, 73, 100, 118

DECEMBER 29, 2015

12/29/2015 TUE			This is considered a NEGATIVE day for you						Shiva
Moving	*Shopping*	*Health*	*Investing*	*Gambling*	*Love is*	*Wedding*	*Travel*	*Work/Job*	*Planet*
Bad	Bad	Bad	Bad	Good	Bad	Good	Bad	Bad	Venus

KEYWORDS ARE: God - Karma, Association, Accidents, death, Illnese, children, hypertension, Sickness - cold, Legal matter, Co-operation, Karmic debts

Lotto #'s	*play 4 #s*	*play 3 #s*	*Ruling Angel:*............	*Color Sugestion:*............	*Ruling Deity*
10,4,33,31,20,17	7076	998	Raziel	Red/Yellow/Pink	Durga

ADVICE & DETAILS	MANTRA FOR TODAY
Today is a great day to enjoy friends, associates, to venture into partnerships and to listen to and honor teachers. You could also lose or end a relationship with a lover.	*Om Hareem Nama Swaha..Shri Maha Laxmi Aye Namah swaha 12 times Om maha laxmi cha vidmahe vishnu pataya dhi mahi tanno laxmi pracho dayat Om hareem namam swaha 9 times*

BIBLE VERSES: (Proverbs)

25:17. Withdraw thy foot from the house of thy neighbour, lest having his fill he hate thee.

READ PSALMS #'s: 2, 11, 29 ,38, 47, 56, 74, 101, 119

DECEMBER 30, 2015

12/30/2015 WED	This is considered a NEUTRAL day for you								Shiva

Moving	Shopping	Health	Investing	Gambling	Love is	Wedding	Travel	Work/Job	Planet
Fair	Fair	Fair	Fair	Good	Bad	Good	Fair	Bad	Mercury

KEYWORDS ARE: IRS - Law, Communication, Denial - Doubt, losses, Stress with Bosses, Legal matter, Abusive, Groups - Parties, God - Karma

Lotto #'s	play 4 #s	play 3 #s	Ruling Angel:...........	Color Sugestion:...........	Ruling Deity
2,4,34,32,20,19	8450	199	Zadkiel	Green/Sky Blue/White	Saraswaty

ADVICE & DETAILS	MANTRA FOR TODAY
You may hear news of possible pregnancy of birth of a baby. Tension over children or younger people. You must watch your health today. You will be stressed.	Om Ganga mataye nama swaha Om Varuna Devta aye Pahimam 11 times Om hareem mama sarva shatru janam vashee kuru kuru swaha om hareem ksham kasham kasheem kasheem swaha 9 times

BIBLE VERSES: (Proverbs)

25:19. To trust in an unfaithful man in the time of trouble, is like a rotten tooth, and weary foot,

READ PSALMS #'s: 3, 12, 30 ,39, 48, 57, 75, 102, 120

DECEMBER 31, 2015

12/31/2015 THU	This is considered a POSITIVE day for you								Shiva

Moving	Shopping	Health	Investing	Gambling	Love is	Wedding	Travel	Work/Job	Planet
Good	Excellent	Good	Good	Bad	Excellent	Good	Excelle	Good	Pluto

KEYWORDS ARE: Accidents, Tiredness, death, finish, Traffic problems, Tickets, Abusive, Karmic debts, Laziness, IRS - Law

Lotto #'s	play 4 #s	play 3 #s	Ruling Angel:...........	Color Sugestion:...........	Ruling Deity
3,5,34,31,20,21	5199	2910	Metatron	Dark Blue/ Purple/ Mauve	Ganesh

ADVICE & DETAILS	MANTRA FOR TODAY
There is the possibility of tension at work with coworkers. You may have group projects that may create conflict. Coworkers are friendly but tense.	Om Namo Bhagawate Mukhtanandaya, 108 times AUM KRSNAYA VIDMAHE DAMODARAYA DHIMAHI. TANNO VISHNU PRACODAYAT. 9 times

BIBLE VERSES: (Proverbs)

25:21. If thy enemy be hungry, give him to eat: if he thirst, give him water to drink:

READ PSALMS #'s: 4, 13, 31 ,40, 49, 58, 76, 103, 121

Section 19

WHAT MAKES YOU HAPPY?

A Note from Swami Ram Charran

Now I know what makes me unhappy and what makes me happy. IT'S MY MIND!! When I am watching movie I am in a different world and I am so much concentrated on the movie that everything here in the real world does not matter, I am so intensely enjoying the movie that I do not even think about food or going to the bathroom or even if other people are around me. Just like in a movie theater, there are hundreds of people around me, but each person is enjoying the move in their own mind with the same intensity as I am. When there is a funny moment in the movie, every person experiences happiness and when there is a sad moment everyone experiences distress in their mind all at the same time. Its amazing director who created the scenes has thousands of people showing the same emotions at the same time and same moments. Movies are one of the great gifts to mankind as it takes away the boredom and routine out a person's life.

However when the movie is finished and we are back to reality then what is the mind going to do? Imagine you have all the money in the world and you never have to work for anyone, you never have to pay any bills…what else is left for you to do? You have to eat, so food is necessary. You have to watch your health so it's necessary that you eat healthily. You have to have love as no man or woman can live without love. No matter what happens you need feel that someone cares for you. It is an inbred natural feeling that you have whether you like it or not. Whether it's a sister, a brother, a mother, a father, child, lover or a friend, you must enjoy some connection in some way, or a sense of belonging. A Priest gets his love from his congregation as he seeks the love of the people through knowledge. An investor gets his love from his thrills when he buys and sells the stock s. A president gets his love when he sees the higher poll in his favor from the people. A calf of the cow gets his love by sucking the breast of the cow, the same as a young child. The joy of the mind is enjoyed when there is sexual contact between a male and female but even though that orgasm will last for a few seconds, it can change the whole world and destroy countries and millions of people as we have seen when great women spurned their lovers…

Every person likes to be heard in some way. Deep down inside every human being is a soul that yearns to teach, preach, and be accepted in thought and words. This is what sows the seeds of very other type of love. Every person wants to be a showman. Writers like to be heard in their books. That is why books such as The Bible, Ramayana, Bhagawat Gita, The Quran and others have changed the world in many directions. Just like a movie, a writer can change the person as well as the world. Many movies have been made as a result of books. When a person is reading a book, he or she is also in a different world and can remain there until the book is finished and then s/he is able to come back to the real world. The mind enters the mind of the writer and the reader starts to experience what the writer conceived in his/her own mind. The actual movie takes place in the mind of the reader s/he visualizes every scene the writer paints in his mind. What a great escape for humankind because life would surely be boring if there were no books to read. Besides the fact that the whole progress when books are written, one can conclude that one writer can change the whole direction of the world. The Authors of the New Testament change the whole direction of Christianity. Mohammed in writing The Quran changes the whole direction of the Indus valley and changed the maps of the world, so did Gautama Buddha who changed the Chinese population and their beliefs.

The action of one man can control the whole world. Every preacher, congressman, president of a country can create one action that will change the direction of the world. It is obvious in this internet age, that one man who made the world direction made a 360 degree turn was Bill Gates. His ideas on computers made others create changes but if it was not for him there would be no GOOGLE or facebook etc... Here as you can see how one man, Bill Gates became the "God" of the technology world.

The action of each person in the world is important and each person's action controls everyone else in the world. The rice or bread you eat started with the action of one person who planted the seed perhaps in Ceylon, India or China. The faster we realize that we all depend on each other the faster we will see the power of 'God' in every one. So one of the ways of finding happiness is to see the "God" or divinity in all people whether it's black, white, red or purple. Chances are that the jewelry you are wearing was made by a person in South Africa or Kenya. The computer you are using has chips that were made in China. The car you are driving has parts from Germany or Japan. The clothes you wear are from India or Saudi Arabia. So as you can see each person has a hand in creating the world and so each person has a spark of divine power within them. So we must see everyone as an incarnate of God, bow to them and say "Namaste" which means 'I bow to the God within you.' This kind of humility will make everyone happy in the world and more peaceful.

So as we can conclude from the above so far, the mind's happiness can be affected by the following
1. WHAT YOU SEE –Movies, Books, Nature
2. WHAT YOU TASTE– Food, to enjoy the taste of something
3. WHO YOU TOUCH – Embracing others
4. WHAT YOU HEAR – Music or words
5. WHAT YOU SMELL – Cleanliness is next to godliness

Happiness is connected to the senses. In the end it is the senses that provide all happiness to the mind. If a person enjoys movies, reads books, keeps himself clean, eats good foods, expresses himself to help others and see the God in everyone then he will experience barrels of happiness.

Based on the above, the following are Permanent factors of happiness….

PURPOSE & MOTIVATION
CONTENTMENT
CHILDREN
SEEKING KNOWLEDGE
RELATIONSHIPS
PRAYER AND CONNECION WITH THE UNIVERSE
HUMILITY – REALIZING THE GREATNESS OF THE UNIVERSE

So I have concluded that there is lots of happiness around me but they are all temporary. They are as follows:

FOOD	YOGA	EARNING MONEY
MUSIC	MOVIES OR TV	PAYING BILLS
SEX	TRAVEL	PLAYING THE STOCK
BEAUTY	KISSING	MARKET
DANCING	GOSSIPING	PRAISES AND
MEDITATION	READING	FLATTERY

The destroyer of happiness is as follows:

CRITICISM	JEALOUSY	BAD LOVERS
REJECTION	LUST	
EXCESS DESIRES	BAD FOOD	
EGO	BAD CHILDREN	

Section 20

QUALITIES OF A DEVOTEE

There are twenty-two qualities that a devotee must master. These qualities are of course qualities that the Guru possesses and surpasses. These qualities are:

1. Be kind to everyone: devotee is well wishing friend to all living entities.
2. Does not quarrel with anyone
3. Fixed in the Absolute Truth :not distracted by Maya
4. Equal to everyone: Sees the soul, the divinity in everyone and everything.
5. Faultless: Surrendered to God in words, deeds and mind.
6. Charitable: Distributes all that has been given to him without selfish motives and promotes the work of his guru.
7. Mild: Remains peaceful because he is satisfied with Krishna consciousness.
8. Clean, Pure: External and internal purification through hygiene, sacred baths, mantras, prayers and meditation.
9. Simple, without material possession: The highest realization is to see everything as the property of God.
10. Benevolent: since Krishna Consciousness affects the heart of every living entity, the welfare work of a devotee is not restricted to specific race, species, etc, but for the benefit of all living entities.
11. Peaceful: To experience real peace in one's relationship with the Divine.
12. Completely attached to Krishna: This is developed by practicing devotional service, giving of your time and talents to your guru that provides you with the knowledge that frees you from suffering.
13. Desireless: Has no material hankering, knows that all desires are fulfilled through service to the guru and his teachings
14. Meek: A true devotee will use things in service of his master or Supreme Being but will not be attached to them.
15. Steady: The deep realization of a devotee will keep him dedicated to his spiritual master and will not be influenced by temptations.
16. Self-controlled: A true devotee controls the negative qualities of anger, lust, greed, illusion, madness and envy.
17. Does not eat more than required: Does not eat too much or too little.
18. Sane: Never intoxicated by material enjoyment. He is always in perfect balance.

19. Respectful: A devotee offers respect to others without expecting anything in return.
20. Humble: To be humble means that one is not hankering to be worshiped by others. Humility should not be artificial but honest, deep, and natural
21. Grave: The devotee is constantly thinking of the ultimate goal of life- spiritual development.
22. Compassionate: The essence of compassion is the distribution of transcendental knowledge.

Swami's Rules for Devotees

1. Seek more profound knowledge, apply in your life and spread the knowledge of the Guru.
2. Perform a yearly puja with the Guru.
3. Protect the name of your Guru, do not allow anyone to desecrate his holy name.
4. Donate your time and talents to the temple or the work of your Guru.
5. Donate or make a sacred offering every time a prosperous situation comes into your life. All good things come through your Guru's grace.
6. Try to have a diet as vegetarian as possible as this shows your respect for all life created by the Divine.

Swami Ram's Product Line has been especially designed by him for your well-being and to help you control all types of health and spiritual issues.

Asthma & Acid-Reflux Control Kit

Alleviate the Stress and Symptoms Associated with Asthma and Acid-reflux to Live a Healthier and Manageable Life.

This life-changing kit is designed to help relieve asthma, as well as the related Gastro-Esophageal Reflux Disease (GERD), which has been shown to worsen asthma symptoms. The combination of herbs in this kit, designed by Swami Ram™, has been used in Ayurvedic medicine for thousands of years, and has been carefully selected and put together into an easy to use powder and teas to accommodate to the modern lifestyle. *

* These statements have not been evaluated by the FDA

Swami Ram's Rejuvenating Bath is a product that can naturally promote tranquility, well-being, balance chakra energy and help reduce stress. It is a scientifically proven method to drive away negative energy that causes headaches, back pain, stomach and chest pain. The results are amazing. Your aches and pains will disappear, you will sleep better and the quality of your life will dramatically improve. This is a pure Ayurvedic mixture of herbal plant elements that has been especially prepared to help you feel well.

Rejuvenating Energy Bath Kit

Revitalize and Restore good energy back into your mind, body & soul.

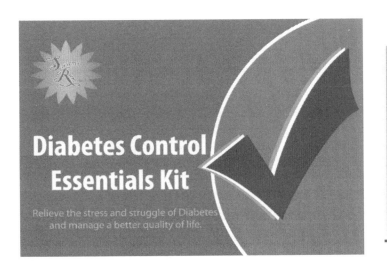

Diabetes Control Essentials Kit

Relieve the stress and struggle of Diabetes and manage a better quality of life.

Swami Ram's Diabetes Kit™ is a Life Changing product. It is designed to prevent diabetes before it appears in the cases of pre-diabetic patients and alleviate diabetes in patients with pancreatic diabetes Type 1 and Type 2.*

*These statements have not been evaluated by the FDA

A Vedic Ritual or Sacrifice performed by Hindus. It is mentioned in the Vedas as a way to bring healing, purification and protection to the Universe and the performer. This kit with complete instructions written by Swami Ram is available at Heendu Learning Center.

Fire Ritual Kit

Agni Hotra

Healing & Purification for Universal & Individual Wellbeing

Hair Rejuvenation kit

Stops falling hair, prevents hair loss and enriches hair growth.

Revitalize your thinning hair and strengthen it NATURALLY! Swami Ram's Hair Rejuvenation Kit contains an Herbal Shampoo, which removes impurities while adding shine to EVERY STRAND and a specially formulated Hair Crème mixture that contains a unique blend of 10 essential nutrient oils proven to aid hair GROWTH and THICKNESS while preventing further hair loss.

Avoid wasting time and money on treatments and medications filled with chemicals that cause harmful side effects! Swami Ram has designed this kit that contains capsules with certified organic and natural herbs proven to help overall health & control different illnesses and conditions.*

*These statements have not been evaluated by the FDA.

Health Maintenance Essentials Kit

For renewal of Mind & Body; Helps regulate digestion & maintain normal blood pressure, good bone health, proper circulation & Chakra energy.

Home Energy Cleansing Kit

Purifies Home/Business To Drive Away Negative Energies & Invite Divine Forces

1 Day

Swami Ram's Home Energy Cleansing™ is a Life Changing product that can naturally promote tranquility and well-being in your home. It is a scientifically proven method to drive away negative energy that causes headaches, back pain, stomach and chest pain. The results are amazing. Your aches and pains will disappear, you will sleep better and the quality of your life will dramatically improve.

Mantras are words of power spoken in Sanskrit; An ancient Hindu language based on the scientific laws of sound and vibration. Meditating and chanting these sounds creates
a vibration through the universe bringing love, health, wealth, prosperity, knowledge, positivity and the ever presence of the

Meditation Mantra Kit

Swami Ram™

Includes 10 Mantra CDs with Corresponding Cards & Instructions

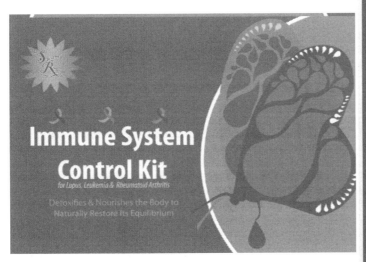

Immune System Control Kit
for Lupus, Leukemia & Rheumatoid Arthritis
Detoxifies & Nourishes the Body to Naturally Restore Its Equilibrium

This kit was developed to help those afflicted with autoimmune diseases like Lupus, Leukemia, and Rheumatoid Arthritis. It is designed to lower the inner toxins and help relieve the chronic and systematic inflammation. Targeting the different weaknesses each individual may have in their body and system, this all natural assortment of remedies will aid the control and maintenance of living these unbearable diseases. The contents of this kit were specifically assembled to detoxify and nourish the immune system to balance itself back to its natural state of equilibrium. *

*These statements have not been evaluated by the FDA.

Swami Ram has especially designed this oil mixture to make you healthier. The curative qualities of this oil mixture are amazing. They have been used in Ayurvedic Medicine for thousands of years and have been known to rejuvenate the digestive system, remove chronic stomach problems, chronic diseases and improve circulation. It has also been known to help healing leukemia and lupus. It restores skin cells and when a mother-to-be drinks it, it protects the unborn child. It removes blockages to progress that appear when the health and energy of the individual is not optimal. It also improves sexual energy.*

*These statements have not been evaluated by the FDA.

Ayurvedic Oil Healing Kit
Improves Body Circulation, Removes Pains, Aches, Blockages & Enhances Sexual Energy

The Pregnancy Kit

Prevent Stretch Marks, Menstrual Problems, Miscarriages,
And Promotes A Successful And Complete Birth

When a baby is developing in the womb, the emotions of the mother are absorbed by the baby as it develops. It can be love or anger that decides the type of child that will be born. If born out of love the world will rejoice and if out of anger it will be distressed. The products in this package help the mother develop a beautiful inner environment for the child so that when the child is born it brings prosperity and happiness to the couple. Swami Ram's™ method has been very effective in helping more than 10,000 women have safer and complete pregnancies.

*These statements have not been evaluated by the FDA.

This kit contains a unique mix of natural oils and herbs that aids men with any reproductive problems or sterility. It detoxifies the body, removes impotence, back pains and body aches; helps maintaining everyday health of the prostate and indigestion issues. Enhance your quality of life in various aspects with just one easy to use package specially designed by Swami Ram™.*

*

Virility
Essentials Kit

Promotes Male Circulatory
Health & Sexual Enhancement

THE HEENDU LEARNING CENTER

In 1990, The Heendu Learning Center, also known as JYOTISH ASHRAM was established. Swami Ram Charran established it with the purpose of bringing back ancient Vedic Scientific knowledge that had been lost in history. Originally, the Heendu Learning Center and the Hindu Society of America Temple Of South Florida were affiliated. Originally, Pundit S. Doobay, a Hindu Priest, and Swami Ram Charran joined efforts and contributed more than $70,000 towards the building of this temple.

As of 1993, the Heendu Learning Center separated from the Hindu Society of America and formed its affiliation with AMAR JYOTI MANDIR (Temple) OF SOUTH FLORIDA. Since 1993 Swami Ram Charran and the Heendu Learning Center has assisted over 10,000 people. His contribution towards the return of ancient knowledge back to Hinduism has resulted in the changing and improvement of many people's lives.

The Heendu Learning Center publishes many books and periodicals; the general concentration is on Vedic Astrology, ritual science and scientific analysis of universal forces. The Center publishes the results of continuous research in an annual magazine called, THE PATRA. The Heendu Learning Center has combined its efforts as a member of the AMERICAN FEDERATION OF ATROLOGERS to provide easy and simple understanding of the exact sciences of Vedic Astrology.

Swami Ram Charran had promoted this Vedic knowledge through many seminars, lectures, television and radio interviews, yagans, astrological conventions and many other types of media. The Heendu Learning Center distributes his video tapes, cassettes and books.

The intense work carried on by the Ashram Center in the promotion of knowledge survives on donations provided by the members and the management group. We receive donations to the HEENDU LEARNING CENTER INC. for the management of the religious and spiritual services provided. The Ashram also promotes the teaching of Vedic Astrology, Learning of Hindu Music, Courses on the Vedas and Puranas, the science of Vedic Rituals and Pujas and much more information on the Vedic Sciences. All questions, subscriptions, memberships and comments are welcome.

The Heendu Learning Center is located in South Florida at 12201 S.W. 128th Court Miami, Fl 33186. This location is the headquarters consisting of the Temple, the Retail Office, and Stores. The head of the Learning Center is Swami Ram Charran, his son (Lucas), and two daughters (Luana & Lueresa) assist in the running of the Center, his wife (Seeta) manages the Puja and Ritual Services Department. You can monitor or reach the center on the following website www.swamiram.com. The following information can be useful to contact Swami Ram Charran.

Swami Ram Charran travels frequently to different locations...

HEENDU LEARNING CENTER DISTRIBUTORS

SWAMI RAM BOOKS, CDs & DVDs ARE AVAILABLE AT THE FOLLOWING LOCATIONS:

HEENDU LEARNING CENTER INC.
12201 SW 128th Court Ste 102 Miami Fl 33186
(305) 253 5410

NEW YORK

DJ SARI HOUSE
12406 Liberty Avenue, Richmond Hill
New York 11419
(718) 843 6100   (718) 843 6100

NUVEENE ENT. – DANIEL SINGH
8824 204 Street, NY, 11423
(718) 926 1952

CANADA

MAHARANI EMPORIUM
1417 E. Gerard Street, Toronto,
Ontario, Canada M4L127
(416) 466 4286

TRINIDAD

DOODNAUTH –PUNDIT SHIVA
(954) 892 3776,(954) 892 3776
(518) 374 2655

PREM SINGH STORE
24 Eleanore Street, Chaguanas
Trinidad & Tobago, West Indies
(868) 672 4423 (868) 740 5470

GUYANA

JOSEPH SATRO STORES
268 Forshaw Street Queenstown,
Georgetown, Guyana,
(592) 642 7743

INDIA

SHARAD GUPTA
House no 900, Sector 29, Faridabad
(NCR Delhi) India 121008
Tel No +91129-2505356,+91129-
2505356, 9467213553

BOOKS ARE ALSO AVAILABLE AT:
Shop.Swamiram.com * Avatarcode.com * lifecodebook.com

Swami Ram Charran's Websites

http://astrocienciavedica.com

http://astrovedica.swami2.renderhosting.net

http://avatarcode.com

http://avatarcodes.com

http://blog.swami2.renderhosting.net

http://data.swamiram.com

http://equationoflife.us

http://exactuniverse.com

http://greatnessofwomen.com

http://guruvsevil.com

http://lifecodebook.com

http://lifecodeguru.com

http://lifecodeseries.com

http://myavatarcode.com

http://mylifecodeguru.com

http://myquantummath.com

http://mysexualvirility.com

http://pujaswami.com

http://quantumdeity.com

http://quantumlifecode.com

http://quantumswami.com

http://ritualscience.com

http://scienceofhindugods.com

http://secretofgreathealth.com

http://spanish.swamiram.com

http://swamiram.com/consultations

http://theherbalcures.com

http://vediclocation.com

http://vedicnamecode.com

http://vedicpastlife.com

http://vedicpatra.com

http://vedicsexualcode.com

http://vedicwavecycle.com

http://whatsmylifecode.com

http://yogiphysicist.com

OTHER WORKS PUBLISHED BY THE AUTHOR

Life Code Series

The Life Code
Equation of Life
Square of Life 1
Square of Life 2
Life Code Annual Series
Vedic Sexual Code
Sexual Death
Location Code
Secret to Great Health 1 & 2
Challenging Temptation
Science of the Hindu Gods

Vedic Patra Series

Vedic Patra: Annual Edition 2013, 2014
100 Year Patra Volume 1
100 Year Patra Volume 2
100 Year Patra Volume 3
100 Year Patra Volume 4
100 Year Patra Volume 5

Puja Series

Antyesti Puja
Durga Puja
Ganesh Puja
Ganga Puja
Garbhadan Sanskar
Guru Initiation Puja
Hanuman Puja
Havan Puja
Laxmi Puja
Moola Puja
Nav-Graha Puja
Panchaka Puja
Pitri Puja
Saraswaty Puja
Shiva Puja
Sat Narayan Puja
Surya Narayan Puja
Vijay Bhava Puja
Vivaah Puja

Español

Código de la Vida
Código de la Vida Anuarios

Vedic Financial Books Series

THE VEDIC CYCLES OF THE STOCK MARKET $99.00
A book that predicts the monthly waves of individual stocks including 10,000 stocks, ETFs and Metal Companies

THE DAILY STOCK MARKET CYCLES FOR 2012... $149.99
This is a yearly manual for daily traders. This book also contains a listing of over 10,000 stocks

THE VEDIC CYCLES OF THE STOCK MARKET ETFS... $199.99
Manual for traders that want to predict ETFs and INDEXES on a monthly basis. Contains over 2,000 ETFs and INDEXES.

THE VEDIC CYCLES OF THE FUTURES MARKET.... $249.99
A Handbook for commodities and futures traders who wish to use the Vedic Codes for predicting the futures markets on a monthly basis. This book also contains a listing of over 100 commodities and futures

THE PDF REPORT ON ANY STOCK OR COMMODITY... $299.99
A SPECIAL REPORT for any ONE commodity, futures or stock using the Vedic Codes forecasting the markets on a yearly , monthly or daily basis. Trader will specify which instrument and provide IPO dates as well as the company profile, for an accurate report.

Invitation to All the Deities and Gods

Bowing To All the Elements That Makes Up the Universe

OM NAMO NARAAYANA NAMA (6 Times)

Oh Universe Come to me as the Lord – this location

JAI Indra MATA AYE NAMA (2 Times)

Oh light come to this Yagna – this location

JAI SHREE GANAPATI AYE NAMA (2 Times)

Oh Remover of Obstacles Come to me as the Lord

OM HANUMANTA AYE NAMA (2 Times)

Oh Lord of the air Come to me as the Lord

SHRI GOBINDA AYE NAMA (2 Times)

Oh Lord of the Cows Come to me as the Lord

SARASWATY MATA AYE NAMA (2 Times)

Oh Knowledge Come to me as the Lord

OM MALI MATA AYE NAMA (2 Times)

Oh Destroyer of Evil, Come to me as the Lord

OM SURYA DEVTA AYE NAMA (2 Times)

Oh Sun-God Come to me as the Lord

OM CHANDRA DEVTA AYE NAMA (2 Times)

Oh Moon – God Come to me as the Lord

OM DURGA MATA AYAE NAMA (2 Times)

Oh Mother of the Universe Come to me as the Lord

OM GOWRIMATA AYE NAMA (2 Times)

Oh Mother of Love Come to me as the Lord

OM GANGA MATA AYE NAMA (2 Times)

Oh Mother of the Seas and Waters come to me as the Lord

PRITIVI DEVTA AYE NAMA (2 Times)

Oh Mother Earth Come to me as the Lord

OM AGNIR DEVTA AYE NAMA (2 Times)

Oh Fire God Come to me as the Lord

OM PAWAN DEVTA AYE NAMA (2 Times)

Oh Father of all Wind come to me as the Lord

NAVGRAHA DEVTA AYE NAMA (2 Times)

Oh – 9 – Planets come to me as the Lord

OM RAMA CHANDRA AYE NAMA (2 Times)

Oh Protector of the weak, Come to me as the Lord

OM BRAMHA DEVTA AYE NAMA (2 Times)

Oh God of Creation, Come to me as the Lord

NAMA INDRAYA NAMA INDRAYA (12 Times)

Let us all enjoy the Bliss of Time, Space and Oneness

With the Universe – the Abode of Indra – God of Gods

A CD-ROM is available for this prayer from the Heendu Learning Center

195